The Sunburnt Queen

"This fascinating volume conveys the researcher's commitment and thrill of the chase as she hunts down sites and oral sources. Her enthusiasm for the story takes it to a fresh level, leaving the recent regurgitated account of the *Grosvenor* castaways in the dust. It is wide-ranging, quirky and deeply endearing."
- **Patricia McCracken,** *Farmer's Weekly*

"While it may appear to be no more than the sweet, romanticised tale of a little girl lost, it is in fact a well-documented account of 18th and 19th Century South African history."
- **Winnie Graham,** *Cape Argus*

"The reader is never left wanting for excitement in this book… The story of *The Sunburnt Queen* is a true story and will open up vistas to the reader not seen before."
- **Paul Murray,** *The Cape Times*

"If Gquma's life is remarkable, so is the book's revelation of the frontier region – with its turbulent history of war between Xhosa and settler. The races are not so far apart as we think."
- **Gill Moodie,** *Go Newspaper (East London)*

"[*The Sunburnt Queen*] is a fascinating account of a part of our history… providing insight into the tragedies and triumphs of cultures and nationalities as they clashed and, on occasion, gelled. It's a story of massacres and genocide, frontier wars and famine, survival and endurance."
- **Lindsay Ord,** *The Daily News*

"Crampton's style is compellingly diverse – her account of shipwrecks and treasure-hunters, her exposition of character, subvert the stereotype of 'a history book'… As a reader, I was invited to delight, to analyse, to contemplate, to empathise, to speculate, to critique – what more could one ask of such a text?"
- **Wordstock,** *Grahamstown Arts Festival*

"… a labour of love."
- **Beverly Roos Muller,** *Tonight*

The Sunburnt Queen

a true story

Hazel Crampton

Related titles by Jacana

The King's Shilling
The Notorious Syndicalist
Mr. Chameleon
Drum Cafe's Traditional Music of South Africa

First published in 2004 by Jacana Media (Pty) Ltd.
Reprinted 2005 (twice), 2007, 2008

10 Orange Street
Sunnyside
Auckland Park 2092
Johannesburg
South Africa

ISBN 1-919931-92-9
      978-1-919931-92-0

Cover design by über
Set in Goudy 11/13
Printed by CTP Book Printers, Cape Town
Job No. 000594

See a complete list of Jacana titles at www.jacana.co.za

for

Kash and Ky,

splendid men of the future

Acknowledgments

Tons of love and thanks
(for keeping me alive, in different ways) to:

Didi Moyle
Judy Repanis
Fi Macpherson
Erin Muller Euijen
my sons Kyla and Kashka Crampton
and my brothers Mark Lawrie, Dimitri Repanis and Kobus Botha

Thanks, too, to Zweliyanyikima Vena
James McFarlane
and especially to Maggie Davey

Contents

List of Genealogies

List of Maps

Chapter One

The Legend of Gquma[1]

One cold and bitter night in the autumn of 1737, a violent north-westerly struck the small Dutch settlement of De Kaap on the southern shores of Africa. Out in Table Bay a fleet of nine ships rode at anchor in the rapidly mounting swell. Homeward-bound for the Netherlands, they were ready for sailing, loaded with the treasures of the East and with their full crews on board.

As day broke the gale mounted, the wind increasing in velocity as it swung round to the west, whipping the waves into towering walls of water and tearing the fleet's rigging to shreds. The Bay was white with foam, the mountainous waves storming in between Robben Island and Green Point, and flinging the tiny wooden vessels this way and that. One by one their anchor-cables began to part. The first to go was the *Ypenroode*, driven aground at the mouth of the Salt River with such violence that its masts were torn from their mountings and fell into the surf. The vessel shattered into fragments, and only a few frantic survivors managed to fight their way to safety. The *Goudriaan* followed. Striking the shore broadside-on, with its stern in the mouth of the Salt River, the ship went to pieces at once. The *Flora* was next, breaking up so rapidly on impact that only six of her crew made it ashore. The *Paddenburg* followed, the power of the elements so awesome that the ship was carried *over* the other wrecks by a mountainous wave and flung far up the beach, smashing the ship but saving the crew from drowning. By half past two in the afternoon, the *Westerwyk* too had been driven high up the beach. Inexorably, the other ships followed – the *Buys* striking close by, the *Duynbeek* beached and shattered as night fell, the *Roodenrys* wrecked at the same place in the pitch dark and, almost simultaneously, the *Victoria*, tossed ashore like a child's toy by a huge wave. The crews were decimated, the fleet destroyed.

When the tumult subsided and calm was restored, only two ships remained afloat.[2] The Cape of Storms had once again earned its name.

Over the centuries the Cape has continued to claim its victims, vessel after vessel succumbing to its wild tempests.

While the passing years have wrought spectacular changes and the little village on the Bay has grown into the beautiful city of Cape Town, the one constant has been its infamous storms. Raging in from the Antarctic, the gale-force winds perform a grotesque pirouette here at the junction of the Atlantic and Indian oceans before sweeping eastwards along the southern coast of Africa and, a day or so after leaving Cape Town, storming up the eastern seaboard to the Wild Coast. Stretching from the Mtamvuma River in the north to the Kei in the south, the Wild Coast is less than 300 kilometres long, running along the shores of the former Transkei, a region bounded in the west by the magnificent peaks of the Drakensberg, rising to over 3 000 metres above sea-level, and falling in vast undulating grasslands to the warm waters of the Indian Ocean in the east. The coastal plateau, dissected by numerous large rivers, some of which have carved themselves deep gorges, and many smaller streams, is perfect cattle country, and the Xhosa-speaking peoples who inhabit the region have always maintained large herds. Fringed with exquisite beaches and punctuated by rugged spurs, plum-pudding hills and clusters of tropical bush, the beauty of the Wild Coast belies its treacherous nature, for the coastline is aptly named, dotted with hidden reefs, subject to storms so violent and waves and currents so unpredictable that it has become a veritable ships' graveyard.

It was on this notorious coast, at about the same time that the Dutch fleet was destroyed in Table Bay in 1737 – perhaps even during the same winter storms – that Bessie, a little English girl, was cast ashore at a remote spot known as Lambasi, the Bay of Mussels.[3] Better known nowadays as Port Grosvenor, after the famous English East Indiaman wrecked there in 1782, the Bay lies some ten kilometres south of the Msikaba River where the Portuguese ship *Sao Bento* was wrecked in 1554, and not far north of the 1635 wreck of the *Nossa Senhora de Belem*, at the mouth of the Mzimvubu River near the present town of Port St Johns.

I fell in love with the Wild Coast the first time I ever went there. I was six years old and had been raised on the sweltering north coast of KwaZulu-Natal, so I wasn't exactly unexposed to wild and beautiful beaches, but there was something about the Wild Coast that knocked my socks off and kept me going back again and again as I grew up. It was a strange and mysterious place; nothing was quite what it appeared at first glance. Everything had a story to tell, every feature of the landscape seemed to conceal its own private tale of mystery and tragedy – the gloomy mountain, site of a tragic plane crash, that seemed always to be in shadow no matter how bright the sunshine or the time of day, the cannons salvaged from a shipwreck which were my jungle-gym at the wildly misnamed Royal Hotel, and the awesome monolith of Executioner's Rock, which dwarfed our little car as we rattled down the dusty switchbacks to the sea. There was something unfathomable and untameable about it.

By way of contrast, I remember a Greek island I visited years later: it was the height of the 1985 summer season and the Mediterranean was greasy with suntan lotion, the wavelets flopping without enthusiasm or vigour onto a beach that was wall-to-wall with northern Europeans sunburnt down to raw meat and then again. I have to admit that my perceptions were

coloured by homesickness – I'd been in East Germany at an MK training camp for several months and Greece was just a cover-up for the time I'd been out of South Africa (MK, or Umkhonto we Sizwe, was the military wing of the African National Congress, which was then still banned by the apartheid government) – but even so, that wasn't a beach! I had a sudden and overwhelming longing to be back on the Wild Coast, so I got on a plane and did just that.

It was a crazy journey because I had to stop over in Zimbabwe to get my passport sorted out – there was a big gap in the dates because I'd gone out through Zambia and Angola without it being stamped – but my commander had malaria[4] and didn't keep our rendezvous, so I took a chance and went through Jo'burg airport anyway, shit-scared but well tanned and in my shortest shorts and a little vest, and it worked and I was safe. A few hundred kilometres later and it was just how I knew it would be: the waves were real-sized, big and clean and loud, the water saltyfresh-smelling, the only other creatures on the beach a herd of cows, and I felt as though I could breathe again. An old man was struggling up the steep grassy slopes of the hill above the beach, with a coffin on his back. It was new, the pine still very pale. I hoped it wasn't his, and then I did, because he was old and if it was, then someone dear to him hadn't died and he wasn't heading back to a home full of pain and sadness.

13

There is no place like it.

But despite its awesome beauty, the Wild Coast is not a picture-postcard, happy-holiday kind of place; it is also violent and cruel.

The former Transkei is dirt-poor and its people often desperate, its hinterland a crazy patchwork of tiny plots unable to sustain the burgeoning population. Under apartheid it was the first of the mickey-mouse 'homelands' to become 'independent' of greater [ie white] South Africa; flags flew, bands played, money changed hands, government stooges got richer and the rest of the population poorer.

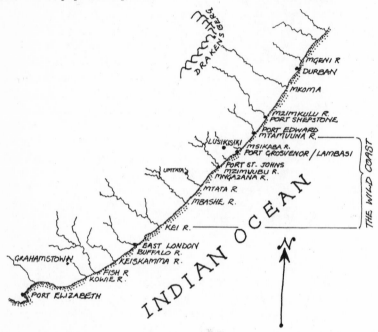

The Wild Coast

The majority of young men worked in the mines and on the farms of white South Africa, and Transkei became a country of women and children, a dumping ground for the old, the infirm and the unemployed who were forcibly removed from the white cities. The legacy remains: Transkei and its Wild Coast are still a developmental backwater and, even though we've had a democratic government since 1994, delivery has been so slow that for many of its people things haven't improved much. Tourism will, it is hoped, boost the local economy in the future and there are several initiatives, marketing drives, the planned coastal road, etc, aimed at bringing in both local and international tourists, but the region's reputation for violent crime remains an enormous deterrent. Hijackings, kidnappings, taxi-wars, military-style heists, political assassinations – the local population has seen it all, but when a group of British tourists is gang-raped at gunpoint or a family of holiday-makers is ambushed and slaughtered on the way to their beach-cottage, it tends to scare away anyone who has the choice of going somewhere else.

It was on that Wild Coast trip – fleeing the Greek idyll – that I first stumbled across Bessie's story. A keen reader of southern African history, I had recently discovered that in olden times a number of castaways – shipwreck survivors – had settled on the Wild Coast, marrying local black women and raising their families there, and it intrigued me. God knows why – it was quite logical that they should – but I suppose because of my apartheid-era schooling, where history was all black and white and the two never mixed, unless it was in battle and the whites won, as at Blood River, I found the whole thing new and intriguing. Talking it over with the friends I was visiting, however, I found it was common knowledge around there and one of Max's patients at the local mission hospital was a descendant of white castaways, a black guy with blue eyes who spoke no English and was a Pondo through and through. I didn't know it at the time, but we were only five or so kilometres, as the crow flies, from where Bessie had lived.

With hindsight I wish I had run off and interviewed Max's patient then and there. Instead I threw myself into beaching and basking in the sun, and it was a couple of years before Bessie and I crossed paths again.

It was in a bedtime story read to me one evening by my boyfriend. Written in the late 19th century, 'Gquma' or 'The White Waif'[5] was a romanticised account of Bessie, but it caught my interest because the author's source was the Tshomane, the people who reportedly adopted the little castaway and with whom she had spent her life. I realised there was enough truth in the tale to bear further investigating. So on a trip to Transkei soon after that we went into the archives in Umtata, the capital, and did just that, learning to our amazement that a whole clan of people descended from castaways lived not far off, at Xora River mouth on the coast, black people known as 'the Whites' or abeLungu.[6] We went down there to interview them and, because we knew practically nothing, asked all sorts of un-informed questions and probably blew an amazing opportunity to really learn something. Fortunately, however, we did tape the whole thing,[7] since the elderly men and women who had so kindly gathered to share their oral history with us were extremely enthusiastic and voluble and our translator, a beaming priest with a startling line of introduction – 'Good day, young lady. I am the Reverend Xoswa. I shall now pass water' – was not always able to keep up with them.

We were working on a documentary on the Thembu at the time, so on our return to Johannesburg we didn't immediately have the tapes translated. Then real life took over for a while. It was an exciting time; the African National Congress and Pan-Africanist Congress were unbanned and Nelson Mandela and other jailed leaders were set free, followed by the birth of my sons, Kyla and Kashka, but I continued to read and gather information on Bessie, and within a couple of years I became a kind of Bessie-bore. The

stuff I was discovering was so exciting to me that I kept telling my friends
stories about it, bending their ears so much that eventually one of them,
Erin, diplomatically suggested that I write it down instead. This book is the
result. It's been a labour of love, but it's been a long journey, sometimes
literally – I've travelled thousands of kilometres across South Africa, visiting
archives, taking photographs and meeting people, some of whom are
descended directly from Bessie. It's been so many years in the making that
my sons have grown up with it – they're 10 and 11 as I write – travelling far
and wide with me and seeing and doing some amazing things in the process,
and I realise that my fascination with the Wild Coast is being passed on to
them, wedged like a little thorn in their hearts, and that wherever they may
end up in the world as adults, it's a part of Africa that will always be a part
of them.

They were five and six years old when I first took them to Lambasi Bay,
where Bessie was wrecked – almost the same age as she had been when she
was cast ashore. The drive down to Lambasi from our home in Johannesburg
took us through the south coast of KwaZulu-Natal. After crossing the
Mtamvuma River, which divides the latter province from the former
'homeland' the road was tarred and in good shape for all of 100 metres, just
enough to get clients to the Wild Coast casino without damaging their cars,
but thereafter it deteriorated rapidly into a pot-holed mess and quite
suddenly we were in the Third World. Transkei roads are notorious for car
crashes, and with good reason. Many of the vehicles that use them shouldn't
– some are so unroadworthy it's a miracle they even go – and the same is
true of many of the drivers. It's pretty standard stuff on a blind rise or a
blind corner to discover a bus or truck barrelling down on you on the wrong
side of the road, or to hit the brakes in a rush of adrenaline because a car
has stopped dead in the middle of the road in front of you with its lights off
in the middle of the night. A lot of the countryside is unfenced, so
wandering horses, pigs, cows and goats add to the hazards, along with
occasional drunks (motorised and pedestrian), children, potholes big enough
to conceal a small goat, overloaded taxis competing for the land-speed
record, ambulances doubling as taxis, etc. And that's the *main* roads.

At Lusikisiki (the name is onomatopoetic for the sibilance of wind in the
reeds) we hit the dirt road to Msikaba, about 60 kilometres away on the
coast, where we camped for the night, and the next morning doubled back a
few kilometres to Lambasi Bay, or Port Grosvenor. The track down to the
Bay wasn't long but it was rough and, even in my 4x4, a slow crawl over the
jagged rocks, but once we hit the flatter grass slopes nearer the sea the going
was easy. At the time of Bessie's wreck, the lush and rolling grasslands
around the Bay were used by the paramount chief, Matayi, as winter grazing
for his herds[8] and today, more than two and a half centuries later, the hills
are still dotted with the cattle, humble homesteads and scattered fields of
the Mpondo who have inhabited this part of the African coast for longer
than human memory.

The Bay itself is an extraordinary place: enormous rusting chunks of machinery litter the rocky shelves against which the great ocean rollers thunder, silhouetted against the wide blue sky like weird monuments, cast-offs from the failed *Grosvenor* salvage attempts in the early 20th century. The sheer scale of the abandoned machinery is a story in itself, a struggle of wit and will and haemorrhaging bank accounts. If the place is inaccessible and remote today, how much more so it must have been a hundred years ago, when ox-wagons were the only means of transport. In the rocks, up against the sea is another monument to futility: the entrance to a collapsed tunnel which, its creators hoped, would eventually come up directly under the wreck, and into which wealth unimaginable would pour. Unfortunately the only thing that did pour into the tunnel was – surprise, surprise! – the Indian Ocean. The undersea tunnel at Lambasi really cracked Kyla and Kashka up, which, considering how young they were, doesn't say much for the geniuses who conceived it, let alone the poor sods who financed it.

Port Grosvenor, looking across the lagoon towards the cottages

Beyond the tunnel is a handful of seaside cottages, to the west of which the Tezana stream, its banks dense with coastal bush, milkwoods and intertwining palms, broadens into a lagoon before flowing into the sea over a small but lovely beach. A stone's throw beyond the mouth the rocky shoreline is broken by a sudden cleft with a spit of sand at its heart. It was in such a cleft that Bessie was found one autumn morning.

'The wind had been blowing strongly from the south-east for several days previously and the sea was running high…,'[9] but stormy weather is not unusual here and the day probably began like any other for the Nanga. Well-built, brown-skinned people with a penchant for elaborate hair-styles, they were a sub-clan of the Mpondo, under the authority of Matayi, a member of the Mpondo royal family.[10]

The lives of the Mpondo were intimately bound up with and dependent on their herds. Cattle played a profound role in their religious practices, as sacrifices in appeasing or communicating with the ancestral spirits; they were used to strengthen marital ties, were the measure of a man's wealth and the means whereby the chiefs secured their authority and status: 'Whatever a man desires, cattle can give him,' it was said.

'Does he want another wife, cattle supply her. Does he want respect from his neighbours, the possession of cattle secures him this. Does he wish to honour a chief, a friend or even an ancestor, the killing of a beast is a full and sufficient means. Does he wish for riches, cattle will multiply their numbers....'[11]

The cattle were the sole domain of the men – women were not permitted to tend or even milk them and were not allowed into the cattle-kraal except on the occasion of their marriage – and they spent enormous amounts of time, interest and energy on their beasts, singing praise poems in honour of their favourites and training their horns into elaborate and unnatural shapes.[12] They knew all their beasts by their own names and trained them to come at a whistle, like well-trained dogs. Early each morning the cattle were taken from the safety of their kraals and led into the veld to graze, where they were guarded by small herdboys.

Perhaps it was one of these youngsters, the earliest to rise or the one with the keenest eyes, who first saw the alien vessel in the soft pre-dawn light and raised the alarm. Or perhaps it was one of their mothers, gathering fuel to rekindle the cooking fires, who lifted her eyes to the exquisite expanse of silver ocean below, gasped in surprise and alerted her companions.

'Just outside the fringe of breakers an immense "thing" was rolling about helplessly in the ocean swell. This "thing" looked like a great fish, such as on rare occasions had been stranded in the neighbourhood, but it had a flat top from which thick, irregular stumps, like trunks of trees, protruded. Moreover, long strings and objects resembling immense mats were hanging over the sides and trailing in the water. As the rolling brought the flat surface into view, strange creatures resembling human beings could be seen moving about on it.'[13]

News of the wreck spread quickly and as the day progressed more and more people gathered on the shore, but there was nothing they could do to assist the unfortunate souls aboard, for although the Nanga lived close to the ocean they had no power or mastery over it; their lives were so firmly rooted in the land, so entwined with their beloved beasts, that they did not even eat fish, had no boats and were neither sailors nor swimmers. Besides, it was probably not the safety of the mariners which was foremost in their minds as they watched the stricken vessel, but that of their own families and herds, since they knew from the collective experience of generations that there was much to be feared from foreign ships.

The earliest sea-borne visitors to the Wild Coast are said to have been Arab slave-traders. Mpondo legend describes the arrival – long before the first Europeans – of long strange ships which anchored off the shore and at night sent a number of small boats through the surf with musket-bearing men, dressed in white headdresses and long flowing robes, who carefully hid themselves away. At daylight, it is said, other boats brought ashore more men who cast quantities of red stones or beads on the beach, and seeing them then return to the ship, the local people who had been watching from the surrounding hills congregated on the beach and began gathering the precious beads. 'Thereupon the concealed men in flowing garments would rush the beach from both sides and carry off the women....'[14] Perhaps that is partly why red beads became known as *umgazi* – the word comes from *igazi* or blood.[15]

Ironically, these incidents may have been the result of a simple misunderstanding: the Arabs' action suggests not a pre-planned slave-raid but what is sometimes called the 'silent trade', a method of commerce without interpreters once used across north Africa and which dates back to at least the Carthaginians. The Greek historian, Herodotus, describes how the merchants of Carthage, on arriving at a given location, would place their commercial wares on the shore, light a fire to draw the local people to the spot, and retire to their ships. On examining the goods and ascertaining their value the locals would place what they considered an appropriate amount of gold next to them and also retire, a process that was repeated again and again until both parties were satisfied.

The same method was successfully used by Arab merchants from Axum to Zimbabwe, from the 6th to the 16th century AD.[16] Unfortunately, being somewhat outside the usual reach of the Arab vessels – the monsoons/trade winds on which the latter depended peter out around Inhambane in southern Mozambique – the inexperienced Mpondo did not recognise the rules of the game. This is not to say that Arab, Indian and Chinese merchant-ships *never* visited our shores, just that it may have been on an accidental or irregular basis. 'Mali' which means money in Arabic, has exactly the same meaning in isiXhosa,[17] and agate-like beads, 'red in colour, of various wrought shapes and... evidently antique', can even to this day be found here and there on the Wild Coast, particularly on the north shore of the Mzimvubu mouth at Port St Johns, known for obvious reasons as Agate Terrace.[18]

But if the Arab abduction was simply a trading initiative gone horribly wrong, for the Mpondo it was a communal tragedy. And most future encounters with foreigners were to prove equally destructive.

With the Portuguese discovery of the sea route to the East Indies in the late 1400s, increasing numbers of European vessels began passing along the eastern seaboard and an increasing number of ships were wrecked. The survivors systematically abused the people living along the Wild Coast, stealing their cattle, burning their homesteads, beating and shooting them, and on occasion even cannibalising them. The survivors of the *Sao Joao Baptista*, wrecked in 1622 near today's holiday resort of Kenton-on-Sea, were particularly sinister. When 'all the whites and negroes that died' of natural causes had been roasted and consumed, they began sentencing their fellow castaways to death for the most trivial misdemeanours. These included two children, the elder of whom was 12, and the others 'were very careful to give [them] the usual burial of those who died'[19] – namely, eating them. News of these atrocities naturally spread quickly up the coast and as the survivors made their way northwards, towards the Portuguese settlement at Mozambique, they found the local communities pre-warned by at least two days of their arrival and well-prepared to defend themselves: 'they had been told that we ate men and therefore they were in arms.'[20]

With bogeymen like the *Baptista* cannibals on the loose – and Portuguese brutality was so prevalent that of all the thousands of castaways of that nation only one group of survivors did *not* attack the local inhabitants[21] – it was with understandable trepidation that the Nanga people at Lambasi gathered to watch the slowly sinking ship.

> 'All day long the monster lay wallowing. The trailing ropes and sails were cut away, and the great East Indiaman, impelled shoreward by the swell, was just able for a time to maintain her distance from the land. The current sucked her slowly southward, and the crowd of natives silently followed along the shore. Late in the afternoon the breeze died down, and the doomed vessel rolled nearer and nearer the black rocks. Just after sundown she struck with a crashing thud, and thereupon a long wail of agony arose from those on board. Then she heeled over somewhat, and it soon appeared as though she were melting away in the water. By the time night fell, strange objects which the people feared to touch had begun to wash up; these were stranded by the receding tide. Nevertheless, the outline of the dark hulk could still be faintly seen when the startled people withdrew to their homes, where they talked until far into the night, over the wonderful and unprecedented events of the day.'[22]

By now the Nanga must have realised that there would be few, if any, survivors and at daybreak they began gathering on the beach again.

> 'The vessel was no longer to be seen, but the strand was strewn with wreckage of every description, a quantity of which had been flung high and dry by the waves. When the sun arose the people gained confidence and scattered about examining the different articles,

which were distributed over an extent of several hundred yards of beach.'[23]

Iron was highly prized for making tools and weapons, but as the Wild Coast has few deposits of iron or copper, these commodities could be acquired only through trade with the baSotho and baTswana far inland, or the amaHlubi and amaZizi hundreds of kilometres to the north[24] – or from the occasional shipwreck. Experience had taught the Nanga that pieces of metal and other useful items could be found amongst the debris, and that by burning the planks of a wreck they could even recover the iron nails, but their foraging was interrupted by a sudden outcry and the people on the beach and in the rocks dropped what they were doing and rushed 'to a certain spot where, in a wide cleft of the black reef, which was floored with gleaming white sand, a strange object had been discovered. Huddled against the rock on one side of the cleft lay a child, a little white girl....'[25]

The child was not alone, but exactly who the other castaways were remains something of a mystery to this day. Several accounts have survived the intervening centuries, but they are fragmented and contradictory, falling largely into two camps, one in which the girl's companions are said to have been white men, and the other in which her companions were black. For me, the most credible of all these sources is Ngcetane, the castaway's grandson who, having 'resided with her until he came to years of maturity, and with whom she spent her last days,'[26] obviously knew her better than most. According to him

> 'five persons besides his grandmother "came out of the *Ulwaanhla* [sea]"; and that the following were their names, viz., Ibadi, whom he calls her father; Upaneya, a brother; Bomboss, another brother; Noqualekiza, a sister; and Colaz, another sister.'[27]

That they were all members of the same family should not be taken literally; it probably arose more from

> 'their all "coming out of the sea" together, rather than to any relationship', since the people of the Wild Coast lived in family groups 'and their dwelling together would further strengthen, in the native mind, the idea of their being all of one house.'[28]

The child's 'brother' Bomboss, for example, is described as having been a black man,[29] while one 'sister' is said to have been Indian or Arab.[30] That the girl's companions were people of colour was confirmed by another source: 'Several slaves were with her... black people with long hair', the Thembu councillor Xelo reported to the 1883 Native Commission. 'I myself married a girl descended from one of these slaves,' he added, stating that 'no white man had come in the small boat with her.'[31]

The other account, recorded by the Xhosa-Scot historian JH Soga, from oral sources in the 1920s, maintains the exact opposite – that all the castaways were white,

> 'four in number, three males and one female child. These the Natives named, respectively, Bati, Jekwa, Hatu and Gquma. According to Native ideas, as they came from the same "house" (viz the ship), they were necessarily all relatives one of another. This need not, however, be accepted seriously. The two first named were supposed to be brothers, and the young girl Gquma was supposed to be the daughter of Bati.'[32]

Oral history was – and is – a form of entertainment as well as a tool for passing on a cultural identity and a system of values, and different storytellers at different times surely added or subtracted details to enhance Bessie's tale. Filtered down through several generations, in the telling and retelling, different patterns have been woven into the whole, but the basic fabric holds true and somewhere among the layers of fact and fiction is a girl coming of age in a wild, strange land, living a life that can be described only as one of the most cross-cultural experiences ever. The Xhosa have a saying, '*Indaba ye-tyel ayikoli*': if you want the truth, get it from the original, rather than from one who heard it second-hand,[33] and in this case it is Ngcetane's account that is closest to the original source – his grandmother – while Soga's was written nearly two centuries after Bessie was wrecked, long after the death of all who had known her and the other castaways personally. About the only point they have in common is that the little girl, Gquma, was white and that Bati or Badi was her father. This does not mean Soga's account is devoid of truth, and it should certainly not be dismissed out of hand. The three white male castaways certainly existed, and – as we shall see later – introduce a whole new dimension to Bessie's story.

Thrown up literally out of the blue, the castaways provoked enormous curiosity and Cimbi, the Nanga chief, sent word to his overlord, Matayi, informing him of their arrival.[34] The local grapevine was a highly efficient system:

> 'Seldom does anything new transpire in the land without the knowledge of the principal chiefs, as scores of persons are daily running about in every direction, for the purpose of bringing them information'[35]

and, as word spread, people began assembling from far and wide. It was the girl-child who inspired the greatest interest. She was very young,[36] as little as seven years old, it is said,[37] yet she was already strikingly beautiful: her pale skin contrasted sharply with her long black hair,[38] which was the perfect foil for her eyes, a startling blue, 'the hue of the sky', as legend would have it, 'a colour never previously seen by any of the spectators in the eyes of a human being.'[39]

A great meeting was held, so vast in size that it was still spoken of over a century and a half later: '...[M]uch wonder and surprise was felt. The people asked [the girl] where she came from and she pointed towards the sea, signifying that she came from a country in that direction....'[40] Despite her youth and the lack of a common language, she was evidently intelligent and understood what was being asked of her. She appeared eager to communicate and talked quite freely, and although much of what she said was lost on her hosts she made sure that they understood that her name was Bessie. The little mite was so adamant about this that although many other aspects of her story have been lost or contradict one another, all accounts concur on this one point: 'She said that her name was Bess,' and 'One word she repeated over and over again – pointing the while to herself: "Bessie, Bessie".'[41] In time she also acquired a Xhosa name, Gquma, which means 'the roar of the sea', in honour of her strange arrival: 'She had come… when the sea was raging and thundering against the black rocks, so her name, said the sooth-sayers, must be called "Gquma" – "the roar of the sea".'[42]

Though Gquma was the one by which she was most generally known, she never forgot her original name, and years later she named her daughter Bessy.[43] A diminutive of Elizabeth, a very popular English girl's name during the 18th century, it suggests she was English, as does the name of her grandson, Johnny, who died in 1829.[44] This is supported by Henry Francis Fynn, who, in about 1826, was the first English trader to enter the region and one of the first white men to meet Bessie's children. He described her as having been 'an English lady.'[45] The accounts of the travellers and missionaries who followed him, and those of Bessie's own descendants, concur.[46] In the words of Reverend William Shaw, who met Bessie's son Mdepa in 1828:

> 'It is highly probable that the European ancestors of the mixed race under Depa were English, from the names by which the three Europeans mentioned by his family were called. As these names had, however, been somewhat Kaffirized by the native pronunciation of them, this is not put forth as a very certain criterion for testing this point....'[47]

From the moment she arrived the little castaway was embraced with warmth and hospitality by her adoptive people; they taught her isiXhosa – 'which she learnt to speak well afterwards,'[48] and she responded to them with trust and love and adapted to her new environment with apparent ease. She was by all accounts a kind and endearing child, blessed with a sweet nature: 'Nor was it her colour merely that secured… general esteem; she manifestly possessed a noble and generous spirit which rendered her greatly beloved among the people.'[49] Her western clothing did not last long in the rough terrain of the Wild Coast, and when it began to fall apart, '… [t]he people slaughtered a beast, and with its skin made the white [girl] a kaross,'[50] a blanket of animal skin tanned and treated with great skill until the leather was wonderfully soft, to be worn over her shoulders in cold weather. In warm weather like the other young girls she wore only a small skin apron, and busied herself with childish things:

> 'Her favourite ornaments were cowrie and other sea-shells. Being always regarded as the child of the sea, her fondness for bathing was looked upon as appropriate and natural. On the level sandy beach[51] ... on sunny days, Gquma with her body-guard of boys and girls would sport and swim, diving through the combers, and then looking back to see them curl over and dash with a thud on the hard smooth sand. On summer days, when the sun beat fiercely on the beach, they would spend hours on the banks of one of the many streams that trickled down through the forest, plunging every now and then into some crystal-clear, fern-fringed pool.'[52]

Although she possessed 'one of those natures – more common among women than men – which can easily assimilate themselves to new surroundings,'[53] the past occasionally intruded. It is said that the things salvaged from her wreck had been placed in two storage huts and that one day, as the girl stood watching one of the wooden chests being unpacked, she caught sight of a pair of hairbrushes and a large mirror. Bursting into tears, she grabbed them and ran off. Later she was observed setting the mirror up against the wall of a hut, sitting before it and solemnly brushing her hair.

It became a ritual that she clung to for years, and long after all other evidence of her past life had crumbled to dust, the

> 'one conventional practice which she continued was the brushing of her hair. Before the wreck she had evidently been taught to take care of her locks, for from the day on which she wept at seeing the hair-brushes and the mirror, she had each night and morning brushed her hair carefully. At night, before sleeping, she would twist it together, and then coil it around her neck. In the morning when she arose she would shake it out until it fell over her shoulders to below her waist. Gquma's brushing of her hair was looked upon as a sort of rite, and the function was regarded with the deepest respect, more especially as she often wept softly during its performance.'[54]

Many years later her daughter Bessy, then well into middle age, still remembered her brushing her hair. As she told Mrs Palmer, wife of the resident missionary, 'her mother used to use combs and brushes for her long hair such as Mrs Palmer used.'[55]

It is not clear how long Bessie remained with the Nanga, but it was probably only a short while, for she appears to have been placed under the protection of the white castaway, Badi. For an unmarried girl like Bessie to remain alone or have to fend for herself was unheard of in Mpondo culture, and so Badi was appointed to be her 'father' and it was at his homestead that she lived until she was old enough to marry and move to her husband's homestead.

According to legend,

> 'Three white cows had been assigned from the chief's herd for Gquma's support, and soon afterwards a law was enacted in terms of which all pure white calves born in the Tshomane herds were regarded as "Gquma's cattle", and had to be delivered, when a year old.... This tribute was submitted to cheerfully by the people, and it was considered a token of good fortune when a cow gave birth to a white calf. In those days virulent cattle diseases were unknown, and in a few years "Gquma's cattle" had increased to a herd of several hundreds. The fame of "the child of the sea" spread far and wide, and people used to come great distances to see her and her wonderful herd of white cattle.'[56]

The Tshomane lived in extended-family groups or *imizi*, rather than villages.[57] Each *umzi* or group of huts had its own name, chosen by its headman. (One *umzi* I read about was known by its neighbours as 'the place of tricks' because of its wily old owner, and no one but he used the more reputable name he had chosen for it.[58]) The Mpondo were polygamous. The inhabitants of the average *umzi* consisted of a senior man, his wives and children, his married sons and their wives and children, and his unmarried daughters, the numbers fluctuating as one of the men took another wife or a young woman married and went to live with her husband, but even when a homestead became quite large – sometimes as many 20 married men of a single heir might be found living in one *umzi*[59] – it remained a closely knit family group, working, eating and playing together. The children were expected to show the same respect for all the adults of the homestead as they did for their biological parents and it was customary for them to refer to all adult men in their *umzi* as 'father' and all the adult women as 'mother'.[60] Family ties were so close that, to early European travellers, it seemed the children of one wife belonged

> 'also to the other. I could never discover from one of my [men] the identity of his natural mother. His father had five wives; he pointed them all out to me and said, "Here are my five mothers", and each one in turn embraced the tall young man with a warmth which I found incredible.'[61]

The terms 'brother' and 'sister', likewise, had a wider application and meaning in isiXhosa than in English[62] and it is in this context that the relationships of Bessie and her fellow castaways should be understood.

Badi and the two other white castaways, Jekwa and Hatu, had established themselves as men of importance under the protection of Matayi, chief of the Tshomane and paramount of the Nanga, who lived at

Lambasi Bay where Bessie was shipwrecked. Matayi was a powerful ruler whose grandfather Qiya had been king of the Mpondo and in whose veins ran the blood of the Royal House,[63] and he controlled an extensive territory extending from Lambasi, where he at one stage had his Great Place,[64] as far as the southern bank of the Mtata River. It appears that Jekwa in particular had become a firm favourite of his, and Matayi bestowed on him the huge honour of *ixiba*, or caretaker, of his late father's House.

> 'Puta, father of Matayi, died about 1735 or '40, and his son, Matayi, ruled in his stead. As the grandfather's house had no male representative alive, his son, Matayi, placed the European, Jekwa, in Puta's kraal to keep the house "alive".'[65]

thus ensuring the continuation of his line through the white man's descendents. As the families of Puta's counsellors, who were amongst the most influential in the community, were attached to Jekwa as the representative of that prestigious House,[66] and as it was customary for the *ixiba* to marry a daughter of the deceased[67] – the chief's sister – Jekwa had become an important and influential figure.

Tshomane society was very conservative – as were most Xhosa-speaking peoples of the period. It was a community in which everything and everyone, particularly the women, knew their place, a system designed to maximise social stability by putting the good of the community first, rather than the needs of any individual. Yet in many ways Bessie had a lot of freedom. Sex, for example, was freely discussed before children and understood from an early age, and as she grew up Bessie and her peers were allowed to explore their sexuality with the knowledge and support of their elders. Pre-marital heavy-petting was permitted – although penetration was not – and this 'sweet-hearting' (*ukumetsha*) as it was known, was common for boys and girls from as young as eight or nine: 'The young people of one small local district – perhaps all those who live on one ridge – gather in the evening in a secluded spot in the veld or in a deserted hut. They dance and sing, then pair off to sleep together.'[68] While Bessie and her companions would have been permitted to have several of these affairs during their adolescence, they were strictly monitored by their elders; cuddling, fondling and mutual masturbation were considered normal and healthy, but under no circumstances was the young girl's hymen to be ruptured, since it was only within marriage that full sexual relations and the conception of children were socially acceptable.[69] After any gathering of young people, at a wedding or initiation for example, the girls who took part would be examined by the older women, and if one was found to have lost her virginity, then the boy with whom she had slept was held responsible and obliged to pay her father a fine in cattle; an even larger fine was payable if she became pregnant. The girl was generally held as having disgraced both herself and her peer group,[70] and in some cases she and her girl friends would go together to the boy's home and beat him with sticks. Not surprisingly, pre-marital pregnancy was not common.

While she was growing up, Bessie, like the other girls in the homestead, would have been taught how to assist the women of her *umzi*, learning from an early age to care for the babies and small children of the family, clean and maintain the floors of the huts by applying fresh cow-dung to them,

MPONDO MAN

and gather firewood. As soon as she was able to carry heavy loads she would also have helped to fetch water, learning how to balance the pot on her head without holding it with her hands, and acquiring the incredibly graceful woman's walk, head high, back straight and hips swaying in sweet soft rhythm. As Bessie grew to adolescence the small animal-skin apron she had worn as a girl was replaced by a knee-length oxhide skirt.[71] Unlike their northern neighbours, the Zulus, Mpondo women and girls did not bare their breasts but covered them with a cloth of softly-tanned leather. Young boys and men were more casually dressed, in nothing but a penis sheath (*isidla*), which was a small cover of skin[72] or a small calabash into which the penis was inserted,[73] then pulled up tight against the body with leather thongs and tied at the back. Girls often gave their 'sweethearts' beads and little bells to decorate their penis sheaths and make them more conspicuous, and much pride was taken in making them attractive. The girls liked their men to be tall and well built and the men in turn liked their girls to have well-rounded hips, generous breasts and strong calves, with a slight gap between the two front teeth being particularly admired.[74]

Cleanliness, too, was considered attractive; Bessie and the other young girls paid careful attention to their *toilette*, adorning themselves with necklaces of sweet-smelling wooden beads and wild mint and rubbing butter into their skin to keep it soft and shiny. They brushed their teeth with a certain fibrous root[75] and, as protection against the sun and insect bites, painted their faces with red clay – against which Bessie's blue eyes must have appeared even more startling and unusual. Both the men and the women plaited their hair, arranging their braids in a variety of elaborate styles and Bessie adopted the fashion, 'twisting or plaiting her hair into cords which extended to her waist, and covered, or rubbed over with red clay.'[76] The widespread use of red ochre meant that everything else in the homestead also had a reddish tinge, since as the clay dried it rubbed off on whatever it touched, so much so that – as the missionaries later reported – even the domestic chickens turned pink.[77]

Bessie was renowned for her love of ornament. 'This white girl,' it was said, 'put more ornaments on her dress than the ordinary native woman did;'[78] strings of shiny shells and bright seeds encircled Bessie's neck and around her wrists and ankles she wore numerous bracelets and bangles. She was growing into a 'most lovely woman. Her skin had browned to a rich glowing tint, and the healthy, natural life she led developed her form to the highest degree of symmetry.'[79]

Adolescence brought several changes to her life and more responsibility; she learnt how to prepare and serve food and with the onset of menstruation she became an *intonjane* (initiate) and together with several other young girls underwent a period of semi-seclusion, observance of certain taboos, ritual dancing and sacrifice of beasts, signifying her passage to womanhood and preparing her for marriage.[80] The *intonjane* usually emerged from the enforced seclusion and inactivity somewhat paler and plumper than usual, both of which traits were much admired.[81] Bessie, of course, was already overly pale, but the additional kilograms would certainly have added to her already substantial charms. She was, by all accounts, 'remarkably handsome,' elegant and possessing 'extreme beauty,'[82] and with her sweet nature, exotic past, and powerful connections she was undoubtedly extremely desirable.

It is hardly surprising, therefore, that she caught the eye of one of the most powerful men around – Tshomane, Great Son of the Tshomane chief Matayi, a prince of the blood, descendant of the ancient Mpondo kings, whose line dated back to 'time immemorial'. Legend traces the origin of the Mpondo, Xhosa, Mpondomise, and Thembu peoples to a mysterious river called the Dedesi, which is thought to have flowed through a pass in the Drakensberg Mountains and been a tributary of the present Mzimvubu River.[83] Long, long ago, it is said, they began moving down towards the coast, where they eventually settled. The genealogies of subsequent Xhosa, Mpondomise and Thembu chiefs goes back hundreds of years, to at least 1300 AD, but archaeological evidence indicates that the Xhosa were already present as far south as Grahamstown in the 1000s.[84]

No physical description of Tshomane has survived and little is known about him, perhaps because he died at a relatively young age, but we do know that when Bessie reached marriageable age – for Mpondo girls usually between 16 and 18 years old,[85] which in her case would have been in about 1746–48 – Tshomane already had several other wives,[86] so he was probably older than she was. A chief usually married his first wife soon after his initiation into manhood (she was known as the *umsul'udaka*, or the one who wiped away the clay left over from his circumcision ceremonies), and as he grew in stature and wealth he acquired more and more wives – but no matter how many he had, none were as important as his Great Wife, whom he usually only married later in life. This was possibly in order to avoid disputes about succession (although it did not always work) since it was only through his Great Wife that the chief's line could continue; even if, as was often the case, he already had several children by his existing wives, he was not considered to have an official heir until such time as his Great Wife bore her first son (the Great Son).[87] Consequently the most important marriage of a chief was to his Great Wife, and it just so happened that Tshomane had not yet taken his Great Wife when Bessie reached marriageable age.

Perhaps it is not entirely accurate to say that Bessie caught the eye of one of the most powerful men around, but rather of all the powerful men in the clan. Since a chief did not normally choose his own Great Wife, Bessie would first have had to win the approval of Tshomane's *amaphakati* or counsellors, men of proven wisdom and influence before whom all matters of importance were discussed and decided.[88] And the castaway certainly had her detractors: 'What chief,' they laughed, 'would marry a frog, a thing that comes out of the water?'[89]

Chapter Two

The Husbands

The union of Bessie and Tshomane was one hundred percent an arranged marriage and in that sense was not much different from contemporary European royalty. By modern standards and expectations the latter, in fact, was probably worse: at the double wedding between the royal families of Spain and Portugal in 1785 neither the grooms, the infante Don Gabriel of Spain and infante Don Juan of Portugal, nor their brides, the infanta Donna Mariana Victoria, princess of Portugal, and infanta Dona Charlotta of Spain, had ever set eyes on each other before. Their personal desires or opinions were of no import: the marriages were arranged solely 'to heal the jealousies and differences which had so long prevailed between these courts, and to unite the two kingdoms in the closest bonds of amity'[1] – a political convenience of which the Mpondo elite would have heartily approved.

Mpondo commoners had it much easier, and generally seem to have been permitted to marry the partner of their choice as long as they did not break any incest taboos.[2] If a girl caught the eye of a man and he wished to marry her, he would ask his parents to facilitate the match. Once they had obtained the girl's father's permission, the girl was approached for her assent and if she was willing a formal courtship could commence.[3]

The marriage of a chief, however, was an arranged and carefully calculated affair, and exactly how much say Tshomane had is debatable. The match was usually initiated by the bride's father, especially when she was a woman of high rank,[4] as Bessie evidently was, though generally only after consultation with the prospective bride. Although public opinion acknowledged a father's right to choose his daughter's husband, it did not approve of him forcing her into 'a distasteful match.'[5] The groom had far less say in the matter than the bride: he could choose his concubines and on occasion his junior wives, but only rarely his more important wives. Occasionally a chief would be permitted to select his Great Wife from among his existing spouses but only if his people agreed with his choice – before she could be 'promoted' her position had to be publicly accepted and declared by a full *ibandla* or gathering of the people[6] – but in the majority of cases his senior wives-to-be were simply sent to him. Sometimes messengers were sent by the bride's father to sound out his opinion beforehand, but usually the girl herself arrived at the chief's *umzi*, unexpected and unannounced. And the more important the chief, the greater the chance of his being 'surprised from time to time by the arrival of a bridal party, bringing with them as his offered bride some chief's daughter whom he has never seen before.'[7]

As a chief grew older and richer, women of higher rank and greater status were sent to him, and even if he not could bear the sight of a potential bride he was often obliged to marry her. Refusal to do so could be dangerous, since it meant publicly insulting her people, scuttling potential alliances or even causing a war. The Xhosa King Ngqika is said to have disliked his Great Wife Msutu so much that he refused to have anything to do with her, yet the marriage ceremony proceeded despite his objections, and although there were persistent rumours that Ngqika was not the father of her Great Son Sandile, the boy was nevertheless recognised as the official heir.[8]

It was on this issue – the production of the heir – that so much depended and that made the selection of the chief's Great Wife such a complex and vital issue. It was important that the girl fulfilled certain criteria – she had to be of high status and preferably not one of his own people, so that the marriage could be used to strengthen or forge political alliances, but it was not only her status and connections that mattered. Because of the power invested in her as the future queen-mother, it was essential that the Great Wife conduct herself with honour: ideally she had also to be wise and of sound morals.

Bessie's prospective in-laws were only too aware of what could happen if they chose the wrong woman, since it was largely through his Great Wife that Tshomane's great-grandfather Qiya had lost the Pondo throne in 1677. Qiya, the heir to the Mpondo king Cabe, is said to have fallen out with his younger brother Gangata, and, in the fighting that ensued, was forced to retreat across the Mtata River. Qiya settled on its western bank, but his Great Wife refused to move to the new country with him. She was taken to wife by her husband's rival, Gangata, and the son that she bore him was then acknowledged as the Great Son or heir, and so it came about that the kingship of the Mpondo passed from Qiya's line to that of his younger brother.[9]

Consequently, as the whole clan stood to lose or gain by the woman chosen as the mother of their future chief, it was not a decision the chief alone could make but one determined by his *amaphakati*, or counsellors.

Bessie's protector Badi, as the 'father' of Tshomane's prospective bride, also had to discuss the matter with his family, his wives and adult sons, if any, and his 'brothers', or fellow castaways, Hatu and Jekwa. Following Bessie's consent, their major concern would have been for her continued welfare, and only once they were satisfied that Tshomane and his family would treat her well[10] would Badi have condoned the marriage.[11] There was also the question of *ukulobola* to be discussed – although that would not have been finalised until after the wedding had taken place, since chiefs, unlike commoners, dealt with the 'bride price' only after the ceremonies were over.[12] As the Mpondo had no written records, *lobola* served as proof that a marriage had indeed taken place, and no union was recognised by law until the groom or his family had paid *lobola* by handing over the agreed number of cattle, or *ikhazi*, to be shared amongst the bride's male relations. There was a strong religious aspect to this, as the presence of the groom's cattle in the bride's family kraal was thought to put her in closer contact with his family's ancestral spirits,[13] but it also served as security for the bride and the children she would in time bear. By law the *ikhazi* was held in trust so that should she become a widow she would be entitled to demand assistance from anyone who had received the cattle, and her children too could apply to them for help in starting out in life.[14] Upon receipt of the *ikhazi* the bride's family was expected to give the groom's family gifts of similar value. These transactions helped to stabilise the marriage, keeping the couple together and mutually respectful by involving not just the two of them but their families as well. If a husband deserted his wife for no good reason, or mistreated her, his family lost the gifts they had received. Likewise, if a woman deserted her husband without adequate reason, her family were obliged to return the cattle they had received.

When everything had been arranged to the satisfaction of both Bessie and Tshomane's families, the marriage ceremonials could begin. Bessie set off for the wedding place, accompanied by selected companions of both sexes,[15] and probably in tears, for it was customary, if not obligatory, for a girl who was about to be married to weep and fuss when leaving her home for another. A second customary ritual was played out upon meeting Tshomane's family, with Bessie's party pretending not to know their hosts and treating them as perfect strangers, and Tshomane's family acting as though their guests were totally unexpected, even though they'd been preparing for their arrival for some time. As 'unexpected' guests, Bessie's entire party, men included, were accommodated in one hut. The next morning a goat was brought out and killed for feasting. The contents of its gallbladder were poured over Bessie's head to ensure that she would be faithful to her husband. This was the bride's last chance to prevent the marriage: if Bessie had not wanted to marry Tshomane she could have refused to have the gall poured over her, and flung it away. As a willing bride, she sat quietly through the ritual and afterwards accepted a special piece of the goat's foreleg to eat. The rest of the meat was shared amongst the bridal party and their hosts, barring Tshomane himself. Although the groom was not permitted to partake of the feast, if he was really hungry, it was said, he could creep into his mother's hut 'and, seen by no one, gobble it.'[16]

The actual wedding was held two days later – a complicated ceremony, from which Tshomane was again excluded. Towards sunset the bride and her

companions left their hut in single file, Bessie and the other unmarried girls
dressed in their finest ornaments, but hidden behind straw mats so that they
could not be seen.[17] Blindfolded, they walked close together so as not to

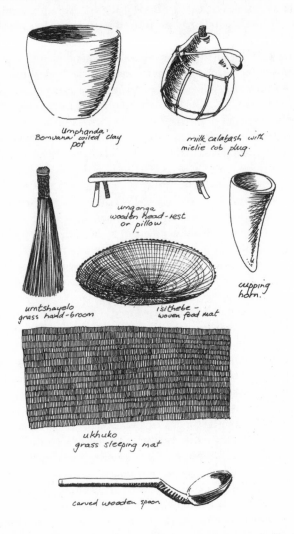

Umphanda:
Bomvana coiled clay
pot

milk calabash with
mielie cob plug.

umqonqa
wooden head-rest
or pillow

cupping
horn.

umtshayelo
grass hand-broom

isithebe –
woven food mat

ukhuko
grass sleeping mat

carved wooden spoon

stumble, with a lead man knocking aside any sticks or stones that may have
been in their way. Then, with their straw mats and blindfolds removed, and
dressed only in long skirts, but with a full complement of bracelets and
ornaments, they stopped first in front of the men of the groom's family and
then in front of the women to be inspected, and their attributes – or lack
thereof – loudly commented upon. Then they returned to their hut while
the groom's mother and the other women of the homestead ran to and fro,
dancing and chanting a kind of pagan Protestant work ethic: 'Here we sow,
here we weed, here we reap, here we grind [corn for] beer, here we work,

here we do not sleep all day.' The men of the bridal party distributed gifts
to the groom and his family, such as specially made *karosses*, or animal-skin
capes, and sleeping mats, and while these were being admired Bessie brought
out her finely woven grain baskets, food mats and other household goods,
half of which were for her own use and half for use in the Great House of
her husband.[18]

With the formalities over the party could begin. Anyone who wished to
be there was welcomed as a guest and given meat and beer. Out of respect
for Tshomane's status as a chief of high rank, the guests numbered in their
thousands, consisting not only of the greater portion of his own people but
also all the other chiefs within one or two days' journey, who were expected
either to attend in person, or send their representatives, along with their
favourite racing oxen.[19] Cattle were driven up and a number slaughtered
and prepared for the coming feast, and the men began preparing for the
ox-racing (*uku-leqa*), which would complete the festivities.[20]

Over two hundred years later the abeLungu at Xora mouth described the
closing events of a wedding day, the basics of which had not changed since
Bessie's time: 'There will be a chase,' an elderly woman told me, 'but by this
time they'll be finished with slaughtering.' 'They choose some oxen and
take them to the top of the hills,' an old man elaborated. Their voices were
raised and joyful, excited by their youthful memories:

> 'Boys look after them there. Meanwhile they slaughter a cow at the
> Wedding place, then they cover it. Thereafter we're told to bring the
> oxen back: that is traditional. Everyone is outside singing, others are
> on horses along the road. Then the oxen come running towards the
> [bride's] hut. When they are there the men praise them according to
> their praise-names.... They call this game "Kukhutsh'umnyama".'

Another mLungu butted in: 'Oh, by then the place is crowded with
people!' 'They are happy,' the first man joined in again. 'The excitement is
about the oxen who are running and are winning the race. Those who enter
the kraal first the owner will praise with his own praise-name.' Crowded
together in a bare storage shed alongside the local trading store, the elderly
descendants of the castaways shared their age-old traditions with us *abelungu*
from Joburg, as all around the real abeLungu women were getting into the
party spirit, swaying and ululating, 'KiKiKiKiKi', orchestrated by our
interpreter-priest: 'Ladies must please, the Ki-ki, when men are praising.'[21]
It was loud, hot, dramatic and sweaty, an outpouring of energy and passion,
yet infused with pathos. Beyond the shabby building the land fell away to
dense subtropical bush and beyond that to the river; it was beautiful, but the
whole place seemed to be inhabited solely by old people. They were humble
folk, some in traditional dress, most in neat but threadbare western clothing;
all were thin, some painfully so. Hard times had come to the abeLungu, but
it had not always been like this. The founding fathers of the clan, Badi,
Jekwa and Hatu, had been men of substance.

In about 1810 political discord had caused the abeLungu to migrate south from their previous home near today's Port St Johns and settle at the Xora River, under Nogaya, a great-grandson of the white castaway Jekwa. But the relocation had not affected their material well-being, for their new home was a land of plenty, bursting with produce and game.[22] Their fields, it is said, were on an island between two arms of the river, where they grew peaches and bananas: 'They used to cross the Xora in their boat, load it with fruit and bring it back to their kraals.'[23] As the peoples of the Wild Coast were not exactly renowned for their water-borne activities, the boat must have been a complete novelty in that time and place, probably a legacy of their shipwrecked ancestors, and the fruits they cultivated were also uncommon in the region, imports from far-off lands which had also probably been brought in by the castaways. Like immigrants the world over, the abeLungu had been innovative, even opportunistic, and they had flourished.

Their descendants, however, were now obviously in severely reduced circumstances, and as we started back towards Umtata at the close of day, and my eyes drifted over the spectacular physical beauty of the river, I felt that, for all their warmth and dignity, the abeLungu had become like travellers without a road. An enormous sense of loss – loss of youth, of comfort, of security – pervaded the place. Their history, too, was being lost: the elders could relate the basics of the clan's past, but the details were becoming a mere jumble of names and generations. Judging by the day's proceedings, their knowledge of Bessie seemed about as garbled as my own was at that stage.

TRADING STORE & ABELUNGU: XORA MOUTH.

According to custom, Bessie and Tshomane would have slept together for the first time on the night of their wedding feast and being, in all likelihood, a virgin, it would have been her first experience of penetrative intercourse. The other girls of the bridal party paired off with the men of the *umzi* for the first night; they could not refuse their partners, but only external sex was permitted, and it was only on the following night that they were free to sleep alone, if they so chose. Then, with the ceremonies over, the bridal party departed for home, leaving Bessie at Tshomane's Great

Place, his primary residence.[24] This was, from now on, her official home, although she was free to return to her father's *umzi* from time to time for short visits. Badi, however, seems to have disappeared some time after Bessie's marriage. It is said that 'a vessel arrived off the mouth of the Lwambaso River' and that, making over all his property to his fellow castaway Jekwa, Badi had 'decided to leave in her.'[25]

Except for the comings and goings of his *amaphakati* and other powerful men, Tshomane's Great Place was not much different from those of the common people, consisting of a semi-circle of wattle-and-daub huts facing east, with the cattle kraal at the open end. The hemispherical or beehive-shaped huts were built with a framework of supple green branches, plastered over with *daga*, a mixture of clay and cattle dung. Their only opening was a low doorway through which some of the smoke from the central fire escaped, the rest filtering out through the roof. There were no windows and the smokiness of the interiors was a common complaint among the early white missionaries to the region. The missionaries were also to complain bitterly about the bugs, a great variety of which made their home in the walls. (Insects were also a big bugbear, incidentally, for visitors in the Dutch houses down at the Cape.)

Opposite the gate of the cattle kraal, in a most important position, was Tshomane's mother's hut, where the young wife was expected to live for the first year of her marriage, cooking for her mother-in-law and learning to observe the traditional rules and taboos of her new position.[26] Mpondo society, as I've mentioned before, was tightly regulated and conservative. Strict rules and taboos governed every single aspect of the people's lives, even the way they addressed one another.[27] According to this custom, which was known as *ukuhlonipha*, Bessie would not have been permitted to use Tshomane's name, for example; as a sign of respect she could refer to him only obliquely, but even that was littered with verbal pitfalls, since she not only also had to avoid words in which the principal syllable was similar to the principal syllable of his name but also of the names of his elder brothers, his father and *his* brothers, and even his father's father, whether they were living or dead. In addition to all that she was also expected to avoid using the personal names of her husband's mother, paternal aunts, and elder sisters, although not words similar to them.[28] Similar rules applied to Tshomane, who had to avoid using Bessie's home name, her sisters' names and the names of all her female progenitors. The parents of a married couple also had to *hlonipha*, and could not use each other's names when addressing one another directly.[29] The upshot of all this was that people probably had to think long and hard before saying anything, which, to me, doesn't seem a bad thing at all. Taboos extended to a whole variety of other things as well: men could eat eggs, for example, but young girls and unmarried women generally did not because – perhaps because they were similar in shape to testicles – it was believed that they excited passion.[30]

With the wedding ceremonies over, it was time to settle the matter of Bessie's *lobola*.[31] The number of cattle which her family expected to receive from Tshomane was customarily decided by the bride's father according to the wealth and standing of both himself and his son-in-law. Tshomane's high status was undisputed; he was a prince of royal blood and heir to the powerful chief Matayi. Bessie had no such proud genealogy, and yet, although she was a mere foundling, an unheard-of number of cattle were asked for her hand in marriage.

Part of the answer to this small mystery lies in the fortunes of the three white men under whose protection she had been placed. In the years following the wreck of their ship the castaways had flourished and become wealthy enough to have several wives each.[32] Though there was no legal limit to the number of wives a man could have, commoners usually only had one. Only chiefs and rich men could afford to *ukulobola* more.[33] Jekwa, Badi and Hatu had become members of this privileged class, and their descendants had become so numerous as to constitute a separate clan with its own distinct identity, the abeLungu, or 'the Whites', whom I met and interviewed at Xora mouth. But, there were other factors besides the stature of her family that determined the size of a bride's *ikhazi*. Beauty, for example – and Bessie's beauty, as we already know, was legendary, so much so that years after her death, a traveller remarked, '… her extreme beauty is the occasion even to this day of the people in that part of the country in their general exclamations of praise'[34] – and her suitability as Queen Mother. The latter was important: since the Great Wife's *lobola* was paid not by the chief but by his people as a whole, its size was largely determined by how worthy *they* perceived her to be, and could vary from ten to a hundred cattle.[35] By comparison with these figures, Bessie's *ikhazi* was enormous: a marmalade-dropping 300 head of cattle.[36] As the *ikhazi* was most frequently fixed on only *after* the marriage was consummated,[37] it is tempting to assume that Bessie was a kind of goddess in the sack and mentally congratulate Tshomane on a great wedding night, but while that may well have been the case, the size of her 'dowry' affirms the esteem in which the Tshomane as a whole held Bessie. Although her beauty was much admired, it was her compassion and generosity that won their affection and admiration: 'When Quma our eyes saw,' the Tshomane said, 'the hungry were always fed.'[38]

> 'She was always called the *inkosazane* [queen], and treated with great respect,'[39] and her husband Tshomane shared his people's affection and esteem. 'He was more than ordinarily attached to her, and therefore constituted her head of his household, which gave her great power and influence.'[40]

According to an early Natal settler, Henry Francis Fynn, it was not all domestic bliss. Bessie, he says, 'would not consent to live with her husband if he retained the women he had already married. He consented to put them aside.…'[41] It is difficult to reconcile this statement with the fact that, as Bessie had been raised as an Mpondo, polygamy for her was the accepted norm. Nor does it fit her reputation: such an incident would have caused enormous mischief within Tshomane's household and had serious political repercussions for both him and his people, and although the oral historians did not hesitate to record the misdeeds of Great Wives who were malicious or even stingy,[42] they do not mention it. Probably Fynn was simply projecting his own marital problems onto Tshomane, since at the time of his own marriage to a white woman, he was already married to several Zulu women. In any case, Bessie, as Tshomane's Great Wife, was the only one of his wives to live permanently at his Great Place, the junior wives being resident at his other homesteads elsewhere in his territory, all of which were similar in design and construction to the Great Place, and he was obliged to travel about to visit them, since a man was expected to pay equal attention to all his wives and treat them with equal respect.[43]

This could not always have been easy, but helped to minimise domestic conflict. Jealousy between wives was by no means unknown, but it does seem that peaceful co-existence was more the norm. Women sharing the same husband were often united by very close bonds and the presence of other wives could help to lighten a woman's workload. Besides the digging of grain pits and construction of fences,[44] nearly all other building, including the erection of dwellings, was done by women, and any number of their daily chores, such as fetching water and collecting or chopping firewood for cooking, must have been easier if they could be shared between several wives. There was an economic factor too: tilling the soil, hoeing and planting were also done by the women, and consequently the more wives a man had, the greater the prosperity of the family unit as a whole: 'The work of each woman provides a surplus and as more wives are acquired so the surplus is increased.'[45]

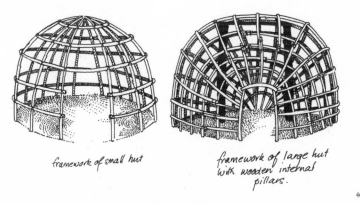

framework of small hut

framework of large hut with wooden internal pillars.

46

As Tshomane's Great Wife Bessie enjoyed certain privileges: she had the help of other women from the community in her agricultural and domestic chores, for which they were remunerated, and they also provided her with companionship.[47] As a general rule the wife of the Great House was also provided with an *iqadi*, or wife of the supporting house, who, in the event of her being barren, could provide her with a Great Son.[48]

Bessie, as we shall see, was not barren, but she never did provide Tshomane with an heir – or any other children for that matter.[49] The chief is said to have died shortly after their marriage, in unknown circumstances. Despite having had sons by his other wives,[50] because he had not yet produced a Great Son Tshomane left no official heir. Consequently, the chieftainship passed to a close relative of his, a man by the name of Sango, who is sometimes also referred to as Xwebisa.[51]

inyango :
store for tobacco,
pumpkins, seed.

udladla :
wickerwork
granary

isisele :
underground
grain pit

The scandal broke out almost before Tshomane's body was cold.

The new chief Sango, it is said, had fallen in love with Bessie and, blatantly disregarding the strict incest taboos which forbade him marrying her, had announced that that was exactly what he intended doing.

Shock and dismay rippled through the community, but despite his people's disapproval, Sango refused to back down. It was a critical situation both for the Tshomane, since failure to observe taboos could anger the ancestral spirits, and for their new chief, since by going directly against the will of his people, he could easily have lost their support and been replaced as chief. He was undeterred, however, arguing 'that as [Bessie] was a foreigner, their own customs, which would not allow of such a marriage, might in this case be set aside; to this proposal the counsellors acceded, and Sango married the white female....'[52] In the words of his grandson, 'Usangoo must have her; and therefore Usangoo, in this case, sets the law aside.'[53]

Exactly who this passionate and determined man was is not entirely clear. Sango is remembered as 'a man of wisdom, who loved peace, who kept his clan as much as possible within its own territory'[54] and, by avoiding disputes over land and cattle, lived in peace with his neighbours. But his exact relationship to Bessie's late husband – and therefore to her – is open to debate. Some say he was Tshomane's younger brother,[55] a very loose term which could mean anyone from a full blood-brother to a close relative, and from his junior in years to a member of a junior House.[56] The question of taboo may cast a little more light on their relationship. As far as I have been able to ascertain it was not only acceptable but even common for a man to take his deceased brother's wives as his own. A marriage was 'not necessarily dissolved by the death of a husband. A widow may remain at her deceased husband's *umzi*, be taken by a younger brother... of the deceased, and continue to bear children, which are looked upon as the children of the deceased.'[57]

In this case, the incest taboo would not have been an issue. It would, however, if Sango was Tshomane's brother's son,[58] or his own son by a junior wife. The latter appears the most likely, and the historian Soga even refers to Sango as the 'Principal Son of Tshomane'[59] – not the Great Son, but the next one in line; according to the prevailing rules of inheritance, in the absence of a Great Son, the heir was the eldest son of the Right-Hand house (and failing him, the son of the Left-Hand house, and so on).[60]

Whatever the case may have been, Sango won the day – and Bessie. Their union appears to have been passionate, enduring and unorthodox. In complete contrast with her first – arranged – marriage to Tshomane, the wedding feast appears to have taken place on the beach, and despite their initial opposition to the match, was attended by all the amaTshomane.

> 'By advice of the soothsayers the great dance took place at the seashore, and instead of following the custom in terms of which the bride should have been led to her husband's dwelling, Gquma and her maidens stationed themselves midway in the cleft of the black reef, where she had been tenderly delivered by the destroying waves, and thither the bridegroom went to ask his bride of the Ocean. Gifts of meat, milk, and beer were cast into the foam, and the soothsayers read the signs of the murmuring water as propitious to the union.'[61]

If this was intended to placate the water spirits it worked, for the marriage seems to have been a long and happy one:

> 'With him she retained all the power and influence vested in her by her former husband; and had, moreover, the first place in his affections, as well as the highest in his house.'[62]

Sango is said to have had two other wives[63] but I have been able to establish neither their names nor anything else about them and their children. Bessie, however, is known to have borne him at least 'five children who lived to years of maturity, and two or three others that are said to have died in childhood.'[64] Bearing a child and losing it was the worst thing that could happen to a woman, even worse than being barren. The Mpondo doted on their children; a deep and enduring love bound mother and child, but fathers too were devoted to their youngsters, making

> 'much of them when small, carrying them about in their arms, fondling them, playing with them, and teaching them to dance....

Parents [had] fierce arguments as to whether a child's first word was
mama (mummy) or *tata* (daddy).'[65]

It was this devotion that was, in fact, one of the primary reasons why the
Dutch totally dismissed the possibility of slave trading on the Wild Coast.
In the words of a Dutch official, writing in the late 1600s: 'Here it would
be impossible to trade for slaves, as they would not be parted from their
children for whom they have an outstanding love and affection.'[66]

Culturally and socially indistinguishable from the rest of the Tshomane,
Bessie and Sango's children were markedly different physically: 'This lady's
children were yellow in colour, having long hair and blue eyes.'[67] Several
were girls, the eldest of whom was called Kye,[68] and there were at least three
sons, Mlawu the Great Son, Gala and the youngest, Mdepa, who was born
in about 1753 when Bessie was in her early twenties. Many years later, in
about 1766, she had another daughter. The naming of a boy was the sole
preserve of the father, but it was the mother's privilege, sometimes shared
with the father, to name a female child,[69] and to this, her youngest child, she
gave the name Bessy,[70] the one which years ago had been supplanted by her
Xhosa name Gquma, but which at the time of her arrival on the Wild Coast
as a little girl she had clung to, repeating it 'over and over again – pointing
the while to herself: "Bessie, Bessie".'[71]

Sango's *imizi* must have housed an unusual collection of people: there
was the black chief himself, his hair braided and his arms adorned with
ivory bands and, as we shall see later, a wealth of imported glass beads, his
white wife with her long black braids, blue eyes and many bangles and
bracelets, their yellow-skinned, blue-eyed children, and his black wives and
their children. Another resident, or at least a frequent visitor, was a Lascar
woman who was said to have been wrecked with Bessie and remained her
life-long companion.[72]

At some stage, the Tshomane and abeLungu had relocated from their
lands near Lambasi Bay and moved southwards, crossing the Mzimvubu and
settling at Mngazana[73] which is about 15 kilometres, as the crow flies, down
the coast from the town of Port St Johns. In the 1990s Mngazana was still a
difficult spot for the average traveller to reach; the broad dirt road that turns
off the main Umtata–Port St Johns road at the small trading post of Tombo
deteriorated rapidly into a deeply rutted track which, in the rainy season,
was passable only in a 4x4. Because of its relative inaccessibility, it remains
a lovely and largely unspoilt spot, a string of pristine beaches punctuated by
dark shelves of flat rock used to great effect by seabirds and fishermen.
Between the outcrops and beaches are scatterings of shells, broken and re-
sculpted by the action of the waves, and drifts of perfectly smooth stones
and pebbles of every size and colour. Plum-pudding hillocks line the dunes,
rounded grassy mounds often 45 degrees or steeper, rising abruptly from the
sea and dropping as suddenly and symmetrically to the lagoon beyond and its
maze of islands, sandbars and intersecting channels, its edges dense with

mangroves. A sprawl of holiday cottages have been built over the past century on and in the slopes and hollows of the hills above the beach, the older ones crouching modestly amongst the wild-banana palms, the newer ones stark, mismatched and more exposed to the beautiful sea views but also

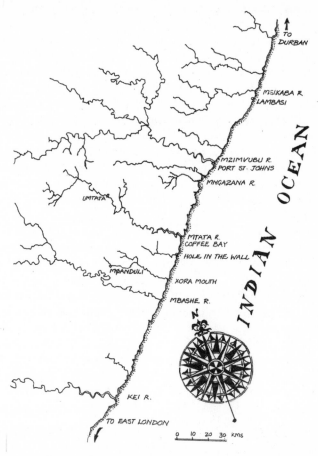

to the elements. Since the tides penetrate quite far upriver, the lagoon water is salty and unsuitable for crops or drinking purposes. The cottages all have rainwater tanks, but Bessie's people would have been obliged to settle further upriver, building their *imizi* on east-facing slopes in order to catch the first rays of the rising sun and disperse the pre-dawn cold in their cattle-kraals.[74] The most ideal place is probably on the western banks of the river, about a kilometre inland, where the freshwater Ngcelora stream joins the Mngazana, a spot now occupied by a trading store.

Five kilometres to the south, at Isilimela, where my doctor friend once tended his blue-eyed Mpondo patient, is another trading store, which, in the early 1990s was, and perhaps still is, owned by a man named Hermanus. On 13 April 1993, in one of those periodic outbursts of hate and rage that blight South Africa's history, Hermanus' son was part of a small group of renegade MK cadres, armed with automatic weapons, who ambushed a family of holidaymakers on a fishing trip. Three of the holidaymakers escaped with their lives, two of them children aged 8 and 12, but Alistair and Glen Weakly died in a hail of bullets. Their assailants were jailed for life but, although they had not been acting under orders, their appeal that their actions had been politically motivated – in retaliation for the recent death of MK commander Chris Hani, shot and killed outside his home by a right-wing white – was granted by the Truth and Reconciliation Commission in 1999 and they were released.[75]

The owner of the Mngazana trading store, Bryan Haynes, has taken a more reconciliatory approach, naming his shop Codesa, in honour of the conference that ended apartheid rule. He claims to be descended from a survivor of the *Grosvenor*, the East Indiaman wrecked at Lambasi a few decades after Bessie, through his maternal grandmother, whose maiden name was Berry.[76] I checked the ship's crew-list for him and found that a seaman called Charles Berry had in fact survived the wreck and was left by his comrades on the south bank of the Mtata after swimming across the river with three others.[77] Although several later settlers in the area also bore names like Berry and Barry, it is quite feasible that Charles Berry the castaway survived among and joined the local people, raised his family there, from which Bryan is descended.[78] I stayed in one of his cottages at Mngazana in the winter of 1999: it was right on the beach but, despite the serenity of the place, I found it difficult to sleep. It was strange lying in my bed at night, listening to the roll and surge of the ocean and imagining Sango and Bessie – born literally worlds apart, brought together by the same big Blue – listening to the same roar, the same song, of the same shore.

Mngazana is an exceptionally beautiful place, but it was not for aesthetic reasons that the Tshomane and the abeLungu had relocated here from Lambasi Bay. According to Soga, the move was forced on them by the very people who had found Bessie at Lambasi, the Nanga, who had 'attacked the abeLungu clan, being jealous, probably, of their growing numbers and strength,' defeating them and driving them south, across the Mzimvubu River.[79]

What had inspired such envy and hatred among their neighbours at Lambasi, I wondered? Generally speaking, clans and chiefdoms were able to increase in numbers and power only if they had something of value to draw more supporters to them.[80] I turned the problem over and over, but for a long time it remained a mystery. There seemed to be no explanation for the abeLungu's sudden growth, nor any indication of what lay behind and incited such simultaneous popularity and unpopularity.

And then, quite suddenly, I found the answer. Looking through some old archival material one day, I stumbled across a report on the Hubner murders. This was a small party of Dutch colonists-cum-traders who in 1736 had set out secretly from the Cape in search of ivory, and had penetrated as far as the remote regions of the Wild Coast, over a 1 000 kilometres to the east, where they not only discovered a haul of ivory rich beyond their wildest dreams, but also three mysterious English castaways, who may or may not have played a role in the subsequent violent deaths of Hubner and his men. The report describes a vital, flourishing trade in ivory between particular Mpondo clans and individual Cape traders, and two things struck

Mngazana, Great place of Sango

me immediately. First, anything as lucrative as this had the kind of power to attract followers to, and increase the size and influence of, the clans involved in it. Secondly, there were startling similarities between the three Englishmen described in the Hubner report and Bessie's three Englishmen. Their locality, period, and even their names bore a remarkable resemblance to Jekwa, Hatu and Badi. I knew from my research that there were many more wrecks on the Wild Coast than appear on the official lists and obviously many more castaways than is generally realised, but even so, the chances of two different but almost identical groups living in the same region at the same time seemed pretty remote. I figured Hubner's Englishmen *had* to be Bessie's companions, and soon discovered I wasn't the only one to have made the connection – the pioneer historian George Macall Theal had come to a similar conclusion in the late 1800s: 'It is… certain that [Bessie] belonged to the same shipwrecked party as the three Englishmen with whom the colonists under Hubner's leadership had dealings in 1736.'[81]

There was just one problem: as Bessie seems to have been wrecked around 1737–40, and Hubner's three Englishmen (as the report makes clear) were wrecked more than a decade earlier, Bessie could not have come off the same wreck as them.

As it turned out, the problem was also the solution: the discrepancies between Bessie's grandson Ngcetane's account and Soga's account now began to make sense. I had struggled to reconcile the fact that although the two stories were obviously connected – with both Ngcetane and Soga, for instance, referring to Badi as Bessie's father – there were also obvious differences. Ngcetane, for example, described Bessie as having arrived in the company of Lascars, while Soga maintained her companions were the three white men. One reason for these differences, I had assumed, was that they were the histories of two different clans. Upon her marriage Bessie had ceased to be abeLungu: thereafter she – and her children – had belonged to her husband's people. Her story as told by her grandson Ngcetane is the story of the Tshomane according to the Tshomane; Badi is mentioned because he was her 'father', but because they had no direct place in the clan's genealogy the other two white men are not. By the same token, the story of Jekwa, Hatu and Badi was the story of the abeLungu's ancestors, as told by the abeLungu; Bessie's novelty value ensured a passing mention in connection with Badi, but her descendants had no place in the abeLungu's genealogy. While this remained true, there was also a second and much simpler reason: the differences lay in the fact that there had been two different groups of castaways wrecked on two different ships, years apart. The similarities arose because their destinies had, for at least a brief time period, overlapped. Bessie had not been wrecked together with three white men; she was only linked to them later. Neither Ngcetane's nor Soga's account, after all, had said that Bessie and her 'father' had arrived together, merely that there had been four castaways who had come from the same 'house', ie were white. It was a possibility I had considered many times before, but, until the Hubner report, had had no evidence to support it.

Even more important, though, than sorting out these tangled threads, was the Englishmen's involvement in the ivory trade, which, the Hubner report makes clear, was of a quite spectacular magnitude. More than two and a half centuries after the Hubner murders, the survivors' skeletal report had fleshed out Bessie's companions a little, fingering the instrument of the abeLungu's and Tshomane's wealth.

Genealogy of the amaTshomane[82]

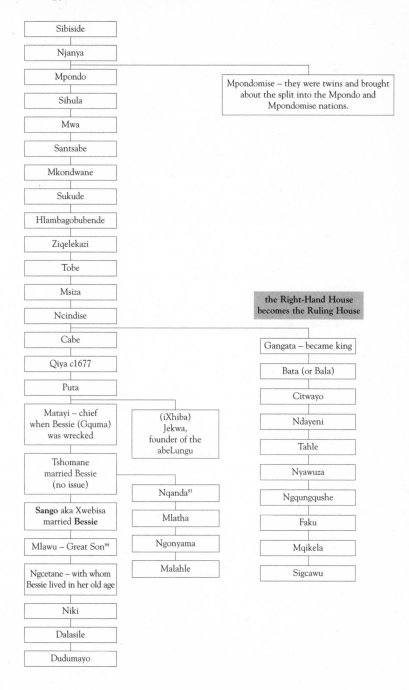

Sibiside

Njanya

Mpondo — Mpondomise – they were twins and brought about the split into the Mpondo and Mpondomise nations.

Sihula

Mwa

Santsabe

Mkondwane

Sukude

Hlambagobubende

Ziqelekazi

Tobe

Msiza

Ncindise

the Right-Hand House becomes the Ruling House

Cabe

Qiya c1677

Puta

Matayi – chief when Bessie (Gquma) was wrecked

(iXhiba) Jekwa, founder of the abeLungu

Gangata – became king

Bata (or Bala)

Citwayo

Ndayeni

Tahle

Tshomane married Bessie (no issue)

Nyawuza

Nqanda[83]

Ngqungqushe

Sango aka Xwebisa married **Bessie**

Mlatha

Faku

Mlawu – Great Son[84]

Ngonyama

Mqikela

Ngcetane – with whom Bessie lived in her old age

Malahle

Sigcawu

Niki

Dalasile

Dudumayo

47

Genealogy of Sango and Bessie[85]

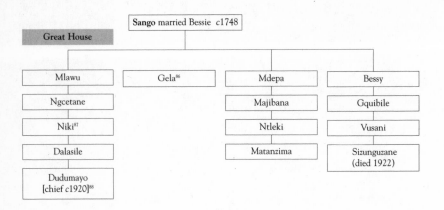

Great House	Sango married Bessie c1748		
Mlawu	Gela[86]	Mdepa	Bessy
Ngcetane		Majibana	Gquibile
Niki[87]		Ntleki	Vusani
Dalasile		Matanzima	Sizunguzane (died 1922)
Dudumayo [chief c1920][88]			

Genealogy of the abeLungu [I]
According to Zali, 1889, one of the oldest abeLungu then living[89]

1.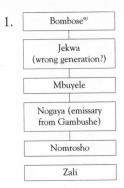

'I am therefore a direct descendant of the chief of the survivors.'

2.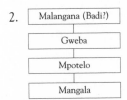

'His descendants are now among the Tshomanes'
(They have almost exactly the same names as the ones Soga lists under Jekwa's Great House see below).

3.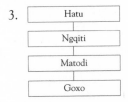

'... his descendants are also among the Tshomanes in the Mqanduli district.'

Genealogy of the abeLungu [II]
According to Soga, the descendants of Jekwa and Hatu are as follows:[91]

1.

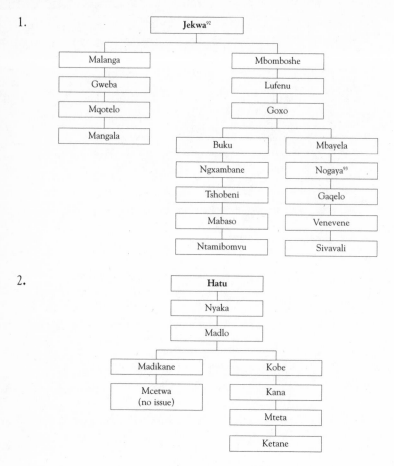

2.

Chapter Three

The Three Mysterious Englishmen

When the ill-fated Hubner party set out on their expedition in 1736, the huddle of whitewashed houses at the base of Table Mountain that would one day grow into the beautiful city of Cape Town was just a village, an outstation of the Dutch East India Company, which owed its origin to the spice trade between Europe and the East. When the overland route between India and Europe was blocked by the establishment of the Ottoman Empire in the 15th century, finding and establishing an alternative route became a matter of urgency.[1] The first Europeans to do so were the Portuguese: in 1497–98 Vasco da Gama broke through to the east by sailing around the southern tip of Africa and up its east coast to Malindi. At that time the trade between India and Africa was the preserve of the Arabs and Indians. It was their pilots and navigators who knew the secrets of the seasonal monsoon winds blowing between the two continents, and it was from them that the European explorers derived their own knowledge.[2] It was an Asian pilot, for example, who guided Da Gama from Malindi across the Indian Ocean to Calicut, and who taught him on his return journey to wait for the north-easterly monsoons of February and March to blow his vessels back towards Africa.[3]

Scurvy raged rampant on the long voyages between Europe and the East. Born of severe vitamin deficiency due to a prolonged lack of fresh fruit and vegetables, the disease took a terrible toll on the ships' crews. The death rate was so high at times that whole ships were lost – and stories of ghost ships like the 'Flying Dutchman', which drifted unmanned on the southern seas, arose from their crews having succumbed to scurvy.[4] Fortunately there was a life-saving landfall at the Cape of Storms, which was ideally placed, roughly halfway between the East and Europe, and blessed with fresh produce and water to revive the ailing crews. Situated at the foot of a huge flat-topped

mountain which could be seen from far out to sea, it boasted a sheltering
bay of spectacular but harsh beauty: 'This remotest part of Africa is very
mountainous, over-run with wild beasts, as lions, tigers, wolves, and many
other beasts of prey…,' wrote one early visitor.[5] The pros apparently outweighed
the cons, however, and the Bay at the Cape was acclaimed for its sweet
water, abundant fish, moderate climate and 'fragrant herbs'. The Cape was
more than a useful stop-off point; it was a sanctuary

> 'where our ships companies, when they have often-times there arrived
> with very weak and feeble bodies, usually by that sea-disease, the scurvy
> … have often found here much good refreshing; for besides a delectable
> brook of pure good water, running hard by out of a mighty hill (called
> from its form the Table…) there are great stores of cattle… called by
> the barbarous inhabitants Boos; and sheep, which they call Baas….'[6]

The Portuguese were the earliest to grasp the Bay's potential, but their
love affair was short and ended violently. Early in 1510, a group of extremely
important Portuguese officials and aristocrats on their way home from the
East stopped in Table Bay[7] to take on fresh water. Their leader was Dom
Francisco de Almeida, the first Portuguese Viceroy of India.

Nobleman, confidant of the King, hero of the war in Morocco and conqueror
of the rich East African ports of Kilwa and Mombasa, he was also a man of
brutal temperament.[8] Following a triumphant attack on the Muslim-held
island of Diu, Almeida had celebrated his victory by dismembering his foes
and firing their heads and limbs into the town centres of neighbouring ports.[9]
From the shore of the Bay, the indigenous Khoikhoi watched the arrival
of the Portuguese aristocrats with interest. They were keen traders and
welcomed the newcomers warmly.[10] Between the two groups there could
hardly have been greater contrast, the Khoi naked but for their leather

cloaks or *karosses*, their slender coffee-coloured bodies smeared with strong-smelling animal fats to protect them from insect bites, the pale, black-bearded Portuguese richly clothed and sparkling with jewels, their swords flashing in the sunlight. After months aboard ship, the Portuguese smelt as least as rancid as the Khoi but, fresh from their victories over the indigenous peoples of the East, they were convinced of their superiority and openly contemptuous of the Khoi. They were not the only ones: every European account of the Cape for the next few hundred years denigrates the Khoikhoi: 'miserable folk who went quite naked, except that they had a cloak of sheep or other skin bound about their neck, and the tail of such hanging before their privities.... They clucked like turkeys and smeared their bodies so they stank disgustingly;' 'They always stank greatly, since they besmeared themselves with fat and grease...;' 'they lived upon the guts and filth of the meate which we did cast away, feeding in the most beastly fashion, for they would neither wash nor make clean the guts....'[11] Perhaps the real issue behind all this ranting was the Khoi's possession of the Fairest Cape; as one visitor put it, 'it is a greatt pittie... such creatures as they bee should injoy so sweett a counttrey.'[12]

Their arrogance led the Portuguese straight into trouble. On their return from a food-bartering expedition at a village in the vicinity of today's suburb of Mowbray,[13] Almeida's men tried to force one of the Khoi back to their ship. It was just a prank, they claimed later, saying they had not intended to harm him but only to amuse themselves by dressing the poor fellow in European finery. If it was a prank, it misfired tragically. When the Khoi saw their comrade being dragged away, protesting and screaming, and with a dagger at his throat, they dropped everything and rushed to his assistance, driving the Portuguese back to their ship with bloody noses.[14] Bored and inactive during their long voyage and eager for some action, their outraged shipmates leapt to the attack. At midnight, 150 of them piled into the boats and hurried back to shore.[15] They were so over-confident and arrogant that they did not bother with armour or firearms, but took only their swords and their lances. Almeida himself went along, albeit with less enthusiasm: 'Where are you taking [a man of] sixty years?' he complained.[16]

Their attack on the Khoi village was a fiasco and their first casualty an own-goal (Fernao Pereira, who was stabbed through the grass wall of a hut by a fellow Portuguese who mistook him for the enemy).[17] Then the Portuguese seized some Khoi children, but instead of intimidating their parents it had the opposite effect. The Khoi were outraged and, in their efforts to save their children, became utterly fearless. Mounted on war oxen and armed only with slingshots and sharp, fire-hardened sticks, they totally routed Almeida's men. Many of the wounded Portuguese were trampled beneath the oxen's hooves. Those who could still stand fled back to the shore, only to find that their boats had returned to the ship. In a futile attempt to save themselves many rushed chin-deep into the icy Atlantic. Others floundered about in the soft sand, outmanoeuvred by the Khoi, 'so light-footed and nimble that they appeared to be birds.' Almeida's scarlet cloak made him an easy target;

beneath the brooding flat-topped mountain the Victor of the East met his
death, with a humble wooden lance through his throat. In a final humiliation,
his killers stripped him of his fine clothing, leaving the body of the man to
whom the King of Portugal himself had said 'I give you power as though it
were to my own person' sprawling naked in the dirt, until his men eventually
felt it was safe to return and bury him.[18] The place where he and his men
were buried was marked by a pile of stones near the Salt River mouth.
Almost half of his men had died with him: of the 150 who had gone ashore
to teach the Khoi a lesson, 65 had lost their lives,[19] 12 of them captains –
noblemen belonging to the most aristocratic Portuguese families.

Round one to the locals.

The Portuguese steered clear of the Cape from then on,[20] but others soon
followed. The success of the Portuguese trade, the silks and damasks, spices,
and saltpetre – an essential ingredient in making gunpowder – inspired a
wave of European traders and adventurers to head East. Spices in particular
were eagerly sought after: 'men were prepared to die in search of them, and
many did; no gift was more acceptable, and to be well supplied was a mark
of status; wealth could be measured in spices.'[21] They were the basis of many
medicines and, besides adding flavour to a variety of foodstuffs, were particularly
valued as preservatives. Fresh meat was available to the European population for
only a few months of the year and, without spices, much of the rest would have
been not only unpalatable but even inedible.[22] (It was spices acquired from
India, incidentally, that the Egyptians used for embalming their dead.[23])

As the sea-borne traffic between Europe and the East increased in
volume and scurvy took its toll on the crews and their ships – and on the
pockets of the merchants who funded them – the Cape became especially
important as a place where fresh food could be bartered, water obtained and
health recovered. More and more vessels from many European nations began
to make use of Table Bay, and as the struggle for domination of the sea route
to India and the Spice Islands grew, the Cape became a coveted strategic
prize. It was only a matter of time before someone had the bright idea of
securing it for their exclusive use, and in 1613 the English sailed into Table
Bay with just that in mind. On Captain Towerson's orders two Khoi men
were forcibly abducted and brought aboard the *Hector*. The intention was
to take them back to England, in order for the English authorities to learn
as much as possible about the Cape and its inhabitants, but one of the
kidnapped men died on the return voyage ('merely out of extreme
sullenness', according to his captors.[24]) The other, whose name was Xhore,
survived and adapted very well to his new circumstances – perhaps too well.

The English never did manage to learn Xhore's language, while he not
only learnt to speak theirs[25] but also had the opportunity of studying them in
their natural habitat. As a result he learnt substantially more about them
than they did about him, and by the time he was returned to the Cape just
over a year later Xhore knew just how essential his people's fresh meat and

produce were to the foreigners – and immediately increased the price on all trade goods.

Where once the Khoi had been content to barter a little scrap iron in exchange for their cattle, now they would accept only brass and the irate English realised too late that it 'would have bynn much better for us and such as shall come hereafter yf he [Xhore] never had seene Ingland....'[26] Their interest in the Cape continued, however, and in the following year, on 5 June 1615, another English fleet sailed into Table Bay. On board was

AFTER COPE, "KING OF THE HOTTENTOTS"

a small party of convicts, nine men and a boy, who had been granted reprieve in exchange for setting up an establishment there and exploring the surrounding countryside.

The fact that our first European settlers were criminals has received little publicity, but then – unlike the convicts who colonised Australia – they left no descendants.

From the start they were less-than-enthusiastic immigrants; one absconded even before their ship had left England and several others escaped by dying on the voyage out.[27] On their arrival in Table Bay the convicts were given some bread, wine and fish and sent ashore with a couple of pikes and swords to defend themselves against the wild beasts which roamed the foreshore. The fleet then sailed on to Surat,[28] but one English vessel, the *Hope*, remained at anchor in the Bay while its crew recuperated from scurvy and, seeking safety in numbers, the convict-settlers hurriedly joined their camp, near the foot of present-day Adderley Street, beside the little stream flowing down from Platteklip Gorge.

The leader of the convicts was Captain John Crosse, a well-educated individual who had been born into an upper-class family. He had once been a member of the King's Guard, but by 1614 had swopped careers and become a highwayman instead. He had been arrested and was languishing in Newgate Prison under sentence of death when he received his 'reprieve'.[29] A 'very stout and very resolute man'[30] and an expert swordsman, Crosse was, however, also a difficult and quick-tempered individual known to have killed several men and, under the circumstances, probably not the best personality for the task at hand.

It was not an auspicious time to begin a new settlement at the Cape. Xhore, who was still chief of the local Khoi, was deeply suspicious of the convicts and quick to 'demaund wherefore those men were lefte behinde.'[31] His control of the foreign market had recently come undone and other Khoi groups were underselling his people in the supply of cattle to European vessels, and civil discord was the order of the day. The situation deteriorated further when four of the convicts, sent to a village by the captain of the *Hope* to obtain cattle, were attacked, leaving one dead and two injured. Xhore hastened to assure the English that the attack was the work of a small unruly faction, and sent a group of Khoi women – in 'noe waies inferior to the men for dirte and greace' – to pleasure the sailors and allay their fears.[32] But the incident had raised doubts about the convicts' safety and before departing, the *Hope's* crew handed over four muskets and a small boat. Left to fend for themselves, the convicts' best hope of survival would have been to establish a mutually beneficial relationship with Xhore, who not only spoke their language but could have afforded them his protection, as well as food, shelter and even wives. But Crosse had neither charm nor diplomatic skills, and failed to realise just how precarious his position was, 'quarrelling with and abusing the natives.'

Within a very short time relations with the Khoi deteriorated to the point where he and his men were forced to flee in their boat to the safety of Robben Island, a bare rock a few kilometres out in Table Bay which would one day become one of the world's most infamous prisons – probably the only occasion in South African history of convicted men fleeing *to* the island! Some of them were eventually rescued by a Portuguese vessel and three others were picked up by a homeward-bound English ship (they deserted while it was in the Downs, took a purse within three hours, were captured and executed).[33] Crosse was not among either group. According to one report he was drowned when a whale capsized his boat near the island, according to another he was killed by the Khoi, who 'fell upon him, and with their darts and arrows shot him, stuck his body so full of them, as if he had been larded with darts and arrows.'[34]

Round two to the locals.

Xhore continued to reign at the Cape for several years, and in time established a large village for his followers, settling them in the manner he had observed in England, for as a well-to-do trader 'that dogge Corye', as the English now referred to him, the nomadic existence of his Khoi forebears no longer served his needs.[35] By 1627 he was dead, allegedly hanged by the Dutch for refusing to trade with them. The Dutch were notorious for their ill-treatment of the Khoi[36] and were involved in a number of violent confrontations with them,[37] but for the crews of European ships the Cape remained a life saving stop-over. As one contemporary visitor reported,

> 'no words could express the joy and happiness of those on board whenever the Cape was sighted: the lame, the cripple, and those who were just able to crawl – all tried to catch a glimpse of the majestic mountain that guards the entrance to Table Bay.'[38]

Over the years several attempts were made by both the French and the English to settle the Cape, but it was the Dutch who are credited with establishing a permanent settlement there. This is rather ironic, first, because it was not their intention to set up anything more than a refreshment station and, secondly, because most of the original settlers were not Dutch; 91 of the 100-strong party were German Lutherans and seven Scottish or English.[39] Their commander, an ex-surgeon's mate named Jan van Riebeeck, had instructions to make 'everything out of nothing.'[40] A touchy little man whose nickname was 'thorn-back', Van Riebeeck took the bit between his teeth and did just that. At one stage, for defence purposes, he even proposed turning the Cape Peninsula into an island by digging a canal from Table Bay to False Bay, but the plan was dropped because of the cost. Six thousand acres were cordoned off from the locals by means of a wild almond hedge,[41] excluding them from land that was really theirs, and within 10 years the Dutch had established a fort, an array of other buildings and planted extensive gardens of fruit, vegetables and exotic trees, which were soon rated among the most beautiful in the world.[42] (The Company Gardens still flourish in the heart of Cape Town, a lush, sweet-smelling green lung in the middle of the city.) As only three of Van Riebeeck's party were women, it was not long before the settlers' intercourse with the Khoi was more than just social, and it continued in this vein even after girls from an Amsterdam orphanage had been sent out to swell the settlers' ranks.[43]

As the years passed and the settlement grew, the original Khoi occupants lost more and more of their lands to the settlers, and were forced to move further afield or lose their independence and become the servants of the Cape burghers. The break-up of Khoi clans was compounded by the devastating smallpox epidemic that swept through the Colony in 1713. While the colonists suffered heavy losses – one in four dying[44] – the Khoi were literally decimated, especially the children, for they had no natural resistance to the disease: '[T]hey died as if by hundreds, so that they lay everywhere along the roads as if massacred as they fled inland with kraals, huts, and cattle, all cursing the Dutch who they said had bewitched them....'[45] For the colonists this was all rather inconvenient, as Valentyn, on a visit to the Cape a year later, noted:

> '[V]ery few Hottentots [Khoi] were to be seen here compared with previously, this causing very great inconvenience to the Burghers and other inhabitants who now lacked their service, both for cleaning and scouring almost everything in the house at low pay....'[46]

The colony was growing, despite its makers' intentions. The Dutch East India Company had never meant its refreshment station to become a permanent settlement, but its employees had somehow mutated into burghers (citizens), and were soon spilling out of the narrow confines of the Bay and spreading beyond the mountains which rim the Cape Peninsula, seeking grazing and trading opportunities further afield. To the north the hinterland of Africa was guarded by the dry Namaqualand, to the north-east by the Great Karoo, a land of few and unreliable sources of water.

To the east, however, the land spread out seemingly without end, a rich mosaic of rolling grasslands, *kloofs*, mountains, vast forests, waterfalls and lagoons. Within forty years of Van Riebeeck's arrival at the Cape, a Dutch expedition had penetrated as far eastward as present-day Port Elizabeth, encountered members of the Xhosa, and killed several.[47] It was not the first incident of black and white conflict, but a beginning, nevertheless, of escalating violence between the two, as they came into more and more frequent contact, particularly through trade.

In an attempt to control and monopolise the economy of its growing colony, the Dutch East India Company periodically outlawed private trade between the colonists and the indigenous people, threatening to execute anyone caught doing so. But the Dutch in South Africa were anything but tulipy: a tough and individualistic lot, they were not intimidated by a mere law, and the trade continued, albeit secretively.[48] Authoritarian but averse to authority, they were a new breed, no longer Europeans but Dutch Africans, or *Boers*.[49] Born in Africa, they adopted whatever tools and traits of the land and the indigenous people – including in many cases the gene pool – they required to survive. They were excellent shots, restless adventurers and were built like giants. Slowly at first and then in increasing numbers and determination, the farmers and hunters spread out into the southern regions of the dry Camdeboo and eastwards to the rich grasslands of the eastern Cape, steadily drawing closer to the Wild Coast where Bessie would one day make her home. They were sometimes a little vague about their exact whereabouts, as the title of a 1661 journal in the Cape Archives reveals – 'Journal kept by me Cornelis de Cretzer of a journey to and fro in the land of Africa…' – but that did not keep them from exploring further and further afield. By 1689 a Dutch expedition had reached as far as Algoa Bay, where the attack mentioned above took place.[50] In 1702 there was another clash between a party of colonists and a group of Xhosa near the Great Fish River, some 160 kilometres north-east of present-day Port Elizabeth and about 1 000 kilometres from the Cape. It is unlikely that these Boers were the first to penetrate the region; we probably know of them only because 'barter took the form of exchange of bullets for assegais,'[51] and attracted the attention of the Cape authorities. Many more illegal hunters and traders must have made the same journey undetected. As Mostert says in his brilliant history of the eastern Cape: 'Somebody knew the way.'[52]

Hubner probably knew the way too, from personal experience. When the trader set out from the Cape, with his companion Hendrick de Vries and three heavily laden wagons, at the beginning of the winter of 1736, it appears not to have been his first expedition to the remote eastern seaboard. It was, however, to be his last.

As the Cape dropped away behind them the traders were joined by the rest of their party, De Vries' brothers Johannes and Daniel, Jan van Vooren and his son Gerrit, the brothers Hendrick and Coenraad Scheffer, Jan Bruijns, Christoffel Hoogreefde and Louis Cloete. All were second- or third-generation settlers, Cape-born and raised in Africa. The majority were in their late teens and early twenties; only their leader Hermanus Hubner and Jan van Vooren were older. Besides the 10 traders there was a contingent of Khoi servants, none of whose names have been preserved, spare draught oxen and horses, and 13 wagons laden with 'trader's goods and powder and lead.'[53] Each was drawn by 12 to 16 oxen yoked in pairs, at the head of which ran a young Khoi *voorloper,* to guide them in the right direction. This was a tiring and unpleasant task, for if the lad slowed down he was apt to find – as one young Englishman did – 'two pairs of horns in rather close proximity to my behind.'[54]

The first part of their route took them through today's district of Swellendam and on to Mossel Bay. This was the least difficult part of their journey; sustenance was easily obtainable, the sandy *vlakte* teeming with food on the hoof and flocks of ostriches, and although there were no towns or even villages, the territory was already sprinkled with farmers from whom both help and hospitality could be had if required. Greater difficulties lay further east, where the land became rougher, sandwiched between the

Indian Ocean and massive mountain ranges, dissected by steep ravines and thundering streams. Known today as the 'Garden Route' for its colourful *fynbos* and wild flowers, it was a near-impenetrable wilderness dense with mighty yellowwoods: 'forests of several days' travel' wrote an early traveller, 'where the intertwined branches and broad-leafed scrub which frequently filled the intervening spaces, intercept all the rays of the sun and prevent them from penetrating.'[55] In the dim light exquisitely plumed Knysna Turacos and other birds 'of all species and size, whose screeches echoed through the forest, shared their solitude with the elephants... in numerous troops....'[56] The only paths were game and elephant tracks, constantly rising or descending over the broken terrain, jagged with rocks and tree stumps and impeded by thickly interlaced creepers and vines. It was impassable by ox-wagon and the traders were forced to turn inland, dragging their heavy wagons through the rugged Attaquas kloof, near the present Robinson Pass between Oudtshoorn and Mossel Bay, to the long, eastward-running corridors of the Langkloof and the Kromme River kloof beyond.[57]

Their journey took them through a region where two climatic zones overlap: the winter rainfall of the south-western Cape and the summer rainfall of the eastern Cape. Every day was spent in the saddle, and the men were exposed to the harsh rays of the sun and to downpours that, to another early traveller, 'resembled cloudbursts.'[58] At night they fell asleep on the hard earth without removing their clothes, using their saddles as pillows. As the traders proceeded further east and the land gradually became flatter, they would have begun to catch glimpses of the sea before, at length, they reached the flat sandy surrounds of Algoa Bay, at present-day Port Elizabeth. The journey, which today takes just an hour by air, had taken the traders months – a long, bone-jarring journey, at once dangerous and monotonous, the excitement of hunting probably the only real break from the tedium of the plodding oxen. Ahead of them lay a tougher stage, a rougher and barely known terrain that promised them much more excitement. So much so, that, had they been blessed with foreknowledge, even the bravest and most adventurous of the young bucks in the party would surely have abandoned the trek then and there.

At Algoa Bay the coastline broke away to the north-east and the wagon-train followed it, through territory that the survivors later described as 'the country of the Gonaquas [a mixed Khoi/Xhosa clan] over whom Captain Babbelaan exercises authority.'[59] In order to avoid the deeply scoured, heavily wooded river valleys of the coastal plains, the traders struck inland. Their base camp appears to have been Hermanus Kraal, a *drift* or ford on the Great Fish River named after their leader Hermanus Hubner.[60] The fact that it bore his name suggests he was a regular visitor to the spot, and it was well placed as a departure point into Xhosa territory, offering not only a crossing over the river and plenty of fresh water, but a place where the traders could rest and gather their strength for the hazardous, even hostile, terrain that lay ahead – the deep valleys and ragged *kranzes* of the Fish, Keiskamma and many other rivers, where leopards, baboons, scorpions and snakes still lurk in the tangled scrub and dense thorn bush. Thorns of every kind are everywhere, grasping at and shredding skin and cloth, the most prolific easily as long as a man's fingers, pale and slender but as strong and sharp as stilettos. In those days great

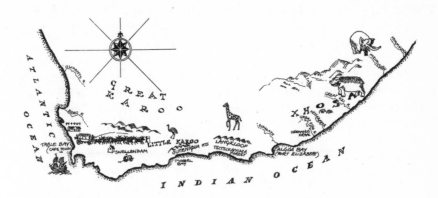

herds of elephant swarmed through the bush, lions and buffalo roamed the countryside and hippopotami wallowed in every river. During the frontier wars of the nineteenth century Hermanus Kraal became strategically important because of its position on the main road from the Colony to Xhosaland,[61] but even in Hubner's time it appears to have been a well-established trade route to the north. Government reports just 30 years after the Hubner expedition refer to 'a road which had formerly been used,' between the Colony and 'the so-called Hermanus Kraal, and [leading] consequently to the abodes of the [Xhosa]… about two short days' journey from this place.'[62] Before 1752 Dutch names had already replaced the original Khoi names of many of the rivers in the area, confirming that from an even earlier date, colonial hunters and traders were visiting the region on a regular basis, and were in contact with the Xhosa and probably also with the Thembu and Mpondo beyond.[63]

Continuing their journey, the Hubner traders entered Xhosa territory, where they paid a visit to 'Captain Bange', chief of the amaNtinde ('a stout man' reported a later visitor, 'who wore ornaments made of beads – obtained from elephant hunters – on his head and hanging from his ears,'[64]) then pushed on to the Great Place of Phalo, king of the Xhosa, in the vicinity of present-day Butterworth. The Xhosa were a proud and handsome people; their physiques were much admired by early travellers, the women possessing 'very sleek soft skin, beautiful teeth, pleasing features, expressive of great cheerfulness and content, and a slender form,' their men 'handsome, strong-made, and their limbs exquisitely proportioned…. They hold themselves exceedingly upright; their step is quick and dignified; their whole exterior denotes strength and spirit.'[65] A further one and a half months' travel through Xhosaland took the traders to 'the country of a certain nation called Tamboegis, which was situated beyond that of the [Xhosa].'[66]

At a pre-arranged spot they linked up with another party of traders –
Antony Lotze, Andries Esterhuijsen and Philip Constant, under the leadership
of Hubner's brother Fredrick[67] – and the two groups then travelled further up
the Wild Coast together, penetrating, in the words of the survivors,

> 'as far as the land called Adera diera de Natal, where the inhabitants
> are known by the name of Nomotis. Among the people of this nation
> they found three Englishmen whose names were Tomas Willer, Hendrik
> Clercq and Willem Bilyert, who, many years before, had been stranded
> there by a shipwreck, and who had remained there living just like the
> inhabitants of the interior, taking to themselves wives and begetting
> children and completely adapting themselves to the life of the
> heathen natives.'[68]

AFTER DERRICOURT,
"BEYOND THE CAPE FRONTIER", PG 75.

'There can hardly be a doubt that the Pondos are the people referred to,'
wrote the historian Theal of the 'Nomotis.'[69] I would go even further: the
Nomotis were not only Mpondo, I believe, but the Tshomane. For a start,
like the 'Nomotis', the Tshomane lived beyond the Thembu ('Tamboegis').
Derricourt, in his map of the Transkei for 1700–50, places the Nomotis on
the Mzimvubu River,[70] bang in the middle of Tshomane territory. Secondly,
at the time of Hubner's visit 'Adera diera de Natal', the land of Natal,
referred not to the province which today bears the name, but to a region
further south, stretching from Brazen Head to Waterfall Bluff[71] – the very
same territory that belonged to the Tshomane chief Matayi. Thirdly, there is
a distinct phonetic similarity between Nomoti (no-mor-tee) and 'Tshomane'
(cho-mar-nee), suggesting the former is merely a corruption of the latter. The

Dutch, incidentally, were abysmal with Xhosa names, in one case rendering 'Mlawu' as 'Oom Louw' (uncle Louw,)[72] and the fact that the Hubner traders would have had to communicate with the Tshomane through interpreters could not have improved the situation.

The names of Hubner's three Englishmen and the three white castaways, Jekwa, Hatu and Badi, are also similar, although once again it may not be immediately obvious, since the Dutch butchered English names as badly as they did isiXhosa. 'Translated' into English, however, 'Hendrik Clercq' becomes Henry Clarke; 'Tomas Willer', Thomas Miller; and 'Willem Bilyert', William (Bill) Elliot or perhaps even Billy Hart, and when these are juxtaposed with the names of Bessie's white men, the result is striking: 'Hatu' resembles 'Henry' and 'Badi' 'Billy' enough to suggest the former are simply Xhosa-ised versions of the latter.[73] There is independent evidence of a white man called 'Biale' (Billy?) having lived among the Tshomane (exactly when is not stated, only that he died sometime prior to the 1820s.)[74] In addition, Bessie's son Mdepa told a missionary in the 1820s that one of his mother's companions had been a white man called 'Tomee', which as the Reverend Shaw was quick to note, was 'probably a native corruption of Thomas.'[75]

If Henry and Billy were Hatu and Badi, Thomas Willer (or Miller) must have been the man known to the Tshomane as Jekwa. It was customary for a man to take on a new name when he became chief – and in fact still is – and his Xhosa name Jekwa was probably bestowed on him when his mentor chief Matayi appointed him *ixiba*, head of his late father's House, or to honour his position as chief of the abeLungu.

The dangers and hardships of mounting an expedition deep into the Transkei and so far from their homes and families at the Cape had paid off handsomely for Hubner and his men. They found the countryside rich with game: lion, leopard, giraffe, zebra, jackal, hyena, wildebeest, antelope of every kind, hippopotamus, rhinoceros and herds of elephant, and through hunting and bartering they had already acquired five wagon-loads of ivory by the time they arrived in Nomoti/Tshomane territory. They found the

English castaways particularly well prepared for trade and, in exchange for copper, iron and beads, were able to fill their remaining wagons, obtaining no less than five full loads of elephant tusks. As a wagon could carry anything between two and seven tons, that means they had a *minimum* of ten tons of ivory.[76] No wonder later colonists referred to the Mpondo – which of course includes the Tshomane – as 'people of the elephants' tooth'![77]

The Mpondo valued ivory for its ornamental use, the men adorning their upper arms with bands of ivory, but the possession of such a vast quantity suggests the 'Nomoti' were deliberately stockpiling it – and that it was specifically for trade. It is a well-established fact that European vessels had been visiting the Pondoland coast to trade since at least the 1680s, exchanging beads and copper for ivory[78] – but the Hubner account suggests that the overland route from the Cape via Hermanus Kraal was also bringing traders far up the Wild Coast on a basis that was regular and lucrative enough for the Tshomane, at least, to actively accumulate vast stocks. In any event, the rewards must have been great, since ivory was by no means easy to obtain. Elephant hunting was an extremely dangerous and difficult undertaking.

Since – as the Hubner report makes clear – the Englishmen had been shipwrecked many years before the traders' visit, even if they had firearms they are unlikely to have had any ammunition, so the tusks were probably obtained by traditional methods of hunting. This involved a party of considerable size and required the approval of their chief. Armed with spears, the hunters could kill just one elephant at a time: they used dogs as bait to separate a single beast from the herd, trapped it within a circle of fire and, advancing from all sides, threw their spears simultaneously and with great force. The kill had to be made as quickly as possible – pursuing a wounded elephant was enormously dangerous and it could take days before the animal succumbed. Once the tusks had been cut out of the carcass they became the property of the chief and it was strictly forbidden to dispose of them without his consent.[79] Faku, a nineteenth-century Mpondo king, is said to have demanded a tribute of half of all tusks traded by his people, but even if the Tshomane chief Matayi's cut was the same, judging by the amounts traded with Hubner, the Englishmen's share would still have made them very wealthy.

In 1782, more than 50 years before traders from Natal and the eastern Cape began to bring a regular supply of beads into the region, a shipwreck survivor reported that the Tshomane were richly dressed in imported goods, with 'beads about their necks, brass rings about their wrists, pieces of copper in their hair, large white and blue glass beads about their waists....'[80] We know that Hubner paid for the ivory with ample quantities of beads, copper and iron. The metal was probably the Tshomane's primary incentive for trade: the peoples of the Wild Coast are known to have smelted ore and they certainly worked iron, but the evidence of shipwreck survivors as well as modern archaeology indicates that metal of all kinds was in short supply.[81] But the beads too were highly sought-after commodities, and were easily exchanged among the neighbouring people for cattle, the main source of a man's wealth. No wonder the Tshomane's neighbours were jealous of them! No wonder Jekwa, Hatu and Badi could afford any number of wives.

Hubner's men had also done extremely well for themselves, almost too well in fact. They now had enough ivory 'to load ten wagons fully, each with from eighteen to nineteen hundredweight of good tusks.' Unfortunately this haul was too great to get to the Cape in one go, and so it was decided that some would be left behind to be collected by Hermanus Hubner on a future expedition.[82]

With heavy wagons and light hearts, the traders prepared to return to the Cape. They tried to encourage Miller, Clark and Elliot to go with them, but the castaways showed no inclination to be 'rescued'.[83] They did, however, agreed to accompany the traders part of the way,[84] but they refused to go beyond Xhosa territory. According to the Hubner report, this was because the three Englishmen 'wished first to discover how and under what conditions His Excellency the Governor would receive them at the Cape.'[85] It is hard to imagine what they were afraid of – the Dutch and English were not at war with one another in 1736, nor had they been for many years – but whatever it was probably holds a further clue to their identities, since Thomas/Jekwa and his comrades obviously had something to hide. Perhaps they were not the castaways they claimed to be, but deserters from the Cape garrison; not only Dutch soldiers served at the Cape but men of all European nations, and there were many runaways, some of whom sought refuge among the Xhosa.[86]

A later Dutch account, however, makes it more likely that they *were* castaways. In 1757, twenty-one years after Hubner's visit, the crew of a Dutch ship, the *Naastigheid*, which was stranded at Delagoa Bay (today's Maputo), made several journeys southwards down the coast, hoping to reach the Dutch settlement at the Cape. One of these took them as far as the Wild Coast.[87] There, on the banks of a 'Wyde Rivier', they met an extraordinary man. To the sailors' surprise, this black chief, living among people who customarily did not fish or sail,

> 'knew the difference between the Dutch, English, and French flags and informed the sailors that a Dutch hooker [in those days a kind of ship] had recently put in farther south and taken a cargo of forest timber to supply the Cape.'[88]

His knowledge of European ships and shipping suggests that he himself must once have been a sailor, a castaway Lascar perhaps. Communicating through Pieter Willemsz, a sailor who spoke 'the language of the land', the chief warned the *Naastigheid* crew that their path to the Cape would be filled with danger: 'Beyond, and farther still to the south, he said, there were "savage Hottentots", living like wild men in the rocks, who killed and ate all strangers.' This was too much for the Dutchmen, who decide to retrace their steps to Delagoa Bay, but before they left the chief told them that 'many years before an English ship had been wrecked there, from which two men of that nation had remained; each one married a woman, and raised children, who were still alive....' These children 'were distinct, like the whiteness of paint, and could clearly be recognised as bastaards [mulattoes] of the European nation.'[89]

The phrase – 'like the whiteness of paint' – immediately evokes the name of Jekwa and Hatu's descendants, the abeLungu or 'the Whites', who, incidentally, have always claimed to be of English descent: 'Siz' Englandi! [We are Englanders].'[90] The historian Mackeurtan believed that the 'Wyde Rivier' where the chief lived was probably the Mzimvubu and in fact 'Wijd' is one of the names by which the Mzimvubu was known at that time.[91] Given the locality, time period, their nationality and the fact that Badi, as you will recall, had disappeared soon after Bessie's marriage, there's a strong possibility that the two castaways were Jekwa and Hatu.

Given that they were castaways, they may nevertheless have been castaways with a secret past, such as convicts, perhaps, or even pirates. Several of the ships wrecked on the Wild Coast had convicted men among their survivors, men who had obvious reasons for not wanting to return to European society. Castaway pirates would have had similar reasons. Pirates of all nations were active in the Indian Ocean throughout the 18th century, with strongholds on islands off the south-east African coast, and there is evidence that some visited the mainland. The old Customs House that once stood on the east bank of the Kowie River at Port Alfred, south of the Wild Coast, was built in 1826 on the ruins of an earlier structure rumoured to have been a 'house of correction' belonging to slavers or pirates. One fictionalised account describes how until about 1830 or 1840, in a small vale nearby, there was a pile of human skulls 'laying about in such close proximity to one another, as proved that they had met with a sudden and untimely death' and that their formation and long hair 'proved them not to be those of natives of this soil.'[92] A tombstone found near Durban, north of the Wild Coast, bears the inscription 'Here lived in Anno 1718, a penitent Pirate, who sequestered himself from his abominable Community and retired out of Harm's Way'. The historian Graham Mackeurtan believed the stone was connected to a group of English pirates who sacked the Dutch fort at Lourenço Marques (Maputo) a few years later, in 1722.[93] Led by Captain Taylor, 'a fellow of a most barbarous nature who had become the most prominent by reason he was a greater brute than all the rest,' the pirates overwhelmed the Dutch garrison, looted the fort and then settled in for the next few months.[94] They took prize several Dutch vessels, including the *Kaap* which, commandeered by a Scottish pirate called Elk, then 'vanished over the horizon to an unknown end'[95] – all of which took place at roughly the time the three Englishmen were wrecked on the Wild Coast.

At any rate, accompanied by the Englishmen, Hubner's party began the slow trek back towards the Cape. The first leg of the journey passed without incident and after travelling through the land of the Thembu, they arrived at last at the Great Place of the Xhosa King Phalo, 'safe and sound.'[96]

Phalo is an interesting man and an important figure in the history of the Xhosa people. He was also the great-grandfather of Mdushane, husband of Bessie's granddaughter Nonibe – but more of that later.

Phalo was the posthumous son of King Tshiwo, son of Ngconde and direct descendant of Tshawe, founder of the Xhosa Royal House, who met his death on a hunting trip shortly after marrying his Great Wife. As she was still a young woman and had not yet borne children, she was sent back to her father to spare her a prolonged period of mourning. Although it was not realised at the time, she was in fact already pregnant, and when Phalo was born a few months later the boy was proclaimed heir, sparking a war with Tshiwo's eldest son Gwali, who coveted the throne for himself. The latter was eventually defeated, and when Phalo came of age he assumed the kingship.[97] At the time of Hubner's visit he was in his early thirties, a wise and popular ruler, and a man of 'fine character and temperament, which was fostered and confirmed by the wise guidance of his father's councillors.'[98]

Beyond Phalo's Great Place lay the deep gorges and dense bush of the Kei River, a daunting prospect under any conditions for any early traveller. For the Hubner traders and their over-laden wagons it represented a serious barrier and promised to test their endurance, and especially that of their oxen, to the utmost. On a level road with a moderate load the pace of the draught oxen was only equal to that of a fast walker, but with a heavy load of ivory and rough terrain the pace was even slower and the beasts were easily exhausted.[99] In order, perhaps, to rest the weaker animals, Hubner divided his men in two groups. An advance party would push on to the Kei with seven of the wagons and the three Englishmen, while he and the rest of the traders remained at Phalo's, where they had been 'received in friendly fashion there as they had been everywhere else by the other tribes.'[100] There was nothing to indicate that the Hubner Expedition was about to change its name, in history books like this one, to the Hubner Massacre.

Sitting outside his tent a few days after the departure of the advance party, Hubner was approached by one of his Khoi servants. The man wished to have some gunpowder, he told the trader, so that he could defend himself if they were attacked; he had seen one of Xhosa brandishing an assegai at Hubner, he explained, and, he warned him, they were 'not intending to be friendly.' Hubner, far from taking the warning seriously, rebuked the man and, in a major setback for international sign language, claimed that 'the brandishing of the assegai was a sign of friendliness.'[101] Soon after this exchange the friendly assegai-brandisher returned with many other equally friendly fellows, offered Hubner eight oxen and then stabbed him in the side. Tearing out the blade, Hubner tried to grab his rifle, but was struck again and fell over backwards. His companions were still asleep inside the tent. Shouting 'Thrust and cut it open; it is not made of wood,' the Xhosa stormed it from all sides, killing Hubner's brother Fredrick, Andries Esterhuijsen and young Gerrit van Vooren. Philip Constant and Antony Lotze managed to escape from the tent but not from their killers.[102] Two of the Khoi servants were badly wounded but several managed to get away. The attackers then turned on the traders' wagons. As they unloaded them big three casks of gunpowder, each weighing 50 pounds, were smashed up and when the wagons were set alight they exploded, killing and wounding many of Phalo's people. Enraged and thirsty for revenge, the rest set out after the traders' advance party.

They were not far off. Although more than a week had passed since leaving the Great Place, the traders had only managed to reach the Kei; the river was in full flood, a vast and fast flowing, chocolate-coloured, silt and tree-laden, dangerous wall of water, impossible to cross. With nothing to do but wait, they outspanned and set up camp. This was probably near Old Kei Drift, about 30 kilometres from the mouth of the river as the crow flies.[103] The contours here are less steep than elsewhere, allowing relatively easy access to the great river and it was 'in consequence, in those days the main crossing place for hunting parties of Europeans with their wagons.'[104] On the eighth day, just as the floodwaters were beginning to drop, the group, which consisted of the three De Vries brothers, the two Scheffer brothers, Christoffel Hoogreefde, Louis Cloete, Jan van Vooren, Jan Bruijns, a number of unnamed Khoi and the three Englishmen, were startled by the sudden appearance of the Khoi who had managed to escape the massacre at the Great Place and who hurriedly informed the traders of the deaths of their comrades.[105] Realising that their gunpowder supplies were too low to hold off an attack, the traders decided to brave the swollen river. The three Englishmen, however, chose to remain where they were, and even persuaded one of the traders, Louis Cloete, to stay with them, 'telling him that if he went along with… his fellow travellers he and they would be murdered by the [Xhosa].' With an attack imminent, there could hardly have been time to use an interpreter. If they were deserters from the Cape garrison they would certainly have been able to speak to him in Dutch, but perhaps they just used exceptionally eloquent sign language, the meaning of which Louis, unlike his late leader, was quick to grasp.[106]

No sooner had the traders crossed the river than a large troop of Xhosa,

> 'among whom were several of the sons of the supposed Englishmen, attacked them, threatening them with assegais, so that they were forced to open fire on them to save their own lives, and with such success that about ten of them were shot.'[107]

But without adequate gunpowder the traders' defence crumbled and they fled, abandoning everything – wagons, tons of tusks, oxen and all their personal possessions. The Xhosa pursued them in a running fight that lasted three days and two nights, but eventually the traders broke through to Gonacqua territory and found refuge with the friendly chief Babbelaan. After a torturous journey, during which they abandoned a weakened Christoffel Hoogreefde near the Fish River (he was never heard of again), the survivors eventually made it back to the Cape, where they gave an account of the massacre to the authorities.[108]

Exactly what precipitated the attack on Hubner and his men is a mystery. Some writers have suggested that the murders arose from Phalo's desire for the bits and pieces of iron holding the wagons together,[109] but the fact that, even after killing Hubner's group and burning their wagons, the Xhosa pursued the survivors in a three-day running battle, suggests they were deeply outraged, rather than merely acquisitive. The surviving traders themselves did not know the reason for the attack. They said only that the Khoi who had escaped to warn them, 'pretended that they did not know' what had prompted it.[110] It is a strange turn of phrase, and an interesting one – given that the Xhosa themselves laid the blame on the Khoi.[111]

In 1752, sixteen years after the massacre, an official expedition from the Cape under the leadership of Ensign Beutler visited Phalo's Great Son Gcaleka, on the west bank of the Kwenxura, just north of today's East London. Questioned about the traders' deaths the Xhosa blamed Hubner's Khoi interpreters who had, they said with spectacular understatement, 'caused a misunderstanding.'[112] Beutler, who seems to have been a rather nervous individual – he ordered a drum to be beaten all the way from Cape Town to the eastern Cape and back, scaring away all the game and almost causing a mutiny amongst his men[113] – did not force the issue. He was smart enough to realise that if a mere misunderstanding could provoke a massacre it was best not to make the Xhosa *really* angry.

Whatever it was that sparked the Hubner attack must have been of an extremely serious nature, since Phalo was evidently no stranger to white traders. He is said to have 'repeatedly received visitors from the colony,'[114] and it was probably in his interests to encourage them, as they would have brought him and his court presents of beads and other exotic goods – and the whole affair is, in fact, so similar to a later case amongst the Zulus as to suggest that the killings may have been triggered by some sort of sexual assault on one of the women at Phalo's *umzi*. In Natal in 1827, two Khoi servants of a party of traders raped the wife of a Zulu chief. In retaliation, Shaka threatened to kill not only the rapists themselves but also their white trader employers – much to the latter's alarm – stating that 'if he killed one, he must kill all.'[115] It is possible that the Xhosa king, Phalo, faced with a similar crime, was simply dispensing what was considered appropriate justice: the extermination of the entire party.

Finding the Hubner report solved a puzzle that had perplexed me from the first – Jekwa, Hatu and Badi's surprising evolution from helpless castaways to men of affluence and influence. Their wealth, I was now certain, had come from beads and metal obtained through the ivory trade, goods which they could re-trade locally at great profit in exchange for cattle.

Their role in the deaths of Hubner and his men is less clear. There is no evidence that they initiated or even anticipated the first attack, nor did they participate personally in the attack on the surviving traders. But their sons did – the survivors stated quite clearly that among their attackers 'were several of the sons of the supposed Englishmen'[116] – and the latter certainly benefited, since with Hubner dead and his men slain or routed, the excess ivory the traders had left behind for collection on a later expedition would have remained with the Tshomane. No wonder Matayi heaped honours on Jekwa – through him and his companions the chief had not only obtained a cut of the trade goods but also retained part of the ivory.

The fact that their sons were old enough to participate in the attack allows us to estimate the date of the Englishmen's wreck. Only those regarded as men were permitted to fight[117] and as circumcision, which marked the passage to manhood, took place only after puberty, say at 16,[118] their fathers must have been shipwrecked in at least 1719, but probably earlier.[119] With this time frame in mind, I set about establishing the name of their wreck. Of all the known wrecks along the Eastern seaboard the *Bennebroek*, which sank in 1713, seemed the most likely candidate. Although the vessel was Dutch, I knew that did not preclude the presence of other nationalities amongst its crew, including Englishmen.[120] Besides, there were also a number of criminals and convicts on board, who – like Hubner's Englishmen – would have had reason to fear contact with the Dutch authorities. What I did not realise was just how many possibilities there were, but as time went on and my research became more intensive, I began to realise that the Wild Coast was simply *crawling* with castaways....

Chapter Four

The Wrecks

A triangular wedge of land jutting out into the southern oceans, South Africa is surrounded by sea on three sides, to the west, south and east. It has an exceptionally long coastline and has seen more than its fair share of wrecks over the centuries – an average of one per kilometre[1] – but of the entire stretch it is the Wild Coast that is most feared by mariners.

The Wild Coast is one of the few places in the world which experiences true freak waves. Its killer waves are the spawn of titans, born when a howling south-westerly, driving massive swells before it, encounters the opposing force of the mighty south-streaming Agulhas current. The embrace of these titans compresses the distance between the waves and accentuates their already dizzying height, increasing their size to awesome proportions and, every so often, superimposing one upon another, piggyback-fashion, to create a freak of nightmarish dimensions and power,

> 'a single wave of frightening proportions, reaching up to 20m in height – as tall as a five-storey building! Such freak or killer waves are periodically responsible for massive damage to ships, the bows of the ship dipping down into the trough that precedes the wave and then being crushed as the oncoming mountainous wave breaks down onto the deck.'[2]

It was probably one of these freaks that caused the famous and mysterious disappearance of the *Waratah* in 1909. The liner had sailed from Durban harbour on 26 July (the height of the winter storms) with more than 200 souls on board, and was headed for Cape Town via the Wild Coast when it simply disappeared. No survivors or wreckage were ever recovered, and for almost a century the fate of the ship remained one of the great mysteries of the sea. It was only in 1999 that a wreck thought to be the *Waratah* was located, 11 kilometres off the mouth of the Xora River, where Jekwa and company's descendants live. Despite the enormous depth of the water in which it sank, the ship had slammed into the seabed with such force that its bows had been shattered and its hull fractured in several places.[3] Even modern liners, such as the 7554-ton *Oceanos*, which went down off Coffee Bay in 1991,[4] have fallen foul of the Wild Coast. Pity, then, the poor souls of earlier times who faced its naked violence in tiny wooden rat-traps.

Examples abound of vessels that disappeared along this coast. A glance at the list of ships missing in the area in the 19th century reveals something of the spooky destructiveness of its seas: in 1824 the *Julia* sailed from Durban, headed south for Cape Town, and was never seen again. A year later the *Bridekirk* left the Kowie River mouth at Port Alfred for Port Elizabeth, but never arrived. In 1828 the *Frances* also sailed from the Kowie and disappeared and the *Circe* vanished with all hands somewhere south of Durban in 1835. In 1875 the *Africana*, en route from New York to Bombay, appeared off the Kowie with all sails fully rigged but with not a soul visible on board, then drifted off never to be seen again and in 1891 the 401-ton German steamer *Emin* also disappeared in this area.[5]

Captain Benjamin Stout, who lost his ship, the *Hercules*, just south of the Wild Coast in 1796, gives a vivid description of the full-blown fury of these seas:

> 'Although bred to the sea from my earliest life, yet all I had ever seen before, all I had ever heard or read, gave me no adequate idea of those sublime effects which the violence and raging of the elements produce, and which, at this tremendous hour, seemed to threaten nature itself with dissolution. The ship, raised on mountains of water, was in a moment precipitated into an abyss, where she appeared to wait until the coming sea raised her again into the clouds. The perpetual roaring of the elements echoing through the void, produced such an awful sensation in the minds of the most experienced of the seamen, that several of them appeared for some time in a state of stupefaction; and those less accustomed to the dangers of the sea, added to this scene of misery by their shriekings....'[6]

If the freak waves did not get the early mariners, other factors conspired against them. Navigation was crude and often faulty. Maps were not widely available and, in any case, were almost criminally inaccurate. Prior to the first real hydrographic survey of the south-east African coast in the 1820s, cartographers drew the seaboard a long way west of its true position. Consequently, ships coming from the East often encountered land well before they expected to – with dire consequences – while those coming from the Cape tended to round the continent near present-day Port Elizabeth too sharply and frequently found themselves ashore where no shore should have been. Anders Spaarman, the Swedish botanist, witnessed a near-miss one evening near Port Elizabeth in 1775, watching in amazement as a ship came straight for the shore under full sail and then, at the last possible moment, suddenly pulled away:

> 'I afterwards learnt at the Cape, that this was a Dutch vessel; and that from the chart she carried with her, she had not expected to

come upon the coast nearly so soon, nor had she perceived it till just before she had tacked about.'[7]

In a similar but separate incident around the same period, Jacob Kok, a farmer and elephant hunter who had a loan-farm just north of Port Elizabeth, saw a ship come in so close to the shore that when he bumped into its captain some weeks later at the Cape the man recognised him![8]

Perhaps another reason for the surfeit of wrecks along the Wild Coast is its lack of protected bays in which a ship could find shelter from bad weather, or where its crew could carry out repairs to damage sustained in a mid-ocean storm or in one of the frequent sea battles that characterised the European powers' struggle for domination of the trade routes to the East. An exacerbating factor was the unpredictability of the currents, both the localised rips and the dominant Agulhas. The Agulhas is strongest close to the edge of the continental shelf, and as the width of the shelf changes – from as much as 30 kilometres wide off the mouth of the Great Fish River to only eight kilometres wide off Port St Johns – so does the speed of the current; in certain places, such as Cape Padrone, it's been seen 'running like a race or overfall' even in calm weather.[9] It is this kind of localised change and unpredictability which, even more than the more obvious dangers of hidden reefs or sandbars, probably accounts for the multiplicity of wrecks in particular places along the Wild Coast.

The earliest wrecks were probably Asian, one of which may have been the source of the cornelian beads which are intermittently washed ashore at Msikaba: 'Native tradition has it that a bird with two large wings came out of the sea and was smashed upon the reef – possibly an Arab Dhow.'[10] The Arabs are known to have been involved in the African coastal trade as early as the time of the Queen of Sheba – the tenth or ninth century BCE.[11]

Over the centuries Arab and Indian traders and immigrants penetrated further south along the east African coast, contributing to the evolution of a unique language, Swahili – a name derived from an Arab word meaning 'of the coast' – and trading silk and cotton cloths, chinaware and beads with African traders in exchange for gold, tortoise-shell, rhino horns, slaves and especially elephant tusks.

By the eighth century AD the Arabs had a trading settlement as far south as Chibuene, opposite the Bazaruto Islands, in south-central Mozambique[12] and seem on occasion to have penetrated even further, blown off course by violent storms perhaps, as far as the ivory-rich Wild Coast. Early castaways on our southern shores may also have included Indians and Chinese, who are also known to have traded with East Africa.[13] In the mid-1400s, for example, an Indian ship was driven

'by stress of weather, in a course out of the Indian ocean, for forty days, beyond the Cape of Sofala and the Green Islands, towards the west and south-west, and that in the opinion of the astronomer on board (such as all the Indian ships carry), they had been hurried away for 2 000 miles,'

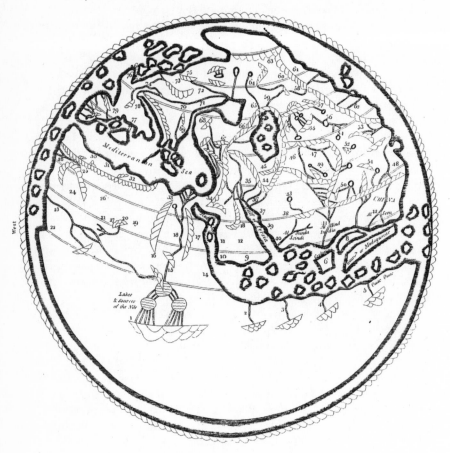

Arab map of the world from the 12th century AD[14]
(showing Africa as circumnavigable 300 to 400 years before Dias and Da Gama rounded the Cape)

a distance which would have taken the vessel as far as the Cape of Good Hope, if not actually round it, decades before the Portuguese succeeded in doing so.[15]

The first Europeans to discover the sea route to the east were the Portuguese. The first Europeans to sail in South African waters, they were naturally also the first to be wrecked on its Wild Coast. As the years passed and other nations came to dominate the trade routes, the wrecks were more often Dutch or English. Portuguese survivors made their way north towards their trading establishments on the Mozambican coast; English and Dutch castaways tended to go south towards the Cape. Regardless of which route they chose, however, the hardships they faced often seemed insurmountable and many succumbed to the hazards of the journey. Extremes of temperature, flooded rivers, hostile locals, snakebite and attacks from wild beasts, to name just a few, took a high toll. Starvation, too, caused much suffering, which has always struck me as bizarre on a coast renowned for its excellent fishing. Fed by the warm Mozambique current, as the Agulhas is known much further north, the Indian Ocean offers an abundant harvest – even with today's depletion of the world's marine resources – yet even survivors who were sailors seldom seem to have tried fishing, contenting themselves with foraging for shellfish instead. Many survivors ate their shoes in a desperate effort to obtain what little sustenance they could from the dry leather, a self-defeating exercise, because without shoes they could not walk far – the terrain was simply too rough. One group of castaways hungrily

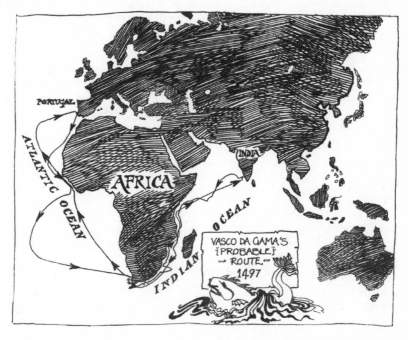

devoured a mariner's chart, which, far from keeping them alive, killed all who ate it 'because of the mercury in the colours.'[16] Others killed and ate each other, like the survivors of the *Sao Joao Baptista*, sunk near the Fish River mouth in 1622. This terrible deed 'was overlooked, and no charge laid,' complained a survivor who drew the line at eating his companions, but admitted that, when cooked, they 'smelt most excellently, like pork....'[17]

Thirst was another problem: many shipwreck survivors died of dehydration, others were reduced to drinking their own urine, yet the Wild Coast cannot by any stretch of the imagination be described as a desert. It is well watered and criss-crossed by streams and rivers, which are brackish only where they enter the sea. The survivors, however, do not seem to have realised that if they went just a little upstream they would have found the water pure and fresh, and spared themselves much suffering.

Because the conditions were so harsh, it was generally the lowest of the low who survived, men such as sailors, criminals and slaves, who were accustomed to living under the worst of circumstances, while the European elite, the officials, merchants and aristocrats, dropped like flies. One Portuguese castaway, a nobleman by the name of Dom Sebastião Lobo da Silveira, was so 'very much burdened with flesh and having other complaints, that he could not take a few steps on his feet.'[18] Too obese to walk to salvation, he offered up his most precious jewels to anyone who would *carry* him to the nearest port, which lay at least a 1 000 kilometres away over terribly tough terrain. Sixteen strong sailors accepted, and set off with Dom Sebastiano's huge bulk slung between them in a fishing net, but their enthusiasm decreased with the distance travelled and, a little way past today's Port St Johns, they eventually abandoned him,

> 'without any food whatever, for there was none, and all parted from him with just sorrow [and some relief, I imagine], leaving him under a little cloth tent, fat and in good health, with his strength unimpaired, because he would not venture to proceed on foot.'[19]

Like the dinosaurs of old, the pampered elite were unable to adapt to their altered circumstances. Some went mad, others abandoned hope. One who did both was Dona Eleonora Sala, survivor of the *Sao Joao*, which went aground in 1552. The daughter of the Viceroy at Goa and wife of an exceptionally rich nobleman, Manuel de Sousa de Sepulveda, the Governor of the Castle of Diu,[20] Dona Eleonora was flung without warning from a life of unimaginable luxury onto the naked dunes and tumbled rocks that today separate a police holiday camp from the waves at Port Edward, on the KwaZulu-Natal south coast. She asserted her right to certain perks and when the survivors set off on their long journey north towards Portuguese Mozambique she and her children were comfortably ensconced on litters borne by their surviving slaves and servants. By the time they had been travelling for three months, however, Dona Eleonora's slaves had either died or absconded and with no one left to carry her, the noblewoman was forced to make her own way on foot. The final straw presented itself shortly after the survivors reached Delagoa Bay (present-day Maputo in Mozambique) where they were robbed again and again by the local inhabitants, losing first their weapons and finally even the clothes they wore, leaving them stark naked. Dona Eleonora is said to have fought back feistily, but was restrained by her husband who feared she would be killed. He tried to cover her nakedness with a shawl but Dona Eleonora 'cast herself upon the ground and covered herself with her hair, which was very long, while she made herself a pit in the sand in which she buried herself to the waist, and

never rose from that spot.' Disregarding the welfare even of her two small
children, she refused to budge. It took the three of them several days to die.
Manuel de Sousa de Sepulveda, who had already lost his illegitimate son
–'the desire of his eyes'[21] – on the journey, buried his wife and children in
silence, walked off alone into the bush and was never seen again.[22]

Sporadic warfare between the major European powers both at home and
abroad, the rapidly expanding Eastern sea trade and competition for foreign
markets and territory meant that various nationalities soon established
separate refreshment and refuelling stations for their ships. With the Cape
a no-go area following the massacre of d'Almeida and his men, the Portuguese
began using Mozambique Island and Sofala. The English based themselves
at St Helena and the French at Mauritius. The Dutch, as we have seen,
secured the Cape for themselves in 1652 and by the beginning of the 18th
century very few ships belonging to other nations stopped in at Table Bay. Even
so, from January 1726 to December 1750 nearly 2 000 ships called at Table Bay,
with an additional 77 putting in at nearby Simon's Town between 1742, when
it first came into use, and 1750.[23] Although this number constitutes only a small
percentage of the ships sailing to and from the East, it gives some indication of
just how many vessels were out there, on a regular basis, just off our shores.

It is impossible to estimate how many of the thousands of ships engaged
in the eastern trade ended up as wrecks, but the losses seem to have been
astronomical. In the 16th century, almost *half* of the vessels that left Portugal
for the East never returned.[24] As all ships sailing between Europe and the
East Indies had to pass South Africa, it is probably safe to assume that the
sailors, soldiers, merchants of exotic fabrics, spices and human flesh, officials
from the lowest civil servant to the highest order, men, women and children
of every age and nation, who were wrecked on that particularly treacherous
stretch, the Wild Coast, numbered in their thousands, if not tens of thousands.
Only a few made it back to their homelands. Many, of course, died before
reaching the shore and others succumbed while trying to reach European
settlements in Mozambique or at the Cape, but the majority simply remained
where they were wrecked. Up and down the Wild Coast, women and children,
the tired, the elderly, the sick, weak or injured, and even the pampered and
obese, were abandoned with monotonous regularity by their stronger comrades
and, although some of the weak or injured died, many more survived.
Practically every group of castaways reported meeting castaways from
previous wrecks, some of which can be identified and others not. All of
these survivors had been assimilated into the local peoples, Mpondo,
Mpondomise, Xhosa or Thembu. Well-to-do castaways, like the overly fat
Portuguese nobleman mentioned earlier, would have experienced huge culture
shock in adapting to their new surroundings, but for the majority of common
people their new lives would have compared more than favourably with their
previous lives as slaves, seamen or artisans or just plain women.

And it was not only those who were too weak or too young to make it
to the nearest European outposts who stayed. Many who were strong and

healthy, had no loved ones they yearned to return to in Europe, and were bright enough to recognise a near-paradise when they saw one, also chose to remain on the Wild Coast, marrying and raising families thousands of kilometres from the lands of their birth. Bessie was by no means the only castaway on the Wild Coast, but because of a double fluke – as the Great Wife of an Mpondo prince she earned a place in oral history, and as her children were still alive when the first English missionaries arrived in the region and discovered their exotic ancestry, she found a place in written history – her story has survived, while those of most other castaways have not. In cases where none of the survivors of a particular wreck made it back to their home country or to one of its colonial settlements, not only the details of their subsequent lives but even the names of their ships and where they foundered went unnoted and remains unknown.

Establishing the location of even the known wrecks can be problematic. Before the invention of the chronometer in 1755, there was no way of establishing longitude accurately, which meant it was impossible to establish a ship's exact position at sea. Nor was there any accurate way of measuring the speed or drift of the vessel, particularly in unfamiliar currents (one method was the Dutchman's Log, by which the time taken for a piece of wood thrown from the bows of the ship to reach the stern was estimated according to set chanting by the crew). Castaways' estimates of distances as they journeyed overland were also unreliable, since the hardships they endured tended to exaggerate in their own minds the distance covered. Survivors frequently had only the vaguest notion of where they had been wrecked, but even in cases where they thought they knew, the place names don't usually match the ones used today, so at times being a detective becomes the greater part of being an historian. The *Johanna* is a good example: it was lost in 1682 'somewhere about De la Goa'. Because of its name the wreck-site was presumed to be Delagoa Bay (today's Maputo) about 2 000 kilometres from the Cape, despite the fact that the survivors' overland journey to the Cape lasted just 40 days. The wreck was located and salvaged in 1984, a few kilometres west of Cape Agulhas, less than 200 kilometres from the Cape and less than halfway between it and Plettenberg Bay, or 'das Alagoas' as it was sometimes called.[25]

Similar confusion surrounds the term 'Natal', which in earlier times, as I mentioned briefly in the previous chapter, referred not to the province which today bears the name, but to the Wild Coast further south.[26] According to Manuel de Mesquita Perestrelo, a master mariner shipwrecked on the Wild Coast in 1554, who covered much of its coastline on foot and surveyed it by royal decree 20 years later, 'The First Point of the Land of Natal is in latitude thirty-two degrees. The Last Point is to the northeast inclined to north, at a distance of 45 leagues [about 230 kilometres]. Its mark of recognition is a great rocky point....'[27] In other words, the southern-most point of Natal lay just south of the Kei River mouth, its middle point was bang on the mouth of

the Mzimvubu River, and its northern boundary was the Mtamvuna River –
the *southern* boundary of present-day KwaZulu-Natal.[28]

The territory we now call Natal seems to have got its name from the
mistaken belief that Vasco da Gama, *en route* to India in 1497, celebrated
Christmas off today's city of Durban, a myth that has been debunked by Eric
Axelson, the foremost authority on early Portuguese navigators. Da Gama
was actually 'off Port St Johns, or in that area, on Christmas Day 1497,'
Axelson says, 'and it was only much later when the English began their
settlement of Port Natal in 1824, that mapmakers moved "Natal" northwards.'[29]
Because of this confusion, many of the ships thought to have been wrecked
on the present coast of KwaZulu-Natal were probably really wrecked on the
Wild Coast, the territory *previously* known as Natal. The famous wreck of
the *Stavenisse* is a case in point.

The story begins on 24 November 1684 when the *Good Hope,* a 50-ton
ketch, mounting six guns, set out from the English port of Gravesend. The
crew had been engaged to take the small vessel to Cadiz in Spain, but once
they were at sea they were informed that their actual destination was much
further away and their mission substantially more dangerous: the little vessel
was headed for the east coast of Africa, to engage in the ivory and slave trade.
The voyage took many months and it was only towards the middle of the
following year that the *Good Hope* reached the south-east African coast.
Finally, on 9 May, it lay off Rio de Natal (the River of Natal); a few days
later, as the crew were hauling the vessel over the bar at the mouth of the
river, a sudden squall blew up from the south, flinging it against the north
shore, where it settled. Concluding there was no chance of refloating it, the
seamen removed its cargo of trade goods and ammunition for storage in a
hut they had built on the southern shore of the river, then set to work
assembling a decked boat that they had brought with them from England.[30]
Four of the sailors and a boy died of dysentery, but work on the boat
continued. It was nearly complete when, at the end of July, another English
ship, a 35-tonner under Captain Wynnford, arrived.[31] Like the *Good Hope,*
its primary purpose was trade and in due course, having procured both ivory
and meat from the local inhabitants, and with four of the castaways on
board, the ship left for Mozambique. The following day, those of the *Good
Hope*'s crew who had stayed behind launched their own boat. The captain,
John Adams, hoped to trade northwards along the coast to well past
Mozambique, after which he intended visiting Madagascar to procure a
cargo of slaves to sell in Jamaica.[32] With him went nine men. Five others,
led by John Kingston, elected to remain at Rio de Natal. In lieu of the
wages owing to them, they received an assortment of trade goods ('68 lbs
Copper arm, neck, and ear rings, and 14 lbs of beads' each) and weapons
('7 guns in all, with some powder and lead').[33]

John Kingston's little band remained at Rio de Natal for several months,
exploring the surrounding countryside and learning to speak the local language.

They found the locals 'a very friendly and hospitable people,' generous with both food and accommodation. The Englishmen lived by bartering their beads for bread, meat, beer, milk, fruit and roots. The copper they traded for elephant tusks, and within a short time they had amassed no less than three tons of ivory.[34] Some nine months after the *Good Hope* had run aground, news reached them that another ship had been wrecked a little way to the south and two of the sailors, together with a group of locals, set off to find the survivors.

The wreck was the *Stavenisse*, a Dutch East Indiaman skippered by Willem Knyff. The ship had been homeward-bound from Bengal when, in the dark, overcast and very early hours of 16 February 1686, the lookouts had suddenly shouted out that they could see land. The mate and officer of the watch, however, assumed that the lookouts had simply seen a bank of mist and, instead of checking for himself, 'threatened to kick their backsides since they were fully 200 miles from the coast.'[35] The lookouts' next warning was almost drowned in the roar of surf and even the officer could not mistake the white foam of the breakers. Captain Knyff, asleep in his cabin, knew nothing of the drama being played out overhead until his door flew open and the cabin boy ran in screaming. The alarm sounded and all hands sprang on deck. Two anchors were immediately dropped, but it was too late; the *Stavenisse* was already in the breakers, drifting inshore with waves streaming waist-high over the deck. Then an anchor cable snapped and the vessel smashed into the rocks and began to fill rapidly with water. Some of the crew tried to save themselves by launching a small boat, but it capsized, drowning several. Sixty survivors, including the captain, managed to swim ashore.[36]

They remained on the beach for three days, living in a tent constructed of sail and wood salvaged from the wreckage along with some food, clothing, firearms, ammunition, compasses and maps, then the main body of men set out to find help. Leaving behind the surgeon, the gunner and the boatswain's mate, who had been injured getting ashore, they headed south in the hope of reaching the Cape. On the first day out the captain grew too tired to continue and returned to the tent at the wreck. On the fourth day eight more turned back. Further on, the carpenter dropped out, a seaman drowned crossing a river, then the trumpeter and the quartermaster who were too weak to continue with the others, were left behind. As the journey progressed more weakened and were left behind, scattered along the coast among the local people, until only 18 remained. The party split; 15 of the healthiest went off on a separate route,[37] but were attacked by a group of Khoi, the 'Hagriquas' or Hoengiqua, who killed the cooper, put out the sailmaker's eye, and took everything they possessed, even their clothing, leaving them quite naked:

> 'They were then obliged for some days to beg their food in the kraals or villages of the Magosse [amaXhosa] Africans, until at length they were distributed in the surrounding villages or neighbourhood, and there were very well treated.'[38]

Already living among the Xhosa they found a young French boy of about 14, Guillaume Chenu de Chalezac.

The boy had an interesting tale to tell. His ship, the *Bauden*, had been attacked by pirates near the Cape of Good Hope and both the captain and pilot had been killed. Without the latter, the crew became increasingly unsure of their position as the ship sailed on. So a party of eight sailors, of whom the boy was one, was sent ashore to make enquiries. The shore was too rocky for their boat to land and after trying for three days, and with their provisions gone, they attempted to return to the *Bauden* and found, to their dismay, that it had already left. They followed the coastline for another six days, and finally landed at Cove Rock, near today's East London. There they got into a fight with a group of amaXhosa. The boy was the only one of the castaways to survive the altercation, and was subsequently adopted by a Xhosa chief, Sotope or Sesse. He had been living at his *umzi* for over a year when the Dutchmen arrived.[39]

The battered and naked crew of the *Stavenisse* were treated with similar kindness. Unlike that of the majority of Portuguese castaways, their behaviour towards the Xhosa appears to have been respectful and non-violent, and they were well treated, each receiving some cattle and land to plant crops. Thanks to this generosity, the castaways were not only no longer destitute[40] but probably better off than they had been as sailors. Their hosts, they later reported,

> 'are well formed in body, swift runners, and live under the gentle monarchy of their King Magamma, who is a very friendly, good hearted, young, and active fellow…. They are generally kind, compassionate, and hospitable, but lazy in their nature, for the women perform all the work… while the men do nothing but milk the cows and make the *kraals*.'[41]

The countryside was well watered and extremely fertile, with all kinds of crops growing in abundance, and it swarmed with wild animals, many of which the castaways had never seen before. All in all, it was not a bad place to be and, when their rescuers did finally arrive, in February 1688, some chose not to leave.[42]

Meanwhile, those of their comrades who had remained at or returned to the site of the wreck had been busy repairing the *Stavenisse's* boat. Within two weeks it was seaworthy and loaded with salvaged bread, salt pork and a container of fresh water, but when it was launched they could not get through the breakers; the boat capsized and broke up in the surf. Everything was lost, including the compass and quadrant, and the castaways were left in desperate straits. The local people had long since realised that they did not have to barter their bread and corn with the castaways in exchange for bits of metal from the wreck but could simply help themselves, 'and by chopping and burning [they] fully supplied themselves with iron,' a castaway reported later, 'we not being at first aware that it was so much regarded, nor daring to prevent them for fear of provoking them, as they had sometimes fully a thousand armed men; they had everything in abundance, while we suffered from want.'[43]

It was at this low point that salvation arrived, in the form of the two Englishmen from the *Good Hope*. While one of the Englishmen tended the injured, the rest of the Dutchmen were taken back to Rio de Natal where the *Good Hope* had been wrecked, some 20 *mylen* to the north.[44]

The records of castaways on the Wild Coast are, more often than not, a litany of selfishness, self-preservation and inhumanity towards others. The men from the *Good Hope* were the exception that proves the rule. They had nothing to gain from helping the *Stavenisse*'s crew, yet, as the latter themselves remarked, 'they willingly offered us their assistance towards our mutual preservation, together with a share of their merchandise, consisting of copper rings and common beads,' which was – they added with relief and optimism – 'enough to find them and us also in meat and bread for fifty years.'[45]

After a few months of idleness the castaways decided to build themselves a boat. Several trips were made back to the wreck of the *Stavenisse* to fetch iron and fittings. They had no saw, so the indomitable John Kingston 'turned a stout iron ring into a tool that answered for one,' using one of the anchors as his anvil.[46] The Englishmen's supply of beads and copper rings enabled them to employ local people to carry timber from the nearby forests and cut it into planks.

As the work went on, early in 1687 they were joined by the crew of yet another wreck, the *Bonaventura*, which had gone aground much further north. A small vessel of just 20 tons and a crew of nine men and a boy, it had sailed all the way from London to the east coast of Africa, only to overturn in a river mouth on Christmas day 1686. The second mate was drowned, and the incoming tide had washed the ship 'fully five German miles' upriver, leaving the crew stranded.[47] Shortly after the *Bonaventura* sailors arrived at Rio de Natal, the castaways put the finishing touches to their new boat. Not all were keen to leave, however. Three Englishmen from the *Good Hope*, and a Frenchman and an Englishman belonging to the *Bonaventura*, chose to remain, the former having established 'connections with the natives, and contrasting [their] ease of life… with the hardships endured at sea, they clung to the former.'[48] I would probably have done the same: a 17th-century sailor's life was a continuous cycle of mental and physical abuse, disease, lashings, inadequate water, rotten food, crowded, unhygenic and stench-ridden sleeping and living quaters, corrupt stewards, drunken officers and terrifying storms. The majority never learnt to swim and, in the event of their being washed overboard or shipwrecked, were guaranteed a watery grave. Under the circumstances the only surprising thing is that so few chose to remain at Rio de Natal.

As the rest prepared to leave, vast quantities of meat and corn, a couple of hundred fowls and twenty goats were purchased from the locals and loaded on board, together with fresh water and the three tons of ivory mentioned earlier. Setting off with neither a map nor a compass, the castaways had to sail close to the coast, heading south. Their luck held and in just ten days they arrived safely in Table Bay. Eleven were survivors of the *Stavenisse*, seven of the *Bonaventura* and two of the *Good Hope*. Had they not reached the Cape, there would have been no official record of any of these three wrecks; like so many others along our coasts they would simply have disappeared, their fate unknown.

The survivors' sudden appearance triggered a flurry of reports and rescue operations. Three separate expeditions – including one on which the rescuers themselves were wrecked – went east to bring back as many of the remaining survivors as they could find. A total of 24 were found, the largest group being the *Stavenisse* survivors who had attempted to walk to the Cape and who were living, along with the French boy, near Cove Rock, about 11 kilometres south of today's East London.[49]

It is generally accepted that the *Stavenisse* sank on the coast of modern-day KwaZulu-Natal. This, I think, is largely because influential historians such as Theal, Moodie and Bird assumed that the 'Terra de Natal' of the survivors' accounts was the same region as modern Natal, and that the Rio de Natal where the *Good Hope* went aground, about 20 Dutch *mylen* or 80 kilometres north of the *Stavenisse*, referred to Port Natal, now Durban.[50]

The evidence, however, does not bear this out. The survivors said that the people living around the *Stavenisse* wreck-site were Mbo, that is, Mpondo or Mpondomise, and that as they moved south, they found

> 'five sorts of Hottentots they travelled through, among them some so simple that they helped carry the sailors' guns, named Semboos [Mbo] beginning at the wreck, the Mapontemouse [Mpondomise], the Maponte [Mpondo], the Matimbes [Thembu], the Magryghas, the cruelest of all, who had robbed them of everything, and the Magosse [Xhosa], where they were received with every kindness....'[51]

Barring the 'Magryghas' (Hoengiqua), a Khoi group who resisted Xhosa domination and refused to pay them tribute,[52] all these people were black, had cattle-based economies, similar cultures and spoke the same language, isiXhosa. This latter fact presented Theal and company with a slight problem, since the black inhabitants of Port Natal were traditionally Zulu-speaking. To get around this they hypothesised that when the *Stavenisse* was wrecked the Xhosa were in the process of migrating southwards and had not yet reached their present positions on the Wild Coast and beyond, but that theory is easily nixed: as Monica Wilson says, 'Xhosa-speaking people [were] as far south as the Mtata River in 1593, and there is no indication that they had only recently arrived there.'[53] This is confirmed by the graves of their kings, all of which are located on the Wild Coast and not one of which lies within present-day Natal.[54]

The assumption that Rio de Natal, where the *Good Hope* was wrecked, is Durban also seems hopelessly incorrect – the two just do not match. The captain of the *Noord*, the vessel sent to rescue the survivors of the *Stavenisse* and *Good Hope* in 1689, left a detailed description of Rio de Natal. At the mouth of the river was a sand-bar, to the north lay beaches 'very steep, but all clear sand, without rocks' and, at a distance of about 2 *mylen*, a small river which was not navigable, as the channel was very narrow – all of which could apply to any of a dozen or more rivers besides Durban. His description of the entrance to the river, however, is more specific: 'it was a 'gat' (hole), in a

> 'high bluff point (<); this < bore S.S.W., one-sixth *myl*; from this < there extends a reef of rock N. by S., over which the sea breaks; around the point lie rocks which shew themselves in the water like a fence or breastwork....'[55]

" THE GATES "– MZIMVUBU MOUTH
LOOKING TOWARDS SEA.

The place this immediately brings to mind is the Mzimvubu River, the Portuguese cartographer Perestrelo's Middle Point of Natal. The mouth of the Mzimvubu is famous for its unique and dramatic 'Gates', a huge bluff lying parallel to the sea and cleft in two by the river mouth, with the twin precipices rising to a height of 1 200 feet on either side. The Gates have formed a prominent and well-known landmark for ships at sea from the earliest times, and must surely have caught the attention of mariners, such as Captain Wynnford and the crew of the *Good Hope*, looking for a sheltered place to trade. The entrance to Durban Bay is far less noticeable; partly concealed by the Bluff, it is not a very obvious topographical feature when viewed from the sea.[56]

The River of Natal, according to an account written in about 1696, is 'the principal [river] of the Country of Natal, and has been lately frequented by some of our English ships....' Although there was a bar at the mouth, the report continues, the river 'opens pretty wide and is deep enough for small Vessels.' A vessel under Captain Rogers visited the place on several occasions in the 1690s to trade for 'Elephants Teeth'[57] – which is just what the *Good Hope* had been doing when it went aground a few years earlier.

As its name suggests, Rio de Natal (River of Natal) was primarily a river rather than a bay, and again the description matches the Mzimvubu. According to one early traveller the river was 'the best in South Africa' after Delagoa Bay. 'Over 300 yards wide, an average depth of 20–30 ft and in some places nearly 100 ft it is navigable for about 12 miles.'[58]

In the 1800s it became a popular stop-off point for small vessels and despite its shifting sand-bar, boats of 80 tons were also able to enter its mouth.[59]

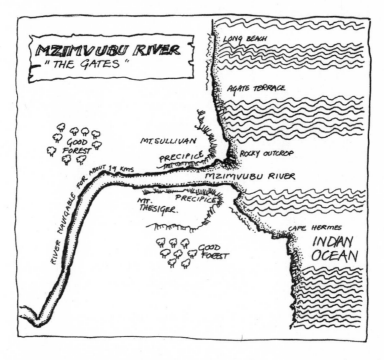

Durban is a bay, rather than a river: 'The harbour at Port Natal is wide, beautiful, and circular in shape. The water is not very deep, and in the centre there are two little green islands.'[60] 'Little' is a misnomer: the islands are big enough to have warranted a mention by the captain of the *Noord* and the survivors of the *Good Hope* and *Stavenisse,* who after all resided at Rio de Natal for months on end. That none of them did mention them can be due to only one thing – there were none; *ergo* Rio de Natal was not Durban.

According to the *Stavenisse* survivors there were substantial forests ideal for shipbuilding at Rio de Natal, and we know there was an enormous forest at the mouth of the Mzimvubu – the Gosa forest, which extended for 16 miles.[61] Practically the only fact militating against the Mzimvubu is its latitude – it lies over one degree south of the latitude estimated as Rio de Natal's by the captain of the rescue ship, the *Noord*.

The Portuguese appear to have been the best and most meticulous of the early navigators, and they guarded their knowledge jealously. The English and the Dutch were rather less accurate in their geographical calculations: in 1783, for instance, the English East India Company's hydrographer set the latitude of the Fish River at 30° S, more than 3° north of its actual position. The Dutch Academy of Sciences openly admitted their longitudes were sometimes as much as 100 leagues out, and that latitudes too were frequently erroneous.[62] According to the captain of the rescue vessel *Noord*, on 4 January 1689, Rio de Natal's latitude 'by reckoning, was 29°28', but the meridian latitude gave us 30° 1'.' The mouth of the Mzimvubu, however, lies at about 31° 37'S. Could he really have been so far out in his calculations? The temptation is to say yes; on its very next voyage to the Wild Coast the *Noord* itself ran aground and sank.[63]

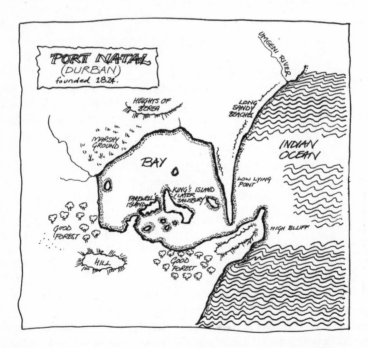

Meanwhile, back at the Cape, much interest in Terra de Natal had been generated by the *Stavenisse* saga, and at the beginning of 1689 an overland expedition was sent out to look for survivors, trade for cattle and probably ivory, and find out if there was anything else there that might be advantageous to the Colony.[64] The leader was Ensign Isaq Schryver, who had won fame in 1686, picking up the pieces, both literally and figuratively, of the *Nossa Senhora Dos Milagros*.[65] The Portuguese vessel, under the command of Don Emmanuel Silva, a personal friend of the King of Portugal, had been homeward bound from Goa when the lookouts reported a cape ahead one night. Five hundred and fifty souls, including several Jesuit priests and three Siamese ambassadors bearing gifts from the Emperor of Siam to the King of Portugal, Louis XIV of France and Charles II of England, were at stake, as well as a king's ransom in jewels. Without bothering to check for themselves, the captain and pilot assumed that they were passing Cape Point, the western-most 'corner' of the subcontinent, and ordered the course to be altered north. The ship came about and sailed, not up the western shore of the Cape but straight into the rocks at Cape Agulhas, about 200 kilometres short of Cape Town. The Siamese ambassadors were among those who managed to reach the shore safely, but when the party set out for the Cape they could not keep up with their Portuguese companions and were left behind to fend for themselves. Starving and disorientated in this strange land, they would surely have died had they not been rescued by a band of Khoi who taught them how to eat frogs, grasshoppers, dung beetles and the leaves of various bushes, and guided them towards the Cape. Two of the Eastern aristocrats, greasy and dirty from the rigours of their ordeal, their silken robes a little worn but still of the most exquisite texture and colour, their pampered courtier's skin blistered by the southern summer sun, finally reached the safety of the settlement.[66] Their Emperor's diamonds and other jewels had disappeared into the pockets of various Portuguese or Dutch officials, and his fine silks, exotic spices and other gifts were either at the bottom of the ocean or had been looted by Dutch salvage crews[67] – it was a diplomatic disaster. As heads rolled and careers floundered in the fall-out, one of the few to emerge with his reputation unblemished was Ensign Schryver. Two years later he was entrusted with the leadership of the Natal expedition.

Travelling light – for those times – with 18 or 19 well-armed soldiers and two wagons, the round trip of about 1 600 kilometres took the party only a little over three months. It was an incredible accomplishment, especially as not a single man died or was even injured. Schryver never reached the east coast, turning back within a few days' travel of it, near today's small city of Grahamstown,[68] but he did learn something of its Xhosa inhabitants: '[they] inhabit small houses of clay and are a numerous people rich in cattle.... This tribe is provided with beads, copper and iron which they know how to obtain from stranded ships.' Living among them were 'people of our fashion,' he reported. These men may have been survivors of shipwrecks or perhaps runaways from the Cape garrison, but Schryver made no effort to find out more about them or to reach them, concentrating instead on acquiring cattle to take back to the Cape. His main trading partner was a chief of mixed Xhosa-Khoi ancestry, whom he refers to mistakenly as Hykon of the Inquahase. This was not the chief's name, but a misnomer arising from sloppy or ignorant interpreters. 'Take us to Chief,' the Dutch probably demanded on their arrival in baby Dutch or broken Xhosa, eager to start trading for cattle. 'Hayi khon inkosi' (or Ayikho'nkosi) – 'Chief no here,' the people answered in simplified isiXhosa, and a verbal hiccup entered the Cape records and official credibility. Chief 'Hykon' pops up from time to time, even today, in (otherwise) sober historical tomes.

Among the survivors left on the Wild Coast were the three Englishmen of the *Good Hope*, who had chosen to remain at Rio de Natal rather than sail for the Cape with their comrades. If, as I believe, this river was the Mzimvubu, they lived in the same locality as Hubner's three Englishmen of 1736. In all probability, though, the *Good Hope* survivors were not Jekwa, Hatu and Badi; even if their average age was as little as 20 when they were wrecked, they would have been around 70 at the time of the Hubner expedition – too old to have accompanied the traders all the way to Phalo's kraal and certainly worthy of mention had they tried. The fact that they lived peacefully and 'formed connections with the natives', traded and raised families in the middle of the territory belonging to the grandfather and father of the Tshomane chief Matayi, would explain why the castaways Jekwa, Hatu and Badi met with a favourable reception. Some of Matayi's people, perhaps even members of his own family, could have been the children of these earlier English castaways. When I asked the abeLungu at Xora mouth if they knew which ship their ancestors had come off, they had answered simply that there was more than one wreck.

Some castaways were not the victims of shipwrecks: in December 1705, nearly 20 years after the *Stavenisse* was wrecked, the crew of the *Postlooper* found an Englishman named Vaughan Goodwin, one of three sailors who had been left on the coast of Natal (read Wild Coast) in February 1699, under orders from Captain Stadis of the *Fidele* to establish a settlement there.

> 'They were to purchase ivory from the natives, for which purpose goods had been left with them, and were to keep possession of the place until Captain Stadis should return, which he promised them would certainly be within three years....'

Nearly seven years had passed, and Goodwin was still waiting.[69] His two companions had become robbers and been killed by people who lived further inland, but he had prospered and had two wives and several children. 'The life which Goodwin was leading seemed so attractive to two of the *Postlooper's* crew that they ran away from the vessel.'[70] There is no indication of exactly where this all took place, though, and in any case they too would probably have been too old by 1736 to have been the men encountered by Hubner. The maths works better, though, with regard to the survivors of the *Bennebroek*.[71]

The ship was wrecked on 16 February 1713, exactly 27 years to the day after the *Stavenisse*, and there are other similarities between the two vessels. Both were Dutch, both had spent some time in the East and both were homeward-bound when the tragedy occurred. Both fell victim to terrible storms and both crews thought they were well out to sea when their ships struck.

Only a third of the *Bennebroek*'s complement, 77 souls, made it safely to the shore. They were a motley collection, 20 were black and 57 European,[72] and included convicts, slaves and seamen. They were probably of all nationalities, as the *Bennebroek* had been travelling in the East for almost three years and recruitment would have been essential to replace crewmen lost through death, disease and desertion.[73] The captain was not among the survivors and, despite a search, his body was not found. '[O]n account of the storm' nothing much could be saved from the ship. As night fell and the noise of the storm gave way to the strange cacophony of the African bush, the battered and hungry survivors must have huddled together for warmth and protection, their minds yearning for the dawn, their hearts longing for their own homes. By the following morning, as debris and cargo began washing ashore, news of the wreck spread inland, and the local inhabitants 'appeared on the scene in thousands' and began searching through the wreckage, salvaging what they could and burning the timber for iron and brass nails and fittings. The survivors joined them, managing to retrieve five firearms, some gunpowder and a supply of salt beef and pork. With these they were ready to attempt a journey to the Cape.

Like that of the *Stavenisse*, the exact location of the *Bennebroek* is debatable: Mackeurtan places the wreck north of the Mzimvubu River and so does Willcox.[74] Turner favours a position much further south, just beyond the Keiskamma River.[75] The late Graham Bell-Cross suggested a site a few kilometres away, two kilometres south of the Mtana mouth.[76] Wherever they were, like the men of the *Stavenisse*, the *Bennebroek* survivors didn't get very far. Their overland journey to the Cape was an abysmal failure; some died and others dropped out along the way. The lucky ones found food, comfort and shelter with the local people. Four of them lived in this way for over a year: the land was fertile and quite lovely, and there was no shortage of food, for it was rich in birds and other wildlife, and filled with 'very fat horned cattle.' The local grain made wonderfully nourishing bread, while 'the goats were almost as large as cows.'[77] Then one day a small boat appeared in the river nearby. It belonged to an English ship on its way to India, the *Clapham Galley* – though it may have been the *Clapham*, and the boat the *Clapham* galley. The galley (or *Galley*'s galley) had been dropped off 'in the neighbourhood of Terra di Natal'[78] with orders to trade along the coast and then proceed slowly to the Cape and there rendezvous with its parent ship. Evidently the ivory trade was already a well-known and thriving industry, as the boat had been built expressly for that purpose. Its mission was so successful that, although it was only 28 by 9 feet, when it eventually arrived at Table Bay, it was carrying over 3 000 lbs of ivory.[79] Also on board were three of the *Bennebroek* survivors, the fourth having chosen to remain on the Wild Coast. Like other castaways before and after him he had weighed up the odds and found life in 18th-century Europe, for all its apparent wealth and elegance, clearly lacking:

> 'Crime was rife in the cities… and citizens were likely to be robbed and assaulted in broad daylight. Absence of law and order was partly due to the poverty and misery in which a great part of the population lived, but a greater cause was simply the lack of an efficient police force and honest magistrates.'[80]

Public hangings were common, with more than 100 every year in London alone. The Wild Coast was altogether far more civilised.

Only one other man who is thought to have been a *Bennebroek* survivor made it to the Cape, a Malabar slave called Mieje – I say 'thought to' because Mieje, who together with his brother and several other slaves had been shipped aboard a Dutch vessel at Sri Lanka, apparently did not know the name of his ship nor that of its captain, only that it was one of a fleet of five in which the Fiscal of Ceylon was a passenger. During a storm at sea the ship had lost two of its masts and the rest of the fleet and shortly thereafter had struck a rock about half a mile off the African coast. The crew cut down the remaining mast, but the vessel was beyond saving and Mieje had seen the skipper abandon ship and leap into the sea. He himself had reached the shore in the ship's boat, together with five other slaves. Only 23 whites and 14 blacks had survived, he said (less than had come ashore from the *Bennebroek*, incidentally) and added that he had no idea where the wreck had occurred and would not be able to recognise the site if he saw it again. He had begun his overland journey towards the Cape accompanied by several others, but one by one they had fallen prey to hunger or been drowned trying to cross the rivers which barred their way, until he alone had remained. He reached the Cape nine months after the ship had gone ashore.[81] What happened to Mieje following this incredible journey is unknown, but one hopes that his ordeal won him his freedom: it would have been really tragic if he had struggled all that way – through a land of free black people – only to be enslaved again on reaching 'civilisation'.

The *Postloper* was sent out from the Cape on a six-month search for additional *Bennebroek* survivors, but failed to find any. Nothing further is known about them, but at least some lived out their lives on the coast where they had been wrecked: 'There seem to have been certain European survivors who intermarried with the natives,' a Transkei resident and Xhosa linguist remarked with regard to the *Bennebroek*, two centuries later, '[and] there is extensive native tradition on the subject.'[82] Unfortunately, he didn't elaborate.

Known wrecks c1500–1800, between Port Elizabeth and Port Edward

1552: **Sao Joao**, off Port Edward, just north of the Mtamvuma River on the Wild Coast border.[83] Many of the survivors were left along the way as the party journeyed north towards Portuguese Mozambique.

1554: **Sao Bento**, Msikaba Island, west bank of Msikaba River mouth.[84] As the survivors made their way along the coast, many were abandoned by their stronger comrades, as many as five or six being left behind every day in the latter stages of the journey. On several occasions the survivors met castaways from the *Sao Joao* living among the local people, one of whom, ' a naked man with a bundle of assegais upon his back,' turned out to be a fellow Portuguese named Rodrigo Tristao. Although he had been wrecked just three years before, 'exposed to the cold and heat of those parts, he had so altered in colour and appearance that there was no difference between him and the natives.'[85]

1593: **Santo Alberto**, near Mtata River mouth.[86]

1608: **Santo Espirito**, between Double Mouth and Hagga-Hagga.[87]

1622: **Sao Joao Baptista**, Cannon Rocks near Woody Cape.[88] Many of the castaways were left behind to fend for themselves. Just north of the Mzimvubu River the survivors met members of the 1593 wreck of the *Santo Alberto*. They tried to take these people with them but they refused: 'they would not desert their wives [who were very much in the plural] or their children [of whom one man had 20].' [89]

1635: **Nossa Senhora de Belem**, mouth of Mzimvubu River[90] (today's Port St Johns). Again many of the survivors were abandoned by their fellows. Near the site of the wreck they met a couple of survivors from the *Santo Alberto*, wrecked more than 40 years before, who helped them barter meat from the local people. They also met a survivor of the *Sao Joao Baptista*, which had sunk in 1622.[91]

1643: **Santa Marie Madre de Deus**, Bonza Bay, East London.[92]

1647: **Santissimo Sacramento** in Cannon Bay near Port Elizabeth. Many survivors were left along the way to fend for themselves or to integrate with the local communities. Those who reached Delagoa Bay in Mozambique reported meeting survivors of the *Belem*, sunk in 1635, of another unknown Portuguese wreck, and of the *Sao Joao Baptista*, sunk in 1622.[93]

1647: **Nossa Senhora da Atalaya do Pinheiro**, near the Cefane river, northeast of East London.[94] Somewhere south of the Mzimvubu River the survivors met a castaway from the *Sao Joao Baptista* and, further north, survivors of the *Santissimo Sacramento*.[95]

1685: **Good Hope**, at Rio de Natal, possibly the Mzimvubu River mouth.[96] The survivors met others from the *Stavenisse*, as well as some from the *Bonaventura*, which was wrecked on the coast of present-day KwaZulu-Natal.

1686: **Stavenisse**, possibly near Coffee Bay (about 80 kilometres south of Rio de Natal).[97] The survivors met crew from the *Good Hope* and *Bonaventura*, as well as a French boy who had been living among the Xhosa, and an old Portuguese man, from an unidentified wreck many years before, living among the Mpondo. Several of the *Stavenisse* crew remained on the coast.[98]

1713: **Bennebroek**, near Mtana River mouth, between the Fish and Keiskamma rivers. Many of the survivors were left behind by those attempting to walk to the Cape. They met an old Frenchman from a wreck about 40 years before.[99] The location of the *Bennebroek* is also the location of at least two other unidentified wrecks. Samples of ceramics found at the site indicate one was the *Bismarck*, a 19th-century wreck, while another was from the 16th century.[100]

1747: **Dolphin**, possibly on Bird Island, off present-day Port Elizabeth.[101]

1755: **Doddington**, on Bird Island, off Port Elizabeth.[102] The survivors met a young white boy with blond hair near present-day Port St Johns. Aged about 12–14, he may have been a survivor of the *Dolphin*, which went missing, presumed wrecked, in 1747.[103] There are several other unidentified wrecks at the same site.

1782: **Grosvenor**, at Lambasi Bay, just south of the Msikaba River.[104] Very few of the survivors reached the Cape and some were rumoured to have married into the local communities.[105] Bessie's ship was lost at the same site several decades earlier.

1796: **Hercules** near Begha River mouth, between the Keiskamma and Fish rivers.[106]

1796: **Ann and Eliza**, off present-day Port Elizabeth.[107]

c1799: At least one, and possibly two other unidentified wrecks occurred in about 1799. In October 1800, the missionary Van der Kemp was told by the Xhosa 'that three Englishmen had started up out of the sea upon a piece of wood....' It took him a full month to discover their fate, which he duly recorded in his diary, on 7 November 1800: 'Two of them were killed by Umlao, some by Gika's [King Ngqika's] men. The third being stripped of his clothes made his escape, but one of the Caffrees threw a club after him by which he was knocked down, and then [as they thought] killed by blows of clubs; but after they had left him motionless, one said, "let us go, and cut his throat, otherwise he may revive!" He then sprang up, and threw himself into the river T'Kauwi [Kei], which he crossed by swimming and so providentially escaped.'

What happened to the poor man remains unclear. As this was at the height of the Third Frontier War (1799–1802) between the Xhosa and the

Dutch settlers, when any stray white would have been perceived as the enemy and therefore fair game by the Xhosa, his chances of survival would not have been high, particularly as he was alone, naked and wounded. He was probably also half-starved; Van der Kemp says that the castaways had been living 'upon raw coffee beans of which they had two bags.' Some of these beans, he adds, had been given to him 'and now serve for our use,'[108] so they were presumably still fairly fresh.

Ludwig Alberti, a Dutch official, also refers to a wreck in the area, at about the same time: in 1803 at the *umzi* of a Xhosa chief called Buchu he discovered two Mozambican slaves 'who had saved themselves some months previously in that area from a stranded ship laden with slaves, and whose crew had been murdered by them.'[109]

The English traveller John Barrow also refers to an unnamed vessel, 'from India under Genoese colours' which was wrecked between the Bushman's and Sundays rivers, just north of today's Port Elizabeth, in 1796.[110]

The above list is misleadingly short, partly because it covers such a small portion of the South African coastline, from Port Elizabeth to Port Edward, the northern half of which comprises the Wild Coast. The main reason, however, is that it covers only the period up to 1800 and contains only *identified* wrecks and generally speaking, the earlier the wreck the less likely it is to have been identified or even recorded.

The Portuguese alone lost between 112 and 130 ships *en route* from Lisbon to Goa in the years 1550 to 1650. That's about 120 wrecks over a distance of 16 000 kilometres, at an average of one wreck per 133 kilometres, yet despite its notorious reputation, there are only about a dozen known wreck-sites *of all nationalities* on the South African coast for that period, an average of one wreck per 216 kilometres[111] – far below the Portuguese average alone. Obviously our knowledge is incomplete. That the number of actual wrecks far exceeds the official list is underscored by the fact that the survivors of practically all the recorded wrecks encountered survivors of earlier wrecks and/or the remains of the wrecks themselves. Some they were able to name, but others, like one from which the survivor was an old Frenchman who had been a cook, remain unidentified.

Modern salvage teams have found evidence of previously unknown wrecks, but most of them have also not been identified. Frequently multiple wrecks are located in one place: in the 1980s, for example, a salvage team recovering the *Doddington*, wrecked in 1755 on Bird Island, off Port Elizabeth, discovered evidence of several additional, but unidentified, wrecks. The *Doddington* survivors themselves had reported finding the remains of two previous wrecks at the same site as their own, one English and the other Dutch, neither of which were known of at the time, nor identified before or since. Another example of an unlisted wreck is the one off the Mtentu River about ten kilometres north of Mzikaba mouth, where a chiselled cross, roughly the size of a man's hand, has been discovered near a small freshwater spring on the beach. Nearby grows a species of South American palm tree – the only place in South Africa where it is found.[112] The wreck from which both came was probably Portuguese, but because its details are unknown it also does not appear on our list.

The list is restricted to large ships only; it does not include smaller vessels, such as the boat that Beutler's expedition found in 1752 near the mouth of the Swartkops River in Algoa Bay. Nine sailors and an officer had come ashore in it from a French ship, the *Necessaire*, but the boat had been swamped and the ship had sailed away, leaving them stranded;[113] or the one from the *Bauden*, which had brought ashore the French boy, later rescued along with the *Stavenisse* survivors. The list also excludes ships that sank offshore, of which three examples will suffice. There was the richly laden *Sampson and Amstelveen*, which went missing during a storm off the southern African coast in 1722;[114] the *Mentor*, lost in 1780, whose fate would never have been known had not two of its crew been found by a passing ship, clinging to a fragment of wreckage;[115] and the *Penelope*, an outward-bound English vessel, which disappeared shortly after rounding the Cape in 1591.[116]

Although castaways on the Wild Coast were predominantly European, they included large numbers of people of other races and cultures, for example the black, Japanese and Javanese slaves wrecked aboard the *Sao Alberto* in 1593,[117] or the Lascars wrecked with Bessie in about 1740. There is an entire clan on the Wild Coast that is descended from black castaways. With the passing of time it has become less easy to distinguish the amaMolo, as they are known, from the other Xhosa-speaking clans, but even 60 or 70 years ago their foreign origins were still evident in their features. They are said to have had 'an Arab look about them' and their hair, being straight and black, was quite unlike that of their neighbours. The amaMolo women were renowned for the length of their hair, which reached well below their waists.[118]

The amaMolos' story, as told to JH Soga in the late 1920s by Nwantsu, Great Son of their chief Mxaga, is as follows:

> 'On a certain day, in their own country, Bhayi, his wife, and two others called Tulwana and Pita, walked down to the shore near their home to bathe. While in the water, they were suddenly surrounded by white men, captured, and placed on board of a ship. In the course of the voyage the ship was wrecked on the coast of Pondoland.'

Bhayi, his wife, and 'another man, Mera' were washed ashore. Liberated from one catastrophe by another, their first thought was to find their way home:

> 'Imagining that they could reach their own country by following the coastline eastwards, they walked for many days but lost hope in the end and, turning south once more, they determined to settle among the Pondos.'[119]

By now they seem to have been joined by two other castaways, uMbhetha and Nosali, also said to have been Bhayi's wife.[120] As she was barren Bhayi married an Mpondo woman, by whom he had six children, 'named Poto, Mngcolwana, Mnyuli, Mgareni and Falteni, the last two being twins, and finally, Nyango.' Bhayi made his home at Brazen Head, three or four kilometres south of Mngazana where Bessie resided, and soon established himself as a craftsman of renown. He carved ivory earrings and armbands from elephant tusks, crafted brass bangles and even worked gold, it is said, smelting the metal in a furnace he had built in the forest.[121] For reasons unknown, he periodically had himself lowered by rope into the Ndluzula,[122] a deep and dangerous gully into which the sea rushes in great swells, breaking onto a small beach. In the early 20th century two residents of the Wild Coast, Frank Guthrie and Harry Clarke, let themselves down there on ropes and pulleys in the hope of discovering Bhayi's ivory and gold but, although they almost killed themselves in the attempt, could find nothing.[123]

Bhayi and his companions' origin is a bit of a mystery, but the general consensus is that they were Indian. JH Soga, who met their descendants in 1924, thought they might be Malagasy but were more probably Malay or Indian,[124] while William Bazley's research positively convinced him that they were 'descendants of Lascar people.'[125] Professor Percival Kirby went so far as to state 'Molo = Moro = Moor = Lascar.'[126] I find that a bit too speculative, yet the amaMolo's physical description, coupled with the fact that 'Mera' is an Indian name (a girl's name incidentally), inclined me to think that Bhayi and his companions probably were Indian. The mystery was solved by my friend Nidhi Raina; born and raised in India, she immediately recognised their names as Hindi in origin. 'Bhayi', she said, comes from 'bhay' or brother. 'Pita' – with whom Bhayi was captured – means 'father', and 'Poto', the name of Bhayi's eldest son, is a corruption of 'pota', meaning grandson. As for the rest of his children, 'Mngcolwana' comes from the Hindi word 'Mukulwan', meaning 'the beautiful one', and 'Mnyuli' derives from 'Mayuri', or 'peacock'. One of the twins was probably a girl, Nidhi told me, as 'Mgareni' comes from 'Megharani' or Queen of the Monsoon, while 'Falteni' may be a corruption of Falguni, meaning Monsoon or Spring.[127] These are names of great beauty; Bhayi must have been a very proud parent.

A look at amaMolo genealogy suggests a possible date for Bhayi's wreck; we know that his descendant Nwantsu already had his own Great Son in 1924, but was not yet a grandfather, so he was probably around 40 years old, born about 1884. Applying the convention of 30 years per generation[128] gives us an approximate date for Bhayi's birth of 1764, and as he was already married when he was captured, ie he was at least 16 at the time, his wreck could not have occurred much before 1780.

Although the time lines suggested by oral genealogies are by no means infallible, there does happen to have been a very well-documented wreck on the Wild Coast at almost exactly that time; the East Indiaman *Grosvenor*, which sank in 1782. Among its survivors were 25 Indian seamen, many of whom broke away from the other groups of survivors in the vicinity of the Mzimvubu River,[129] just a few kilometres up the coast from Bhayi's home at Brazen Head. Another survivor of the same wreck was an Indian maidservant called Mary,[130] possibly an Anglicised version of Bhayi's fellow castaway Mera, who was also last seen near the Mzimvubu – in the company of another Indian woman, Sally, whose name bears a remarkable similarity to Nosali, Bhayi's wife. Neither Mary nor Sally, incidentally, was among the survivors who reached the Cape.[131]

The *Grosvenor* captured the public's imagination in a way no other wreck on our coastline has done before or since, and has continued to do so in the more than two centuries that have passed since it occurred, partly because the ship was believed to be carrying treasure of fabulous proportions, but also because of the unknown fate of its women and children. So pervasive has the legend of the wreck become that almost everything that has happened on the Wild Coast seems to be linked in some way.[132] Bessie, for example, was rumoured to be one of the *Grosvenor* survivors, although she clearly was not. Nevertheless, it was due to this ship that we have an account of Bessie's only confirmed meeting with whites from the outside world.

Genealogy of the amaMolo[133]

Kumkati

Jafilita ['Pita'? – father]

Bhayi
(married unnamed
Pondo woman)

Six Children

whose descendants are as follows:

1.

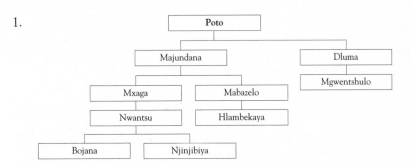

Poto

Majundana — Dluma

Mgwentshulo

Mxaga — Mabazelo

Nwantsu — Hlambekaya

Bojana — Njinjibiya

2.

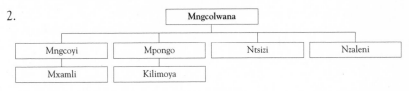

Mngcolwana

Mngcoyi — Mpongo — Ntsizi — Nzaleni

Mxamli — Kilimoya

3.

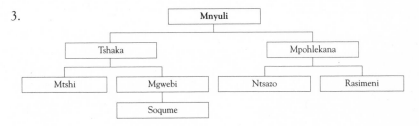

Mnyuli

Tshaka — Mpohlekana

Mtshi — Mgwebi — Ntsazo — Rasimeni

Soqume

The twins

4.

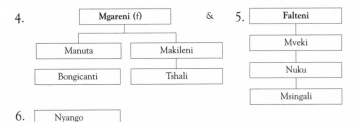

Mgareni (f)   &   5.

Manuta — Makileni

Bongicanti — Tshali

Falteni

Mveki

Nuku

Msingali

6.   Nyango

Chapter Five

The *Grosvenor*

The Hoseas' baby almost saved her parents lives.
'Mrs H will be brought to bed by the 15th of the next month at
furtherest,' wrote William Hosea in November 1781. The wealthy
English East India Company official and his family were due to leave for
England aboard the *Grosvenor* at the beginning of January, and with luck
the baby would be born in time for them to keep their passage. The recipient
of his letter was a dear friend, Lady Frances Chambers, who was making
arrangements for his wife's confinement in Calcutta. Hosea added that he
hoped to employ 'a Portugueze or Mohometan Wetnurse to go with us to
Europe,' and offered to look after any children Lady Chambers might wish
to send to England.[1]

Tragically, she did.

Lady Chambers, the wife of Sir Robert Chambers, Judge of the Supreme
Court of Bengal, was 'a beautiful creature not more than eighteen years of age,'
remarked a visitor who had met her five years earlier. Hardly more than a child
herself, she already had two children.[2] By the time her friend Hosea made his
offer, her son Tom was almost seven years old, and the Chambers decided to
avail themselves of this seemingly perfect opportunity for him to begin his
schooling in England and escape the unhealthy climate of eighteenth-century
Calcutta. In exchange Lady chambers offered to take care of the Hosea's infant
while they were away.

The baby, however, was late. By 15 December she had not yet arrived;
the beginning of January came, and went – and so did the *Grosvenor*, sailing
from Calcutta without the Hoseas. Their baby was born a few days later, and
it would have been better for all concerned had they just accepted the way

things had turned out and waited for another homeward-bound ship, but they had two children already back in England, a passage booked and business to attend to, and William Hosea had not become Chief Resident of Murshidabad and survived nearly two decades in the East India Company by simply accepting things as they were. Within two days of the baby's baptism, he and his wife, together with their 16-month-old daughter Frances, seven-year-old Thomas Fitzgerald Chambers, several servants and 29 trunks, were aboard a coastal vessel and soon intercepted the *Grosvenor* and the rest of the English fleet at Madras, on the east coast of India.[3]

The baby remained behind in Lady Chambers' care, too newly born to be exposed to the long sea voyage that lay ahead. The decision to leave her must have been a difficult one for both her parents, but particularly for her mother. Unlike her go-getter husband, Mary Hosea was, said an intimate acquaintance, 'one of the most amiable women I ever knew; it is impossible to do otherwise than love her....'[4] As traumatic as their departure must have been for her – the anxiety and discomfort of her late delivery, the agony of birth, the stress of nearly missing their ship, the mad scramble to catch the East Indiaman before it left Indian waters and the terrible separation from her newborn infant – she nevertheless found time to write to her friend Lady Chambers, consoling her over the recent loss of her mother, who had died, and the imminent loss of her son Tom, albeit – or so they thought – not permanently. 'I had flattered myself that I should have behaved with more philosophy at the parting with my child, but the moment of separation was too acute and I have really been ill ever since the day I left her,' she added in a letter taken ashore by the pilot as the *Grosvenor* headed for the open sea. 'I own myself a coward, and as much as I wished to embrace you before I left India, I am glad I did not see you just at the instant of my departure. We had both, my friend, more than we were able to support.'[5]

In the confusion of leaving, a trunk of Tom's clothes and Hosea's books were left behind, but as things turned out, neither would be needing them.

For the 150 men, women and children on board the *Grosvenor*, the voyage must have seemed cursed from the start. Just two days after leaving Madras the English fleet was involved in a fire-fight with a French ship of sixteen guns – Britain and France were at war with one another yet again – and less than a week later it ran into the French fleet proper. Outnumbered and outgunned, the English ships sustained heavy damage, delaying them off Sri Lanka until the middle of June 1782.

Generally East Indiamen travelled in convoy – as soon as a war was declared, insurance underwriters increased their rates, encouraging merchants to seek safety in numbers by offering a reduction of 5–10% to any whose ships travelled in convoy.[6] The fleet with which the *Grosvenor* had sailed, however, had commitments in the East, while its own route lay westwards, and at Trincomalee they parted company. More bad luck followed when the East Indiaman missed a rendezvous with another English ship, and was forced to sail on alone. It was dangerously late in the season to be making the homeward voyage. They were sailing directly against the prevailing winds (the south-westerly monsoon, which blew from April to September) and the winter storms had already begun in the southern ocean.

The voyage was rough and the ship sustained damage, particularly to its mainmast, in a mid-ocean storm. The chief mate Mr Logie fell ill and was soon too weak to perform his duties. As the vessel closed with the African coast the weather deteriorated further, making accurate navigational readings impossible.[7] On 3 August when, according to the captain's calculations, the ship was at least 300 kilometres out at sea,[8] it was in fact close to land – and drawing nearer with each fleeting hour.

In the early hours of 4 August several sailors were sent aloft to take in the topsails; the wind was freshening and the mainmast was taking strain. On the horizon a couple of the men saw lights – 'two very large lofty spreading lights' according to a 20-year-old seaman, William Hubberly – and reported them to the second mate and officer of the watch, Mr Shaw. The lights disappeared soon afterwards, but although it was agreed that they had probably been some kind of atmospheric phenomenon, 'something similar to the Northern lights', the seamen remained uneasy. They had no way of knowing, until much later, that far from being 'lights in the air', they were fires on the ground. It was common in those days (and for that matter, still is) for the people living on the south-east African coast to burn their grasslands in winter, to stimulate new growth for their cattle.[9] It was these veld fires that the sailors had seen. The *Grosvenor* was dangerously close to shore.

When the morning watch came on deck at four o'clock Mr Shaw told the third mate Mr Beale about the lights and warned him to keep his eyes open. About half an hour later through the pre-dawn gloom a dark smudge could be seen low on the horizon. Some of the sailors thought it was a squall or fog but others thought it might be land. Within moments it was clear that the latter were right. The quartermaster ran to alert Mr Beale, who was not only dismissive but would not even walk to the other side of the ship to check for himself. Realising the situation was critical the quartermaster bypassed the usual chain of command and ran straight to Captain Coxon, who came on deck immediately and at once ordered the ship to go about.[10]

It was too late; the *Grosvenor* was already in the grip of unexpected and powerful currents, and as all hands on deck fought to hoist the mizzen staysail and veer away, it struck an offshore reef, smashing into the hidden rocks with such violence that it seemed the masts themselves would be ripped from their mountings. Torn from their slumber by the crash and noise of the impact, the Hoseas and other passengers scrambled to the deck in the pitch dark, the wind lashing their faces with rain and spray. In the sporadic flashes of lightning, it was obvious from the wild waves careering all around them that it was impossible for a boat to be launched, let alone to carry them safely to the unseen shore. 'Despair was painted on every countenance. Mothers were crying and lamenting over their children; husbands over both; and all was anarchy and confusion.'[11] Nobody knew what to do; sailors and officers ran this way and that, some shouting out to God to preserve them, while others were struck dumb with terror. Two broke into the grog store, thinking perhaps that death by alcohol was preferable to death by water.

The ship did not go down immediately, however, and as dawn broke the wind moderated and swung round to an offshore breeze. The crew began packing on canvas in order to pull the ship off the rocks, but in doing so they ripped out its bottom. Water began pouring in and, as the ship began drifting out to sea again, the men who minutes before had worked so hard to get the *Grosvenor* off the reef, were fighting desperately to get it back on again.[12] By now the boats had been broken up by the waves and a makeshift raft had met with the same fate, but two Lascars swam a line to shore and an Italian seaman swam in and helped secure it.

The place where the Indiaman had run aground was Lambasi, the same bay where Bessie had been cast ashore some 40 years earlier, her ship probably victim to the same currents and rough conditions as the *Grosvenor*, and perhaps even to the same submerged reef. Just as it had been in Bessie's time, the area was well inhabited; the Mpondo King Ngqungqushe's *umzi* was about 30 kilometres inland and, it being wintertime, all the inland cattle were down at the sea,[13] enjoying the seasonally sweet coastal grasses. As day broke large numbers of people gathered on the shore. As two amaMpondo told their sons years later:

> 'We got up one morning and saw the ship on the rocks, so we went onto the beach and the sailors threw us a rope which we fastened round a rock and the white people came ashore by this…. The wreck broke in half, and half went into the sea….'[14]

By some miracle, a huge wave had lifted and flung the starboard quarter, on which most survivors were crowded, into shallow water and, as this was also the portion attached by the hawser to the shore, everyone on board was pulled to safety, including the women and children. This was a long drawn-out process, and it was only towards nightfall that the last of them reached the shore, more than 12 terrifying hours after striking the reef.[15]

The survivors numbered 125, a strange and very varied collection of souls, a mixed bag of tough British, Indian and Italian seamen, aristocratic French prisoners of war, British army officers and bureaucrats, their wives and Indian maidservants, and six young children.[16] Some were battered and bruised, others more seriously injured, some were calm, some fearful, others still in shock; all were trying to come to grips with their new and frightening circumstances. Slowly they began gathering what they could – hogs, geese, tools and valuables – from the debris strewn about the rocks and beach, and managed to erect two sailcloth tents. While all this was going on, the Mpondo were also busy amongst the wreckage. Far from being 'dumb with astonishment' at the sight of the Indiaman, as one colonial writer would have it,[17] they were fully cognizant of the wreck's material value and highly efficient in securing it: 'We carried stuff from the wreck and hid it a little distance from the shore,' an unnamed Mpondo told the settler Zacky Bowles many years later.[18] With their ochre-painted skins, near-naked bodies, their hair twisted into long braids or curled into conical shapes and decorated with feathers, the Mpondo must have appeared both strange and frightening to the castaways, and although they did not harm them, they took whatever they liked and even removed stuff from their tents.[19] Mostly, however, they were preoccupied with the wreck itself, its cargo, its ropes, planks and even the nails holding them together, and paid little attention to the foreigners: 'the white people… stayed nearby for a little, but eventually went away westwards….'[20]

Like so many other castaways before them, the survivors had decided that their best option was to make for the safety of the Cape, a journey which Captain Coxon estimated would take about 10 days, 16 or 17 at the utmost. It was his second critical mistake – the first had been his assumption that the ship was still far out to sea when it was practically on the rocks – a tragic underestimation of the distance to be covered and the dangers of the route, and it was to have fatal repercussions. The journey that followed was to prove worse than their worst nightmares, and very few would survive.

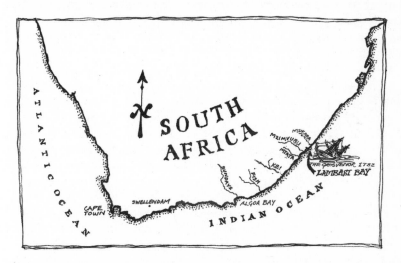

Only two of the survivors were fortunate enough or smart enough to stay at the wreck, Joshua Glover who, ironically, was described as 'a fool', and John Bryan, a discharged soldier who had injured his leg in getting ashore and was unable to walk. He planned 'to get some pewter and lead from the wreck, of which he would make little trinkets to amuse the natives, hoping thereby to ingratiate himself with them, and learn their language….'[21] Whether or not he succeeded will be dealt with in a later chapter.

The journey that lay ahead of the *Grosvenor* survivors has much in common with the accounts of the preceding chapter, but for one detail: before leaving, they buried something near the site of the wreck. The Mpondo were watching, of course, among them a group of small herd-boys. One of them, years later, when he was very old and almost blind, recalled: '[I]n the early morning when looking for cattle, they saw the *Grosvenor* ashore, and the white women and children that came out of the sea…. [H]e saw them carry something along on a pole a little inland and bury it.'[22]

Another elderly Mpondo had a similar story to tell: 'Keeping hidden in the bushes he had seen a group of them bury what he described as a fair-sized box a short distance inland.'[23] Since more than a dozen of their companions had died in the wreck, it is possible that the survivors were just burying their dead, but the connection between the *Grosvenor* and hidden treasure had taken root; over the centuries the myth slowly grew and grew, until the size of the treasure reached fabulous proportions, muddling men's minds with greed and producing fantastical plans for its recovery – the nuttiest of which was probably the underwater tunnel described in the first chapter of this book.

On 7 August 1782, the fourth day ashore, the survivors set out to walk to the Cape. The trouble started almost immediately. According to young William Hubberly:

> 'Soon after we moved forward we were surrounded by a great number of the natives, who began throwing stones at us and holding their lances in a threatening manner and seemed desirous of preventing us from proceeding.'[24]

The Mpondo threw stones at the survivors and took some of their possessions, including food, before being driven off. Shortly afterwards they reappeared in a more orderly fashion, with a chief at their head 'which alarmed us very much.' 'The chief then stepped forwards and made a short speech, they all behaving themselves very peaceable.' The captain gave them some gold lace and they left again, and the survivors proceeded with their journey. A day or two later, in the vicinity of Mbotyi, the local people came out of their huts and gathering together, drove the castaways off. Those who could fled, but the stragglers were robbed, the women among them lost their earrings and, their hair 'coming down', the jewellery they had hidden in it was discovered.[25]

For reasons not entirely clear, the *Grosvenor* party was subjected to an unusual amount and degree of violence. Although the coastal peoples had been assaulted, shot and robbed by castaways for centuries and were understandably fearful and suspicious of foreigners, particularly in large groups, even the sizeable *Stavenisse* and *Bennebroek* parties did not provoke the animosity the *Grosvenor* survivors did. Some historians have speculated that the outbreak of war between the Xhosa and white Settlers further south two years before the wreck of the vessel, news of which would certainly have travelled quickly northwards, had something to do with it, but the survivors' own behaviour was almost certainly a contributing factor.

Hubberly's and the other survivors' accounts give the impression that they were largely the innocent victims of unprovoked aggression, but an Mpondo account suggests otherwise. In 1896 an elderly man named Ubawa-Mkulu told a Cape Mounted Rifles trooper, who was hunting on the Pondoland coast, of a great ship wrecked more than 100 years before some way north of the Mzimvubu River – the same period and location as the *Grosvenor*. The survivors, he said, had promised the local people, under a man called Bungana, that in exchange for their help they would reward them with presents. For three days Bungana

> 'brought fruit for the white women and children, and meat for the men. At the dawn of the fourth day from the coming of the white people, Bungana and many others went to them to get the presents for helping them, but they found that, save only two men, all the others had gone.'

Bungana and his people set off in pursuit but when they caught up with the castaways, were told that they would be paid only once the whites had succeeded in reaching their own people again. Angered by the castaways' duplicity, they crowded round them, stripping the women of their jewellery, whereupon the white men leapt forward with big knives and drove them off.[26]

According to Ben Dekker, a long-time resident of the Wild Coast who drew my attention to Ubawa-Mkulu's story,

> 'Bungana was a M'Pondo headman from Quibeni, then about five miles due north east of its present site – then it was at the headwaters of the Umlambomkhulu River – the one that forms the double waterfall on Waterfall Bluff...'[27]

In other words, only a few kilometres from the wreck-site.

'Bungana's dates are difficult to establish,' Ben cautioned, 'and could refer to any of a dozen wrecks.' Yet the details of Ubawa-Mkulu's account match those of the survivors so closely (it *was* on the fourth day that the castaways began their journey south, two men *did* remain behind, etc), I have no doubt that the wreck referred to was the *Grosvenor*. His story offers a credible explanation why the people living at and around Lambasi Bay, who had shown no aggression towards the survivors on their arrival, should suddenly have become violent. One of the survivors, an able seaman named John Hynes, seems to support this contention when he says that the party's Mpondo pursuers called out 'Zembe', which he took to mean 'Give us something' (the word was probably 'ntsimbi', meaning 'metal'), and that three of them held an assegai at Captain Coxon's throat 'several times.'[28] All of which sounds more like a demand for payment than an outright assault. When the captain, at last 'irritated beyond his patience,' grabbed the assegai and broke it, the men went away but they returned the next day and attacked the castaways with a large force of armed men. When peace was restored over two hours later, several of the *Grosvenor* men cut the buttons off their coats and gave them, along with other items, to their Mpondo attackers; 'upon which they went away and returned no more.'[29] Which, to me, sounds very much as though, restitution obtained, Bungana and his men considered the subject closed.

Ubawa-Mkulu's account also explains the continuing hostility that the castaways encountered as their journey continued. Cheating Bungana's people would have initiated a self-perpetuating cycle of violence. News spread quickly on the coast, especially bad news about bad castaways. Just as people had known about the *Baptista* cannibals fully two days ahead of their arrival,[30] people further down the coast were forewarned of the *Grosvenor* party – and forearmed.

The survivors' difficulties were exacerbated by the fact that their ship was wrecked in winter – a season in which the local people did not slaughter their beasts, except as sacrificial offerings to their ancestors,[31] and obtained most of their meat from hunting. Frustrated and outraged by their refusal to sell or trade their cattle, the starving survivors stole to feed themselves. It was a vicious circle: the locals would not provide them with food so the survivors stole their cattle so the locals attacked the survivors:

> '… [S]o apprehensive were the natives of the strangers stealing their cattle, that they constantly drove them away as they approached the Kraals. Nor was their precaution confined to this point; wherever the English came, they were driven away with sticks, stones, and other missile weapons.'[32]

Some of their tradable goods were stolen in these skirmishes, particularly iron objects such as knives and nails. Metal was so highly prized that even the tiny cogs of their pocket-watches were taken.

The survivors had managed to save some firearms from the wreck, but as they had no gunpowder were unable to procure food by hunting. The sight of the firearms, though, seems to have provoked the local people: one elderly man

> 'came out with a lance in his hand, which he levelled at our people, making, at the same time a noise somewhat resembling the report of a musquet. This was supposed to mean, that he apprehended they would kill his cattle; for he instantly drove his herd into the Kraal….'[33]

Evidently he had had first-hand experience – and that not good – of men with guns.

Sometimes innocent victims, sometimes agents of their own misfortune, the outcome was the same – the survivors were always the losers. Hungry, frightened and angry they struggled on. The countryside was extremely rugged, broken by countless small streams and many large rivers, rough *kloofs* and dense bush, making their passage a relentless ordeal. Just south of the wreck rearing up out of the sea are the great cliffs of Waterfall Bluff, so called for the great waterfall on the Mlambomkulu (Big River) which tumbles directly into the sea far below. The survivors' progress was painfully slow, their pace compromised by the weak, the young and the injured. As the days passed and the wreck dropped further and further behind them, their supply of salvaged and scrounged victuals diminished quickly; and their relationships with one another, which had begun civilly enough, deteriorated with equal rapidity.

It has been estimated that it takes over 250 kilograms of food to feed five men for six weeks;[34] with the *Grosvenor* party numbering 123 that amounts to several tons of foodstuffs – an amount they simply did not have. Without adequate food the children, in particular, weakened rapidly. There were six altogether: the Hoseas' two-year-old daughter Frances, Lady Chambers' seven-year-old son Tom, two other boys of the same age, Thomas Law and Robert Saunders,[35] and two little girls, Mary Wilmot, also seven, and Eleanor Dennis, aged three. By the third day the party was already starting to disperse along the shore, the fit, young and strong leading the way, while the captain, a number of his officers and several strong seamen, who had been promised a reward if they stayed to help the passengers and the sick, brought up the rear. Among the latter was the first mate, Alexander Logie, who had to be carried in a hammock. He had married shortly before the *Grosvenor* sailed, and his pregnant bride Lydia was among the passengers. Other passengers included Mr and Mrs Hosea, an elderly couple, Mrs James and Colonel James, a French officer, Colonel Charles Francois d'Espinette, several other French prisoners-of-war and four Indian maidservants, Sally, Mary, Betty and Hoakim.

On 11 August, four days into the journey, the party of castaways broke up. The first to leave was a mixed group of about 50 European and Lascar sailors, 'saying it was of little use to stay and perish with those they could not give any assistance to.' One of the children, Thomas Law, went with them.[36]

The captain left the same day, abandoning his charges. Despite the fact that he himself was a father of a small child (whose third birthday he had celebrated the day before the wreck), Coxon left the children, the women, including the pregnant Mrs Logie, and the rest of the passengers under his care, to fend for themselves. They were ill-equipped to do so, with even the adult men among them in a sorry shape: Colonel James, for example, was 'unable to move without assistance' while the injured Mr Logie 'was almost dead,' according to a maidservant who was the last to see them alive.[37] They were still about two days' march north of the Mzimvubu River at that stage.

We know that Captain Coxon reached the river, because members of his crew saw him there and, later, at the Mtata River much further south,[38] but he was not among those who succeeded in reaching the Cape. What became of him is not known. What became of his abandoned charges is also not certain. Only two of them were to reach the Cape – Mrs Logie's maid Betty and Mrs Hosea's maid Hoakim, and they left soon after the captain. The other two Indian women who accompanied the passengers, Sally and Mary, may – as I suggested in the previous chapter – have been Nosali and Mera, who settled just south of the Mzimvubu with Bhayi and are numbered among the progenitors of the amaMolo clan.

What became of the rest of the group is fraught with rumour, often contradictory. According to William Bazley, an old Natal settler who was to spend much time during the following century in Pondoland investigating the *Grosvenor* story,

> 'many of the captain's party got drowned in crossing the St John's River [Mzimvubu] on a catamaran or raft of driftwood. This raft was smashed by a big cow [sea-cow, ie hippo] and many were drowned, including some of the children, and at least one of the grown-up ladies,'[39]

whom Bazley thought was the elderly Mrs James.[40] One little girl, whom he calls 'Minna' – probably a corruption of Mary, the seven-year-old Ms Wilmot – was carried across by a Lascar man.[41] The other children and women remained north of the river. One of the women, said Bazley,

> 'committed suicide by strangling herself with a silk scarf or shawl; a second lady died after giving birth to a little girl baby, five months after the wreck.... This I know because the wreck took place on the 4th of August, about mielie planting time, and when the woman was confined the natives gave her young unripe mielies, still milky, to eat, which brought on dysentery, and she died within a few days of the birth of her child.'[42]

This must have been Lydia Logie, the first mate's wife who, as mentioned above, was pregnant when the *Grosvenor* was wrecked. But let us return for a moment to Ubawa-Mkulu's story of Bungana, the man who supplied the survivors with food for three days at the wreck-site and received nothing in return. Many days after the survivors' departure, said old Ubawa-Mkulu,

> 'Bungana found two white women in the bush nearly dead from hunger, and he brought them to his kraal. One of them he made his wife; and the other, Nomedola his brother, took as his wife, and both had children whose offspring live among us even now.'[43]

Bungana, as mentioned above, lived at Quibeni, between the wreck of the *Grosvenor* and the place where Captain Coxon abandoned the women and children's party.[44]

It seems quite feasible to me that after the captain left, some of them turned back and began retracing their steps to the wreck, where they knew they could find John Bryan and Joshua Glover, and that on the return journey the two women, too weak to continue, were found by Bungana. It was customary among the Mpondo never to harm women or children, even in warfare. They had very definite traditions of courtesy and hospitality towards strangers and, although they were obviously afraid of the *Grosvenor* party as a whole, the women and children, being the most vulnerable, would have posed no threat to them.

That the *Grosvenor* women married Mpondo is confirmed by Bessie's daughter, Bessy, who was about sixteen when the Indiaman was wrecked. The women and female children, she told a party of English missionaries in the 1820s, were spared and many of their descendants were still to be found among the Mpondo,[45] but their male companions were killed by order of the Mpondo king, whose 'jealousy and fear were excited by the large number of [Europeans] who thus suddenly appeared in his country.'[46] Her mother – in her late forties and living just south of the Mzimvubu – evidently also knew of this incident: according to an independent source Bessie's hair 'turned white in a single night at the news of the tragedy....'[47]

Various other sources also indicate that some of the women and children survived. Bazley, for example, who spent much time investigating the *Grosvenor*,

> 'found a very old white woman living exactly as a native between Springvale and Highflats somewhere between 1860 and 1870 or so, she then being about 86 years of age and speaking only Zulu. He could not get her name, but thinks it must be Hosea. He got full accounts of her having been saved from drowning and then concealed by natives. The relief party that came failed to find any of the survivors in consequence of natives being loath to deliver up wives so cheaply secured,'[48]

that is, for whom they had not had to pay *lobolo*. Too much time had gone by for the woman to have been Mary Hosea, but she may well have been her daughter; aged two at the time of the wreck, Frances Alicia Hosea would have been in her mid-80s by 1865.

The following report by Mahaya ka Nongqabana may be connected. Mahaya, whose immediate ancestors had been embroiled in the Shakan wars near Highflats, where Bazley met his old white woman,[49] claimed descent from a white woman who was found 'in a state of destitution' after a ship was wrecked

> 'at the Lwambazo near the Msikaba river, where these rivers enter the sea. It is said nowadays that this woman had come from the ship.'

Two men and one girl, says Mahaya,

> 'came out on a piece of the wreckage. They rolled a safe or chest of money along and buried it. They then wrote on a rock, saying that [the two of them] and a girl had escaped. The two men lived on wild

plums (amatungule), and afterwards died of fever. Black men came along to gather mussels,[50] and found the girl and tended her. They reported this. "We saw a white person with long hair, a wanderer or waif." They said they had come out of an *uqwembe* [wooden meat tray], not knowing what a ship was. Their chief, whose name I forget, then told them to go and "catch her" on the beach. The girl cried. They escorted her back to the chief. They saw she had breasts and was a woman. She lived on fowl's eggs chiefly. She then saw that no harm was intended and was happy.'[51]

In her case tradition was carefully observed and Bazley's claim that no *lobola* was paid for female castaways seems unfounded. The chief acted as the castaway's father and sought out a man of property as a suitable husband for her. In those days it was customary for a father to send to a man of importance asking him to give his daughter a snuff spoon – which meant an offer to marry – but the chief was unable to find a suitable man amongst his own people, and so the application for a snuff spoon was made further afield – to Mahaya's ancestor Mbukwe, and in time the girl became his wife.[52] The couple had a girl and two boys, one of whom was Mahaya's grandfather Mntengwane. 'He was a "bastard" (ibastela),' Mahaya recalled, 'light in colour, as was his hair.' His daughter Nqalo was Mahaya's mother.[53]

Of the 123 *Grosvenor* survivors who undertook the journey to the Cape, only six succeeded in reaching the Colony, while another 14 were found later by a rescue expedition. Many of the remainder undoubtedly perished along the way, but none of the women and only one of the children was among the deaths reported by eyewitnesses. The exception was seven year-old Thomas Law.

Genealogy of Mahaya[54]

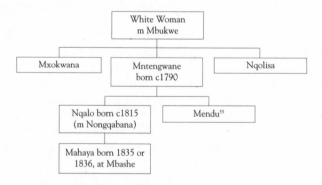

The son of an English aristocrat and an Indian lady, Thomas was a feisty little boy who had joined a breakaway party of sailors, led by the ship's carpenter, and won a special place in the hearts of his tough companions:

'When the road was even and good, he walked, and was able to keep pace with the party; but when they came to deep sands, or passed through high grass, which was often the case, the people carried him by turns.'[56] Perhaps he was a kind of good-luck mascot; certainly he was a repository for all the humane feelings they denied their weaker comrades – from whom they literally walked away – since they even carried him when they themselves could barely walk any more.

Although they had begun as some of the strongest of the survivors, things did not go well for the carpenter's party. Five of them died in the rugged terrain south of Brazen Head, including the carpenter, who had eaten poisonous fruit.[57] The steward, Henry Lillburne, became their leader, and took young Master Law under his personal protection.[58] The going was hard and once, in extremely long grass, they found a mass of trees torn up by their roots and, minutes later, stumbled on a herd of thirty or forty elephant and were fortunate to get away unnoticed and unscathed.[59] Despite their hardships, the boy bore up well and even made himself useful: 'When they went on fishing parties, he was stationed near the fires, in order to keep them alight; and on their return was rewarded with a part of the spoil.'[60] Just past the Bushman's River, near today's popular holiday resort of Kenton-on-Sea, they met up with another group of *Grosvenor* survivors, who gave them the remains of a whale they had found.[61] Intended as an act of kindness, it had tragic repercussions, for the meat poisoned the steward and his little ward. It is a measure of the sailors' affection for the boy that, instead of abandoning him as they usually did when one of their number fell ill, they waited a whole day for him and the steward to recover. On the following night, to the grief of the latter who 'had provided for [the boy], swam with him on his back over rivers, and nursed him with all the tenderness of a father,'[62] the child died. The sailors did not bury him, but simply left him where he lay, next to the fire, as if asleep.[63] It was 11 November 1782, the castaways had been walking for three months and covered a lot of ground; they were only 50 or 60 kilometres from the nearest Dutch farms. Had it not been for the rotten meat the lad would probably have made it to safety.

Like other shipwreck victims, the *Grosvenor* party left many of their companions behind them on their journey along the Wild Coast. Like them, they found evidence of previous wrecks, in one case some planks with a few nails in them, from which they fashioned crude knives[64] and in another, a boat upset on a beach.[65] They also saw 'on the shore, an old rotten mast and not long after they past the Great Fish River, they saw a small old topgallant mast in a freshwater creek.'[66] Just north of the Kei River one group of them met a 'black Portuguese who could speak Dutch very well,' who showed them much kindness and cooked them a meal.[67] They also met runaway slaves, one being a Malay called Trout who spoke Dutch and recognised them as English, calling 'Engles, Engles!' He lived at Mbotyi, a little way south of wreck, and had clearly been resident there for some time, as he already had a family.[68] News of the *Grosvenor* had preceded the castaways and Trout was on his way to see what he could salvage.[69] He warned the survivors that the Cape was further away than they estimated, but flatly refused to join them as a guide, even when they tried to bribe him with a fortune. He was last seen returning from the wreck, looking rather dashing in a long morning gown.

Some of the survivors also met Bessie's people. William Hubberly was a member of a party led by the second mate, Mr Shaw, that had turned inland at the Mzimvubu to find a place higher up the river where it would be easier to cross and, having done so, headed back towards the sea a little south of the river, in Tshomane territory. They would have been surprised to discover that they were entering the territory of a people whose queen was, like them, a castaway.

It was two weeks since their ship had gone down and the castaways were hungry and weakening rapidly – although they had passed many homesteads, the inhabitants had refused to part with their fine cattle. After a day-long struggle through head-high grass without the aid of footpaths, they reached the coast at Mngazana, where Bessie lived with her husband, the Tshomane chief Sango.

> 'This morning we started very early, in hopes of procuring on the seashore some shell-fish, and at length gained the beach,'

Hubberly reported later.

> 'It being now high water, we were obliged to halt. Some natives observing us came up, and as they behaved very peaceable, we began our old custom of applying to them for something.'[70]

As they had only encountered hostility and refusal until now, Hubberly and his comrades must have been pleasantly surprised by the entirely different response that met their request for food: 'They immediately after drove a fine young bullock to us, for which we gave a gold watch-chain.' The Tshomane were most accommodating, not only killing the bullock for their visitors but lending them a lance to cut it up, and also fetching some milk for them, which was exchanged for buttons. When the sailors stripped off to cross the river, a couple of men tried to take the clothes but their chiefs stopped them.

Despite their exhaustion and hunger, the sailors realised these

'were certainly a different sort of people from those where the ship was unfortunately lost; their hair being covered with brick-dust and matted with grease had more the resemblance of ropes hanging down than hair.'

Their chiefs were richly ornamented with

'beads about their necks, brass rings about their wrists, pieces of copper in their hair, large white and blue glass beads about their waists, and ivory rings about their arms.'[71]

Their beads and copper, as suggested above, may have been part of the huge haul of goods obtained from ivory traders such as Hubner. We do not know if Bessie was among the people on the beach – dressed in skins, with her long black hair in braids and with 'more ornaments on her dress than the ordinary native woman,'[72] except for her famous blue eyes she probably bore no resemblance to any white woman they had ever met – but her daughter Bessy probably was, since, as she told a missionary many years later, 'when she was about 16 years of age, she remembered the wreck of a large ship, out of which "a whole nation," as she expressed it, of white people came....'[73]

Hubberly and his companions, having divided up the meat and wrapped strips of the hide around their bare feet, took leave of Bessie's people and went on their weary way. Their new shoes did not last long; as soon as hunger set in again they ate them. The other groups of *Grosvenor* survivors were having an equally hard time, and as the journey lengthened more and more dropped out of the scattered little groups or died. Once in a while, however, something wonderful occurred. A large group had split in two, and the ones lagging behind had not been able to locate water. They were weak with thirst, when suddenly they came upon a message from the forward party, scrawled in the sand at the entrance to a deep *sloot*: 'Turn in here and you will find plenty of wood and water.'[74] They did and were saved – at least for the time being.

As the castaways' faltering steps took them further south they drew closer and closer to the war raging between the Xhosa and the Boers, and once more came under attack. William Hubberly was one of a small group particularly violently assaulted at the mouth of the Fish River, the attack probably precipitated by an event which had taken place further inland a year earlier, when a Boer commander, Van Jaarsveld, had tricked the imiDange Xhosa with a present of tobacco and then ordered his men to fire;[75] at such short range the imiDange did not have a chance and many were killed, including the chief's son Jalamba. It was something they never forgot nor forgave: for the three *Grosvenor* survivors it was a tragic case of wrong place, wrong time.

Looking south towards Mngazana from Mngazi

Today a hotel stands just to the north of the river mouth, but it is set well back beyond the dunes and the beaches are just as deserted and rugged as they must have been when Hubberly and two passengers, Williams and Taylor, who were brothers-in-law, made their weary approach, the bank lined with dense bush, viciously thorny and full of snakes, ending in a jumble of rocks at the sea's edge. The attack took them completely by surprise. Hubberley fled into the inhospitable thornbush and in so doing saved himself. Williams, less fortunate, was dragged down to the river mouth and thrown in. As he tried to swim away he was pelted with stones; some struck his head, and he sank beneath the waters. Taylor, who like Hubberly had run for his life, was caught and dragged away, begging for mercy. From his hiding place in the bush, Hubberly heard his cries slowly fade to silence. At sunset, when his attackers finally gave up searching for him and drifted off, he crawled out and found to his surprise that Taylor was still alive, though bleeding badly.[76] With his assistance, Taylor somehow managed to keep going, but as they approached the twin lagoons of Kleinemonde, his condition suddenly deteriorated and within a few hours, unable to eat or to speak, he died. The next morning, too weak to bury him, Hubberly stripped the corpse and shoved it into the river for the tide to carry it away, then continued his journey alone.[77]

Eventually – and just when he most needed it, Hubberly found help, stumbling upon some kindly women, who gave him milk to drink, and their menfolk, who gave him meat. They were Gqunukwebe, a Xhosa people with some Khoi ancestry, under their chief, Zaka.[78] At first they were terribly afraid of Hubberly, for, by his own admission, his appearance was exceedingly strange. In the three months since the loss of his ship, he had barely eaten enough to keep body and soul together. Cadaverous and desperate, filthy and sunburnt, he wore a cut-off pair of trousers with a piece of woman's shawl serving as his shirt, over which he wore a waistcoat and on his head a trouser leg, serving as his hat. He looked so odd that whenever he moved, the people fled in fear – one dropped her infant but was too afraid of the castaway to return, so he picked the child up and gave it back to her. That broke the ice, and he was soon overwhelmed with kindness. As he ate his fill for the first time in ages, the poor castaway was convinced it was all a fantastic dream. This happy interlude was brought to an abrupt end: during the night Hubberly woke up with his tortured guts rebelling against their newfound bounty. Running outside, he relieved himself in the nearest convenient spot. That this happened to be in the middle of the cattle kraal, a sacred spot where the Xhosa bury their chiefs, had unfortunate repercussions. When his hosts discovered his dreadful deed the next day he was cursed and driven away immediately.[79] Hubberly never fully understood why, nor did he know how lightly he had been let off – the punishment for relieving oneself in a cattle kraal, or even against the fence, was usually death.[80]

As the various groups of survivors threaded their way down the Wild Coast, crossing and re-crossing each other's paths in a tragic weave, their individual suffering seems to have made them oblivious to the suffering of their fellows. Generally speaking their story is not one of heroic deeds or selfless sacrifices, but dog-eat-dog – from the captain down. They abandoned the women, they abandoned the children, the sick, the elderly and the weak. In many ways it is a frightening tale, and it gets worse, with hints of cannibalism and a strange tale of an amputated hand.

After the death of little Master Law, the steward's party had continued their journey southwards and soon entered the Alexandria dunes, the largest moving coastal dune system in the world, a waterless 'desert' of sand two or three kilometres wide and thirty or forty kilometres in length, stretching from Woody Cape to just past the mouth of the Sundays River. As day followed day, their thirst grew worse; some of the men, exhausted and unable to keep pace, lagged further and further behind, others died in their tracks, among them the kindly steward, Lillburne. The remaining few struggled on, but their progress was extremely slow; they were desperately weak, drawing on their last reserves, surviving only by drinking each other's urine and sharing half a fish they had found on the beach.[81] Late one afternoon they found a deep gully, which they entered in the hope of finding water. Instead, they found one of the *Grosvenor*'s crew there, dead. He lay flat on his face in the sand, with his right hand cut off at the wrist.

His shipmates froze – for the dead man's favourite expression had been *'May the Devil cut off my right hand if it be not true.'*[82] It would be no exaggeration to say that these men had been dehumanised by their suffering, but even they were spooked. John Wormington, the boatswain's mate, was the first to recover. He had been without adequate clothing since losing his while crossing the Mtata River, a long way back and, seizing the opportunity, he stripped the corpse and put on the clothes.[83] Who the dead man was is not recorded, and it is hard to imagine how he came to be mutilated in such a way in such a remote spot – unless it had something to do with the diamonds.

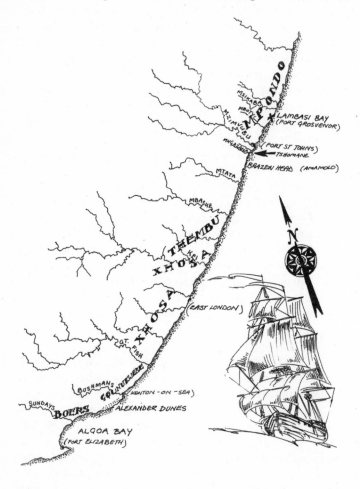

The *Grosvenor* is often supposed to have been a treasure ship, and although that is more myth than anything else, both the passenger Mr Hosea and

Captain Coxon are known to have had a substantial number of uncut stones in their possession.[84] Neither of them reached the Cape and what became of their diamonds has never been ascertained (but see Appendix 4).

The next day another man fell behind and there were now only three left, John Hynes, Jeremiah Evans and John Wormington. Barely able to stand from extreme exhaustion and deprivation, crazy with thirst, Wormington hit on the brilliant idea of drawing lots – the one who lost would have to die, so that the others might survive by drinking his blood. On hearing this, Hynes burst into tears: he 'was grown so weak, that he was almost childish... but he would by no means consent to it' and with tears streaming down his cheeks, said they could do whatever they liked with him once he dropped, but as long as he could walk he would not draw lots! His words sobered the others and the three ragged, filthy men who had come so close to feeding on each other, with great dignity shook each other's hands to show there were no hard feelings. (If it were not so tragic, it would be quite funny.) Then, leaving the semi-demented Wormington, who refused to go any further, Hynes and Evans went on ahead.[85]

Some hours later they saw what they thought were large birds on the heat-shimmering horizon, but, on dragging themselves forward, discovered that the 'birds' were men. Almost blind from the perpetual glare of the sand and sun and nearly senseless from dehydration and starvation, it was a while before they recognised them as their own shipmates, the sailors De Lasso and Barney Leary, Dodge the armourer and Price, an 11-year-old cabin boy.[86] Leading Evans and Hynes to a little spring, they then went back to fetch Wormington, and the two groups compared experiences. Leary reported that they had passed the dead steward on their way south and had come very close to eating him; in fact they had already decided to do so and had just turned back 'in order to cut off some of the steward's flesh,' when they discovered a seal and ate that instead. Someone else mentioned how nice the steward's clothes had been, and Dodge suggested that if Evans would show him the way, they should go and fetch them. It was a crazy idea, since they were exhausted and the steward had died three days' walk back, yet the next morning the two set out across the burning sands. By nightfall Evans was back, alone. Despite his weakened conditioned and the short time that had elapsed, he claimed to have reached the place where the steward had died, but had not been able to find the body. Dodge, he said, was lagging behind. Dodge, however, never rejoined them, and was never seen again.[87]

It is not known whether Evans, alone or with the collaboration of his companions, was responsible for whatever had happened to Dodge, but certainly they had endured so much that all taboos had fallen away. Survival had become their only concern, and survive they did. Hynes, Evans, the boy Price, Wormington, Leary and De Lasso eventually reached the Dutch farms just outside today's Port Elizabeth, where they were discovered by the servants of a Boer named Christopher Roostoff.[88] From there they were taken to Swellendam, 240 kilometres east of Cape Town, to recover. On

21 December 1782, some four and a half months after the *Grosvenor* was wrecked, an expedition under the leadership of Heligert Muller set out in search of the remaining survivors, with Evans and De Lasso acting as guides. They found William Hubberly near the Bushman's River and, in the same vicinity, two European sailors, Feancon and Lewis, together with three Lascars.[89] Near today's city of East London, three more Lascars were found, one of whom was a Bengalese named Bemmers. North of the Kei River amongst the Thembu they found one more Lascar, and Mrs Logie's and Mrs Hosea's maids, Betty and Hoakim.[90] Also just beyond the Kei they recaptured a runaway slave named Anton, who told them that he had seen two survivors, a man and a woman, on the beach not long before, but a search revealed nothing but five skeletons.[91]

Because of the unsettled nature of the Frontier and the recent war with the Xhosa, Muller's expedition was strong both in numbers and firepower, consisting of 109 colonists, 200 Khoi servants, 47 wagons, 81 spans of oxen (with 10–12 oxen per span), 216 riding horses and a supply of slaughter oxen,[92] but its size was no guarantee of success – and it did not even reach the wreck-site. On the expedition's return to the Cape the handful of survivors were repatriated. In an incredible stroke of bad luck, the Lascars, Bengalis and the two Indian women, sent home on the *Nicobar* to 'Tranquebar and Bengal… under the express condition that [the captain] will treat them well during the voyage…,'[93] were wrecked *again*, at Cape Agulhas. Five of them died, including one of the women. The remaining woman and five men returned to India,[94] probably determined never to set foot aboard a ship again.

About 18 months after the wreck of the *Grosvenor*, a group of Xhosa travelling down the coast arrived at a Frontier farm belonging to Stephanus Scheepers, who had been a member of Muller's expedition. Were any of the survivors still alive, the Xhosa were asked. Yes, they replied, the English people were alive, but their own people 'were dying in great numbers. It would appear to be pox.' The disease must have brought ashore by one of the *Grosvenor* survivors, probably the cook, since he is known to have died of 'the children's sickness', as smallpox was sometimes called.[95] It is impossible to say exactly how many died but it must have spread like wildfire along the coast. The effect was catastrophic: by 1790 the country between the Kei and the Mbashe rivers was almost uninhabited, reports the historian Theal, 'the Tembu clans who had lived there having been almost exterminated by an attack of the small pox….'[96] In 1807 a traveller reported that people in the region still bore the scars of smallpox: 'numbers of men not more than thirty years of age are now to be seen exceedingly marked with it.'[97]

In the years following Muller's expedition, rumours about the *Grosvenor* castaways continued to surface at the Cape, persistent tales that they were still alive and living amongst the coastal clans. The fate of the white women caused particular concern; one London newspaper stated categorically that they had been 'dragged up into the interior parts of the country, for the purposes of the vilest brutish prostitution….'[98] The thought of Fair Maidens Alone on a Remote

Coast (at the Mercy of Dusky Pagan Men!) caused the imaginations and emotions of white males to run riot and gave rise to quantities of bad prose: 'How cruel a situation for women! Condemned to drag a painful life in all the horrors of agonising despair….' The racism underpinning all the hysteria attained its zenith in novels of the time. One describes how the hero, setting out for Africa to find out for himself the fate of his relatives, passengers on the *Grosvenor*, discovers 'with rapture… that he has no Kaffir second cousins….'[99]

A second rescue attempt was made soon after Muller's expedition, but because of the chaotic situation in the eastern part of the Colony nothing much came of it. There was war and bloodshed in Europe too; the French Revolution was in full swing, and across the Channel the Industrial Revolution was beginning, in its own fashion, to effect equally drastic, if less bloody changes on British society. Eventually, in 1790, eight years after the wreck of the *Grosvenor*, another expedition was assembled and a group of Boers descended on Bessie's remote home with guns, teams of oxen, wagons and horses.

The leader of this expedition was Jan Holtshausen, the fifty-something son of a Swellendam farmer, but as he died on the journey the expedition is known for his successor, Jacob van Reenen, keeper of what must rate as one of the most inadequate and frustrating journals ever. How unfortunate it is that he failed to give us a richer picture of their incredible journey – he barely mentions, and seems utterly oblivious to, the scale and beauty of the wildernesses they penetrated, the spectacular coastlines they explored or the fascinating cultures they encountered, and appears far more concerned with the hunting he and his men enjoyed: 33 elephant, 60 hippo, 8 buffalo, 11 eland, 1 lioness and so on and on, each kill meticulously recorded – and herein lies an important clue to the party's motivation. Rescuing the survivors of the *Grosvenor* was less of a priority than hunting and trading;[100] rescuing damsels-in-distress, the expedition's supposed *raison d'être*, had fallen to last place on the Boers' list of things-to-do.

Chapter Six

The Bastards and the Boers

Despite the inadequacies of his journal, Jacob van Reenen was not a semi-literate country bumpkin unable to see beyond his rifle sights, but a member of a well-to-do Cape family and – despite his obsession with hunting – rather a poor shot. Lady Anne Barnard, who accompanied him on a hunt, reported that his shots were always too high or too low and that even the slave, Adonis, could have done better.[1] Born in 1755, Van Reenen had travelled to Europe at the age of 16 with his father and brought back to South Africa the celebrated (if misnamed) Cape gooseberry.[2] The Swedish botanist Lichtenstein, who met him in 1807, says he

> 'gave me many very interesting details respecting his travels in Caffraria, and evinced a knowledge of the natural history and geography of the country which is seldom to be found among the inhabitants of southern Africa.'[3]

His expedition to find the *Grosvenor*, however, had nothing to do with the natural sciences; it was first and foremost speculative, its motivation more what could be had, than who could be rescued. It included five members of the previous expedition and was funded by the men themselves – they received only the most basic reimbursement from the Cape authorities – in anticipation of the benefits they hoped to reap. They expected it to be profitable, and it was: one of them later informed Lichtenstein that

'the further they went the more elephants they found, so that they
killed them almost daily; indeed, the hope of gain from the elephants'
teeth that they should collect had allured most of the party who
joined in the undertaking.'[4]

The expedition left the Cape in August 1790. Consisting of only 13
colonists and 48 Khoi,[5] it was substantially smaller and more manageable than
Muller's, and could move faster. By the beginning of October they had crossed
the Kei River; their route had taken them further inland than Muller yet in
the cliffs lining a small river nearby they saw, among some San paintings, one
of a soldier in a grenadier's cap.[6] A month later they crossed the Mtata River,
and soon the Mtakatyi, where the previous expedition had turned back.[7] If any
survivors were still to be found, they would probably be located between here
and the wreck, yet instead of turning down to the coast immediately, which
would have been the logical thing to do, the Boers continued on their inland
route for another few days. It was only on Wednesday, 3 November 1790, as
they ventured closer to the coast, that things became more interesting.

Early that morning the party left the forests where they had been
hunting for the past two days, near today's Gcwaleni Forest Station, and
began the ascent to Brazen Head, 'on a height from which we saw many
kraals of the Hambonas, a people quite different from the Kaffers. They are
yellowish and have longer hair, which is all tightly curled up in the manner
of a turban.'[8]

They were not Bomvana, though, but amaMolo: Brazen Head was the
prominent sea-facing bluff where the descendants of the Indian castaway
Bhayi and his companions lived. Van Reenen's mistake may have arisen from
the fact that the amaMolo paid tribute to the Bomvana or through the
carelessness of his interpreters, but it was an unfortunate slip. There is a good
chance, as I mentioned earlier, that the amaMolo's ancestors include survivors
of the *Grosvenor* – the very people Van Reenen was seeking – and had he
taken the time to question them, he would surely have discovered the fate of
at least some of them. But he did not, and it was a sadly missed opportunity.

Instead he sent four of his men with a gift of beads and copper to the
Bomvana chief Gambushe, who in his turn sent five ambassadors to visit the
Boers and take stock of them.[9] In the exchange of beads and information
that followed, recorded Van Reenen,

'They told us that subject to them was a village of Bastaard Christians,
who were descended from people shipwrecked on that coast, and of
which three old women were still living, whom Oemtonone, the
Hambonas captain, had taken as his wives.'[10]

The news must have thrilled Van Reenen and his companions – the
discovery of the white females from the *Grosvenor* was sure to bring their

rescuers fame, if not fortune – yet his journal gives no hint of this. Perhaps the Boers already suspected that these were not the people they were looking for.

The expedition set off for the village the next morning in ugly weather. An hour into the journey the wagons were forced to a halt by the torrential rain and the party continued on horseback.[11] News of their coming preceded them – the travel-stained Boers and their horses, train of wagons, long teams of oxen, noise of whips and guns and their overtures to Gambushe would all have generated much interest and discussion up and down the coast. As they approached the 'Little Mogasie' River on the banks of which the castaways' village stood, its inhabitants, 'a nation descended from whites, also a few from yellow slaves and Bengalese,' according to Van Reenen, poured out to welcome them and 'made a great rejoicing, and cried out "Our fathers are come".'[12]

Now the 'Little Mogasie' River was none other than the Little Mngazi or Mngazana River, where, according to Bessie's son Mdepa, she had 'lived and died,'[13] just south of the Mzimvubu River. It is where Hubberly's party of *Grosvenor* survivors had met the friendly, heavily beaded 'different sort of

people' who had supplied them with a bullock. Hubberly's account does not
tell us much about the Tshomane, because he had stuck to the beach and
Sango's Great Place was situated a little way inland; the castaways had
contact only with those able or curious enough to go down to the beach to
see them and, having no common language, their communication was very
limited. Van Reenen, by contrast, went right into the Tshomane 'village',
the chief's Great Place, and was able to talk to the Tshomane through his
Khoi interpreters. Unfortunately his journal has very little to say: 'We also
met the three old women, who said they were sisters, and had, when children
been shipwrecked on this coast, but could not say of what nation they were,
being too young at the time that accident happened.'[14] Because of their age
it was obvious that their ship had not been the *Grosvenor*, wrecked less than
a decade ago, and Van Reenen adds merely that 'We offered to take the old
women and their children back with us on our return, which, so it seemed
to us, they were very willing to do.'[15]

There is no doubt that one of the women was Bessie. The other two
were probably the two Lascar girls with whom she was wrecked, Noqualekiza
and Colaz, whom her grandson – like Van Reenen – called her 'sisters'.[16] We
will return to them again later, but for the moment, we, like the impatient
Van Reenen, must rush on....

Wasting no time, the Boers rode out again the following day. A few hours
later they reached and crossed the Mngazi, 'the Great Mogasie river, where is
the residence of the Hambonaa captain, Camboosa,'[17] and shot seven hippos,
probably making enough noise to wake the dead, scaring away all the game,
ensuring that people for miles around quickly drove their herds into the safety
of their kraals, and generally warning any runaway slaves or deserters in the
vicinity that if they valued their freedom now was a good time to conceal
themselves: the Boers were coming! Trekking on, they crossed the Mzimvubu
River, beyond which they had been told they would find an Englishman who
was a survivor of the same wreck as the three elderly women. Instead they met
a Dutch-speaking man who claimed to have been wrecked there 'with the
English from Malakka' but whom the Boers believed was a runaway slave from
the Cape. The man agreed to show them the way to the wreck, but when he
did not reappear they were forced to continue without him.[18]

Three or four days later they crossed the Mbotyi River, bringing them
within about 20 kilometres of the *Grosvenor* wreck. Just beyond Mbotyi is a
small beach covered in millions of minute red shells and a little waterfall in
a grove of trees, and it is probably here that they outspanned their wagons
and set up camp. The route ahead was blocked by the rugged bulk of
Waterfall Bluff and, leaving the rest of their companions behind, a small
group of men led by Holtshausen proceeded along the cliff tops on
horseback, and finally reached Lambasi, where the *Grosvenor* had been
wrecked eight and half years before. Jan Holtshausen, incidentally, had
recently fallen into an elephant trap and received a stake through his hand,
but at this stage does not appear to have been troubled by the wound.

There was little to be seen at the wreck-site beyond five cannons, a quantity of iron ballast and, on a rise between two clumps of bush, the remains of cooking fires, which, as it had been raining heavily, must presumably have been of very recent origin. On the same spot 'was a pit,

THE DOUBLE WATERFALL INTO THE SEA — WATERFALL BLUFF.

where things had been buried and dug out again; this confirming to us what [had been] told us; that everything had been dug up and dispersed very far into the country'[19] – including, presumably, the box that the survivors had reportedly buried. There was no sign of John Bryan or Joshua Glover, the two men who had remained at the wreck site, nor could the Boers learn anything regarding them or the other survivors. On at least three separate occasions, though, people living in the vicinity of the wreck offered the Boers gold and silver, probably coins recovered from the site, in exchange for beads and other trifles.[20]

The Boers spent a few hours at the wreck site. According to Van Reenen,

> 'all the natives have promised me that if another unlucky ship should be wrecked there, they will take care of the men, and bring them to us, provided that they are assured that, in return, they will be given beads, copper and iron, and this we have promised to do.'[21]

His confidence in his powers of communication seem to have been misplaced, however: a headman living near the wreck later confirmed that the Boers 'gave away blankets and beads,' but that 'he was unable to ascertain the real object of their visit.'[22]

Back at their camp, the next day the Boers inspanned their oxen once more, turned the wagons around and began the long journey home. For at least one of their number the journey was almost over – old Holtshausen's wounded hand was severely infected and his condition had begun to deteriorate alarmingly. He was soon exhibiting the classic symptoms of tetanus, 'attacked with a locked jaw and violent convulsive fits, so that we expected his death every moment.'[23] The wagons ground to a halt and the men awaited the inevitable, then buried him where he died on the north side of the Mzimvubu River.

It was getting on for mid-summer now, the wettest time of year. It can rain so heavily along here that the tiniest streams become raging rivers. Every summer all along the Wild Coast clusters of frustrated holidaymakers bog down to their axles in the mud, where they remain sometimes for days until a far-off village can send a truck or tractor to pull them all out. Van Reenen's expedition seems to have run headlong into one of these prolonged downpours, and the Mzimvubu had come down in flood. With their crossing delayed for days, it was only on 26 November 1790 that he and his men rode into the Tshomane 'village' once more.

> 'I would now have taken the three old women with us, to which they seemed well inclined, as appearing much to wish to live among Christians, but mentioned their desire, before they could accomplish such a plan, of waiting till their harvest to gather in their crops; adding that for this reason they would at present rather remain with their children and grandchildren; after which, with their whole race, to the amount of 400, they would be happy to depart from their present settlement. I concluded by promising that I would give a full account of them to the Government, in order that they might be removed from their present situation. It is to be observed that on our visit to the old women they appeared to be exceedingly agitated at seeing people of their own complexion and description.'[24]

In actual fact their agitation probably owed less to the thrill of shared pigmentation than to the threat of losing their homes and families. Even with their children, moving to the Cape could have held little attraction for Bessie and her companions. The castaways had nothing in common with the colonists, neither language nor culture nor religious beliefs. Wherever they may have come from as children and whatever they may once have been, from the tips of their toes to the ends of their long black braids they were Mpondo. Epitomising this is the way they spoke of themselves as 'sisters', using the word not in the western sense but in the broader Xhosa sense.[25]

According to Bessie's grandson, she had come ashore with two other women, the rest of her party being men. These female castaways were Colaz and Noqualekiza and, although Bessie was white and they were Asian, the Mpondo considered them to be sisters. Van Reenen used the same word to describe the three castaway ladies he 'found' at Mngazana. Though his journal does not mention their race, it makes it clear that they were not African, and, as we shall see below, he later confirmed that one of them was white. Given the time and place, it is highly probable that the elderly castaways were Bessie and her Asian companions. The Reverend Kay, a missionary who met Bessie's son Mdepa and grandson Ngcetane in the 1820s, concurs:

> 'The number of females mentioned by [Van Reenen] exactly agrees with the account given by Cetani; who, however, does not corroborate Van Reenen's assertion relative to their being all the wives of one chief.'

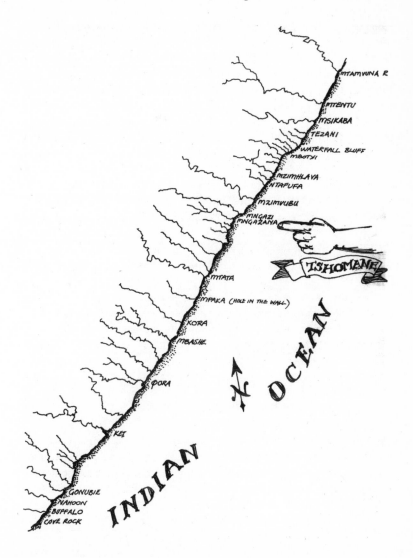

This is confirmed by Van Reenen's own men, Hillegard, Cornelius and Ignatius Muller, who told Vaillant, a year after the expedition's return to the Cape, that only one of the elderly women was the wife of the chief, Oemtonone.[26]

Kay went on to say:

> 'Two out of the three seem either to have married persons of inferior rank, or to have been wives of an inferior order; for very little is now known concerning either them or their offspring.'[27]

The first part of Kay's statement was confirmed by a descendant of one of the Asian women. In 1907 Falilanga, a resident of Elliotdale, told Eliza Conway, Bessie's great-great-granddaughter, that his ancestor, 'the servant girl of the Lady what was married to Sango,' had married 'one of Sango's big counsellors' at the same place where Bessie was married.[28] This would have brought her into frequent, and probably daily, contact with Bessie. She is almost certainly the same 'Lascar girl-servant' whom Bazley's informants described as having been Bessie's life-long companion, aka the 'Arab who stuck to her until she died.'[29] Like Van Reenen's elderly women, the Asian girls who were castaway with Bessie had many descendants. In the words of Xelo, who was married to one of them: 'There are many... the women have long black hair, not soft, and black faces'[30]

The Boers' stopover with the Tshomane was as brief as their first, and the very next day they proceeded on their way back to the Cape. Although there is no mention of any such incident in his journal, one of Bessie's grandchildren seems to have gone with them. Bessie's youngest son, Mdepa, 'had a white son by a black wife,' his son-in-law told a missionary years later,

> 'but then a white man came, and after asking all about the boy, took him away to the Colony, promising his father, Umdepa, that his son should be restored to him; this however has never been done, and the lad was never brought back.'[31]

More than thirty years later his father was still grieving: 'Daapa distinctly recollects the visit of Van Reenen, and many of the circumstances connected with it,' wrote Reverend Kay in 1829.

> 'One occurrence then took place, which, to him, ever afterward constituted a painful memento. A boor [Boer], who journeyed along with Mr. R., succeeded in persuading one of his sons to accompany them back to the colony; whence he never returned.'[32]

Kay tried to comfort Mdepa him by saying he had made enquiries about the boy, that he was alive and well, and would be coming to see him soon. According to William Bazley, however, the boy was 'sold as a slave on the market at Capetown.'[33] The story may well be true, as one of Van Reenen's men was the infamous bounty hunter Jacob Joubert, who frequently travelled beyond the Frontier capturing runaway slaves and bringing them back to the Cape in exchange for a reward from their owners. Joubert had been a member of the first *Grosvenor* expedition in 1783;[34] he knew the territory well enough to do most of the second journey alone, only joining Van Reenen's party when it was well north of the Kei.[35] On at least one earlier

journey he is known to have brought a Xhosa-speaking male back to the Cape with him – though I have not been able to discover his age or identity, or what became of him.[36] Joubert was also the only member of Van Reenen's expedition who did not sign a Declaration to the Governor stating that

> 'no one of us, whoever he may be, shall withhold anything whatever that he may find, shoot or obtain by trade, but shall produce it to us, the undersigned; and that if we find that anything of the sort has occurred and that anything has been concealed, we shall declare and denounce the person concerned as wicked and indecent.'[37]

On his arrival back at the Cape, Van Reenen informed the governor of the 'bastaard' village, but although the matter was put before the Council of Policy,[38] nothing appears to have been done about it and the castaways remained where they were. A footnote to the affair is added by Lady Anne Barnard, an inquisitive and energetic Englishwoman and writer of copious letters and diaries, who visited Van Reenen a few years later.

The English had recently ousted the Dutch and occupied the Colony and Lady Anne had accompanied her husband Andrew Barnard, the new governor's secretary, out to the Cape, where she became one of the first white women to climb Table Mountain. Among her other adventures was the cross-country journey by ox-wagon that brought her and her husband to Van Reenen's farm at the mouth of the Breede River, some 300 slow and bruising kilometres from Cape Town. The last 20-odd kilometres were particularly trying, but on their arrival they were warmly welcomed by Van Reenen and his wife, surrounded by hordes of white and brown children.

Mrs van Reenen spoke almost no English, but Lady Ann was relieved to note that – unlike most Boer women – she still had her front teeth. She was

> 'of the same size and age as all the rest of the married women in the colony, – the moment half a dozen children are born, five-and-thirty and fifteen stone seem to be acquired, of course. They have no idea, I see, of continuing to look handsome to please their husbands....'[39]

A Frenchman who travelled among the Boers was more succinct: 'My God! what oxen! Alas! what women!'[40]

Lady Anne did not leave us with a description of Van Reenen, but she did refer to his quest to find the survivors of the *Grosvenor*, saying he told her

> 'that, although no person remained of the crew, there was an old woman, near sixty years of age, a European, who had been found when a child by the Kaffirs under similar circumstances. She did not know from which country she came, but remembered to have sailed a great way in a ship. He proposed to her to come down and visit the Europeans at the Cape; she seemed intoxicated with pleasure at the idea, but said she could not till her harvest was got. She had been married in the Kafir fashion to the richest man in the tribe, – that is to say, he had more cattle than anybody; and her sons by him were all Captains – a pre-eminence given to them voluntarily by the rest in compliment to her as a white woman. She still lives, and still proposes coming to the Cape; – I wish she would make her words good while I am here; I should be very glad to give old Kaffraria an apartment in the Castle.'[41]

In his journal Van Reenen had remarked merely that the three elderly castaways were of the same 'complexion and description' as the members of his expedition.[42] Some historians have interpreted this to mean that they were white, but as Van Reenen's party included not only Boers but also Cape Khoi, some of whom would have been of mixed blood, he could have meant they were mulatto. His statement to Lady Anne made it quite clear that one of them was white, and should lay to rest any lingering doubt as to whether or not Bessie was one of the elderly castaways. The white woman's age, which Van Reenen's said was 'near sixty', is exactly the same age as Bessie would have been at the time of his visit.[43] It was, in fact, probably because of Bessie that Van Reenen calls her husband 'Oemtonone' rather than Sango: since etiquette prevented her from using her husband's real name, she would have had to *hlonipha* when referring to him and use a substitute instead – such as 'mTshomane', his clan-name.[44]

An independent source confirms that Bessie was the only white female among the Tshomane in her lifetime: Xelo, a Thembu headman who heard all about Bessie from her son Mdepa, whom he knew well, told a government commission in 1883 that besides her, he had 'never heard of any other white woman here.'[45]

Van Reenen, in the only surviving manuscript of his journal written in his own hand, described the expedition's destination as 'naar de River Aderadiera de Natal of anders Caap Natal gestrandt den 4 Aug. 1781 het Engels schip de Grovenour gestrand'[46] – almost exactly the same name, incidentally, as 'Adera diera Natal', by which the Hubner traders called the place where they found the three Englishmen.

Van Reenen also has some interesting things to say about the Tshomanes' crops, growing close by their homesteads on the banks of Mngazana River. They aroused the admiration of the farmer in him, and were, he wrote, 'very extensive and handsome gardens, planted with kaffer corn, maize, sugar canes, plantains, potatoes, black beans, and many other things: they also have some cattle.'[47] Many of the crops were exotic and probably introduced by the castaways; pumpkins, for example, are European and American, while plantains, a small sweet banana, come from south-east Asia. There is no doubt that Bessie's people were well nourished: maize, for instance, has a far greater carbohydrate yield per unit of labour and land than the indigenous sorghum, and in this well-watered region yields two harvests a year, providing an abundance of food, both for consumption and storage in times of need.[48] We already know that the Tshomane had a profitable line in ivory trading, but in the long term their ability to grow such diverse and abundant food would have been as great an asset, enabling the Tshomane chief to attract new supporters and bind them to him in a mutually beneficial relationship.

Each chiefdom consisted of a number of local communities bound by kinship and marriage, its size depending on the chief's (and his counsellors') ability to govern well. Supporters tended to vote with their feet, so that despotic, stingy or inept chiefs invariably lost their followers to wealthier and more benevolent rivals. As there was no such thing as a formal or standing army, chiefs such as Sango depended on their people's ability and willingness to fight for them. By attracting supporters and increasing the size and importance of the Tshomane, Sango would have been able to secure the material resources (land, cattle and water) his people needed, avoid dissidence and consolidate his own position.[49]

His supporters and adherents included runaway slaves from the Cape. I remember reading one chief's comments to a Colonial official that runaway slaves made good fighters, for which reason, he said, he was happy to give them refuge. The Tshomane probably welcomed them for similar reasons – and their willingness to do so probably accounts for the fact that among the more than 400 people of mixed descent that Van Reenen found at Mngazana were people descended 'from yellow slaves and Bengalese.'[50]

Henry Francis Fynn, an ivory trader who visited the Tshomane 30 years later, describes a similar situation. One of the people he met was Mornegal, who, 'though black, has a countenance strongly resembling that of a

European.'[51] Mornegal was one of four sons of Kapa, a cooper who had made pots, tubs and stools and who had died some five months before. Kapa had been informed by his father Jeffrey that the latter had been 'sitting on the rocks picking shell-fish when he was seized by some sailors, put on board a vessel and "fastened", then taken off to where the ship was wrecked,'[52] which Fynn took to mean that Jeffrey had been a slave of European extraction.[53] Fynn also met a runaway slave called Jantze Lapoot, whose master had been 'Baas Kronier' of Uitenhage,[54] and another named Peter, 'of Malabar caste' who was about 60 years old, spoke good Dutch, and at first claimed to have come off a ship wrecked some years before but, on discovering that Fynn was not a bounty hunter, he admitted that he too had once been a slave, belonging to a certain Hendrick Fleck. He must have escaped at least two decades before, as he had a son of about 20 from his marriage to a local woman, as well as several other younger children.[55]

Fynn met Bessie's son Mdepa and grandson Majubana – to whom we shall return later – and learnt of a white man named Biale, who had also lived among the Tshomane but had recently died, leaving a son called Jugugaler. He also met a man called Faku who turned out to be the son of John Bryan, and his story throws a welcome light on the subsequent history of the *Grosvenor* survivor whose lameness had caused him to remain behind at the wreck after the departure of the other castaways on their ill-fated journey towards the Cape. Bryan, whom the Mpondo called uMbethi (the beater),[56] had apparently carried out his plan to build a forge and make assegais and brass rings from metal salvaged from the wreck, with such success that he soon had enough cattle to marry and had taken an Mpondo woman as his wife. Their first-born was a daughter, says Fynn, and the couple was expecting their second child when tragedy struck and Bryan's wife was carried off by people who came from the east. They took her south to the Mtata River, where her son Faku was born. Bryan and his little daughter, meanwhile, 'in despair on account of the loss of his wife,' resided for a time with the amaXolo near the Umzimkhulu, where he built a canoe for exploring the river, then went off inland where he apparently met his death. His daughter later married a local blacksmith and died in 1823, 'in the general slaughter of the surrounding peaceful nations by Shaka,' the Zulu king.[57]

That slaves such as Jantze Lapoot and castaways of little or no means were able to travel vast distances along the coast was largely due to the hospitality of the local people. Other outsiders who found refuge on the Wild Coast included, as mentioned before, deserters of all nationalities from the Cape garrison, Germans, Englishmen, Irishmen, Dutchmen and even Poles,[58] who married local women and raised their children as fully fledged Xhosa, Thembu or Pondo. It is impossible to say just how many foreigners were incorporated into the coastal gene pool in this way, but the numbers appear to have been significant – on one occasion the bounty hunter Jacob Joubert, who had been on both Muller's and Van Reenen's expeditions, found 18 runaways at the same place.[59]

For fugitives who settled close to the frontiers of the Cape there was always the threat of being captured by men like Joubert, or being handed over to the colonists in exchange for trade goods or in fulfilment of some new treaty. It was their distance from the Frontier that probably attracted runaways to Mpondo clans such as the Tshomane; as Jantze Lapoot told Fynn, on his first escape he had been recaptured, so on his second attempt he had taken no chances and, fleeing as far as possible from the Colony, had ended up amongst the Tshomane.[60]

For his predecessors among the Tshomane, a relocation proposal such as Van Reenen's must have been particularly threatening. Their return to the Colony would have represented nothing less than a return to hell: brutal punishment followed by re-enslavement. Even free common criminals were harshly dealt with in the early years of the Colony: sentences included torture, dismemberment, execution and the iconic abuse of their corpses. There was a perverted creativity to it all; simple punishment was not enough – there had to be a symbolic element too: a butcher found guilty of illicit sheep-dealing and fraud in 1680, for example, was locked in stocks placed outdoors for public ridicule, with a sheepskin around his neck, the fraudulent text pinned to his chest and (oddly) an oar in each hand.[61] There is a kind of gleeful overkill to the sentences that verges on depravity, as in the sentencing of the slave, Titus of Bengal and his lover Maria Mouton, for the murder of Maria's husband, who also happened to be Titus' owner. Maria was sentenced to be 'half-strangled, after that to be scorched, and after that strangled unto death,' while Titus was to be impaled and left to die, then his head and right hand were to be cut off and publicly displayed on the boundary of his victim's property.

It took Titus 48 agonising hours to die on the stake that had been driven up into his bowels, perforating his vital organs. Judging by the spirited way in which he handled his prolonged and ghastly torture, he must have been a unique and quite remarkable man. About four hours into his ordeal, he was given a bottle of arrack; admonished not to drink too much in case he got drunk, he replied that '… it did not matter, as he sat fast enough, and that there was no fear of his falling.' He kept his sense of humour right up to the end, vowing never to trust a woman again.[62]

Long after Van Reenen's expedition, rumours about Bessie's people continued to filter through to the Colony. In 1803, on an expedition to the eastern Frontier, for example, his brother also heard of 'a yellow-skinned nation with long hair' living north of the Thembu.[63] His informant, Coenraad de Buys, a notorious rebel Boer of enormous size and huge appetites, knew what he was talking about. Fluent in isiXhosa, he was well travelled and familiar with the territory, one of his wives, Elizabeth, having come from the same vicinity ('geboren in het land v. d. Makinas achter de Tamboekis,')[64] but Van Reenen did not pursue the matter, either because he had already heard it all before from his brother Jacob, or because De Buys had assured him in the same breath 'that the unicorn, the size of the eland and black in colour was to be found there.' Other travellers also mentioned the strange clan; Lichtenstein, for instance, wrote that

> '... according to report, the colour of their skin is yellow, and they have long straight hair, which they do up in locks, and wind round the head. Such an account does not seem deserving of much attention, and appears at first wholly fabulous. But probably Europeans may here be meant, who have from time to time landed upon various parts of the coast....'[65]

Even Captain Bligh, of *Bounty* fame, had something to say. Passing through the Cape six years after the wreck of the *Grosvenor*, he made the acquaintance of Colonel Gordon, the Commander of the Garrison, who had made a number of lengthy expeditions into the hinterland: 'in his travels into the Caffre country, he had met with a native who described to him that there was a white women among his countrymen, who had a child, and that she frequently embraced the child, and cried most violently.' Could this have been the same unhappy survivor who, in the previous chapter, reportedly committed suicide by strangling herself with her scarf?[66] Gordon sent his informant back to the woman with a letter in both English and Dutch, but, receiving no reply, continued his journey and never heard of her again.[67]

All these reports were based on hearsay, however, and Jacob van Reenen's journal remains the only eyewitness account.

He never made good his intention to move Bessie to the Cape and never visited her again, but some of his party quietly – and illegally – established trade links with her people. One was Hillegard Muller, the leader of the first *Grosvenor* expedition, who had accompanied the second together with his brother Cornelius and his son Ignatius. Muller had farms in the eastern Cape[68] and, with the knowledge and experience acquired on these expeditions, was perfectly placed for trade along the Wild Coast. It is thanks to him that we have an idea of when Bessie's husband Sango died: in 1792–93 Muller told a traveller that the Tshomane chief had died shortly after Van Reenen's visit and was succeeded by his son.[69] Sango had joined the ranks of the ancestors, spirits capable of influencing the lives of their descendants who communicated through dreams and were honoured and appealed to through the ritual sacrifice of cattle.[70]

The Xhosa-speaking peoples of the time did not perceive death as an inevitable part of life but an unnatural and evil condition, which could taint relatives and neighbours. Commoners on the verge of death were not allowed to remain in the *umzi* for fear that whatever afflicted them would spread to the rest of its inhabitants. As a Dutch official observed in 1807,

> 'If one sees that a sick person belonging to the ordinary classes is about to die, he is moved out of the hut to the shade of some bushes, a little distance from the abode, and is laid on a grass resting place that has been prepared. A fire is lit near to the dying person and a vessel of water placed next to him…. Apart from the husband or the wife, no one usually remains with the dying person until his death.'[71]

As a chief, however, Sango would have been permitted to die at home, after which his body, wrapped in a *kaross* of soft animal skins, was buried in the middle of his cattle kraal. The Mpondo were firm believers in witchcraft; almost anything belonging to a potential victim could be used in the casting of spells, but the most potent charms were the flesh, bones or hair of a deceased person[72] and in order to protect Sango's body from discovery by wizards and other evildoers a herd of oxen was driven over and over the spot so that no sign of his grave remained on the surface.

His Great Wife Bessie and other junior wives then retired separately into the veld for a period of mourning lasting three days, at the end of which they discarded their clothes, put on grass skirts and returned to the homestead, where certain cleansing rituals were performed. A number of cattle, corresponding to the number of wives, were slaughtered and the hides made into new clothing to replace those they had destroyed. Sango's dwelling was locked, covered with thorn bushes, and left uninhabited and deserted. His spears and other weapons were given to his eldest son,[73] while his ornaments, the ivory rings which had adorned his upper arms, and other bracelets and beadwork noticed by the *Grosvenor* survivors, were buried with him or destroyed. Everything that Bessie and Sango had shared was considered impure, including wooden spoons, woven milk baskets and other household articles, and had to be destroyed and replaced.[74] Bessie kept nothing.[75]

Their Great Son Mlawu, who succeeded Sango as chief, built a new kraal not far from the old one,[76] and it was probably at his *umzi* that Bessie would have gone to live. Mlawu, however, was not destined to rule for long; he died while still a young man, and as his heir Ngcetane was just a child at the time and 'unable to manage his father's clan.'[77] Bessie's youngest son, Mdepa, took over as regent of the Tshomane. Her daughter, Bessy, meanwhile, had married Mjikwa, chief of the Nkumba, son of Wose of the Bomvana royal house, and a cousin of the ruling chief Gambushe,[78] and had gone to live among his people.

This was not far away – Gambushe's Great Place was on the Mngazi River, just three or four kilometres from Mngazana where Bessie lived – but things were about to change.

Gambushe was a man of strong character, whose courage and open-
handedness had won the love and admiration of his own people,[79] but he
earned the everlasting hatred of his Mpondo neighbours when their King
Ngqungqushe was killed in a clash with his men. In the early 1800s
Ngqungqushe's son Faku formed an alliance with the Thembu against
Gambushe, who, finding himself surrounded by enemies and constantly
under attack from one side or the other, decided to move his people to more
peaceful climes. The territory he had in mind lay some way to the south,
between the Mtata and Mbashe rivers, a beautiful tract of countryside, well
watered, fertile and with elephants and antelope in abundance. Although
vacant, it belonged to the Xhosa[80] and before Gambushe's people could
occupy it they were obliged to obtain the permission of the Xhosa king,
Hintsa. In this the descendants of the castaways played an important role:
Gambushe's chief negotiator was Nogaya of the abeLungu clan, a
descendant of the white man Jekwa, a trader in bluebuck skins and sweet-
smelling *mthomboti* necklaces who had travelled widely and was familiar
with the country, while Bessie's grandson Ngcetane, Gambushe's overlord,
helped facilitate the move.[81] The negotiations went well, a tribute of cattle
was paid to Hintsa, and around 1810 the Bomvana and abeLungu moved
south to the Mbashe;[82] with them went Bessie's daughter, Bessy, the *laat-
lammetjie* born at least a decade after her other children and probably her
favourite, since it is said that '[j]ust before she breathed her last, she called
for Bessy, her daughter.'[83]

Bessie had lived to 'a good old age', spending her last years with her
grandson Ngcetane, now chief of the Tshomane. She died sometime around
1810 – her famous long black hair by then completely white[84] – aged about
80,[85] at the same place that she had lived, at Mngazana.

The 19th-century writer WC Scully accords Bessie a very romantic end:

> 'On the day she died she was, at her own request, carried down to the
> cleft in the reef.... She partly lifted up herself, and pointed across the
> sea with her right hand; then she turned... and gave out her life with
> a long-drawn sigh. In the night a terrible storm arose, and the shore
> afterwards was found strewn with myriads of dead fish.'[86]

It's an almost cinematic image, especially against wide-angle backdrop of
Mngazana – the broad clean sweep of breakers and beach, the shimmering
coils of the lagoon – but her burial was likely to have been far more prosaic,
her grave a hole in the centre of the floor of her hut. To avoid contaminating
the living Bessie's body would have been interred soon after death, the grave
filled in with earth and the pillars and foundations of her house dug up and
'thrown down... to decay upon the spot on which her hands had placed
them.'[87] Stones, branches and finally thorn bushes were laid over the fallen
roof to discourage wild animals from digging up the corpse, and for the same

reason – and to ensure that witches did not disturb it – for many nights her grave was visited by a close relative.[88] The mourning rituals included a short period of celibacy for the adults of Bessie's *umzi* and the shaving of the men's and children's heads. Immediately after the burial everyone cleansed themselves by washing in the river; a beast was slaughtered and all the neighbours invited to join Bessie's extended family in eating this 'beast of washing'. No work was done in the fields that day and the *umzi* was filled with the sound of weeping.

In the years following her death Bessie's children were to be embroiled in a series of wars and invasions that swept them from their ancestral home and drove them south. They never returned to Mngazana, and the people who now occupy the land know nothing about her, her history or the whereabouts of her grave. William Bazley made several attempts to locate it in the early 1900s, but, as far as I can ascertain, never succeeded in doing so. We know that as the wife of a chief Bessie would have been buried in her hut where she lived, at Ngcetane's *umzi*, but there is no evidence of exactly where his Great Place stood, other than that it would have been on an east-facing slope, not too close to the coast and with access to fresh water. The only clue is a brief statement by Captain Sidney Turner, trader, farmer and one of the founders of Port St Johns, who visited the site in the 1860s. His guide was Hans Lochenberg, the son of a renegade Boer who had fled the Colony in about 1799 and a Khoi woman. Born and bred on the Wild Coast, Hans knew the terrain like the back of his own hand, had seen Bessie as a child and was familiar with her family. He was fluent in Xhosa as well as English, and worked as an interpreter at one of the Wesleyan missions. A traveller who met him in 1859 described him as

> 'a stout-built man, about 50 years of age, resembling a patriarchal "Boer", but on close examination you find a certain flatness of the nostrils: and crisp hair too strongly testify to the amalgamation of the European with the aboriginal AmaKosa, and which I have learnt is very general in the settlements of the Umzimvoobo.'

If Hans noticed his visitor's sniffiness, he chose to ignore it: 'I am a great man in my country, I have two hundred guns, and nine hundred shields,' he said proudly. 'I am a Kafir and I will die a Kafir.'[89]

Bessie, he told Turner, was 'buried with all her trinkets, which she saved, and requested might be buried with her.' This is supported by Xelo, a Thembu who knew Bessie's son Mdepa well: 'Umdepa had no ornament or anything belonging to his mother, as, according to [our] custom, all effects belonging to persons dying are destroyed. I never heard Umdepa say where his mother was buried….'[90]

Hans Lochenberg, however, had heard, and he pointed her grave out to Turner: it lay 'in a bush almost on the banks of the little Umgazi, not far from the old Dutch road by which Captain Smith passed on his way to

Natal from the Cape' in 1842. Running from Old Morley mission to Old Buntingville and from there to the Mzimvubu, the road crossed the Mngazana about five kilometres upstream from the mouth.[91]

> 'We are such stuff
> As dreams are made on, and our little life
> Is rounded with a sleep.'[92]

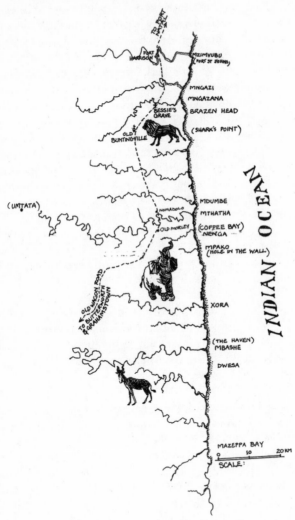

During her lifetime Bessie had won the love and respect of her adoptive people and was 'uniformly acknowledged, and looked up to by the whole clan, as the "great woman," or queen.'[93] Her reputation as a great beauty and particularly as a compassionate and wise woman continued long after her death: '[T]he word of Gquma', it was said, 'was a great word.'[94] Atypically for a woman, since only a man normally has one, she was given an *isinqulo*, an ancestral praise-name used as a prayer, a call for help or even a kind of 'Bless me' when sneezing, and a century after her death, 'Gquma 'ndincede!' was still used by the Tshomane.[95]

Bessie was blessed with a long and interesting life, and was fortunate to live in peaceful times in a stable and well-ordered society. That is not to say that the Tshomane's lives were perfect or idyllic. There was frequent bickering and skirmishing between the various coastal clans and peoples, usually over cattle and their theft and counter-theft,[96] but strict laws of chivalry governed their warfare. The enemy were warned beforehand so that they could prepare themselves for attack, women and children were never killed and prisoners were not put to death, but held to ransom instead. The purpose of war among the Mpondo was not to annihilate the enemy but to acquire cattle and wives, and it was not unusual for the victors to give the losers a number of cattle to ensure that they did not starve. It has even been recorded that '[a]fter a battle the young men of one side would often send home their shields and spears by the attendant boys, and proceed as honoured guests to the kraals of their late adversaries.'[97]

But all that was soon to change.

When Bessie died, it was said, 'good fortune seemed to have departed from the tribe....'[98]

Genealogy of the amaBomvana[99]

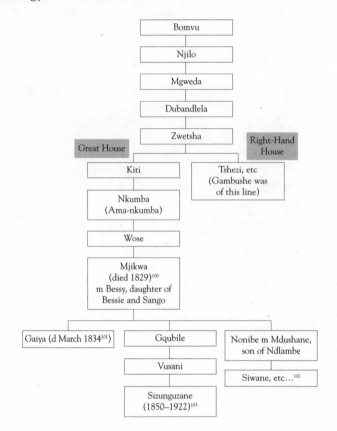

Chapter Seven

The Hunters and the Hunted

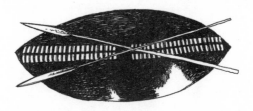

'Truly this land is full of lamentation and mourning and woe.'[1]

M depa was Bessie's youngest son, born in about 1753. He had inherited his mother's striking blue eyes and her sweet nature and was remembered, long after his death, as

> 'a nice gentleman, he had a long nose, blue eyes, a yellow complexion, and long hair. He was a very old man when he died, nearly one hundred years of age, and we buried him. He was a very good gentleman, and much liked by the white people.'[2]

In his youth he had been a spirited fighter, renowned for his bravery, but in his old age Mdepa was to encounter the most fearsome threat the region had ever known, caught up in the mounting terror of the *Mfecane*.

The magnitude of human suffering during the *Mfecane* is unquantifiable. Hundreds of thousands of people were killed, vast numbers of refugees criss-crossed the face of the country. There was widespread starvation and even cannibalism and the very fabric of traditional society was destroyed; the remnants assembled in its aftermath never entirely reflected the original. The destruction spread throughout southern Africa in a domino effect as victims became the perpetrators of the next cycle of violence and their victims, in turn, the perpetrators of the next. Shaka, whose brief but dynamic reign consolidated and militarised the Zulus, is often cited as the main cause of the turmoil, but there is growing evidence 'that violence had been on the increase for up to fifty years before Shaka's time, and that it was no gentlemanly Elysium which Shaka suddenly disrupted.'[3] The *Mfecane* was more than just inter-clan and inter-tribal warfare; it was a full-blown social, political and military revolution,[4] the culmination of a number of intrusive forces, its origins as varied as they were widespread.

By the late 1700s settler expansionism in the south-eastern region of southern Africa had displaced the Khoi population, annihilated the San and triggered a series of wars against the Xhosa in a fierce competition for land and grazing. In the south-west, survivors of the Khoikhoi who had once occupied the Cape Peninsula had retreated before the Dutch settlers. Their remnants, the Korana and Griquas, infused with the blood of numerous

Korana[5]

runaway slaves, renegade Boers and deserters from the Cape garrison, gave rise to the swashbuckling and charmingly named Bastards (the *Basters* of later centuries) who had begun occupying the land around the Orange and lower Vaal rivers from the 1730s onwards, outlaws among them taking refuge on the islands in the Orange River between present-day Upington and the Augrabies Falls.[6]

Their arrival changed the face of the north-west. Skilled horsemen and excellent marksmen, with access to guns, powder and ammunition through illegal trade with individual Boers and itinerant traders, they raided deep into the hinterland,[7] preying on the cattle-rich Tswana, driving off their herds, seizing their harvests and displacing entire communities, which, in order to recoup their losses, in turn attacked and scattered their neighbours. Smaller groups of bandits, outlaw Boers such as Nicolaas and Willem Lochenberg and the Bezuidenhout brothers, or emigrant Xhosa such as the band under Danster, contributed to the disorder, 'subsisting entirely upon the chase and occasional plunder.'[8]

In the north-east, the Portuguese contributed to the general upheaval; renegade noblemen, deserters and criminals, fanning out from settlements such as Sofala and Sena, had established themselves as powerful and ruthless warlords, trading in ivory and firearms and, especially from about 1644, in slaves. They encouraged hostilities between the local chiefs, because war guaranteed them a greater supply of slaves than peace. Beginning as a law unto themselves, they were in time recognised by the Portuguese crown as legitimate landholders and loyal subjects. After 1750 Delagoa Bay became a major trading centre[9] and, as its influence spread in the late 18th and early 19th century, the socio-political dynamics of the region were irrevocably altered. Some idea of the impact of Portuguese activities is suggested by the fact that, in 1823 *alone*, they exported 16 000 slaves from Mozambique to Brazil.[10]

A Bastard[11]

The Zulu-speaking clans to the south of Delagoa Bay, the Mthethwa under Dingiswayo and the Ndwandwe under Zwide, for example, which constituted some of their main trading partners – though not, it seems, in slaves – competed for domination of the lucrative Portuguese trade, and became increasingly militarised.[12] The conflict between them spread and intensified, becoming more systematic after Dingiswayo's death, when

13

145

his ambitious protégé Shaka took over, monopolising the trade routes and annihilating or absorbing all who succumbed to his increasingly powerful army.

As Shaka grew in power and his *izimpi* raided further and further south, rumours of war began to penetrate the Wild Coast region. They were soon followed by refugees; a scattered few to begin with, they increased steadily, until they numbered in their thousands. By 1823 groups of these *Mfengu*, as they were called, had penetrated as far south as the Kei River. The Mpondo, Thembu and the Xhosa under Hintsa and Ndlambe all came under attack at one time or another with greater or lesser success,[14] as whole clans of fighting men, with their women, children and cattle, probed the strengths and weaknesses of the local people, looking for a way to get their foot in the door, hungry for land where they could settle down and rebuild their lives.

For Bessie's Tshomane the first blow seems to have fallen in about 1823–24 when Shaka unleashed an *impi* on the Mpondo, driving them over the Mzimvubu River and into the deep valleys of the Mngazi and Mngazana rivers, in Tshomane territory, where they massed in concentrated defence.[15] It was a new kind of warfare: Shaka's men had no time for chivalry and no interest in mercy; they took what they wanted and destroyed what they did not – and for those in its path it was nothing short of devastating.

At about this time, in 1824, six Englishmen acting as agents for a group of Cape merchants began establishing a trading post at Port Natal (now the city of Durban), between Pondoland and Shaka's territory, one of their principal objects being to procure ivory.[16] The traders had barely settled in at the port when they witnessed the returning Zulu force – an army of such vast proportions that it took until sunset to pass: 'I saw on my right a dense mass of people coming fast from the direction I had come,' wrote 24-year-old Henry Francis Fynn. 'My view extended over several miles of the beach, but I could not see the rear of this immense black and continuous mass of natives, all armed and in their war-dresses.'[17] A short while later Fynn himself headed off to Pondoland, hoping to engage in ivory trading there. As he made his way along the coast he was shocked by the apocalyptic effect of the Zulu army on the countryside and its inhabitants:

> '... [F]rom the Intongati River, 25 miles N.E. of Port Natal up to within a few miles of the Umzimvubu, I did not find a single tribe, with the exception of about 30 natives residing near the Bluff, under the chief Amatubane.... There were neither kraals, huts, [people], nor corn. Occasionally I saw a few stragglers, mere living skeletons, obtaining a precarious existence on roots and shell-fish.'[18]

Fynn's men stopped to help the starving survivors, some of whom were so desperate that they had eaten poisonous roots,[19] but when they themselves began struggling to find food, were obliged to abandon the expedition.

On his return to Port Natal Fynn was immediately summoned by Shaka who, 'having heard in my absence that I had gone off on a journey to the westward, asked me to give him particulars thereof. He laughed heartily on hearing the account... he wanted to know how I could expect to travel through those parts without his assistance, for obviously my troubles had all arisen out of his having killed off the inhabitants of the surrounding countries.'[20]

Fynn, young, ambitious and street-wise, must have understood the subtext of Shaka's words at once: without the king's help he could not hope to reach the Mpondo and their ivory[21] – and that help would not be free. Perhaps the deal was struck then and there; certainly it was not long after this that Fynn set off for Pondoland again and this time his journey was successful, as was the next, which he undertook almost immediately afterwards.

On arriving in Mpondo territory Fynn's party headed for the Great Place of the king, Faku. News of the traders had preceded them and they found a great meeting in progress; the Mpondo were anxiously anticipating another Zulu attack and (quite rightly) suspected Fynn of being a spy, but his vehement denial of all knowledge of Shaka saved his skin and eventually the charges were dropped. Free to go again, Fynn headed south across the Mngazi. The devastation caused by the Zulu invasion, although not as bad as it had been north of the Mzimvubu, was still evident here, and the country was in turmoil. As Fynn ventured further south into Bomvana territory, trading and exploring, he was intrigued to discover that living among them were individuals of obviously white extraction. He began seeking them out and inevitably came across Bessie's descendants. Her daughter, Bessy, it will be remembered, had married a Bomvana prince, Mjikwa, but Fynn also found her son Mdepa and the Tshomane here. It appears that the amaMpondo, seeking refuge from the Zulu army in the Gosa Forest near the mouth of the Mzimvubu River[22] and in the rugged folds and valleys of the Mgazi and Mngazana rivers, had driven the Tshomane from their ancestral lands, forcing them to find shelter with the Bomvana, with whom they had strong kinship ties.

The Tshomanes' world had been turned upside down; along with their land they had lost their crops, granaries, most of their cattle and the graves of their ancestors. But none of this is mentioned by Fynn, who remarks only that Mdepa 'had European blood in him' and was 'the son of an English lady,' who was

'said to have been remarkably handsome... she used to dress in native costume, twisting or plaiting her hair into cords which extended to her waist, and covered, or rubbed over with red clay. It was on account of her extreme beauty that, even to this day, the people when reciting her eulogies use the expression, "Izinkabi zikaDawa", i.e. the oxen of the white lady.'[23]

Fynn's encounter with Bessie's descendants was brief, but he may have been the catalyst for what Mdepa did next. Perhaps the suspicions the trader had awoken in the Mpondo at Faku's Great Place were also aroused in Mdepa. Fynn was not the only spy Shaka had despatched down south,[24] but he was to become a regular visitor to Pondoland, obtaining on his extensive and lengthy expeditions, as far south as the Mtata River and lasting up to nine months,[25] not only a hoard of Mpondo ivory but also an intimate knowledge of their strengths, weaknesses and extensive herds of cattle – information of profound interest to Shaka.

Mdepa may have suspected something of the sort; although he was getting on in years and his physical strength had deserted him, his intellect was unimpaired. At any rate, clearly anticipating more trouble, Mdepa turned to his mother's people for help.[26] The nearest Englishmen were Wesleyan missionaries at Butterworth, a newly established station under the Reverend William Shrewsbury, about 120 kilometres as the crow flies to the south-west. Mdepa must have known that the Wesleyans were already providing protection to the Mfengu refugees who were streaming south; perhaps they would afford his people the same protection.

The Wesleyans had spent the previous few years establishing missions among the amaNdlambe and amaNgqika south of the Kei River and in 1826 had begun preparing for a mission among the Gcaleka Xhosa north of the Kei. To obtain King Hintsa's permission, Shrewsbury had been dispatched to his Great Place on the Gcuwa River, not far from the spot where the Hubner traders had been killed 90 years before. Shrewsbury's single-mindedness was perfect for the task; an austere, judgmental man, driven by his passionate faith, he relentlessly pursued Hintsa, who was clearly ambivalent about the advantages of Christianity. The king soon found himself caught between a rock and a hard place: he was hesitant to offend the Colony by turning away its missionaries, but unwilling to have them stay, lest they alienate his subordinate chiefs.[27] He procrastinated to such an extent that eventually Shrewsbury moved his entire family and servants onto Hintsa's doorstep, began erecting buildings and planting trees and gardens, and by the time permission was granted for its establishment, the station was already two months old and had been named Butterworth.[28] Acting as Hintsa's interpreter during this whole fiasco was Nicolaas Lochenberg, a hunting, shooting Boer, who had known Bessie's family for decades.

Lochenberg had absconded from the Cape Colony with his brother Willem and several other rebel Boers under the leadership of Coenraad de Buys in the 1790s and had spent at least half of his life on or near the Wild Coast. Van der Kemp, the first missionary to visit the region, in 1799, had found him and his comrades ensconced near Ngqika's Great Place on the Keiskamma River, together with their families and servants. Van der Kemp's interpreter, incidentally, was a famous Khoi elephant hunter named William Bruntje who had accompanied Van Reenen on his expedition to find the

Grosvenor survivors, so if Lochenburg had not heard of Bessie before then, he certainly had by 1799.[29]

One of the Boers' entourage was a Khoi woman named Sarah, the wife of a Khoi employed by the Boer Coenraad Bezuidenhout.[30] She began attending Van der Kemp's prayer meetings and eventually became the old missionary's first convert. She had her three children, Hannah, Sarah and Christina, baptised too and, as her eldest child was then just four years old,[31] Sarah was probably still in her early twenties if not younger. Under Van der Kemp's tutelage she learnt to read and write, making her one of the few Khoi women of her generation to do so – an exceptional feat, considering that even a hundred years later 90% of black and coloured South Africans were illiterate.[32] It is not certain what became of her first husband, or of Nicolaas Lochenberg's first wife, a woman of slave descent, Alberta Maria Joubert,[33] but in time Sarah and the renegade Boer formed a liaison and together they had six children, including Hans, who, as mentioned in the previous chapter, pointed out the location of Bessie's grave, and Willem, who later became a lay preacher at Beecham Wood mission near the Mbashe River mouth.

By 1809 the Lochenbergs were living at Mazeppa Bay, on the coast east of Butterworth.[34] 'They resided quite close to the breakers of the Indian Ocean, in a beautifully romantic situation,' wrote an official who visited them there, in 'a collection of huts, some built in the colonial, others in the [Xhosa] style.'[35] With them were several slaves and an Irishman from county Clare named Henry MacDaniel, who had deserted from the 8th dragoons during the time of the first British occupation of the Cape (1795–1803). Another deserter from the Cape garrison, a Dutchman named Peter, had left not long before to live at the Mbashe River further north. Lochenberg, 'whose only covering was a ragged jacket, and a pair of breeches,' and MacDaniel reportedly had two or three Khoi wives each and several children 'and were become [Xhosa] in every respect except in eating fish and poultry, which the latter would not do.'[36]

In 1827, when Mdepa delegated him to present his case to the missionaries at Butterworth, Lochenberg was about 60 years old.[37] Bessie's son could not have hoped to find a more unlikely ambassador: the old Boer, who subsidised his hunting and ivory trading by gun-running and occasionally hiring himself out to the local clans as a mercenary, had very definite reservations about missionaries, English ones in particular. He tried to warn the chiefs about 'the encroachments of the English, for whom he entertained a very natural aversion,' his son Hans said later.

> 'First, said he, would come a missionary, who would beg a piece of land; then would follow traders, and settlers, more and more numerous, until they and the redcoats, by whom they were defended, would cover the land like locusts.'[38]

Hundreds of kilometres north of the Wild Coast and a few years later an exiled Xhosa named Jacob Simbiti was to warn the Zulus in almost the very same words: first, he said, the English

> 'took a part of their land, then they encroached and drove them further back, and have repeatedly taken more land as well as cattle. They then built houses (i.e. missionary establishments) among them, for the purpose of subduing them....'[39]

In terms of birth, race and language, Jacob could hardly have been more different from old Nicolaas, but in their attitude to the British the fugitive Boer and exiled Xhosa were as close as brothers, and in due course their prophesies, unfortunately, proved true. Both met a violent end: Jacob, or Nhlambamanzi as the Zulus called him, was murdered by a settler in the 1830s; Lochenberg's date with destiny was somewhat sooner.

Lochenberg's antipathy towards the missionaries was mutual – one describing him as 'violent and ungodly'[40] – but when he conveyed Mdepa's request to the Reverend Shrewsbury, the missionary wasted no time in securing his services as a guide. Shrewsbury must have heard of the Tshomane before, as he refers to Mdepa as 'the long-talked of white chief, ... a descendant of one of the unhappy females wrecked in the *Grosvenor*,'[41] but Mdepa's dramatic message pushed him into action:

> 'If you don't come soon I shall die, and be buried in the bushes, and my body eaten by Ashes. I want to have a Christian burial as I am descended from Christian People, but if you come while I live you will teach me and my People what white People know.'[42]

Shrewsbury's first stop was Lochenberg's place at Mazeppa, about 50 kilometres as the crow flies from Butterworth. The present road runs over an undulating sea of hills – green hills stepping back to blue-green, then to deep blue in the distance, hillock piled upon hillock as far as the eye can see. It is tarred up to the small trading centre of Kentane, after which it turns to dirt and swings north, narrowing rapidly and pitted with potholes. Following much the same route as the old wagon-trail along the crests of the hills, it winds its way down to the coast where a hotel and a few humble cottages shelter amongst the *Phoenix reclinata* palms and a large suspension bridge, looking quite incongruous, links a small island to the beach. The journey, which today takes about an hour, took Shrewsbury two days by wagon.[43] Then, with Lochenberg as their guide, the party turned north, relying on the traditional hospitality of the local people for accommodation and food along the way. The journey was rough but uneventful. After several days' hard travel they reached the magnificent Hole in the Wall, a mountain of rock set apart from the mainland, sheltering a placid lagoon at its base from the open sea at its back, the waves crashing through a tunnel in its centre.

A little further north they crossed the Mtata River, two hours beyond which they found Mdepa, who was 'exceedingly glad' to see them. Shrewsbury, on the other hand, was singularly unimpressed. Unfortunately, as Mdepa was illiterate he left no record of their meeting and the missionary's is the only account we have – with, of course, his particular slant. He was obviously expecting a much grander figure, a noble white chief cast in the mould of popular novels, and his disappointment shows: 'It was a melancholy introduction,' he wrote. Mdepa was old and worn, and although his features were European, between him and the rest of the Tshomane there was

'not the slightest difference in his habits and manners. I thought on his mother's unhappy lot, and on the little advantage he derived from the mere circumstance of having an English woman for his mother.'

Hole in the Wall, looking across the lagoon towards the sea

According to Shrewsbury, Mdepa could give him

'no information concerning his mother, save that she had by the chief, her husband, 3 sons and 1 daughter; that she died higher up the country.... But I could not learn so much as his mother's name.'[44]

This is an odd statement; none of his contemporaries seem to have had a problem discovering that Mdepa's mother was called Bessie (or even Gquma, for that matter), and may have been due to the fact that Shrewsbury had not yet learnt to speak Xhosa and was dependent on an interpreter. In addition, his visit was very brief; he spent little over a day with Mdepa and, it being the Sabbath, most of it was taken up by his sermon, followed by discussions about establishing a mission. The Tshomane's recent misfortunes had made them 'poorer and much more teachable [than the Xhosa],' noted Shrewsbury with an eye to its advantages, 'consequently amongst them I think the fruits of missionary labours would more immediately appear.'[45]

Yet by February the following year, 1828, Mdepa was still without his mission and had to send another message to Shrewsbury requesting its establishment 'without further delay.'[46] Again no help was forthcoming and his sense of urgency grew as the days shortened: winter was coming and it was the season for raiding.[47]

Shaka, meanwhile, had sent a deputation of important counsellors and chiefs to initiate a political alliance with the British. Led by Sobote and Mbozamboza, they had hoped to meet King George in London but their vessel was impounded at Port Elizabeth, and they were obliged to deliver their message to the colonial authorities there instead. In it Shaka guaranteed the subservience of all the inhabitants north of Mzimvubu River,

Zulu fighter[48]

and expressed his intention of extending his conquest south of the river, all the way down to the Fish River 'thus giving him a common frontier with King George.' He promised to delay conquest for two months 'pending a reply to his question: would the annihilation of all the tribes between the [Mzimvubu] and Fish rivers meet with his new ally's approval?'[49] Before the promised time was up, however, in the middle of May 1828 Shaka's forces invaded Pondoland:[50] 'The Chief Tshaka, or Chaka, is coming down the coast upon the Kaffers with immense hordes of people under his command,' wrote Reverend Shrewsbury,

> 'The troops under him are compared to locusts for number. They are drawn out of several divisions, distinguished by the colour of their shields, as the white, red, black shields, etc; one division goes forth to fight, and the others come to their aid or reserve themselves for securing plunder, as circumstances may dictate.'[51]

The young trader Henry Francis Fynn acted as Shaka's enabler. In 1827 Fynn had established a trading post on the Mzimkhulu River that attracted some two thousand refugees and other local supporters, including a group of trained elephant hunters.[52] It was there that the king stayed, after leading his regiments south in person, while his commander, Mdhlaka, took the *impi* into Pondoland itself.[53] Fynn went with it. He and the other Port Natal traders had acted as Shaka's mercenaries before,[54] and seem to have had no hesitation in doing the same against the Mpondo. Major Dundas, who visited the Mpondo shortly after the attack, reported:

> 'That Fynn was present with the invading army was verified to me beyond a doubt, as a man who had been wounded by a shot from a gun in both thighs was brought to me who said that the person who shot him afterwards saved his life and dressed his wounds and then told him that his name was Fynn....'[55]

Another Cape official confirmed that 'an Englishman of the name of Fynn and some other persons either English or Bastard Hottentots, armed with muskets' were among the invading Zulus, adding that the mercenaries participated in more than one attack, for which they received a share 'in the Plunder as their reward.'[56] A third claimed that Fynn and his fellow traders had actually instigated the invasion.[57]

Henry Francis Fynn in later years[58]

A man of few scruples, whose *curriculum vitae* later included murderer, mercenary, liar, fraud, bankrupt, and possibly even slave-trader,[59] Fynn was not, however, the only one to betray his Mpondo hosts. Mfengu refugees, who had found shelter among the Mpondo and Xhosa, reportedly also acted as spies against their countrymen.[60]

In early 1828, at roughly the same time that Shaka's forces invaded Pondoland, the Ngwane, an independent Zulu-speaking clan, invaded Thembuland. In 1818 they had been attacked by Shaka and driven from their homes on the White Mfolozi River (in northern KwaZulu-Natal), making their way southwards and then across the Drakensberg into Sotho territory.[61] In January or February 1828 they lost many of their cattle and much of their prestige in a raid by Mzilikazi, and their chief Matiwane decided the time had come to move again, although his people were reluctant to do so. His mother is said to have been one of the dissenters, but 'after some thought she said, "We had better go, because he is sure to kill us all".'[62] A ruthless individual who brooked no opposition, Matiwane had already killed at least two of his own brothers.

Routing the Thembu and scattering the smaller clans before them, the Ngwane penetrated to within 100 kilometres of Butterworth, well within Xhosa territory and sent a message full of contempt and arrogance to the king, Hintsa: make sure you keep your cattle fat for us, it said, because we shall be back in three months to collect them.[63] In June 1828 it was Mdepa's turn. Bessie's son may have been a famously brave fighter in his youth, but he was no match for the ruthless Matiwane and the Tshomane were no match for the battle-hardened Ngwane. With their herds decimated and their homes destroyed, they fled south, hiding out in the bush along the banks of the Nenga River, near Coffee Bay, where they lived in constant fear of marauders. They were just beginning to emerge from their hideaways when they received another visit from Reverend Shrewsbury, accompanied by Reverend William Shaw and Reverend Davis. The missionaries arrived at dusk, causing much alarm among the Tshomane, since strangers – who would once have been warmly welcomed in accordance with their traditions of hospitality – were now to be deeply feared, and they were reassured only on recognising Nicolaas Lochenberg in the party.[64]

Mdepa was again 'glad to see us, though he was now without a home,' wrote Shrewsbury, 'in the last wars he lost a considerable portion of his cattle, and was now wandering with the rest and scarcely knowing where to settle.'[65] The enemy had withdrawn only a week earlier and the skeletons of two women could still be seen a short distance from Mdepa's hide-out, while the remains of several of his men who had died in the fighting lay nearby.[66] From the size and quantity of enemy campfires in the neighbouring Ngcwanguba forest, it was obvious that the invading army had been huge, yet the Tshomane had managed to avoid the full power of the attack, losing only a small number of their people. They were, nevertheless, in dire straits: 'Many of the kraals were burnt to ashes, and the poor people reduced to the greatest misery.'[67] They had no corn and no milk – their crops had been burnt and it was not yet calving season – and, reluctant to slaughter their few remaining cattle, Mdepa's people were close to starvation. When Lochenberg shot a hippopotamus they stripped the huge carcass bare in a matter of minutes.[68] The times of plenty in which Bessie and Sango had lived and raised their children were but a distant memory, and the fat cattle and luscious crops that Van Reenen had seen must have seemed a mere dream to her destitute descendants.

Bessie's descendants seem to have fascinated the Wesleyans, far beyond their commitment to establishing a mission station. Many made the long and difficult journey to meet Mdepa and his sister, even during wartime, painstakingly recording their meetings in their journals and agonising over their paganism. One wrote that, on seeing Ngcetane's sons,

> 'some of whom were nearly white, although belonging to the third generation, I could not but reflect, when I saw the colour of their skin, who can tell but some of the ancestors of these children, were as eminent for piety, as these are now for heathen ignorance?'[69]

Sincere as the missionaries undoubtedly were in wanting to bring them once more into the fold, at times they seem less like evangelists than *ky'daars*,[70] and Mdepa was obliged to repeat the story of his ancestry once again – much of which we already know. His mother 'was probably wrecked eighty years ago,' reported Reverend Shaw, 'she has only died within the last fifteen years.'[71] 'He stated also that his mother's father and the other white man married native women, which is not improbable. The family greatly branched out, and the colour of a number of these people proves the extent to which it has increased.' Mdepa was clearly of 'European descent,' the missionary continued,[72] 'an infirm old man,' worn down by trouble though in full possession of his faculties; he had several wives, only one of whom still lived with him, and at least 22 children, eleven of whom were fully grown men, including Majibana, his Great Son. His brothers were dead, said Mdepa, in consequence of which he had inherited his father's chieftainship – a slightly flakey claim since although he was a chief in his own right the head of the Tshomane was really his nephew Ngcetane. His one surviving sibling was his sister Bessy, who lived not far away; the *Mfecane*, in which so many people had been destroyed and so many families broken up over the length and breadth of southern Africa, had, ironically, been instrumental in bringing Bessie's two youngest children closer together again.

But much as he may have enjoyed regaling the missionaries with reminders of their common ancestry, Mdepa's immediate concern was for his people. 'He expressed great regret that the country was in such a state of confusion, [and] intimated his urgent wish that a Missionary might be sent to his tribe as soon as the people were again settled....'[73] The Tshomane's future appeared uncertain and that Sunday, when Reverend Shaw delivered his sermon, he noticed that they seemed rather distracted, no doubt listening with more than half an ear for the return of the dreaded Zulus. Their fear seemed justified when rumours reached them that the 'Fitcani' [a colonial corruption of *Mfengu*] were advancing again, and the missionaries hurriedly took their leave.

On their way back to Butterworth, they stopped at the homestead of Chief Mjikwa, the husband of Mdepa's sister Bessy. Signs of the recent invasion were evident here too: the banks of the nearby Mtata River were littered with the remains of those who had been killed in the recent fighting[74] and many of the Bomvana's choicest cattle had been stolen – by their Xhosa neighbours, complained Bessy. The missionaries found her to be 'a strong lively old woman with truly European features. She received us very pleasantly....' She was a large woman with coarse somewhat grey hair, which she wore long 'like European females,' with a 'dark yellowish complexion and prominent features.' She was probably about 63 years old, more than a decade younger than her brother. 'Some of her children were with her: rather good-looking young people darker than their mother and more like their relations the Natives.'[75] Like Mdepa she was preoccupied with her people's misfortunes but found time, nevertheless, to indulge her visitors' curiosity and answer their questions about her mother; Bessy had been about 16 at the time of the *Grosvenor* wreck and her account convinced the missionaries that Bessie had not been aboard it but 'was an European saved from the wreck of a vessel about 20 years before the loss of that East Indiaman.'

She confirmed that her name, Bessy, had also been her mother's name.[76]

> 'It is highly probable that the European ancestors of the mixed race under Depa were English, from the names by which the three Europeans mentioned by his family were called. As these names had, however, been somewhat Kaffirized by the native pronunciation of them, this is not put forth as a very certain criterion for testing this point. The female who was the mother of Depa and his sister, was called "Besi", "Bessy" or "Betsy". One of the European men was called Tomie, probably a native corruption of "Tommy", or "Thomas"....'[77]

The missionaries went on their way once more, but the crisis in the interior was growing, and Reverend Shrewsbury had no sooner left than he was back again, acting as guide to Major Dundas, who had been sent by the British to try and persuade the Zulus to withdraw. Dundas was a 'tall, well looking but reserved' man in his forties.[78] A veteran of several wars, he had been wounded in Spain and lost his left hand. As Dundas' party entered Bomvanaland they came across the first scenes of devastation and, in the middle of it all,

> 'about seventy persons of a mixed race, descendants, (it is said) of English who were wrecked twenty years before the loss of the *Grosvenor* East Indiaman. The last of these, an old woman, seems to have died a few years ago. Her daughter upon seeing the party of whites, burst into tears; and said they were like her mother whose name was Betsy.'[79]

Leaving the bulk of his party at the Mpako River, where Mdepa's Tshomane were hiding out, Dundas proceeded with nine men, the devastation increasing as they made they way into Mpondo territory. It was a journey into hell, belying Dundas' belief that the Zulus' object had been the acquisition of cattle: every hut had been burnt, every granary destroyed, the children had all been carried off and rotting bodies, including women, lay all about the ruins.[80] After a month and a half of pillage they had recently withdrawn, but as Dundas and his men neared the Mpondo Great Place at Mngazi, not far from where Bessie had once lived, they could hear the invaders 'war cries' in the middle of the night: 'a very peculiar cry; shrill, weird and prolonged and calculated to stir the heart of every man who heard it....'[81]

Later visitors were to describe the Mpondo King Faku, who was to rule for more than 60 years, as a tall good-looking man, who was courageous, strong and forthright: 'How can I distinguish white men again when they are all alike?'[82] he asked a missionary whom he had failed to recognise on meeting him for the second time. Dundas, however, found him 'most abject and dispirited....' This was a bit of an understatement, as the king was lying flat on his face on the ground and barely lifted his head when the Englishman approached. If Faku was on the verge of a nervous breakdown, he recovered sufficiently later to tell Dundas that all the Mpondo's cattle had been stolen and his people had nothing to eat nor hides for clothing. Shaka, who had caused all the trouble, was now offering them cattle 'which were to be received as a token of their dependence upon him and that he was to be Chaka's friend' but, Faku added wryly, 'as he had lost his all it was of little consequence whose friend he was....'[83]

While Faku grappled with his inner demons, the Thembu fought off the real live ones. Matiwane's invasion had swept them from their land and fired their crops and homes; the country was 'in a terrible state – black with the smoke of fires and around the cinders of huts and kraals lay the bodies of men, women and children and their dogs.'[84] At the end of July 1828, the Thembu hit back: 5 000 men led by their king, Ngubencuka, and assisted by Dundas' party of 24 attacked the Ngwane and seized twenty-five thousand cattle.[85] When Matiwane retaliated, trying to recover his cattle, Ngubencuka called on the British for military support. Towards the end of August 1828 Lieutenant-Colonel Somerset arrived with a Khoi regiment under English officers, several hundred armed Boers, and heavy artillery and, with a combined force of Xhosa under Hintsa and Thembu under Ngubencuka, attacked Matiwane at Mbholompo, near the present town of Umtata.

'One day at early dawn,' an Ngwane survivor recalled many years later,

> 'we heard the thunder of the cannons; of course at that time we knew not what it was. Then we saw a file of wagons, drawn by what we took to be hornless cattle, and also men riding on the like. We had never seen mounted men before, and were sore amazed. Moreover, the country was black with Tembus, as though a cloud had obscured the sun and thrown its shadow on the ground. We formed line along one of the banks of the Umtata. The Tembus rushed upon our cattle, but we repulsed them. It was then that the white soldiers opened fire upon us. We knew not then what it was; we heard a terrific noise,

and saw fire and smoke, and deadly burning things pierced and killed us where we stood. It was very terrible for us, as we had only our spears and shields, and could not reach the enemy, who killed us from a distance. Time after time we tried to charge, but our men were killed before they got near enough to strike....'[86]

Matiwane's *impi* was destroyed, many of his womenfolk captured, vast herds of his cattle taken, and his power utterly broken.

One month later, on 22 September 1828, Shaka was assassinated by his bodyguard Mbopha and half-brothers Mhlangana and Dingane,[87] passing into the realms of myth and legend – and becoming a favourite bogeyman for generations to come. A contemporary writer describes how a Thembu woman used his name to great effect on some unruly children:

'She was bulky but not unwieldy, and withal a merry rattling creature. Several little boys came running down to see us, and whether it was out of fun or whether they had left their employment, she called out loudly to them, pointing to us and frequently using Chaca's [Shaka's] name, which made them run off hastily with fear depicted on their Countenances, and she enjoying their fright with a loud horselaugh; the boys however soon returned.'[88]

Shaka's death did little to stem the tide of the *Mfecane*; although the Zulu army itself no longer posed a direct threat to Mdepa and his people, other forces had been unleashed which soon would.

For a short, sweet time, however, it must have seemed to Mdepa that his troubles were over and, as the chaos subsided, traders, travellers and missionaries began filtering back into the territory. Early in 1829 he received a visit from two Grahamstown residents, Dr Cowie and Tiger Green, who were on an exploratory journey from the eastern Cape up the Wild Coast and through Zululand to Portuguese-held Lourenço Marques. It was a journey from which neither was destined to return (both succumbed to malaria further north),[89] but at that stage the travellers were still fresh and were probably drawn to Mdepa's by rumours of his unusual ancestry. They could not have been disappointed; in that remote wilderness, where lions and elephant roamed, where the rivers were frequently impassable and the first wagon road would not be built for another half-century, the old chief must have presented a startling picture with his 'aquiline nose, blue eyes, yellowish complexion and long hair'[90] and, on leaving, they made him a present of a checked shirt.[91] Mdepa set great store by this article and wore it whenever he had white visitors, but as the shirt was worn without trousers, without anything, in fact, except the standard penis-sheath, the effect was quite the opposite of what he was probably hoping to achieve. Instead of emphasising his European roots, it highlighted the void between him and his mother's countrymen, particularly as the years passed and the garment got older, shabbier and dirtier.

The Wesleyan Society, meanwhile, had finally given the go-ahead for Mdepa's mission and in May 1829 the Reverend William Shepstone arrived to establish Morley.[92] Choosing the site proved to be a bit of a political football: the Tshomane comprised three factions under three chiefs, each of whom wanted the mission on his land, Mdepa, Bessie's grandson Ngcetane, and Nqanda, a son of Bessie's first husband Tshomane, a 'tall and very corpulent man' shaped just like his name which meant 'egg'.[93] One of the proposed sites was on the north bank of the Mtata River at a place known as Nomadolo.[94] Situated on a high ridge of land four or five kilometres north of the Mtata and about 20 kilometres from the sea, it was blessed with abundant water – ten or twelve strong springs rising within a short distance to form the source of the Mdumbe River – and the soil was fine and fertile. Its position, though, was strongly opposed by Mdepa, who recognised the value of the river as a natural barrier against further incursions from the north and, following Matiwane's attack the previous year, had sworn never to return to that side of it.[95] Unfortunately, he was overruled.

The Tshomane threw their support behind the mission, donating oxen for food and labour for building and, as they emerged from their hiding places in the forests and nearby hills, many began establishing their homes near the new station: '… [T]he people are flocking over from the southern side of the river,' wrote Reverend Shepstone, 'and filling up their old places round the station from which they were driven last year, by Chaka.'[96] He planned to start a school and Bessie's grandson, Ngcetane, promised to send his children and locate his *umzi* near the mission, as did Nqanda-the-Egg, some of whose people had already selected their sites. Mdepa's sons planned to do the same – the eldest, Bajela, bringing the missionary an ox 'as a present, to thank for the additional pillar in the house of his grandmother…' – and there was a possibility that Mdepa would too. Shepstone was granted unconditional freedom to preach amongst the Tshomane,[97] and for a time it must have seemed to him that everything was coming up roses. However, throughout southern Africa the relationship between the missionaries and the indigenous people was to prove a complex and difficult one. While chiefs such as Mdepa recognised the benefits of having a missionary and Englishman in their midst, they had distinct reservations about the message he preached.

Christianity was directly opposed to the pillars of traditional society – polygamy, *ukulobola* and circumcision – while school diverted the boys from their herding duties, and interfered with economic life. Generally speaking, the chiefs found 'school people' were less amenable to their authority: 'To become a "school" person was to lose a way of life, a culture. It was to accept an education which involved the idea that many of the traditional customs and rites were obnoxious to Christianity.'[98]

The first converts to Christianity were those with the least to lose. The mission provided people on the periphery of society, the lame, the aged and outcast, the sick and the fugitive, with sanctuary[99] and refugees flooded in from the war-torn countryside. The Tshomane seem to have accepted the new wave of strangers as easily as they had once welcomed runaway slaves and castaways, but despite their courtesy towards Shepstone, men such as Mdepa and Ngcetane clung to their ancient beliefs and customs with a tenacity that drove him almost to despair.

For the missionaries, who had chosen to isolate their families from the fellowship and succour of their countrymen in Africa and to subject their frequently pregnant wives and growing children to the dangers of the wild without access to medical expertise, formal educations, or most modern comforts, life was anything but easy. Backsliding among their converts was common and disheartening. They were affronted by the near-nakedness of the people they served, and their letters and journals are peppered with italics reflecting their dismay and outrage:

> '[T]he *most discouraging* fact is the *licentiousness* of the people.
> *It exceeds all description*... the Kaross that is occasionally worn is
> thrown round the body like a mantle *only as a defence from the cold*; at
> other seasons, old men and young men alike are without covering,
> and fathers sit before their children without a single rag upon their
> bodies. This is a *universal* custom....'[100]

There was also the problem of language: the typical missionary, newly arrived in the country, could not speak Xhosa and his interpreter, who was usually Khoi, spoke no English. To overcome this little hurdle, the missionary had to learn a little of the local Dutch, which was already mutating beyond mere dialect into Afrikaans, a language in its own right. With a smattering of this new *taal*, the missionary explained his sermon to his interpreter, who then instructed the missionary how to state these ideas in Xhosa.[101] There was no Xhosa dictionary or phrasebook available until much later and the interpreter was frequently illiterate. As he was also not necessarily a Christian himself and had a shaky grasp of divine matters,[102] the process was open to serious error – and probably accounts for one chief naming his grandsons Adam and Eve.[103] Having written out his sermon in what he hoped was Xhosa, the missionary read it out aloud to his assembled congregation – unfamiliar pronunciation and all – and hoped to God that they understood it. As one historian said, for the missionaries to have converted anyone at all under these circumstances was a miracle in itself. And if the conditions were difficult, so were many of the missionaries themselves. The Reverend Shrewsbury, for example, had the peculiar habit of delivering his sermons lying down. He found the smokiness caused by the central fire inside most huts so bad that he preferred to preach stretched out full-length on his back below the level of smoke, an eccentricity which probably did not add to his chances of making new converts.

Work on Morley nevertheless progressed and amid the ruined homesteads and burnt fields, new buildings slowly grew up. 'When I look round me,' wrote Shepstone, 'and see so many places which have been destroyed by fire, my prayer to God is, that war may no more disturb our repose....'[104] His prayer went unanswered; the horrors the Tshomane thought they had put behind them were once again before them. Ironically it was Nicolaas Lochenberg, who had helped establish the mission, that contributed to its fall.

Following Shaka's assassination, the Zulu throne had been seized by his half-brother and killer Dingane. Nqeto, one of the late king's bravest generals and leader of the Qwabe, had refused to swear allegiance to Dingane and was driven out of Zululand with the usurper's forces snapping at his heels. Leading his people south, he eventually reached Pondoland, where he sent a message to King Faku requesting permission to settle in his territory, but Faku had had it up to *here* with Zulu invaders, and put the emissaries to death. Nqeto chose not to retaliate, but as his people withdrew further south, they were attacked again and again by their new neighbours. Nqeto was a son of Kondlo of the Great House of Malandela, of which Shaka was of the Right-Hand House,[105] and he was not to be trifled with – 'Nqeto *used to spit* in Tshaka's presence,'[106] ran his breathless praises – but even he must have been hard-put to restrain his army, a finely tuned killing-machine with a reputation to uphold. Yet he held his peace. It was only when his enemies recruited Nicolaas Lochenberg, promising him a cut of the Zulu cattle, that the shit hit the fan or, as a contemporary missionary put it, 'was kindled the vengeful flame which soon burst forth with fury.'[107]

Lochenberg, as I mentioned earlier, had a sideline as a gun-runner and occasional mercenary, and with his armed Khoi he commanded a very destructive amount of firepower. However, he feared that this battle would not be so easy. The old Boer began to have premonitions of his own death and for several nights prior to the battle his sleep was disturbed by dreams 'that violent hands had spilt his blood upon the ground.'[108] Nevertheless, having already committed himself, and against his men's objections, he prepared for battle. On the morning he was due to set off he awoke to find his horses gone. They were located only late in the day, so he was forced to postpone his departure, but the next day the horses again disappeared. Once again they were found only after many hours of searching, but Lochenberg refused to delay any longer and rode off to join his allies – and to meet his fate.

Nqeto's Qwabe fighting men watched as Lochenberg and his mounted Khoi led the enemy into the attack. Retreating to the crest of a hill, with their wives, children and cattle hidden behind them, they waited in companies divided according to their shields, white, black and red. Their only weapon was the short-shafted stabbing spear that the Zulus had developed for close-contact fighting, their discipline so strong that they withstood several volleys from the Boer's guns. Holding their positions even when Nqeto was shot in the leg, they allowed the enemy to advance to within a few paces of them. Then, as Lochenberg and his men dismounted to take aim, the Qwabe rose up with a roar and rushed down on them. Lochenberg, taken by surprise and unable to remount, was 'literally cut to pieces'[109] and his retainers and allies decimated. With no one to stop him Nqeto swept through the land, attacking at night, burning and destroying everything before him.[110]

For the Tshomane life was just beginning to return to normal. For a few sweet months the smoke on the horizon had been from cooking fires rather than burning homesteads, and they were slowly re-establishing the timeless routines of traditional life: the boys herding the cattle, the women tending the fields, the girls minding the children, the men hunting and the elderly smoking their dagga pipes and basking in the warm winter sun outside their homes. Even the young bucks were back to normal, involved in an altercation over cattle with a neighbour named Ngezana.[111] The peace was shattered by news of Nqeto's rampage. Having defeated the Mpondo, his forces were arrowing in on the Tshomane, one column coming down the coast and the other down the Mtata River. By 11 August they were just 72 kilometres away from Mdepa's new mission.[112]

Also at Morley was a recently arrived party of English adventurers and traders, who were spending a few days resting themselves and their oxen before continuing the long, hard trek north to Port Natal. Their leader, Francis Farewell, and Nqeto had known each other in Zululand and, on learning that the chief possessed a large quantity of ivory, Farewell decided to drop in on him for a spot of trading – undeterred by Lochenberg's death or by the fact that mid-rampage might not be an opportune moment. Unlike Lochenberg, he seems to have had no inkling of what awaited him: 'I am well acquainted with some of the chiefs of the Quabees and if possible shall have an interview with them,' he wrote on 25 September; 'I shall try to get them to live peaceably....'[113] The traders left Morley the following day, and a few days later located the Qwabe.[114]

Leaving their wagons behind, Farewell, two other traders named Walker and Thackwray, and a number of their Zulu and Khoi attendants, rode on to see Nqeto. Most unfortunately, the party included one of Dingane's spies – the same Dingane who had sworn vengeance against Nqeto and, as the latter knew, was in the habit of sending spies into Pondoland to gain information about him.[115] Nqeto also knew that Farewell was on excellent terms with Dingane and he probably suspected that only a small portion of the muskets and ammunition, with which Farewell's wagons were heavily loaded, was intended for use at Port Natal, with the bulk destined for trading with Dingane.[116]

If he was suspicious of the traders, however, he hid it well, welcoming them and slaughtering a beast to feed them. At nightfall, however, when the Qwabe discovered the spy among Farewell's men, the atmosphere suddenly became charged with hostility. As Nqeto showed the traders the wound he had survived 'from the gun of a white man,' and triumphantly paraded Lochenberg's horses before them,[117] Farewell's Khoi attendants became increasingly nervous. Like Hubner's servants, they were more adept at recognising a dangerous situation than their white bosses. Like the unfortunate Hubner, Farewell dismissed their fears, and retired with his companions to their tent to sleep.

It must have been a hell of a night, since one of the traders, William Thackwray, was an incorrigible farter. According to George Stubbs, who had once been his apprentice, it was so bad he could not even talk without farting. For instance he would say: 'George thou art a fool (Poop) George if thou doesn't alter (Poop) I shall be obliged to (Poop) get rid of thee (Poop).'[118]

But it was not because of Thackwray that the traders did not survive the night – just before dawn Nqeto's men surrounded the tent, collapsing it onto the trapped traders and stabbing them through the canvas. Farewell and his two companions, and five of their attendants who were in a hut nearby, were all killed, only three of the party managing to escape alive. While the Qwabe pillaged the wagons, and took a good haul in trade goods from them, as well as horses and oxen, the occupants fled straight back to Morley where they raised the alarm. Bessie's grandson, Ngcetane, immediately assured Reverend Shepstone of his protection[119] and, while the women and children took refuge in the woods, the missionary and some of the men stood guard at the station, expecting the worst. They must have been scared witless because it took them some time to identify Nqeto's spy in their midst – although he must have been fairly obvious, wearing as he did a portion of Farewell's tent on his head[120] – and when Nqeto was just a few kilometres off and the flames of burning homesteads lit up the night sky, Shepstone decided to abandon the mission and take his family to safety.[121] In order to reach the wagon drift over the Mtata he had first to go straight towards the advancing Qwabe, before turning west for the Colony, but just in time a dense fog suddenly rolled in from the sea, concealing the wagons until they had reached the drift where the bush and broken *kloofs* could provide them with cover, at which point it suddenly cleared again. Shepstone, of course, thought it was a miracle; he got clean away. His flock fared less well. Those who remained at the mission 'were almost wholly destroyed,'[122] but the majority escaped by doing what they had done so many times before: hiding out in the bush, in the *kloofs* along the river, or running blind. Morley was burnt to the ground, less than six months after being built, and the Tshomane, who had only just rebuilt their homesteads and sown 'what little seed-corn they had with difficulty been able to collect,'[123] lost everything yet again.

The perpetrators did not go unpunished: the Qwabe were finally defeated near today's village of Port St Johns. Trapped by Ndamase, eldest son of the Mpondo King Faku, on the great precipices looming above the Mzimvubu, 'a dreadful slaughter ensued. Comparatively few could effect their escape; and numbers, in fleeing from the spear, leaped from the rocks and perished in the river.'[124] Nqeto, still recovering from the wound Lochenberg had inflicted, was not among them and was spared. He eventually returned to Zululand, where Dingane was waiting for him, and there met his death.[125]

Once again peace returned to the region, and once again the Tshomane began emerging from their hiding places. Somehow, in all the confusion and terror, Mdepa had managed to keep his shirt on – literally. He was wearing it when the Wesleyans visited him in 1830, the shabby old checked garment 'his only covering,' sniffed one.[126] The purpose of their visit was to re-establish the mission station. A few charred poles were all that remained of the old Morley buildings and the only living creatures were a few old crones scavenging for food. The state of the surrounding countryside was evidence of the recent upheavals: 'Human bones were scattered about on every side, together with heaps upon heaps of ashes, the only remains of former dwellings.'[127]

On their way up the coast, not far from Mdepa's *umzi*, about three or four kilometres from the Ngcwanguba Forest, one of the missionaries, Reverend Stephen Kay, had picked up a human skull 'with part of the pericranium upon it quite fresh' and, rather thrilled with his find, carried it with him as a curiosity. The skull's previous owner had been one of the amaMolo, the descendants of the Indian castaways who had once lived at Brazen Head not far from the Tshomane and who had remained in close contact with them even in exile. Their unusual appearance, remarked the missionary, marked them as 'persons of a mixed character, chiefly of slave extraction;' although their skins were brown like the Mpondo, 'their unusually thick woolly hair and bushy beards rendered them strikingly singular; and on being challenged, they very ingenuously acknowledged their [alien] origin.' Along with the neighbouring Bomvana the amaMolo had suffered terribly at the hands of the marauders, 'who rushed down from the adjacent heights like a torrent; and while the men were endeavouring to secure their herds, the poor women and children were, as usual, left either to flee or perish.' Most had made for the shelter of the nearby forest, but many had been cut off before reaching it and all around were signs of their desperate but futile flight.

It was Kay's first trip to see Bessie's descendants and he found it all rather exotic. Just beyond the amaMolo the missionaries came

> 'into full view of the deep and sinuous channel of the Umtata. Its banks were here exceedingly precipitous, in so much, that riding down was impossible, and even walking was in some places not very safe. After a fatiguing scramble, however, we reached the bed of the river, and forded it without much difficulty. A mile or two more brought us among those of the natives who claim the honour of European lineage. The appearance of the first we met with particularly struck me, being much whiter than I had expected to find them. On riding up to his *umzi*, he came running out to salute us; and very soon gave us to understand, both by words and signs, that, as he had a special

claim upon our attention, he hoped we should not merely notice the colour of his skin, but leave him a present behind.'[128]

It was time the tourists started paying! A little beyond Mdepa's 'wretched' *umzi*, Reverend Kay found the shattered remains of a homestead belonging to one of his sons and, suddenly embarrassed by the skull he was carrying, hid it under a bush, intending to recover it later.

The Tshomane had not fared as badly as their neighbours in the recent fighting. They had proved themselves 'most desperate warriors' and had even managed to retain some of their cattle. (The invaders had taken everything they could lay their hands on and had even eaten the neighbouring dogs, though possibly not so much from hunger as from the belief that it would render them 'more fierce and powerful in battle.'[129]) Mdepa, who had excelled in the art of war, and been so fearless that his enemies had not dared to attack him unless they had double or treble his force, had chosen the Tshomane's refuge well: set on a hill covered in lush vegetation and at the foot of which ran the Mdumbe River, it overlooked 'several beautiful glens, in which the scenery is rich beyond description; and likewise commands a full view of the ocean, not more than a mile or two distant.' It was not only beautiful but, more importantly, strategically secure: 'Behind are steep ravines; in front the sea; and rivers on each side: so that it appears to be marked out as a place of defence.'

In his prime, when Mdepa's 'warlike exploits [were] greatly celebrated,' he had 'been a powerful and active man; now, he was very thin, an elderly man worn down by warfare and want.'[130] Mdepa and his people had been reduced to extreme poverty. Although amaMpondo generally did not eat fish, famine overcame the Tshomane's reservations and they were now surviving largely on shell-fish. For Mdepa it was fitting that in their hour of need Bessie's children were succoured by the same ocean which had carried her to these shores; when one of the missionaries asked him why he had always resided so near the sea, he replied 'because ... it is my mother. From thence I sprang; and from thence I am fed when hungry.'[131] Although the soil was rich and the region well watered, the Tshomane had not been able to grow food or at least harvest a crop successfully for several seasons because of the perpetual disruptions. The shell-fish were supplemented by foraging for wild fruits in the forest and scratching about in the undergrowth for edible plants and roots. All of Mdepa's people exhibited visible signs of starvation. His son Majibana, who just a few years before had been described as tall and coppery, was now, according to Kay,

'one of the most haggard, filthy, and ill-looking natives I ever met with. Some of the others, also, are anything but handsome: their black shaggy beards, long visages, eyes somewhat sunk, prominent noses, and dirty-white skins give them a wild and very unpleasant aspect.'

One of Mdepa's sons, Johnny, had recently drowned while chasing a buck across a river, his rashness, like his brothers' sunken eyes, probably brought about by extreme hunger. 'The mad fellow,' said his father, 'must needs throw away his life for the sake of a buck....'[132]

Adding to his tribulations was a plague of hyenas: in just a few months there had been no less than thirty attacks. Usually content to feed on carrion, the predators – whose jaws are capable of crushing a buffalo's thighbone – were targeting the children. One of their victims was Mdepa's 10-year-old great-grandson, who was dragged from a hut and out into the veld. Although the child's leg was half-severed he survived the attack; his little brother was not so lucky; he had his face torn half-off by a hyena, followed a few nights later by second attack in which he died.[133]

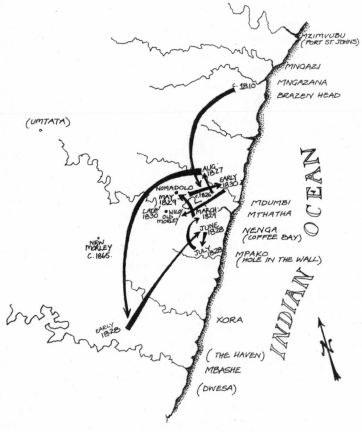

The Tshomane in flight

The missionaries were keen to rebuild Morley, but the Tshomane refused to return to the site. Instead they withdrew to a place called Wilo, south of the Mtata River, where Shepstone rebuilt Morley about six months later.[134]

166

Although it was only about five kilometres from the old one, the new mission was on the other side of the river and in a much safer location.

Nqanda-the-Egg settled within a few minutes walk of the station, the only one of the three Tshomane chiefs to do so, and many of his people began attending church; as things returned to normal and food became more abundant, Shepstone ensured that God got the credit, and the congregation grew. So did the number of children attending school,[135] but although the chiefs maintained a friendly relationship with the mission station they managed to avoid conversion. As I mentioned earlier, the people who joined the mission stations, if not actually 'the worst men in a tribe' as some have claimed,[136] were certainly the neediest. Men of high rank such as Mdepa generally avoided conversion, and the missionaries' journals are peppered with their excuses for not attending church. As Mdepa's age increased he succumbed to a rheumatic disability which provided him with the best excuse of all: 'I would come, I would come to the great place to hear about [God], but I cannot because of my legs,' he told Reverend Palmer, who succeeded Shepstone in 1835. 'It was pleasant when I was there one day; and I would always come to Sunday, but I cannot walk.' His disability did not, however, prevent him from marrying again and fathering a child at the age of 'almost 100.'[137]

His sister Bessy was afflicted with the same rheumatic condition, but hers was so severe it eventually crippled her. Her husband Mjikwa had died sometime in 1829, and when Palmer first met her she was living with her son Gquobile.[138] She was 'a fine-looking old woman, with hair as white as snow,' but her sinews were so contracted that she could not bend her knees at all, not even to rise and certainly not to walk.[139] She asked the missionary to cure her and, when he suggested praying, demanded: 'Where does God live? How can I pray to him when I don't know where he is?' The feisty old lady blamed her mother, Bessie, for not teaching her about God: 'Why did she not? I am her child and God is a person my mother knew. I think she had so much to do with law (meaning politics) that she forgot God.'[140] It was unusual for Mpondo women to be involved in political decisions or deliberations and exceptions were made only in extraordinary circumstances, 'as where a woman has from her age obtained a particular degree of experience, and from her situation commands respect.'[141] That Bessie was so deeply involved in politics is a measure of the esteem in which she was held, but to her daughter it was simple parental neglect, and she sounds almost American in her resentment. 'You are of the same generation,' she told the missionary, 'you must call my mother up again. Why did God let her die?' Before she herself died, Palmer reported happily, Bessy 'sought and found the Lord.'[142] A photograph taken in 1852 or 1853 of her son Gquobile shows a handsome man of strong physique. His beard and hair are neat and trimmed short, the latter decorated with a feather. He wears the ivory armband of a man of rank on his left elbow, and another on his wrist; in his hand he holds a spear and around his neck is a string of what appears to be leopard claws or teeth. His face is calm but attentive, and his features bear the mark of his unusual ancestry, his skin light and his nose prominent.[143] He appears to be aged about 40–45, which means he would have been born between about 1806 and 1811, when his mother Bessy was in her mid-forties.

When Bessy's husband Mjikwa died in 1829, he was succeeded by Gquobile's older brother Gaiya. When Gaiya fell ill and died in March 1834 Gquobile was accused of bewitching him. On trial for his life, he was saved

BESSIE'S GRANDSON (GQUOBILE?)
(AFTER A PHOTO BY CATO, 1853)

from almost certain death by the fortuitous arrival of Reverend Palmer. 'U Pama! I want to go with you. Let me go with you now!' Gquobile shouted and Palmer, realising there was no other way of saving him, took him straight back to Morley mission, where he was joined by his wife and child. How long he remained there – Palmer says he refused to leave[144] – and whether or not he became a Christian like his mother, is unknown.

Despite the inevitable squabbles over cattle and land with the neighbouring people, such as the time when Ngcetane fell out with the Mpondo and named his dog No-Faku (mother of Faku),[145] the early 1830s were a relatively peaceful time for the Tshomane. With no serious warfare to disrupt the region, it was slowly opening up to the outside world and by 1834 there were several traders living at Morley station.[146] Mdepa was still alive in that year,[147] but of such an advanced age that he had not much longer to live. 'He was a very old man when he died,' according to his friend Xelo, 'nearly one hundred years of age, and we buried him.'[148] His grave is

said to lie between Old Morley and Ngcwanguba but closer to the latter, at
the place known as kwaCawu, probably named for his son Cawu.

After his death, Mdepa's principal line moved across the Mpako River,[149]
perhaps fleeing the war that broke out again in 1835. The traders at Morley
fled back to the Colony; Reverend Palmer also left, encouraged by the
Tshomane chiefs.[150] The mission was burnt down for the second time and,
when Palmer returned the following year, only the chapel was still standing,

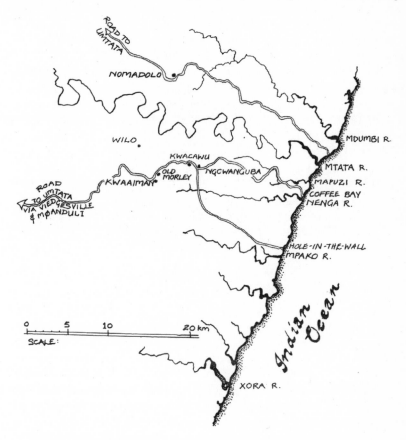

but without its doors and windows.[151] Morley was again rebuilt and for a time
it flourished, but later it fell into disuse and was incorporated into Clarkebury
mission in Thembu territory.[152] It was re-established about 12 kilometres west
in the 1860s by the Reverend William Rayner, a man so diminutive that his
arrival dumbfounded the Tshomane: 'Have all the Englishmen run out?' asked
one after a long pause.[153]

The Tshomane are still to be found in and around Old Morley or
Kwaaiman, as it is known today. It stands on a ridge on all sides of which
the land falls away sharply to the Mtata and its tributaries, particularly to

the east where they flow down to the sea. The gorge is deep and broad, broken into many intersecting *kloofs* crowded with indigenous bush, thick scrubby clusters of dark green tumbling down to the water far below. Morley's elevated position placed it squarely on the route between Xhosa and Pondo territory, and between the Colony and Port Natal, and the many refugees who found a haven at the mission were soon followed by the traders, missionaries, and others. Gradually the footpath along the ridges turned into a wagon track. The modern road follows the same high, winding route of earlier times; tarred from its intersection with the main Umtata road to Kwaaiman, it then becomes a gravel road leading down to the seaside hotel and cottages at Hole-in-the-Wall.

There is little to be seen at Morley today: a police station, an old signboard saying 'Kwaaiman' and a boarded-up trading store, a scattering of huts and a wattle-and-daub church-cum-schoolroom, complete with browsing cows. It is too tiny to be a village, just a slightly denser arrangement of the thatch and mud-walled huts that dot the neighbouring ridges. The only trees are small clusters of wattle and a few towering gum trees, neither of which is indigenous to South Africa. I found nothing at all to hint at the complex histories and the mysteries of the people it once served, but parked in a ditch next to the road was one of those strange and incongruous things so peculiar to the (former) Transkei: a car decorated with lengths of bright ribbons, a wedding carriage with no groom or bride in sight and all its wheels missing.

Genealogy of Mdepa and Bessy

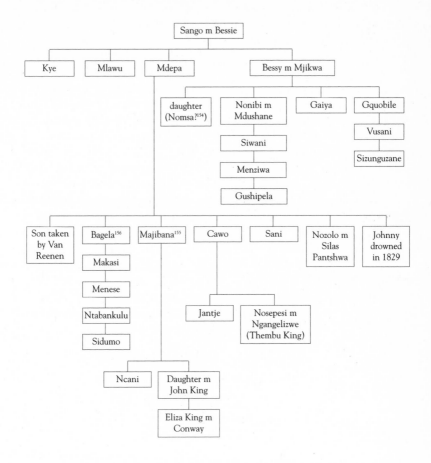

Genealogy of the Lochenbergs

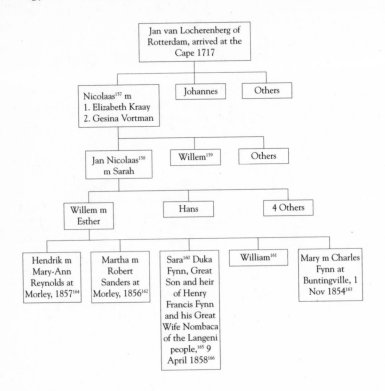

Jan van Locherenberg of Rotterdam, arrived at the Cape 1717

Nicolaas[157] m
1. Elizabeth Kraay
2. Gesina Vortman

Johannes

Others

Jan Nicolaas[158] m Sarah

Willem[159]

Others

Willem m Esther

Hans

4 Others

Hendrik m Mary-Ann Reynolds at Morley, 1857[164]

Martha m Robert Sanders at Morley, 1856[162]

Sara[160] Duka Fynn, Great Son and heir of Henry Francis Fynn and his Great Wife Nombaca of the Langeni people,[165] 9 April 1858[166]

William[161]

Mary m Charles Fynn at Buntingville, 1 Nov 1854[163]

Chapter Eight

The Gathering Storm

'...The descendants of Quma and her unhappy companions are now scattered about to a very considerable extent.'[1]

[2]

It was not only warfare that scattered the children of castaways far and wide across the land but also their powerful connections and, in some cases, their beauty: the infusion of alien genes into the coastal clans, themselves a fine-looking people, produced some real stunners, especially among the women. One of these young nubiles had a British officer in a sweat:

> 'Tall and well made, and wrapped in an ample kaross of white sheep-skin, she had one of the most regular and pleasing countenances I ever saw. Her complexion was light brown; her nose, lips, and teeth beautiful; her eyes "globes of fire"; and her dark hair "ensnaring the hearts of lovers". On enquiry who this African beauty was, I found that she had come from the far Umzimfoobo; was supposed to be of Malay descent; and was now the wife of Mr Ayliffe's bastard wagoner. Lucky bastard!'[3]

Like her, Bessie's female descendants were much admired for their exotic beauty, attaining such celebrity for their looks and charm that they were highly sought after as the wives – frequently the Great Wives and Queen Mothers – of high-ranking chiefs and even kings.[4] As a result the lives of her descendants were entwined with virtually every pivotal event in the history of our country as it was played out on the eastern Frontier. The leader of the most significant attack on the British in the region in the 19th century – the man who nearly succeeded in driving the colonists into the sea, that symbolic dunking in the amniotic fluid of pre-existence which indigenous people across the globe and the centuries tried their damnedest to do, in the hope that it would solve their problems once and for all – was, for example, married to Bessie's granddaughter, Nonibe.[5]

His name was Mdushane, and he was one of most enigmatic of the Xhosa chiefs. A large and widely respected man, he was celebrated for his military skills and renowned for his courage,[6] and he commanded the most powerful Xhosa army ever assembled at that time – yet surprisingly little is known about him. He planned and executed some of the boldest and bravest military manoeuvres against both the British and his rival chiefs – yet he has been virtually ignored by history. He came within a hair's breadth of turning back the tide of British imperialism in South Africa, the only one of all the Frontier chiefs to do so – yet it was his diviner, rather than he himself, who received the credit. And typically, ironically, and despite his achievements, Mdushane appears in our story mainly because of his wife, because she was descended from Bessie.[7]

Mdushane's own ancestry was impressive. The eldest son[8] of Ndlambe, an extremely powerful chief and prince of the Xhosa Royal House, Mdushane was directly descended from Phalo, the king at whose Great Place the Hubner traders had been killed in 1736. Phalo was the last king to rule the Xhosa as a whole; on his death in 1775 there were two main contenders to the crown, and the ensuing power-play split the nation in two.

It was traditional, as mentioned above, for an important chief to marry his Great Wife fairly late in life. This tended to encourage Xhosa expansionism, since the Great Son and legitimate heir was often still a minor at the time of his father's death while his half- brothers, the sons of lesser wives, were frequently fully-grown men with established support bases. And that is exactly what happened when King Phalo died in 1775. His Great Son, Gcaleka, a 'sensitive and sickly individual,'[9] had only just reached manhood, while his older half-brother, Rharhabe, was already in his prime and enjoyed wide support. Although he was not the official heir, Rharhabe was 'a man of public weight, wisdom, and superior courage…. For common sense and physical courage, he was far and away the superior of Gcaleka'[10] – in short, the perfect candidate for king. Rharhabe, however, chose not to usurp the throne and shortly after his father's death he and his followers broke away and moved south-west in search of their own territory, across the Kei River. (Gcaleka and his supporters stayed on their lands east of the Kei River; he remained the paramount Xhosa authority and his people, the Gcaleka-Xhosa, constitute the senior branch of the nation to this day.)

Rharhabe ran headlong into trouble: even as his people were crossing the Kei they came under attack from the Khoikhoi who occupied the country beyond it. Both sides had everything to lose – the Khoi, desperate to protect their families and preserve their land, put up a violent struggle against the invaders, while the amaRharhabe had nowhere else to go but forward – and a violent fight ensued. As they fought hand to hand in the swirling water, the mighty Kei became so choked with the bodies of the dead and dying, it is said, that its waters ran red with blood. Eventually Rharhabe succeeded in driving the Khoi back, but rather than face an ongoing war, he negotiated to purchase their land from them. He paid a great number of cattle to their queen Hoho, whose husband had been killed in the battle, and in exchange obtained a vast territory between the Buffalo and Keiskamma rivers,[11] including the natural fortress of the Amatola mountains. In time he extended his authority further south to the Great Fish River, but he had no jurisdiction over the independent Xhosa chiefdoms there,[12] and in the years that followed, as the Cape Boers spread eastwards and began settling in the same area – causing the Cape government to note with some trepidation that its citizens 'almost live mixed together with the Kafirs'[13] – Rharhabe's people were increasingly caught up in a political firestorm not entirely of their own making.

Initially the Boers had occupied the land only for short periods, seeking temporary grazing for their herds and withdrawing when the season was over, but in time they began establishing permanent farms. Not exactly noteworthy conservationists, they had systematically overgrazed the lands closer to the Cape; one contemporary traveller noted that 'in direct contradiction to the custom and example of the original inhabitants the Hottentots [Khoi], the colonists turn their cattle out constantly into the same fields, and that too in a much greater quantity....'[14] As early as 1772 large parts of the south-western Cape had already been destroyed by the

Armed San[15]

Boers' herds, and as the land became overpopulated or the grazing fell off they simply spread further afield, monopolising the water sources, decimating the wildlife and destroying or displacing the indigenous Khoisan.

With nowhere else to go, and no inclination anyway to give up their bountiful and beautiful land, the Khoisan fought back with every means at their disposal. Following a skirmish in 1777 a San leader called Koerikei or 'Bullet dodger' had a revealing conversation with his Boer opponent. Carefully placing himself beyond firing-range, he called down to Commandant Carel van der Merwe: 'What are you doing on my land?' he asked. 'You have taken all the places where the eland and other game live. Why did you not stay where the sun goes down, where you first came from?' When Van der Merwe was evasive, shouting that the San should try to live in peace with the Boers, Koerikei snapped back fiercely that 'he did not want to lose the country of his birth, and that he would kill their herdsmen, and that he would chase them all away.'[16]

Violence on both sides became an everyday occurrence. Contemporary Cape Dutch dispatches became cluttered with statistics, lives lost, cattle stolen, farmhouses burnt and shelters destroyed. As the situation deteriorated into full-blown guerrilla warfare the Boers resorted to what can only be called genocide, particularly of the hunter-gathering San.[17] The men were hunted down and destroyed; only the children were spared, and occasionally the women, to be carried off into slavery. A typical document of the time reads:

> '2nd September, divided the little Bushmen among our men as follows: J.J. Swanepoel, a girl; Alewyn Johannes, a Hottentot; L.J. Vorie, a Hottentot; David Vorie, a little Hottentot; C. Harmse, a girl; W.S. van Heere, a little boy.'[18]

The blandness of the words masks the terrible tragedy of these children, caught up in the systematic destruction of their entire nation. Hunted like animals, their parents murdered, they faced a lifetime of slavery and abuse. For the Boers, however, it was a convenient – and officially sanctioned – reward for the dangers and expenses of commando duty. Besides their gunpowder, which was provided by the Cape government, everything else they needed on commando had to be supplied by the farmers themselves: the wagons, oxen, horses, manpower, food, etc. When the authorities later tried to prevent the farmers from enslaving the San, the Boers became far less enthusiastic about their commando duties. As one official observed:

> '[T]he prohibition to their carrying off women and children has greatly served to damp the ardour for commandos, and has actuated the farmers as much as humanity in their tenderness to the Bosjesmen, a feeling that their great want of servants has tended to promote.'[19]

The longevity and ferocity of the San resistance meant that many of the Boers found themselves on commando more frequently than on their farms. Happily for them, however, the farm labour shortage was gradually being alleviated by the subjugation of the pastoralist Khoikhoi; displaced and landless, many of them survived by working for the colonists as herders and cowboys,[20] and some of the Boers began to send them on patrol instead of going themselves. Other Boers refused to participate at all and their excuses must surely rank among the most creative in the history of our country. One exasperated commandant, who had ordered a certain C de Klerk to send his wagon on commando and then had to send an additional demand for its tilt (canvas hood), received a very cocky letter instead:

> 'Monsieur D.S. van der Merwe. You write me to send my wagon tilt tomorrow, which is impossible that I can do, as it is the bolster of my bed. I am not unwilling, if I had enough bed clothes, to give the tilt, but I am deficient in these.... The tilt of which I write you, is the bolster for my head, and my wife is my mattrass; so if you claim the tilt by force, order the mattrass with it, as cook.'[21]

As the Boers prevailed against the Khoisan their eastward spread continued; even such incidents as the Hubner massacre did little to discourage it. By 1752 the most easterly Boers were at the Klein Brak River,[22] but within 20 years they had spread into the Zuurveld – the coastal lands running from just north of today's Port Elizabeth to the Great Fish River – and beyond. Even before the Great Fish River was officially proclaimed as the Xhosa–Cape border in 1780, the wild Prinsloos of Agter Bruintjes Hoogte were stealing and killing north of it.[23] Official reaction to the Boers' expansionism varied from decade to decade, but mostly the Dutch authorities simply turned a blind eye. The Frontier, it has been said, was in any case a barrier that existed more in theory than in reality, a shifting boundary of little import to either the colonial or Xhosa cattle farmers. Living cheek by jowl and competing for the same resources, it was probably inevitable that the two would clash. In time what had begun as an uneasy co-existence began to deteriorate into aggression, brutality and, eventually, into open warfare. And if the colonists had struggled to overcome the Khoisan, they had no idea how much tougher the Xhosa would be. The name alone should have warned them: '//kosa' means 'angry men' in the Khoi language.[24]

As the skirmishing and squabbling between the Boers and the independent Xhosa clans of the Zuurveld escalated, Rharhabe – whose lands lay just north of the disputed territory – tried to maintain his neutrality. He 'sent word to the Boers dissociating himself from these disturbances.... He had no quarrel with the whites and desired none.'[25] He had no such reservations about the Thembu, however, and sometime between 1782 and 1787 he invaded their territory and was killed on the battlefield. Rharhabe was about 60 and left several grown sons, but his Great Son had been killed in the same battle and as *his* heir was only 11 years old, the regency fell to Ndlambe, the second son of the Great House and father of Mdushane, future husband of Bessie's granddaughter.

Ndlambe was always smiling, his conversation 'a succession of laughter.'[26] But behind his sunny exterior was a smart and extremely ambitious man, and with him an aggressive new dynamic was born.[27] Intent on expanding his territory and consolidating his power, he attacked the Gqunukhwebe, an independent clan of mixed Khoi-Xhosa origin, and drove them deep into the Zuurveld, where increasing numbers of Boers and their vast sleek herds had settled. The refugees, hungry and smarting from the loss of their own cattle, were presented with a temptation they found impossible to resist; in a flurry of theft and counter-theft, accusations and counter-accusations, war eventually broke out between the Boers and Xhosa in 1779, followed a few years later by a second. So began a hundred years of war.

Xhosa chief, believed to be Ndlambe[28]

Ndlambe, meanwhile, had proved to be an extremely popular regent – so popular, in fact, that when the real heir, his nephew Ngqika, came of age he had to resort to arms in order to claim his crown.[29] In the fighting that followed, Ndlambe was defeated and held prisoner for a time at Ngqika's Great Place on the upper Keiskamma River (the site of the present Fort Hare university), but in about 1799 he broke away with his followers and several of his brothers, and settled in the Zuurveld – right in the gun-sights of the Boers.[30] The increasing population and escalating competition for resources affected adversely the relationship between the Boers and Xhosa, and although Ndlambe tried to stabilise the situation – even, on occasion, personally executing followers found guilty of stealing Boer cattle – even he could not prevent the cattle raiding nor control the minor chiefs who were responsible for the bulk of the depredations.[31] When the third Frontier war broke out Ndlambe, who in the previous war had assisted the colonists against the independent Xhosa, suddenly found himself fighting against them.[32]

His rival Ngqika, meanwhile, aligned himself with the colonists. Fatherless from an early age, he was extremely close to his mother Yese, a skilful politician who advised him on affairs of state and with her own interpreter, a Dutch-speaking runaway Bengali slave from the Cape,[33] accompanied him in negotiations with visiting colonial officials. She was hugely fat – so corpulent that even walking tired her and when this occurred on the way to a meeting she would simply lie down at the side of the road and wait for a special cart to fetch her. She was also a woman of enormous appetites, fond of wine – a partiality that Ngqika unfortunately inherited[34] – and powerful men. One of her conquests was Ndlambe, with whom she had been co-regent during her son's minority. Another was Coenraad de Buys, leader of the rebel Boers (of whom Nicolaas Lochenberg was one) who had taken up residence at Ngqika's Great Place. The affair between this fabulously obese woman and the gigantic De Buys has inspired much interest in otherwise sober historians:

> 'The match between the outsize Boer and equally outsize Xhosa Queen mother probably had its erotic attractions for both. Xhosa widows were notorious for their amorous adventures. De Buys was insatiable in his lust for attractive half-caste or black women. The Boers liked their women large; their own flourished as corpulently as Ngqika's mother; and with both these individuals passion was complemented by the management of power in that wide frontier zone, which both obviously enjoyed.'[35]

Under his mother's guidance, Ngqika's influence had grown and by 1803 the 26-year-old chief was at the peak of his power and extremely handsome, a man possessing 'spirit, determination and character and… an unusually intelligent grasp of affairs,' reported his Dutch allies, '… for a Kaffir….'[36]

The young chief's own people, however, were slowly becoming disenchanted with him. He grew increasingly arrogant and abrasive, and gained a reputation for being 'rude and outspoken in his language and behaviour, and reckless of evil consequences, comporting himself in a manner which often grieved his relatives.'[37] In 1807, he further alienated them by abducting one of Ndlambe's favourite wives, Thuthula, who was reputed to be the most beautiful woman in the land.[38] As Ngqika was Ndlambe's nephew, the seduction was regarded as incest, provoking such shock and disgust that, according to the historian Jeff Peires, the incident was still considered reprehensible nearly two centuries later.[39]

As Ngqika's popularity declined, Ndlambe's was growing, and by 1809 he was the most powerful chief in the Zuurveld.[40] Despite intermittent skirmishing with other Xhosa and the Boers, it was a time of peace and plenty; the amaNdlambe herds were magnificent, their cattle fat and healthy, and their crops were flourishing. Their gardens, wrote a British official in 1811, were 'very large and numerous; and here also are the best garden pumpkins I have ever seen; some of the pumpkins are five and a half feet round, and the corn ten feet high.'[41]

Genealogy of the amaXhosa: Gcaleka and Rharhabe

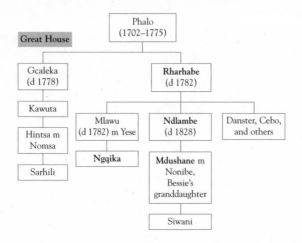

Unfortunately the man who penned these words had been sent to destroy the very gardens he so admired. In 1806 the British had occupied the Cape and ousted the Dutch, becoming the ruling authority of a vast territory that stretched all the way to the eastern Cape – and inheriting all the problems of their predecessors. Now, in an all-out effort to bring Frontier hostilities to an end, the British governor had ordered a military force under Lieutenant-Colonel John Graham to drive all the Xhosa, including Ndlambe, out of the Zuurveld and over the Fish River boundary.

Although the relationship between Boer and Xhosa had been fraught with sporadic outbreaks of violence, in many ways the two were dependent on one another and their interaction co-operative. They frequently engaged in mutually beneficial trade and even military alliances. Besides the obvious similarity of both being cattle farmers, they were alike in many other ways too. Like the Xhosa, many of the Frontier Boers were illiterate, they wore clothes made of animal skins, shod their feet in the same, lived in wattle-and-daub huts and hunted for the pot. They valued the freedom of the vast open spaces, drove a hard bargain and admired the manly virtues of courage and expertise on the battlefield, protecting their womenfolk and providing for their families. The bonds of kinship were powerful factors in the lives of both the emerging Afrikaner nation and the Xhosa-speaking nations. Prior to the arrival of the British, says Hermann Giliomee, 'the European and the Xhosa on the frontier had in some respects resembled a couple in a disastrous forced marriage: they would fear and fight each other, but neither would destroy the other....'[42]

All this changed with the advent of the British military machine. Whereas the Xhosa had concentrated on trying to abduct the enemy's cattle and women – the purpose of warfare for them being 'not the destruction of productive resources, but their acquisition and absorption'[43] – the British employed a scorched-earth policy. Lieutenant-Colonel Graham issued his troops with instructions that if anyone should 'make any attempt to resist they are to be fired upon.'[44] Contrary to Xhosa traditions, the British killed women (the soldiers apparently found it difficult to distinguish between them and their menfolk) and ruthlessly destroyed the Xhosa food supplies. The soldiers drove herds of oxen through their gardens, systematically trampling the summer crops that stood ripe and ready for harvesting.[45] One of Ndlambe's sons sent an urgent request to the British commander to halt the destruction until the harvest was gathered, after which, he promised, his people would move quietly beyond the Fish River; by way of reply the British clapped his messenger in irons and tied him to a wagon wheel with a leather thong around his neck. Taken out the next day to lead the soldiers to Ndlambe, he led them instead on a wild goose-chase, which lasted three days and gave Ndlambe and his sons time to escape. One hopes that the brave messenger was able to do likewise.[46]

The unprovoked invasion drove thousands upon thousands of men, women and children from their land. By February 1812 Graham boasted that 'hardly a trace of a Caffer man remains.'[47] The fertile valleys – 'exceedingly beautiful, much resembling a nobleman's park in England, being covered with the finest grass interspersed with trees'[48] – were empty of all but the ruins of homesteads. Within a year the amaNdlambe alone had lost over 6 400 *square kilometres* of territory.[49] Driven northwards over the Fish, they settled around the Keiskamma and Buffalo rivers.[50] Deprived of their cattle, many struggled to survive[51] and although 27 military posts were established along the Fish River to keep them out of the Colony, it was not long before they were back. Hunger and desperation left them no choice, and the drought of 1813 compounded their predicament, driving the Xhosa back into the Zuurveld in search of grazing for their remaining herds. The Boers and British launched retaliatory raids against them; no mercy was shown and no prisoners taken: 'The orders on the frontier were to shoot all Kaffirs,' said a colonist.[52] From 1815–18 there was another devastating drought, which intensified the spiral of violence, expulsion and return.

As a British ally Ngqika had been spared from expulsion, but the alliance had proved a double-edged sword. He found himself in the impossible position of trying to please both the colonists and his own people, compelled to perform a delicate balancing act by both condemning and condoning cattle raiding, in order to secure British military support against Ndlambe on the one hand and on the other to maintain the support of his subordinate chiefs. Many of his supporters were leaving him in favour of Ndlambe, but despite his waning influence the Cape government chose to treat Ngqika as the paramount authority and supreme sovereign of all the Xhosa: 'the white man made an agreement with the first person he met –

Ngqika, c1803[53]

counting for nothing,'[54] said the poet and historian Mqhayi. When the British appropriated a huge chunk of Ngqika's best land, stretching from the Fish to the Keiskamma River, to establish a buffer zone between the Colony and the ousted Xhosa, he was powerless to prevent it. As the British tightened their grip on the Frontier, immigrants and traders began to flow into the area in increasing numbers; brandy was introduced 'in floods'[55] and Ngqika took to it like a fish to water.[56] It was whispered that he had 'sold the land in exchange for colonial assistance and a bottle of brandy'[57] – land which was not his to dispose of, as it belonged to the people as a whole.

Dagga (marijuana) was a traditional soporific and sorghum beer a traditional drink, but it seems that neither had prepared the Xhosa for the highs – and ultimate lows – of Cape brandy. Its impact on our country's history cannot be underestimated: 'If dagga and tobacco were the first tiny storm clouds to appear in the sky, brandy was undoubtedly the raging thunderstorm itself.'[58] So many chiefs succumbed to alcoholism that it must rank as one of the most effective weapons in the colonial arsenal; not only in South Africa but in Australia, the Americas and throughout the world, indigenous people let their land slip through their fingers as they opened their hands to grasp the bottle. And as Ngqika's behaviour became increasing degraded, fuelled by his taste for Cape Smoke, his followers left in droves. History has judged him harshly: although other chiefs formed

alliances with the colonists when it was expedient for them to do so, it is
Ngqika who is remembered as a sell-out. Ndlambe, by comparison, has
managed to maintain both his dignity and his independence in popular
memory: 'One sees the beginnings of a passionate black nationalism in
Ndlambe,' one commentator has said; not only did he refuse to allow British
and Boer commandos to reclaim cattle from his kraals, he positively

> 'stated that the Xhosa were as much a nation as the English and were
> not to be treated as if they were subjects to the Colonial
> Government. His people entirely agreed with him, as did the subjects
> of Ngqika who again began to drift away from him to Ndlambe.'[59]

Although he had at least ten wives, Ndlambe had never taken a Great
Wife and consequently had no official heir, but if this was a deliberate attempt
to avoid the successionist struggles of his father and grandfather, it was
doomed to failure. His problems began even before the birth of his first child.

Soon after marrying his first wife Ndlambe had gone off to war. Shortly
after his return she gave birth and, suspecting that she had been unfaithful
during his absence, Ndlambe drove her away and refused to recognise the
child as his. The infant Mdushane – who was later to marry Bessie's
granddaughter Nonibe – and his mother were taken in by Ndlambe's brother
Cebo who, having no son of his own, adopted the boy as his heir. By a
strange quirk of fate, Mdushane ended up at the same *umzi* as his father's
rival, Ngqika, the two boys, who were of the same age, growing up together
at their grandfather Rharhabe's Great Place.[60] Hurt and resentful of his
father's treatment of his mother, Mdushane grew up to support Ngqika
against Ndlambe in his dispute over the chieftainship. Had the two young
men remained allies, the political dynamics of the Frontier – and the history
of South Africa – might have been entirely different, but as he grew,
Mdushane's resemblance to his father became increasingly obvious and
because he 'exhibited traits which proved him to be a man of outstanding
ability and, as a Chief, superior to all his contemporaries among the Xosa
chiefs of his day,' Ndlambe's counsellors set about reconciling the two.[61]
Unfortunately for Ngqika it was at this critical juncture that he carried out
his ill-considered abduction of Ndlambe's wife, the beautiful Thuthula, an
action which so offended Mdushane that he broke off their friendship and
joined forces with his father,[62] bringing with him 'such an accession of
strength' that in the subsequent battle, which took place at Amalinde,
Ndlambe was able to defeat Ngqika.[63]

All the preparations for the battle of Amalinde and the assembly of the
amaNdlambe forces were entirely under Mdushane's control,[64] and he used
his resources well. His masterstroke was to forge an alliance with the Xhosa
king, Hintsa. There was no love lost between Hintsa and Ngqika: as a child,
in about 1800, Hintsa had been seized by Ngqika, who then proclaimed
himself king of all the Xhosa, and murdered his uncle. Recently Ngqika had

defeated him again in a clash over grazing rights, and an alliance with the powerful amaNdlambe must have seemed the perfect opportunity for revenge.[65] It was customary, in any case, for chiefs to use their family ties and marital bonds to strengthen or establish political alliances and Mdushane and Hintsa were distant cousins. Their Great Wives were also related to one another, both being members of the Bomvana royal family.

Mdushane's Great Wife was Nonibe, the daughter of Bessie's youngest child, Bessy, and Mjikwa, chief of the Nkumba clan. Hintsa's Great Wife Nomsa belonged to the Tshezi, the ruling clan of Gambushe, the chief whom Van Reenen had met in 1790, at Mngazi near Bessie's village, and who had led the Bomvana south to settle in Hintsa's territory in about 1810. Distantly related on their fathers' side, the two women may have been even closer on their mothers' side.

In *The Cradle Days of Natal* the historian Mackeurtan makes the intriguing statement that 'Nomsa and Nonubie, wives of two Transkeian chieftains, in the early nineteenth century' were both 'of mixed blood.'[66] Although he does not name his sources, it was common knowledge in the 19th century that Nonibe, for one, was descended from a white woman,[67] the castaway Bessie. By the time I came across Mackeurtan's statement I knew enough to recognise that he was right on at least three out of four points; the only point I was not sure about was Nomsa's mixed ancestry. And despite a lot of digging around in old colonial papers and memoirs, the only supporting evidence I found was a fleeting reference describing her son, Sarhili, as 'half-black'.[68] Nomsa's genealogy named only her paternal ancestors – her father was Ntshunqe, Great son and heir of Gambushe[69] – but despite a lengthy investigation I could not find out anything about her mother or grandmother, not even their names. I had, in fact, abandoned the search when I discovered a letter stating unequivocally that Nomsa's grandmother had been a white castaway. In 1877 Nomsa's brother, the Bomvana chief Moni, told WRD Fynn, the author of the letter, about two white women

> 'rescued from a wreck, near the Umtata mouth. Nutshunci was at that time Chief of the Bomvanas, and he took these two women to wife, and these women were the grandmothers of Moni himself, and also of Nomsa, who was Kreli's [Sarhili's] mother, and that is how Kreli came to have a strain of European (Scotch) blood in his veins.'[70]

Moni was in his eighties, blind and physically weak, but there was nothing feeble about his mind: 'his mental faculties were perfect.'[71] Fynn is also a credible source, fluent in isiXhosa and personally acquainted with the chiefs concerned – according to Nomsa's son Sarhili, he was 'born and brought up with me.'[72] Fynn served as Resident to Sarhili from 1865 and Resident to Moni from 1875–78.[73] Yet there is a glaring inconsistency in his story: if the white castaway was Moni and Nomsa's grandmother, she had to have been married to their grandfather Gambushe, not their father Ntshunqe.

Fynn assumed that the wreck was the *Grosvenor,* but since Ntshunqe became chief of the Bomvana only when Gambushe died in about 1826,[74] more than 40 years after the Indiaman was wrecked, he is more likely to have married a descendant of its survivors than the castaways themselves – unless he had a thing for (much) older women. In any case the *Grosvenor* is so ubiquitous to stories of white female castaways on the Wild Coast, it should be taken with a pinch of the old iodised: for all the tales to be true the ship would have needed an exclusively white female crew endowed with long golden hair, becomingly dishevelled bodices and firm morals against cohabiting with swarthy men which were not only easily put aside but were complemented by amazing fecundity.

Although some of the white men from the *Grosvenor* certainly reached the Mtata mouth, as far as I have been able to ascertain seven-year-old Mary Wilmot is the only one of the female survivors to have travelled that far, and she did not stop there but settled much further south.[75]

Bessie's daughter Bessy, however, lived near the Mtata, with her husband the Bomvana chief Mjikwa, from about 1810 until her death. As she was not Bessie's only daughter,[76] it is not inconceivable for her sister, perhaps the eldest one called Kye, to have married the Bomvana Chief Gambushe and been Nomsa and Moni's grandmother. If so, Nomsa's Great Son Sarhili was related by blood to Bessie's son Mdepa. Circumstantial evidence that that was indeed the case is supplied by William Bazley, the old Natal settler and *Grosvenor* fan, who was adamant that Mdepa and Sarhili were related, though he was not sure exactly how.[77]

In the mid-1880s Xelo, a Thembu counsellor who was educated by the Wesleyans and who had known Bessie's son Mdepa personally at Morley mission in the 1830s, told a colonial official that Mdepa's mother had been 'wrecked at the mouth of the Umneno River between Port St Johns and the mouth of the Umtata River.'[78] William Strachan, a trader who knew the locality well, confirmed that the remains of a wreck could be seen at the mouth of the Mnenu.[79] I find it hard to believe that after one hundred and fifty odd years of being battered by Wild Coast storms, Bessie's ship would still have been visible above the surface. Either there was a muddle-up of names – a confusion of the Nanga who found Bessie with the similar-sounding Mnenu river – or the wreck was that of another ship altogether.[80]

According to Fynn: 'The three Chiefs now in Bomvanaland, Serunu, Charlie, and Dumas, are the great-great-grandchildren of those white women, and they are very light in complexion.'[81] Two of them, Serunu and 'Charlie' (Tyhali), were Moni's sons,[82] while 'Dumas' or Ndamase was the eldest son of the Mpondo King Faku, born about 1800 to Faku's Right-hand Wife and favourite, Noqiya. She was a woman of high status, 'intombi ka Nqayiya, Kwa-Bomvana,'[83] a girl of the Nqayiya clan of the Bomvana, Gambushe's brother's line.

It would appear, therefore, that several present-day Xhosa-speaking royal families are descended from white castaways and, perhaps, from Bessie in particular. This fits with the fact that Bessie's female descendants were much sought after as the wives of powerful chiefs. Nomsa's and Nonibe's husbands were certainly powerful, the most powerful men in the region in fact – the king of the Xhosa and the amaNdlambe heir respectively, no less.

Traditionally the Xhosa kings almost always took their Great Wives from the Thembu, yet Hintsa broke with tradition to marry Nomsa.[84] The reason was probably political. Because of their white ancestry Bessie's female descendants were widely regarded as being 'wise and friendly to the white people,'[85] and at a time when the English were the most important single threat facing the Xhosa, having a wife of English descent could be a definite asset.

Genealogy of Nomsa

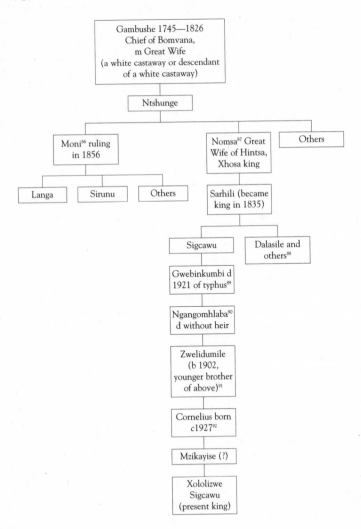

Gambushe 1745—1826
Chief of Bomvana,
m Great Wife
(a white castaway or descendant
of a white castaway)

Ntshunge

Moni[86] ruling in 1856

Nomsa[87] Great Wife of Hintsa, Xhosa king

Others

Langa

Sirunu

Others

Sarhili (became king in 1835)

Sigcawu

Dalasile and others[88]

Gwebinkumbi d 1921 of typhus[89]

Ngangomhlaba[90] d without heir

Zwelidumile (b 1902, younger brother of above)[91]

Cornelius born c1927[92]

Mzikayise (?)

Xololizwe Sigcawu (present king)

The alliance of Mdushane and Hintsa against Ngqika at Amalinde was spectacularly successful. (Amalinde, or Debe Nek as it is sometimes known, is a most extraordinary place, a sea of undulating, shifting green mounds caused by giant earthworms. These creatures, capable of reaching nearly two metres in length, were once found over large parts of Africa, but are now restricted to this small region. The shifting hillocks are actually huge piles of worm faeces endlessly recycling through the bowels of the worms, the soil so hardened with excess calcium that it grinds down the teeth of grazing livestock.) The confrontation took place in October 1818, and was one of the most critical and desperate battles in Xhosa history.[93] Led by Mdushane and equipped with a number of horses and some firearms, the amaNdlambe out-numbered and out-manoeuvred Ngqika's men. Slowly the latter began to give way, retreating – it is said – for the first time in their history, yet still maintaining their discipline and fighting an orderly rearguard action, even as Mdushane's forces cut them down in their hundreds. As darkness fell, the victors scoured the surrounding bush, dispatching their wounded enemies. It was a spectacular victory for Mdushane and an unprecedented defeat for his opponent: all but one of Ngqika's counsellors were killed and some families lost every single one of their menfolk in the battle. Ngqika himself survived, however.[94] Fleeing into the Winterberg, he called on the British to honour their military commitment to him and, on 7 December 1818, they did.

Despite Ndlambe's repeated assurances that he had no hostile intentions against them,[95] the colonial forces attacked, demolishing his Great Place with artillery[96] and taking 23 000 head of cattle. Nine thousand of these were given to Ngqika. For Ndlambe and his 'scarcely-less powerful son' Mdushane, it was the last straw. Turning against the Colony, they raided as far south as today's city of Port Elizabeth, taking as many cattle as they could to replenish their herds, driving out the Boers and burning their farms, and forcing the British from their newly erected forts.[97] On 21 April Mdushane sent a message to the commanding officer of Military HQ in Grahamstown, informing him that he would be joining him for breakfast the following morning. The element of surprise had no place in Xhosa military tradition: no self-respecting chief went into battle without first making a public declaration of war so that his enemy could prepare himself against attack.[98] But Mdushane's message encapsulated so much more than mere protocol. It was a statement of confidence, challenge and wit. The man had *attitude*.

For reasons of his own Colonel Willshire chose to ignore the message. The next morning began peacefully enough, but while he was inspecting his troops at about ten o'clock he was informed that Xhosa had been seen driving the cattle from the commonage, and rode out to see for himself. He was back in town almost immediately, chased by several hundred armed men. The surrounding hills were alive with Xhosa armed to the teeth and in their full battle regalia, and for Willshire the penny finally dropped: 'From their numbers I instantly concluded they intended an attack on Grahamstown....'[99]

From where I sit writing this, in the old Settler quarter of Grahamstown, I can see Makana's Kop quite clearly, the *kopje* and adjacent ridge to the east of the village where the Xhosa gathered in their thousands. It is April, the same month in which Mdushane launched his attack almost 200 years ago, and the recent rains have turned the grassy slopes of the hill, now dotted

Grahamstown, May 1820[100]

with houses, shacks and yards, a deep green and the sky is a bright luminous blue. Against such a blue, Mdushane's forces, smeared with red clay, must have seemed like a slash of newly spilt blood as they massed along the ridge. Willshire must have watched their rapidly swelling ranks with alarm – for they outnumbered his own force by about ten to one – and later he admitted he 'would not have given a feather for the safety of the town.'[101] The Xhosa shared his opinion and were so certain of victory that they had brought their women and children with them, who now waited on the flats behind them with their cooking pots, sleeping mats and food, ready to follow the men into the village after the battle and reoccupy the land which had once been theirs.[102]

Mdushane had laid his plans with care;[103] he had several spies in the village, and from them and his war-doctor Makana, who had frequently visited Grahamstown in the past,[104] he knew both its layout and the strength of its defenders. The garrison was small, consisting of some 450 white troops of the 38th Light Infantry and the Royal African Corps, the latter made up largely of criminals who had volunteered for the army rather than serving their sentences,[105] and their officers, together with 120 coloured and Khoi Cape Corps cavalry under a white officer – a total of almost 580 men.[106] Fewer than that, though, were still in the village: through an interpreter named Hendrick Nquka, Mdushane had fed the British false information about a disturbance near the Fish River mouth, and Willshire had taken the bait, sending 100 men of the 38th under Major Frazer off to investigate – and effectively depleting his defenders by almost a fifth.[107]

Grahamstown had been founded seven years before, in 1812; by 1819 it consisted of only 30-odd buildings, but despite its small size it was an important place, the British military headquarters for the entire eastern Frontier region. Situated in a small valley rimmed by gently rising hills, it was in the heart of what had once been Ndlambe's territory – according to tradition, his Great Place had stood on the site of the present cathedral – and he was determined to reclaim it.[108] The outcome of the battle was therefore of vital importance to both sides and, given Mdushane's experience and numerical superiority, should have been a forgone conclusion. Several factors militated against his success, however. One was his opponent: 'Tiger Tom' Willshire was an experienced officer and skilled tactician who had been a lieutenant since the unbelievable age of seven (his father had purchased his commission as an ensign when he was six, upgrading it a year later).[109] Another was Mdushane's war-doctor, the powerful mystic and prophet, Makana: at a sacrificial ceremony (*ukukafula*) before the battle, Makana harangued Mdushane's forces with prophecies of victory, and fortified them with the flesh of the sacrificial cattle and various battle-charms.[110] Their ancestors were with them, he assured the assembled fighters, and would strike down the English like lightning. The British bullets would turn to water, he declared, and such was the respect he commanded that they believed him.[111] But the primary threat to Mdushane was the British heavy artillery; loaded with round-shot and shrapnel the guns were effective to almost 800 metres,[112] capable of pinning down the Xhosa under a hail of shot from well outside the range of their throwing assegais or the few firearms they possessed.

At about one-thirty, with about six thousand fighting men – 'probably the most powerful army ever assembled in Xhosaland'[113] – Mdushane attacked, sweeping down the hill with two divisions under his command, while a third under Makana made for the East Barracks, which were set a little apart from the village.

> 'The firing of some of the stolen guns among the [Xhosa] was the signal for the onward rush, and then with blood-curdling war shrieks from thousands of throats, the black, or rather red, cloud of death and destruction moved swiftly down the slopes towards the apparently doomed village. Onward they came like an irresistible wave, and yet there were no signs of any intention to check them or to sell life dearly. Nearer and nearer until the foremost were about thirty-five paces from the thin line [of defenders], and just when a few moments more seemed sufficient for the overwhelming numbers to complete their bloody enterprise, the 270 muskets of the defenders rattled and sent forth their leaden hail.'[114]

It's stirring stuff, clearly written from a colonial perspective – and quite loose with the truth. The defenders actually numbered more than 600, about 500 soldiers and townsfolk,[115] as well as 130 mounted Khoi hunters who arrived just before the battle began. Their presence had a significant affect on its outcome, since they were 'some of the best marksmen in the Colony,'[116] yet the above account does not mention them at all. Their leader, a famous elephant hunter named Jan Boesak, was particularly effective: a crack shot, he knew many of the Xhosa personally and 'levelled in a few seconds a number of the most distinguished chiefs and warriors.'[117]

Even so, Mdushane's advance was so swift it threw the frontline of defenders into retreat; at the East Barracks over a hundred of his men actually got within the walls, and in the village itself some even got the meal Mdushane had promised, although it was lunch not breakfast: a Mr Potgieter, who lived in a double-storeyed house at the top of High Street opposite the Drostdy Arch, was just sitting down to eat when a group of Xhosa burst into the dining room and helped themselves to his food.[118]

As the infantry fell back to their trenches, Mdushane's men swept after them. They had almost reached the mouths of the cannon when the guns opened up. The result was immediate and absolute carnage. At such close range every shot worked to devastating effect: as volley after volley ripped through the densely packed amaNdlambe, the shrapnel and grapeshot 'opened spaces like streets in the courageously advancing masses.'[119] Those who were not killed outright flung themselves to the ground, but there was no place to hide. One survivor, who owed his life to a small anthill, later described the shots falling so close to him that they kicked dust into his face.[120] Others,

> 'overwhelmed by the roar, the flame and the smoke of the muskets and cannons… simply sank to their knees in full view of the troops, and, holding up their hands to cover their faces without attempting to use their weapons, remained as if petrified until they were killed.'[121]

By late afternoon it was all over. The defenders, unbelievably, had lost only three (white) men, but the Xhosa had suffered terribly. To this day the battlefield is known at *eGazini*, the Place of Blood. The eastern slopes of the little valley were strewn with the bodies of the dead and dying and the Kowie Ditch or stream was choked with corpses. It is difficult to say exactly how many of Mdushane's men died, as contemporary estimates vary enormously, from several hundred to over a thousand.[122] Among the dead were three of Mdushane's brothers,[123] but he himself survived, as did the prophet Makana.

After the battle the British soldiers scoured the battlefield, killing the wounded Xhosa.[124] To their surprise they discovered that the majority of the fallen fighters had not even used their assegais in the attack: 'the most of them did not, as usual, carry one in the right hand, but kept them tied up together… without their having taken an assegai out.'[125] Makana had assured them that 'the white man's gun would fire only hot water,'[126] and they had died in their hundreds proving him wrong. Perhaps it is because of this – Makana's 'foolishness' and the Xhosas' 'gullibility' – that he attained such prominence in later colonial accounts of the battle. Today it is commonly claimed that it was Makana who led the attack, but contemporary reports do not bear this out.[127] In addition, Makana was not a chief and, as a commoner, he did not have the authority to command the entire force. (It is said that Ndlambe did permit him to establish a Great Place, but whether this was because the old chief 'was genuinely impressed or whether he simply felt that the madman might prove useful is difficult to say…')[128] Mdushane, the real leader of the attack on Grahamstown, has been all but ignored (if he is referred to at all, it is by his clan name 'Ndlambe', thereby confusing him with his father, who, at eighty, was too old to have been present.)[129] Despite Mdushane's careful and judicious planning, despite his efficient use of spies and his perfectly executed foil that sent a hundred soldiers out of Grahamstown immediately before the battle, despite the fact that he came within an inch of driving out the British and recovering his people's land once and for all, his role has been almost totally forgotten.

The backlash was swift and brutal, British reinforcements were sent in and commandos sent out, and another round of burning homesteads, seizing cattle and destroying crops ensued. Ndlambe was declared an outlaw and Willshire went after him and Mdushane in person, although somewhat ineptly at first – he was so unfamiliar with local conditions, for instance, that he equipped his troops with European-style siege ladders.[130] The Xhosa took refuge in the dense thornbush of the river valleys, and the British forces, unable to flush them out, bombarded them with grape-shot and Congreve rockets, indiscriminately mowing down unarmed women and children in the process.[131] For Bessie's granddaughter Nonibe and her loved ones, it was a time of great hardship and terrible suffering. As winter approached, the weather turned icy cold and it rained constantly, but the bad weather also impeded the British troops and the amaNdlambe and their allies were able to escape northwards, retreating across the Buffalo River a little inland of today's city of East London.[132] By the beginning of August they had lost two thousand cattle in intermittent skirmishes; a fortnight later a more serious confrontation with the colonial troops left many amaNdlambe dead and another 6 000 of their cattle were taken. This was closely followed by the news that the herds and horses they had left for safekeeping with Hintsa across the Kei River had been seized.[133] As the situation deteriorated, Makana the prophet decided to turn himself in: accompanied by two of his wives he walked with great dignity into *landdrost* Stockenstrom's camp, near today's village of Peddie, and offered himself up in exchange for a cessation of hostilities to save his people from starving.[134] It was a brave and selfless gesture but also deeply naïve – if not downright stupid – because instead of cutting a deal the British promptly put him in chains. Ndlambe and Mdushane offered to end the war in exchange for his release, but it was too late: Makana had already been shipped off to Cape Town where he was banished to Robben Island. On the night of 20 August 1819, barely a month after his arrival, he was drowned trying to escape.[135]

Back home the rain continued to pour down in torrents, turning the wagon trails into mudbaths, the streams into rivers, the rivers into floods, and effectively hampering Willshire's offensive. The Xhosa, however, were in desperate straits;[136] many were close to starving, and Ndlambe's allies began to surrender one by one. Eventually he was the only senior chief still at large, but his losses had been considerable – of the 30 000 cattle captured by the British, the majority belonged to his people[137] – and as his destitute followers began abandoning him, Ndlambe's power disintegrated. By 16 October 1819 the *Government Gazette* was able to report:

> 'he is so completely a Fugitive, so totally abandoned by his Followers, and so reduced, as well in real strength as in influence, that his mere existence becomes a matter of secondary importance'.

Three months earlier, in July 1819, the British government had launched a scheme to import thousands of its citizens into the eastern Cape to occupy the land from which he and his people had been so brutally expelled. By December 1819, just eight months after Mdushane's crushing defeat at Grahamstown, the immigrants were already embarking on the first of 21 ships. Among them were at least two families whose members, like him, would marry Bessie's descendants.

The immigration scheme had generated enormous excitement and interest throughout Britain. The end of the Napoleonic wars, together with the consolidation of land into big estates, had dumped thousands of landless peasants and demobilised soldiers on an already saturated job market, which, as the Industrial Revolution gathered steam, was increasingly unable to accommodate them. Compared to the slums, poorhouses, rampant gin abuse, disease and miserable weather of Britain, the promise of a 100-acre farm in sunny South Africa was simply irresistible, and more than *ninety thousand* people applied. Just less than 4 000 were chosen, nearly half of them children; of the remainder, 20% were women and 36% men. The majority were of humble origins – unemployed craftsmen and traders for the most part – but there were also a few well-to-do men among them who organised their own parties and equipped themselves with every comfort and tool imaginable – even coaches, although there were no real roads to speak of where they were going. In fact, for rich or poor, a near-total ignorance of their new country seems to have been a common denominator. But while the Settlers' knowledge and numbers were small, their impact on the lives of the Xhosa, and Bessie's descendants, was to be enormous.

After a long and tedious sea journey, the 1820 Settlers (as they were thereafter known) eventually reached Algoa Bay, today's Port Elizabeth, where they were due to disembark. The settlement was a dismayingly isolated clutch of makeshift dwellings on a desolate and windy shore, beyond which were rows and rows of small white tents, the Settlers' temporary accommodation. As the ox-wagons carrying them to their allotments creaked slowly northwards, however, their initial disappointment turned to admiration. The heavy rains, which had so recently hampered the military campaign against Ndlambe, had beautified the countryside and the rolling grasslands were lush and green, the streams and rivers full, and the forests tall with excellent wood for building. The political climate, of course, was decidedly less healthy. As the wagons penetrated deeper and deeper into the hinterland, they began passing the burnt-out shells of Boer farmhouses, and the Settlers glimpsed, perhaps for the first time, the real motive behind the government's generous promises of land, seed and implements, and the pendulum of their emotions swung back to doubt and gloom. The Frontier was not a border, it was a front line, and they were there for one reason only – to form a living buffer between the Colony and the Xhosa. And if any of the immigrants were still ignorant of what lay ahead of them, the locals were not: all night long the Khoi wagoneers gathered around their campfires 'laughing most heartily,' reported a Settler, 'and I fancied that it must have been at our cost for I could distinctly hear them cry out "Englis setlars," and an immoderate "Ha, ha, ha!"'[138]

The settlement scheme failed miserably. Over half of the Settlers were city folk,[139] who knew nothing about animal husbandry or cultivation – stories abound of carrots planted two feet underground or seedlings planted upside down with their roots in the air – and they quickly became disenchanted with farming. Within the first year some were already abandoning their allotments and heading for the towns, where they could make a better and more secure living by resorting to their old trades. The majority settled in Grahamstown, boosting its population and initiating a building boom, and by May 1823 the village had grown from 20 or 25 houses to more than 300.[140] The Settlers who remained on their allotted lands faced a constant struggle to support their families and even the ones with agricultural experience found it difficult; their plots were simply too small for anything but market gardening, yet there were no ready markets for their produce, nor adequate roads or transportation even if there had been. The territory was better suited to cattle, but while the neighbouring Boers had farms of 5 000–6 000 acres,[141] the British government had deliberately limited the Settlers' allotments to 100 acres per adult male, in the hope of creating a close-knit community. To compound the Settlers' misery they were afflicted by bumbling bureaucrats, drought and floods, their wheat was destroyed by several consecutive years of rust[142] and their freedom of movement severely curtailed – they were among the first people in South Africa forced to carry a *dompas*,[143] without which they were not permitted to leave their farms.

Almost from the start there was suspicion and hostility between the recently evicted Xhosa and the new occupants of their land. One point of contention was the Clay Pits just outside Grahamstown, where the amaNdlambe had traditionally obtained the red ochre they used for cosmetic and ritualistic purposes, but to which their access was now restricted. Nonibe was just one amongst many affected: her husband

Mdushane had to apply for a special pass to obtain the clay they so loved, a dark red 'that reminds of dried blood.'[144] Real blood was soon to flow on both sides. Between the Xhosa and the Settlers there was no common ground (if you'll pardon the pun); the latter had little understanding of the Xhosa's prior claim to their lands[145] and the history of their dealings with the British authorities. As their relationship with the Xhosa soured, the Settlers grew terribly fearful of attack. The people who settled at Salem just outside Grahamstown, for example, fled from their beds one night to shouts of alarm – 'The Xhosa are coming! Their camp-fires are in the hills!' – only to discover, when the whole village was up and running about in confusion and terror, that the so-called campfires were just little fireflies flitting through the bush.[146]

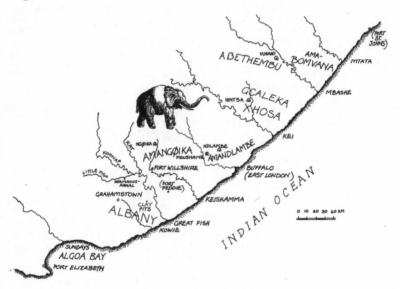

The Eastern Frontier c 1828

But they were right to be afraid. And so were the Xhosa. The future was to bring unspeakable suffering to both. There were simply too many points of contention between them for things to have been otherwise: the deprivations suffered by the Xhosa through the confiscation of their land and the loss of lives, cattle and crops on the one side, intermittent attacks on individual Settlers and increasing theft of their livestock on the other, combined with the ignorance and arrogance of the newcomers and the pitfalls of illegal ivory and cattle trading between the two groups, created a volatile situation. After a number of Xhosa were killed by British soldiers at the Clay Pits, the clashes became more frequent and widespread, the violence feeding on itself and reverberating down the generations, laying the foundations for the divided South Africa of the future.

Ndlambe meanwhile – and despite all British efforts to the contrary – had never been caught or detained, but because of his reduced circumstances he was no longer considered a threat to the new settlement of Albany (as the Zuurveld was now known). Consequently, in a meeting in 1823 with Major Somerset, Commandant of Kaffaria, he and Mdushane were able to secure permission to their people to reoccupy the land between the Keiskamma and Buffalo rivers,[147] less than 100 kilometres north-east of Grahamstown. Slowly Ndlambe's followers began to increase in numbers and in due course he re-established himself as a commanding presence in the region. He had at least ten wives of his own and, despite his advanced age, a lusty eye for everyone else's too.[148] Mdushane, nominally under his command, was a chief in his own right and was recognised as the son 'on whom the government of the tribe was expected to devolve' upon Ndlambe's death.[149] Mdushane's Great Place lay some kilometres west of his father's, in the upper reaches of the Nxarhuni[150] or Nahoon River, and it was here that his Great Wife Nonibe, granddaughter of the castaway Bessie, resided. It is possible that she had borne him a daughter or two by this time, but Nonibe was not to give birth to his Great Son Siwani until 1826.[151] Mdushane already had several sons by his more junior wives, though, at least one of whom was old enough to be circumcised. Among the Xhosa, boys were generally circumcised at about the age of 14.[152] The *abakwetha*, or initiates, were secluded from the rest of the community for a prolonged period of time, the ceremonial removal of their foreskins just one part of the passage from boyhood to manhood. Living in temporary grass huts for between three and eighteen months under the care and guidance of a tutor they learnt the responsibilities and privileges of becoming a man, participated in mock battles and got up to all kinds of practical jokes. It was male-bonding of the highest order and the greatest honour was to belong to the same circumcision class as the son of a chief. In 1825 Reverend Kay described a group of *abakwetha* sallying forth 'under little or no restraint… into the neighbouring gardens, playing the most mischievous tricks. They were all fine, active, and interesting lads; one of whom was Dushani's son.'

> 'Their bodies, from head to foot, were daubed over with white clay; which gave them a singular and very unnatural appearance. On their heads they wore caps made of the palmeet leaf, and from their waists was suspended a kind of petticoat composed of the same material, and in length and shape not much unlike the Scotch kilt. Each seemed to vie with the other in agility and expertness, while the utmost harmony prevailed among the whole.'[153]

Peace lay over the region, but it was an uneasy peace. In 1824, in an effort to minimise cattle theft and legalise and control the thriving but illicit trade between the Settlers and Xhosa, the authorities instituted weekly fairs at Fort Willshire, a military outpost situated in a hot and humid little valley on the Keiskamma River. The fairs were an enormous success, with the trade in ivory alone reaching staggering dimensions – in the first six months 38 424 lbs (about 17 000 kgs) changed hands.[154] On the Xhosa side this trade was largely monopolised by Ndlambe's old rival Ngqika, who visited the fairs regularly.[155] A retinue of about 25 wives and concubines attended him, including the delectable Thuthula, whom he had stolen from his uncle Ndlambe nearly 20 years before. A well-to-do Settler, Thomas Philipps, who met her preparing for the fair surrounded by her attendants, describes her as tall, shapely, and rather charming.

> 'She held out her hand quite gracefully, and her walk was perfectly Courtly. Her head was covered, having just come from under the operation of the Hair dresser who had well clotted it with red Clay, and her whole face, neck, and arms were rouged over with the same material, delicately put on with a piece of Supple Skin. An impartial observer could not but acknowledge that there was no mighty difference between this custom and the powder, pomatum, and rouge of Europe.'[156]

Ngqika was now in his early 50s, but looked 20 years younger: a good-looking, well-proportioned man, he was tall and athletic, with 'limbs of the most perfect symmetry, although now getting rather large.'[157] Despite his healthy appearance he was an alcoholic, and spent a lot of time in the local canteen – 'continually intoxicated,' remarked an English visitor, 'a sunk and degraded being,' who was 'ever ready to sell his wives for brandy.'[158] Occasionally he wandered around the fair, dressed in an old regimental jacket and other odds and ends of western clothing, helping himself to a hefty cut of the Xhosa traders' profits (which did nothing for his popularity ratings). Away from the Fort and the canteen, however, he cut a more dignified figure. His handsome body was naked but for his *isidla*[159] and his leopard-skin robe flung carelessly over his shoulders, signifying his royal status. On his right forearm were a profusion of metal bracelets. Both thumbs and several fingers on each hand were adorned with rings given to him by various visitors. On one was inscribed the word 'Hope'.[160]

While Ngqika dominated the legal fair, Mdushane resorted to illegal trade with the Colony to accumulate the wealth that kept Ngqika's power in check and protected the more vulnerable Xhosa clans from his ambitions.[161] In 1825, in a move designed to appease the British, Mdushane and his aging father, Ndlambe, permitted a Wesleyan mission station to be established in a corner of their territory. Mount Coke, as it became known, was within easy reach of Grahamstown – some 80 kilometres north-east as the crow flies – and, on a visit to the town the following year, the missionary, Reverend Kay, persuaded Mdushane to accompany him. It was the first time the chief had returned to the site of his bloody defeat seven years before.[162]

The wagon road from Mount Coke to Grahamstown brought Mdushane and his companions directly to Makana's Kop,[163] the *kopje* and neighbouring ridge overlooking the village. It was the very same spot from which he had launched his ill-fated attack. Makana's Kop has a commanding view of the valley and one can take in the whole village at a glance: *eGazini*, or the Place of Blood, where hundreds of his men, including some of his own brothers, had died, the flank of the hill sweeping down to the huddled buildings of the old east barracks, now Fort England hospital, and the broken line of the stream where his fighters had sought shelter from the lethal British shrapnel and grapeshot. Kay wrote that

> '[t]he recollection of that day and its scenes made them tremble while approaching the spot, and especially when within sight of the town... all stood gazing for some time in perfect silence, as if doubtful of their safety in entering.'[164]

After a long pause Mdushane broke the spell, observing wryly that 'the kraal was now too large to be attempted.'[165]

The chief's trepidation about entering the 'kraal', was shared by the inhabitants, and his arrival sent a wave of anxious excitement sweeping through the village. It takes more than a few years for the terror of such a violent battle to fade, and the villagers' memories were still playing back in Technicolor. Yet they rose to the occasion and welcomed Mdushane, plying him and his entourage with western clothing (in the hope, no doubt, that they would get *dressed* and cover those damn penis sheaths) and various other presents. Xhosa chiefs were accustomed to being courted with gifts (though they seldom kept them for their own use, but usually immediately shared them out amongst their followers) and were not shy to demand them when the opportunity arose,[166] and in Grahamstown Mdushane did just that, although he apparently felt no obligation to return the favour. Feted by the very people he had sought to annihilate, inundated with goods he would not use and ousted from the land he could, Mdushane cannot have failed to appreciate the irony of his situation.

It was not long after this visit that Mdushane's father died. Ndlambe had been suffering increasing ill-health for some years and in February 1828, aged about 90, half-blind and with 'the infirmities of age bowing him down to earth,' the 'old lion' died. He was buried at his Great Place on the Xinira, a tributary of the Gonubie River, which enters the sea near East London.[167] His rival Ngqika followed him into the grave a year later, riddled with alcoholism and tuberculosis.[168]

With Ndlambe's death his people began to disintegrate. His sons Mqayi and Mhala set themselves up as independent chiefs, each with his own following,[169] and Mdushane, who was generally expected to have succeeded as paramount chief of the amaNdlambe, had neither the power nor the will to prevent them. Ravaged by 'a certain disease', as the missionaries delicately put it, 'which is now lamentably prevalent, occasioned and fostered principally, if not wholly, by his own imprudence,'[170] Mdushane was a shadow of his former self.

Syphilis had been a problem from the earliest days of the Colony, but it became more widespread following the arrival of the British in 1806. By 1811 it was rife in all Cape districts, and seems to have boomed with the arrival of troops and Settlers in 1820. In 1822 troopships arriving at the Cape from the east were automatically quarantined without exception, and

Ngqika's grave, near Burnshill Mission.

by 1833 syphilis featured as one of the Colony's most prevalent diseases (along with delirium tremens and rheumatism). Neither black nor white escaped its ravages. In the eastern Cape the Boers treated secondary syphilis by bathing in hot springs like the one at Fort Beaufort.[171]

But no amount of hot-tubbing could have saved Mdushane. Nonibe's husband had neuro-syphilis. The disease had reached his brain and he was dying.

Chapter Nine

The King-killers and the Queens

'Everything in Africa is in extremes'[1]

Initiate diviner, Mngazana, her face covered in white clay.

Belief in witchcraft was widespread and fervent, and generally speaking, still is – not only among the Xhosa but throughout southern Africa.

It is often said that the causes of disease and misfortune were not generally understood by the Xhosa, that they were believed to be 'the art and machinations of wizards and witches'[2] which, unless exorcised, would follow one illness or death in a family with another.[3] But witchcraft was also a useful tool in the maintenance of the status quo – as one observer put it, a 'state engine for the removal of the obnoxious.'[4] To accuse someone of witchcraft was a sure-fire means by which a chief and his counsellors could rid themselves of powerful rivals and seize their cattle-wealth.[5] It was also a means of isolating, or removing from the community, individuals who were perceived as being divisive.

Xhosa society was basically very conservative, and anyone diverging widely from the norm was seen as a potential danger. In times of uncertainty or conflict, accusations of witchcraft naturally tended to increase,[6] and it was in such a situation and at such a time that Mdushane's Great Wife now found herself. The death of Ndlambe, followed by the rapid deterioration in Mdushane's health, had placed the imiDushane in a very vulnerable position, and their future was uncertain in the extreme. The situation was exacerbated by the fact that they had been dispossessed of most of their territory, stripped of large numbers of their cattle and forced into overcrowded locations. As the Xhosa turned against the British, the cause of their misfortune, they turned too against anyone who favoured them. At a time when her people were growing increasingly antipathetic, Nonibe was openly sympathetic towards the British.

The Eastern Frontier: 1820s[7]

British policy in the eastern Cape had been a series of monumental blunders.

One was their expulsion of the Xhosa from the Zuurveld. Ndlambe had bought the land – twice over it seems, firstly from the Khoi Queen Hoho and then from a Boer fraudster, a *landdrost* from Graaff-Reinet.[8] Even men such as Adriaan van Jaarsveld, the notorious Boer commandant who slaughtered the imiDange in the tobacco incident of 1781 – and hardly a soft touch – acknowledged their right to the land and recommended that the amaNdlambe be permitted to return to the Zuurveld.[9]

Their second mistake was their support of Ngqika. It was, ironically, largely his people who were involved in the theft of colonial cattle and Ndlambe who did the most to try and prevent it, and in taking Ngqika's side against the latter the British became involved in and affected the outcome of affairs which did not concern them. It was their military interference and the confiscation of Ndlambe's land and cattle, on which his people depended directly for their survival, that precipitated the war of 1819 and caused the deaths and untold suffering of thousands.[10]

Yet another blunder was Colonel Somerset's infamous raid of 1825. During a period of relative quiet, when friction between black and white on the eastern Frontier had decreased and trade increased, Somerset launched a vicious assault on the Xhosa. In what was intended as a surprise attack on a minor chief called 'Neuka', or Nyoka, who was reportedly harbouring stolen livestock, Somerset mistakenly attacked a homestead belonging to Botomane, a British ally of long standing, seizing his herds and shooting his women and children, whose bodies were thrown into the Keiskamma River. The Chief himself barely escaped with his life. The incident had serious repercussions, and as Somerset was not only the military commander of the eastern Cape but also the son of the Governor of the Cape, it gave rise to deep and lasting mistrust among the Xhosa. And when a second *umzi* of innocents were attacked and slaughtered, and the real cattle thieves allowed to escape while the commando blundered about,[11] anti-British sentiment grew and spread.

Nonibe was caught in the middle of the rapidly deteriorating political climate. She 'prided herself on having the blood of the white man in her veins,' and it was well known that she was 'the descendant from a white woman, supposed to have been English, who some generations back, was saved from a wreck on the coast, and was taken as a wife by one of the [Xhosa] Chiefs.' According to a missionary who knew her well, because of her claim to kinship with the English she 'refused to sanction any act of hostility against them.'[12] She and Nomsa, the Great Wife of King Hintsa, were among the few Xhosa who remained well disposed towards the British, however, and as relations on the Frontier deteriorated and anti-British sentiment deepened, the two fell victim to political intrigue. The charges came at roughly the same time: in about 1828, in separate incidents, both women were accused of bewitching their husbands.

Clearly their English ancestry, once an asset to their people, had become a liability.

In Nonibe's case it was Mdushane's deteriorating health that forced the issue. As it slowly became clear that Mdushane might be dying, his people were forced to deal with the problem of a successor. His heir, Siwani, was an infant[13] and too young to succeed him, but his Great Wife, Nonibe, on whom the regency was most likely to devolve, was perceived as dangerously sympathetic to the English. To a powerful faction within the imiDushane it was clear that she had to be removed. It was at this critical juncture, and surely by no coincidence, that a powerful diviner was summoned to 'smell out' the person responsible for 'bewitching' Mdushane.

Diviners were widely feared and deeply respected. No one could actually choose to become an *igqirha*; initiates, usually female, were marked by the ancestors at an early age to communicate with the spirit world, a 'calling' which generally manifested itself in the form of epileptic fits, delusions or hysteria. Years of intensive training and ritual followed, setting them apart from lesser mortals.[14] Conspicuously ornamented with bangles, beads, necklaces, body paint and extravagant headdresses of fur and feathers, they inspired great fear among the common people and wielded enormous power. They still do today, for that matter, since the belief in witchcraft in South Africa remains prevalent, but whereas it is now part of a diviner's function to treat the 'witch' and exorcise the evil spirit, in Nonibe's time people who were charged with witchcraft were usually found guilty, tortured and frequently put to death. Their property was confiscated by the chief and by a happy coincidence, as most accused were wealthy individuals, the diviner responsible for smelling them out received a share. That is not to say that the *amagqirha* were charlatans – their training was too rigorous and their functions and skills too diverse to dismiss so lightly – but they do generally appear to have upheld the interests of the elite, the elders and counsellors who were the power behind the throne in every chiefdom.

For the 'smelling out' of Mdushane's malefactor the whole clan gathered at the chief's Great Place. There they formed an enormous circle and began to sing and to dance, the men striking their fighting sticks rhythmically against the shafts of their assegais and the women clapping their hands to the beat. After circling the crowd the *igqirha* was addressed by one of the great counsellors and exhorted to discover the person responsible and make his or her identity known: 'We are all weeping... alarmed on account of the sickness of our Chief, and the mortality among his cattle... and wondering who among us had so evil a heart as to bewitch the Chief.' The dancing and drumming continued while the diviner retired to a hut alone, entering a private world of dreams and visions from which she would emerge only once she knew who was causing his illness. As the hours passed the excitement of the dancers outside increased to fever pitch, so that the diviner's eventual appearance was a moment of high and calculated drama: her left eyelid, arm and thigh were painted white and her right side black, the rest of her body smeared with fat and blood-red clay, the hair of wild animals stood up from her head in two tall tufts and in her hand she grasped three spears. Sweeping through the fearful crowd, she stopped suddenly and made her announcement.[15] It was Nonibe who had bewitched their chief; none other than Mdushane's Great Wife had caused him to fall ill.

The news must have caused a sensation among the assembled people, though it was perhaps not entirely unexpected: as a dissenter she was too close to the throne to be left unneutralised.

Having been found guilty of witchcraft Nonibe could expect to be tortured[16] or even put to death. She herself probably anticipated the worst. Yet given the gravity of the situation her punishment was surprisingly mild, perhaps because Mdushane himself did not wish her serious harm. The sentence must nevertheless have devastated her: 'this otherwise sensible chief... peremptorily commanded her never more to call him husband, or appear in his presence again. He then rose from his seat, and in his fury declared that he would forthwith burn her habitation to the ground.'

Help came from an unexpected source. As Mdushane fell silent, his eldest son suddenly stepped forward from the crowd, and addressed him, saying: 'If my father is resolved to burn the work of my mother's hands, he shall burn me with it.'[17] It was an act of tremendous bravery, given the circumstances and – especially – his age. Seyolo, for that was his name,[18] could not have been much more than 15 at the time. That he acted as he did suggests that he had already been circumcised and, though still a youth, was considered a man and already commanded great respect.[19] What proves him worthy of that respect, and mature beyond his years, is not only what he did but *how* he did it. This was no wild emotional outburst, though he spoke with feeling. It was neither an outright challenge to his father's authority, nor a condemnation of his judgement. It was a simple statement of love and support, made all the more remarkable by the fact that Nonibe was not even his biological mother but, in western terms, his step-mother.

Seyolo's courage and loyalty saved Nonibe, but Nomsa, the Great Wife of Hintsa, who like Nonibe was the descendant of a white castaway and pro-British, was less fortunate.

In a similar trial at about the same time, Nomsa was found guilty of witchcraft and was sent back to her people, the Bomvana,[20] where she remained for several years – effectively neutralising any political influence she may have had over her husband the king or divisions which her support of the British may have caused among his people.

In December 1828 the great warrior Mdushane died and was buried at his *umzi* at Phunzana, about ten kilometres south of Mount Coke mission. He had been 'much beloved... a man of rare courage and energy of mind,'[21] and an even greater number of people – 'so many hundreds of men, women, and children, with their heads shaven... mourning for the Chief'[22] – attended his burial than had attended his father's ten months earlier. The ceremony was traditional, with Nonibe following the age-old rituals that her grandmother Bessie had observed when her husband Sango had died, Only the details were slightly different, the influence of western culture manifest in Mdushane's personal effects, such as his trousers and saddles.[23] These together with more traditional items such as his assegais and ivory armbands were supposed, in accordance with custom, to be interred with his body, but the new missionary at Mount Coke interfered, protesting that to do so was an unnecessary waste.[24] He refused to allow them to be buried and gave them away to his converts. Nonibe and the rest of the family refused to have anything to do with them.

Mdushane's death left a painful vacuum. As the Reverend Shaw remarked,

> '[h]is loss will be greatly felt in this Tribe, for at the present there is no one who can properly assume the supreme authority. Doubtless this will devolve on one or other of the branches of the family, in course of time, but from a variety of circumstances I fear the Tribe will be without an efficient leader for some time, which will necessarily be injurious to them.'[25]

With his heir Siwani still an infant, Nonibe, who was not yet thirty years old, was appointed regent. Women frequently became regents, and these were often periods of great prosperity for their people for, as one old-timer observed,

> 'though the widow possess the full power and authority of the chief, she is not so likely to be arbitrary and despotic, and is less likely than a man to do or permit anything which may bring her into collision with her neighbours.'[26]

In time Nonibe came to share the responsibilities of governance with her stepson Seyolo, whose courageous intervention had been instrumental in saving her from banishment. Despite his evident respect for her, it was an uneasy partnership. Politically the two were diametrically opposed; Seyolo was vehemently anti-British, 'the war-spirit of his tribes,'[27] and when the long-simmering tensions between British and Xhosa exploded into open warfare in late 1834, the divisions between the two deepened critically. Keeping the imiDushane from being torn asunder became a razor-edge balancing act.

Nonibe was then in her mid-thirties. She was 'pleasantly stout, and light brown,' with a distinct squint and an agreeable smile.[28] The majority of Xhosa women, at that time, still wore traditional clothing, a leather skirt or apron and a turban-like headdress consisting of a length of fine thin leather wrapped around the head in many folds and shaped into two points on either side of the head (which young coquettes wore at a fashionable tilt).[29] Nonibe, however, favoured western clothing, 'a blue and white striped dress, with a silk handkerchief round her head,' which was probably due to missionary influence. Prior to the death of her husband Mdushane, Nonibe had lived about eight kilometres from Wesleyville mission station and had often visited the Reverend Shaw there, and it is likely that she was exposed to at least some Christian teachings.[30] The missionaries' influence, however, was not as strong as they would have wished since Nonibe 'by some accident was in the family way.'[31] A Xhosa widow was permitted a lot of sexual freedom 'to raise up seed to her dead husband' – as long as she remained among his people these children would be regarded as legitimate and subject to the usual laws of inheritance[32] – and Nonibe had obviously been doing her duty. I have always thought that the worst possible time to be pregnant must be during wartime, and with her first-hand experience of the horrors of war, when she and her people were hunted down like animals following their defeat at the Battle of Grahamstown in 1819, Nonibe must have felt particularly vulnerable.

The War of 1834 had been a long time coming and the factors contributing to it were diverse. One was the expulsion of the late Ngqika's powerful and respected son, Maqoma, from his lands on the Kat River,[33] but the immediate catalyst was the shooting and wounding of another of his sons, a junior chief named Xhoxho, who had been grazing his cattle in the prohibited territory. Ngqika, it may be recalled, had been a particularly handsome man but the unfortunate Xhoxho had not inherited his looks: 'Look at that thing! Does that look like a chief's son?' Ngqika had grumbled about him. 'My councillors advised me to marry his mother, saying that she was a fine-looking woman, and would bring me fine-looking children; but look at the thing she has brought me!'[34] Xhoxho may have been a disappointment to his father and a bit-player, but to the Xhosa he was still a chief of royal blood and his shooting ignited the Frontier: 'Every [Xhosa] who saw Xoxo's wound went back to his hut, took his assegay, and shield, and set out to fight, and said, "It is better that we die than be treated thus.... Life is no use to us if they shoot our chiefs".'[35]

As all hell broke loose, colonists all over the Frontier piled their families and goods onto wagons and fled to Grahamstown. It all happened so fast that 'meney of them… had to leve thear Plum Cakes and Puddings un baked and un biled,' lamented the settler Jeremiah Goldswain. 'Mr. Richeson's famley had to leve a verey Large plumb cake in the hoven baking.' All was not lost, however: two or three months later a couple of Richeson's sons returned to the area on patrol 'and as they passed near thear house they thought on they plumb Cake wich they had left in hoven and to thear great astonishment they found that the Cake [was] Quite Good.'[36]

In Grahamstown the townsfolk, fearing another attack like Mdushane's, barricaded the streets and set up cannon at strategic points. Martial law was proclaimed and all males were expected to bear arms.[37] The motley collection of butchers, bakers and candlestick makers-cum-farmers prepared themselves for battle with such earnest ineptitude that when their new commander, Colonel (later Sir) Harry Smith, arrived in town after a hell-for-leather ride from Cape Town, he almost died laughing.

It is not my intention to go into the greater causes and repercussions of this war or the ones that succeeded it – others have written far more comprehensive and learned treatises than I could ever hope or wish to write. Our story lies rather in what happened to Bessie's granddaughter Nonibe and her child Siwani during that time, in the troubled years that followed, and the one thing that truly defined their future: the fact that Nonibe opposed the war, and was one of the few Xhosa chieftains to do so. Her political stance was not a popular one: chiefs – and regents – were only as powerful as their people's willingness to support them and, respected though she was as queen-mother and regent, 'as a woman she was quite unable to repress the war-spirit of her people.'[38] As her stepsons Seyolo and Qasana took up arms against the British and the imiDushane followed them almost as one, Nonibe took refuge with the missionaries at Mount Coke. The station was situated on land belonging to her brother-in-law Mqayi who, under the influence of Reverend Dugmore, chose to remain neutral, and was about the only chief besides herself to do so.[39]

As the war spread and the situation deteriorated refugees began pouring into the mission. Many of them were traders, and at least one of them, Richard Bradfield of Clumber, owed his life to Nonibe. The Xhosa seldom harmed missionaries, women or children in wartime, but their attitude towards colonial traders was quite different. They despised them for their

Mqayi[40]

exploitative practices and specifically targeted them, often singling out and killing a trader when others around him were left unharmed. Bradfield, the 23-year-old son of an English settler of 1820, had had the misfortune of being captured by a party of armed Xhosa. As luck would have it, the men not only knew him but were on good terms with him – with some he was even 'something of a favourite'[41] – so his fate presented them with a real dilemma. Torn between friendship and their hatred of traders in general, they began arguing among themselves and, as the debate became more heated, Bradfield resigned himself to a sticky end. Determined that his death would not be slow and painful and figuring that a bullet would be quicker and cleaner than assegais – but only if the shot was accurate – he began teaching his would-be killers how to use his gun. This bizarre scene, and the lesson, was brought to an abrupt end by a message from Nonibe, who commanded the Xhosa to bring Bradfield at once to the mission station. Obediently they escorted him in – shepherding to safety the very man whom, moments before, they had been intent on murdering.[42] Evidently Nonibe still commanded great respect among her people, even among those who supported the war and were prepared to spill blood in its cause.

She also enjoyed the respect of the colonial authorities, largely because of her pro-British stance. Her unusual ancestry attracted much attention and interest, and it was well known among them that she was a 'Lady of European descent'[43] and 'quite evidently of European blood.'[44] In 1835, for example, Robert Godlonton, the proprietor of the *Grahamstown Journal*, an influential Settler paper, wrote a remarkably accurate account of her: on the borders of the Mtata River, he wrote:

> 'reside a people, under the chieftainship of Depa, who is the son of a European mother, but of what country has not been ascertained, though from the name of her daughter it may be inferred she was English. It appears, however, from all that has been gathered, that she, with some others, must have been cast on that shore when very young, more than a century ago.... Of the descendants of these unfortunate females only two can now be traced with any degree of certainty, and these are Depa, the chief, and his sister, a widow; and whose daughter, Nonube, married the Kafir chief Dushanie. She is now a widow, and it is an interesting fact that during the recent commotions she distinguished herself by undeviating kindness to the traders, and attachment to the English cause.'[45]

The governor's aide, Alexander, also knew a substantial amount about Nonibe's history:

> 'The Kaffir queen Nonube, the mother of young Siwana of the T'slambies... is the great widow of Dushani, who with the prophet Makanna attacked Graham's Town in 1819. As I before noticed, Nonube has European blood in her veins, being of the tribe of Depa ... the kaross-covered descendants of Europeans'

living between the Mbashe and Mtata rivers.[46] Elsewhere he refers again to 'the people of Depa, about the Umtata: many of whom, of a light colour and with straight hair, are well-ascertained to be descendants of shipwrecked Europeans.'[47] The Governor of the Cape himself, Sir Benjamin D'Urban, knew about Nonibe and met her personally, and 'on learning her position and submission, treated her with great kindness.'[48]

It was at about this time that the Campbell rumour became widespread. Several contemporary accounts claim that Nonibe was the great-granddaughter of a general of that name. According to one writer, 'General Campbell and his three daughters being wrecked off the Coast of Africa, in the *Grosvenor* East Indiaman, the unfortunate ladies were allotted as wives to the Kaffir chiefs. Nunnube's grandmother was one of these....' Elsewhere the writer reiterates: 'Nonube's mother was the daughter of a Miss Campbell, one of the General's unhappy daughters, who had been seized and retained by a Kaffir chief as his "great wife".'[49] The rumour was so persistent – and so intriguing – that it bears closer attention, and we shall return to it later (see chapter 12).

Nonibe and her young son Siwani remained under British protection for the duration of the war.[50] As the fighting intensified and Mount Coke was abandoned, they retreated with the missionaries, refugees and traders to Wesleyville, just south of today's East London, and when it too had to be evacuated,[51] Nonibe found a mentor in the unlikely person of Colonel Harry Wakelyn Smith's wife. 'Harry Whackalong Smite', as his troops called him, was an abrasive, over-active little man of great arrogance, but his saving grace (to me at least) was his relationship with Juana Maria de Los Dolores de Leon. Smith was 24 years old and still a captain when they first met, and she was a 13-year-old refugee living in the war-torn ruins of her Spanish hometown. When the British troops withdrew Smith took Juana with him, and the following year married her.[52] He remained deeply in love with her for the rest of his life and when circumstances beyond his control conspired to keep them apart poured his heart out to her in passionate letters.[53] The couple was childless and Juana generally managed to travel everywhere with Harry, even to the front when he was campaigning; in 1835 she accompanied him to King William's Town, where he set up his military headquarters on the site of a burnt-out mission station,[54] and it there that she befriended the queens, Nonibe and Msutu, the widow of Ngqika.

Msutu was the Great Wife whom, as I mentioned briefly in chapter two, Ngqika had refused to marry. He already had enough wives, he claimed, and was content with his sons by them, principally his right-hand son Maqoma. His elders and counsellors, however, were determined that their king produce a Great Son and heir, and it was clear to them that Msutu had all the attributes they desired. A Thembu princess of very high rank, she was a woman of keen intelligence and a great beauty, and they were willing to meet the substantial *lobola* she commanded.[55] Despite Ngqika's resistance his counsellors prevailed and the marriage went ahead. Ngqika was furious and, it is said, refused to have anything to do with Msutu. With or without his assistance, however, she managed to produce an heir. Her Great Son Sandile was born in 1820, a bright and beautiful boy with, unfortunately, a deformed leg. When the boy was nine years old Nqgika died and Msutu became regent, a position she shared with Sandile's older half-brothers Maqoma and Tyhali.[56]

When the war broke out in 1834, Msutu was the most influential woman among the amaNgqika. Forty years of age, she was very fair of complexion with high cheekbones, 'and an agreeably plump person.'[57] She smoked a pipe, with an elegant hand-carved stem over a foot long. Sometimes, like Nonibe, she wore European clothes with a striped silk handkerchief about her head, but at other times she dressed in fine skins, with a splendid traditional headdress of bluebuck skins covered with white beads.

Like Nonibe, Msutu had opposed the war, and she tried to dissuade the amaNgqika from fighting. Both women, reported the governor's aide, 'told their people that the English had done them no harm' – which was, of course, untrue – and 'both of them by their influence saved missionaries and traders, and much property,' all of which, he added, just went to show that 'all Kaffirs are not equally bad.'[58] An accomplished politician with a talent for diplomacy, Msutu saw the missionaries as potential allies in preventing Sandile's older half-brother Maqoma from supplanting him as king. She protected them as much as she could, preventing her people from destroying the nearby mission of Burnshill and sending a wagon and escort to carry the Pirie missionaries to safety.[59] Despite this and her resistance to the war she

Msutu, Chieftainess of the amaNgqika c 1840[60]

was forced into hiding, in the foothills of the Amatola mountains.[61] Her hide-out, between Hogsback and King William's Town, was eventually discovered when a British officer literally dropped in on her. In hot pursuit of a party of Xhosa fighters in the tangled bush and dense undergrowth of the *kranses* along the Keiskamma River, Captain Warden almost fell through the roof of what turned out to be a richly decorated cave. It was furnished – in the midst of this most remote and rugged mountain terrain – with a surprising array of western luxury goods, 'carpets, tables, chairs, mirrors, and other European articles,' in and on which Msutu and eighteen female attendants were comfortably ensconced.[62] Warden treated the queen with the utmost courtesy, making no attempt to seize her, and in due course she and her entourage entered the British camp where, in one of those ironic little twists which make life so interesting, Msutu and Nonibe, widows of the arch-rivals Ngqika and Mdushane, became friends, and in another funny twist, also became the 'almost constant attendants and willing pupils'[63] of the wife of their worst enemy, Harry Smith.

As a result – and rather bizarrely – the two most influential women among the southern Xhosa spent the rest of the war learning the art of fine needlework. 'My wife,' wrote Sir Harry with characteristic arrogance,

> 'who took equal interest in the reform of these poor barbarians with myself, was always surrounded by numbers of the chiefs' wives and

hangers-on, particularly the queens Suta and Nonibe.... She taught many of them needlework, and was for hours daily explaining to them right from wrong, and making them little presents, so that she became so popular she could do anything with them.'[64]

Actually Juana Smith comes across as a warm and compassionate woman with a deep sense of fair play and respect for others, and it is not difficult to understand the bond between her and the queens, Nonibe and Msutu. War was their common ground: all three had endured and survived its terrors, all had lost people they loved, all had married warriors, and it was because of war too (although in Juana's case it was voluntary), that they were almost perpetually on the move. And all had children, Nonibe and Msutu their young sons, Siwani and Sandile, and Juana her demonstrative, demanding and sometimes delinquent husband, 'Enrique'.

Harry Smith could be extremely intimidating, but Msutu for one was unimpressed by his bullying condescension. She had several run-ins with him, of which the following exchange is an example:

'On Colonel Smith telling her the Governor would make her son Sandilli a king, she replied, "He is a king already".
"But", observed the gallant colonel, "What's the use of being a king unless he has people and a country?"
Sutu shrewdly observed, "If you let us alone, we shall soon have both".'[65]

Hintsa, King of the Xhosa[66]

Nonibe's countrywoman and fellow descendant of castaways, Nomsa – who had been charged with witchcraft at about the same time as she had and been sent into exile in Bomvanaland – had meanwhile returned to her husband the Xhosa King Hintsa. Nomsa had been brought back at the insistence of her Great Son Sarhili, who apparently refused to be circumcised unless she was present to cook the necessary traditional foods for him.[67]

210

As it was unheard-of for the future king to be uncircumcised, Sarhili had chosen his threat well. It was probably the first indication of the enormous diplomatic and political skills the young man commanded, and which he was to use to such great effect on his succession to the Xhosa throne.

No one could have anticipated that that day lay in the very near future. His father King Hintsa was the most powerful man in the land and in his prime. 'He was one of the most athletic men I ever saw,' wrote an English settler, 'an excellent model for a Hercules.' Aged about forty-five, he was six feet tall and carried himself with dignity. His features had an almost Arabic cast, with a low, aquiline nose, voluptuous lips and deeply hooded eyes. He had a very dark complexion, close-cropped beard and hair. In keeping with his royal status, he wore a beautifully tanned leopard skin *kaross*, with an ivory band above one elbow. He wore a brass belt around his waist, many brass bracelets on his arms and red and white beads around his neck and hanging from one ear; in his right hand he carried a bundle of finely wrought assegais and in his left a buffalo-hide *sjambok*, or short whip.[68]

Although Hintsa's Gcaleka Xhosa were not directly involved in the war, the British suspected the king of complicity and in April 1835 Harry Smith's forces crossed the Kei River and invaded his territory, though officially declaring war on him only 10 days after the fact. The Great Place was burnt down to the ground and Hintsa and his Great Wife Nomsa forced to evacuate so suddenly that the Queen's fine oxhide *kaross* and personal jewellery, 'beedes Bell Buttons Rings for her harms,' were left behind.[69] The war drew to a close shortly after the invasion and while the terms of settlement were being negotiated, Hintsa was brought under guard to Smith's camp accompanied by Nomsa, their son Sarhili and a number of other dignitaries,[70] the idea being that as long as their king and his heir were in British hands, his people would be more than averagely inclined to keep the peace. The British stressed, however, that Hintsa was not a prisoner and were at pains to explain that he was not being held against his will.[71] His safety had been personally guaranteed by the British governor, D'Urban – but within two weeks the king was dead, shot at close range by one of Smith's own men, and his body mutilated.[72]

The circumstances surrounding Hintsa's death raised many questions, which have never been satisfactorily answered, even to this day. The official account suggests some kind of cover-up took place; it has as many holes as a mosquito net and no less a personage than the colonial secretary, Lord Glenelg, queried its veracity.[73] In the end, however, Smith and his men, including Captain George Southey, who fired the fatal shots, were exonerated. The British had become king-killers.

Hintsa's death shocked the Xhosa to their very core. Kings were seldom killed – even in battle it was an almost unheard-of occurrence. As the paramount authority and direct descendant of Tshawe, founder king of the Xhosa, Hintsa's person was sacred, and his violent death – not to mention his mutilation – dismayed his people. On an individual level too, Hintsa's passing was a great loss to both the Xhosa and to the region as a whole. As one English settler wrote, 'Hintsa was a marvellously clever man, the greatest black man I ever knew; and it was, in my opinion, a loss to the country when he was destroyed.'[74]

George Southey, Hintsa's killer[75]

Hintsa's Great Son Sarhili became king in his stead and agreed to uphold the peace treaty. A 'very fine young man' of about nineteen or twenty, he was much admired for his intelligence and presence. Several contemporary accounts remark on his handsome features, dignity, his wit and vivacity.[76] Even Sir Harry Smith admired him, remarking in a back-handed reference to his mother Nomsa's white ancestry: 'You cannot conceive a more handsome half-black fellow.'[77]

The end of the war left most Xhosa worse off than before. The British extended their authority to such an extent that the Governor of the Cape, Sir Benjamin D'Urban, was able to boast to his superiors that a vast tract of land 'running from the sea up the Keiskamma and Chumie rivers to the Winterberg, and the Kye river from its source in the Stormberg mountains to the sea has become the territory of His Britannic Majesty....' The only Xhosa to really benefit from the war were those who had been opposed it – and for precisely that reason. Nonibe was singled out and praised by D'Urban 'for her endeavours to prevent the war; and for her successful efforts in saving the lives and property of some missionaries and traders'. He promised to give her ample land in the newly occupied territory:

> '... [I]n consideration of the excellent disposition and conduct of "Nonube", great Widow of the chief Dushanie, of the tribe of T'Slambie, I will acknowledge and uphold her son, as chief of that tribe, under his mother's tutelage, during his nonage; will appoint ample lands for their reception and support... and will receive under

the protection of the Colonial Government and Laws, such of the tribe as Nonube shall recommend, and who shall not have been engaged in invading the Colony.'[78]

Nonibe was granted land near the Keiskamma River. In the aftermath of the war the government appointed magistrates to oversee each of the main groups of Xhosa. Most were ex-army officers, and the one sent to keep a watchful eye on Nonibe and Siwani was Captain Richard Southey, the brother of the man who killed King Hintsa and, it is said, hacked off his ears as souvenirs.[79]

In about 1844–45 Nonibe stepped down as regent and her son Siwani became chief of the imiDushane. At 18 or 19 years old,[80] he was the ruler of a mere fraction of the people his grandfather Ndlambe had once led. The amaNdlambe consisted of two main factions under Mhala and Mqayi, with the imiDushane as a third and smaller branch. Siwani's succession to the chieftainship occurred at a critical time and his mettle was tested almost immediately. By the mid-1840s the tensions between the colonists and Xhosa that had been simmering since the previous war had almost reached boiling point; cattle raiding across the border had become endemic and there was constant skirmishing. Confined beyond the Keiskamma River the majority of Xhosa lived in desperate conditions, the shortage of land compounded by a burgeoning population and periodic droughts. In 1846 the country was caught in the grip of a particularly bad drought[81] and by April things were becoming critical. Cattle were dying in their hundreds and famine was widespread. As day followed scorching day the land lay baking and seething in the relentless heat. Something had to give.

It was then that Tsili stole the axe.

He was caught red-handed, spotted by a white trader, named Holland, who ran the store on the market square at Fort Beaufort, and Tsili's shoplifting career came to an abrupt end. Tsili, who was also known as *Kleintjie* because he stood just 4 ft 6 inches high, was placed under arrest, handcuffed to a Khoi prisoner to prevent him escaping, and sent under guard to Grahamstown where he was to stand trial. On the way there his escort was ambushed by a group of men led by Tsili's brother. It was a messy, amateurish affair – Tsili was freed by the simple expedient of chopping off the hand of the other prisoner, who subsequently bled to death, and his brother was shot dead by one of the fleeing soldiers[82] – but it became a political football, provoking an unsatisfactory exchange of words between Colonel Hare, lieutenant-governor of the eastern districts, who demanded that the thief and murderers be given up, and Sandile, Msutu's Great Son and recently crowned king of the amaNgqika, who refused to do anything of the sort.

The axe was not worth much – about fourpence – but it was to cost hundreds of lives. The spark had been struck, the whole frontier was alight: the War of the Axe had begun. All minor divisions and altercations among the Xhosa were forgotten and the chiefs, including those who had previously been allies of the British, prepared for war. Even Dyani Tshatshu, the famous Christian convert and amaNtinde chief who had been feted in London, took up arms – later in the war, when English troops broke into his Great Place during a surprise attack, they found he had been priming himself with 'The Wrongs of the Caffre Nation', a treatise on the suffering of the Xhosa at the hands of the British during the previous war.[83] Stokwe of the amaMbalu, who had sworn on his father's deathbed that he would not involve his people in another war, also took up arms.[84]

'*It must be well understood*,' D'Urban had stated on granting Nonibe her land in recognition of her neutrality in the previous war, '*that these Kaffirs will be all British subjects.*'[85] In effect this meant that in the event of another war she and Siwani would have no choice but to support the British or they would be committing treason, an act punishable by death. But Siwani did not hesitate and joined his half-brothers, Qasana and Seyolo, in taking up arms against them.[86]

The Eastern Frontier 1835–1846

The Xhosa had the numerical advantage and many more were equipped with firearms during the War of the Axe than had been the case in previous wars, but it was obvious that they did not know how to use them effectively: 'Very few fired their gun from the shoulder', remarked a British dragoon, 'but discharged it from the hip, with the muzzle elevated so much that their shots nearly all went over our heads.'[87] The Xhosa had had no training in the use or maintenance of their weapons and time and again the British and their Mfengu allies were able to escape unscathed from what should have been devastating fire. The Xhosa were so short of ammunition that they often used almost anything that would fit down the barrel. They did not measure their gunpowder and sometimes used too much, making the older guns recoil so hard they knocked themselves down instead of the enemy. Some of their guns came from anti-British Boers, men such as Louis Trichardt, one of the leaders of the Great Trek into the interior.[88] Many of their guns bore the stamp of the British army, and while some may have been won in battle, the majority appear to have been stolen – although not by the Xhosa. 'We used to buy our guns from the European thieves who used to come and sell us guns at night,' King Sarhili's brother later recalled. Itinerant traders and British shopkeepers in Grahamstown also indulged in gunrunning,[89] importing new weapons specifically for illegal sale among the Xhosa. Some of the Xhosa firearms were so antiquated that they were more of a danger to their owners than the enemy, but on a psychological level even they won a few small victories by turning the tables on their foe: more than a few British and colonial soldiers had the novel experience of being the ones running away as mounted Xhosa sent bullets whizzing all around them.

The first victory of the war went to the Xhosa, when they took and destroyed a massive wagon-train at Burnshill. The wagons had formed a line three miles long, with only a small escort to guard its front and rear sections,[90] and were laden with ammunition, firearms, rations, blankets, tents, cooking utensils and every other item essential to the British military machine, including the vintage wines, silverware and fine china of the officers' mess. Their loss was a severe blow to the British. (Also lost were the Office Books – much to the joy of the reprobates 'whose names were inscribed therein for deeds which do not in general precede promotion.')[91] Inspired by their success, the Xhosa prepared to invade the Colony, but between them and their target, Grahamstown, stretched a line of military posts, running from Fort Beaufort near the Amatola mountains down to Fort Peddie, near the coast. Situated halfway between King William's Town and Grahamstown, Fort Peddie guarded the main route south into the Colony and was the largest of the posts with the strongest garrison on the Frontier. Not far away lived Nonibe and Siwani.

The territory around Fort Peddie supported a large population of amaNdlambe – including the imiDushane – Gqunukhwebe, and large numbers of Mfengu. The latter were a mixed bag of *Mfecane* refugees who, in the early 1820s, had been given refuge by Hintsa's people. Like immigrants everywhere, they were eager to improve their lot and, when the British offered them the opportunity to relocate to their own territory in about 1835 they were quick to seize it, crossing the Kei and resettling south of the river in the so-called Ceded Territory, where they provided the labour-starved colonists with an abundance of cheap workers.[92] The Mfengu also provided the Colony with a welcome buffer against the Xhosa, and bore the brunt of many attacks. In pulling out of Gcalekaland they had taken with them vast herds of King Hintsa's cattle, and there was no love lost between the two. Many Mfengu enlisted in special levies, and they became a vital part of the Colony's defences. It was dangerous work, since they were often deployed in the thick of the fiercest fighting, but were forbidden to carry guns. Armed with only assegais and shields, they seized every possible opportunity to plunder their opponents' herds and often those confiscated by the British too. Their bushcraft made them far more efficient than British troops, though their 'irregular' tactics, which included torture and dismemberment of prisoners, appalled their allies.[93] The levies were led by white officers, usually men who had grown up locally and were familiar with both isiXhosa and the terrain. In a peculiarly South African twist of fate, the commander of the levy deployed against Nonibe's people was Captain Michael Conway, whose son was later to marry another of Bessie's descendants.[94]

On 21 May the Xhosa forces took another large train of 43 wagons and a few days later, in full view of the British troops, an estimated 8 000 Xhosa fighting men from all the major chiefdoms gathered at Fort Peddie to launch another attack; 'the Kaffirs are coming,' wrote one of the whites in his diary,[95] and they locked themselves in the fort with their artillery, leaving their Mfengu allies, including women and children, outside in the ditch to do the actual fighting. The artillery decided the battle and within two hours it was all over. Xhosa casualties were high – between one and two hundred – and it was rumoured that Nonibe's son Siwani was amongst the dead, although that later proved to be wrong. On the colonial side, several Mfengu were killed 'but,' noted the resident missionary, 'not the hair of a white man was touched.'[96] With its supply lines cut, the fort was effectively under siege, its occupants in dire straits. Buck Adams, a private in the 7th Dragoons who had been seriously wounded in the leg, found himself in the 'hospital', a makeshift hut outside the fort, occupied by two others, a blind man and a Boer who had lost an arm. In the event of another attack

> 'the order given by the Surgeon was to be carried out as follows for our safety: As soon as the alarm was given, the blind man was to take me upon his back, and the man with one arm was to lead him into the Fort....'[97]

By the end of May the Xhosa had all but stopped supply wagons from Grahamstown and the British troops had had practically nothing to eat for 10 days,[98] but although they had won individual battles the Xhosa were losing the war. Their losses had been enormous, especially around Fort Peddie, where the fighting was particularly ferocious; within a month of the start of the war the missionary at Fort Peddie noted: 'They have lost many of their petty chiefs and great men.... The Imi-Dushani, especially, are said to have suffered greatly.'[99] More Xhosa were killed in this neighbourhood than anywhere else.[100]

As the war wore on and their losses mounted some of the chiefs began surrendering. Soon others were suing for peace. Nonibe protested that she also desired peace, 'but that Seyolo "has his hand on her shoulder, and keeps her down"....'[101]

It was at this critical junction that Seyolo made his unforgivable tactical error.

Seyolo, half-brother of Siwani[102]

It was he who, as a youth, had saved Nonibe's skin, when she was accused of witchcraft. Ten years older than Siwani, he was now about 30,[103] and as brave as ever, fiercely devoted to the struggle against the colonists and to reclaiming his people's land. In the eyes of the British he was 'a violent and morose savage [who] appears to be one of those on whom no dependence whatever can be placed,'[104] but to his followers he was a hero.

Seyolo, however, was an obstinate and impatient man – a most dangerous combination in a military leader. On the morning of 8 June 1846, he and his uncle, Mhala, began moving their fighters towards the Fish River in preparation for an attack on Trumpeter's Post. Mhala, 'The Wild Cat'[105] wisely chose to travel under the cover of darkness, but Seyolo decided impetuously to delay his departure until sunrise, and by the time his men reached the Gwanga, a little to the north of Peddie, it was broad daylight.[106] While they were fording the river a minor drama was being played out nearby that was to have a major impact on the outcome of the war. A British officer, Lieutenant Bisset, was returning to the fort from a skirmish when his horse suddenly ran away with him. Fighting to regain control of it, Bisset was carried over a hill and suddenly found himself, to his utter astonishment, running parallel to Seyolo's powerful army just as they were crossing the open flats alongside the river. The Xhosa were as amazed as Bisset: 'Org!' they exclaimed in astonishment,[107] their legendary oratorical skills failing them for once.

Bisset's commander was no more articulate when he heard the news: 'Hurrah!' he said and gathered his forces.[108] The terrain was ideal for cavalry and Seyolo was a sitting duck: catching him on the grassy open flats in broad daylight was as good as it got, and the British made the most of it.

With no bush for cover, Seyolo and his men pulled together in a tight mass, bravely standing their ground and waiting until the British were within 30 metres before opening fire. But nothing could save them from the artillery. Grouped together they made a perfect target for the big guns and many were literally torn to sheds. As the survivors broke, the British cavalry swept in for the kill. Some of the Xhosa tried to hood the horses by throwing their karosses at their heads, but the Dragoons 'cut, slashed, and sabred' them ruthlessly.[109] Although he was severely wounded, and it was a long time before he recovered, Seyolo was among the survivors. Two of his uncles, Mxhamli and Zethu, were not so lucky.[110] It was the most disastrous encounter of the war; the British lost only two men, while hundreds of Seyolo's men perished, dying 'almost by families, it being said, that in one place a father and two sons, and in another a father and three sons, and so on, may be seen lying together.'[111] The slaughter was shocking: the whole plain was covered with bodies, and the river so choked with corpses that Bisset's orderly, whom he had sent to fetch water, returned empty-handed: 'Master,' he said, ' I cannot bring the water; it is all blood.'[112]

'After the battle of the Gwanga,' it was said, 'nothing succeeded with the Xosas.'[113] A few months later the British crossed the Keiskamma and struck at the heart of the amaNdlambe.[114] Nonibe, who had already begun negotiating her surrender, was not spared.[115] Under cover of darkness the British force assembled on the hills above her homestead, which lay on an open grassy plain, 'undulating here and there into shallow kloofs and valleys.'[116] The rising sun burnt off the mist, revealing a calm and peaceful scene: Nonibe's people were still asleep in their homes and their cattle still sheltered in their kraals. Without waiting for the artillery and infantry to join them, the British cavalry launched their attack, flying down the hillsides in fan formation at full gallop. Nonibe's people woke to the crash of guns and the panicked stampeding of their cattle. Racing outside they tried to drive their herds to safety in the nearby bush but the artillery was now blazing away and they were forced to save themselves instead. Many were killed, vast numbers of their cattle driven off and their homesteads burnt.

Napier, one of the dragoons, describes entering the remains of the village:

> 'Cautiously descending into the picturesque valley where the skirmish had taken place, and near which stood the kraal of Nonube, the great wife of the late Dushani (a lady of European descent, and mother to Siwana, the actual paramount of the T'Slambies) the first thing we beheld, lying on the green bank of a gurgling brook, was the dead body of a Kaffir. His right hand, firmly clenched, still grasped an assegai; whilst the left one, dangling over the flowery bank into the stream, was gently moved to and fro by the clear rippling waters....'[117]

Napier, incidentally, had heard the same story about Nonibe's ancestry, which had been so widespread in the previous war, over a decade earlier: 'Queen Nonube – whose "capital" we so ungallantly destroyed – is said to be able to trace a lineal descent' to females aboard the *Grosvenor*, one of 'two daughters of a General Campbell, who, it is said, became the wives of a Kaffir chief....'[118]

By the end of 1847 the war was over. In December Nonibe, Siwani, and the rest of the allied chiefs were summoned to King William's Town by Sir Harry Smith, the new Governor of the Cape. Nonibe, who was in her forties, appeared much younger than her years, but the war had taken its toll on her: 'Her hair was long and matted and her whole appearance was filthy in the extreme.'[119] The other chiefs were no better off and all 'looked wretchedly haggard and dejected. They were wrapped in large woollen blankets, and evidenced by their condition that they had suffered severe privations.'[120] Smith compounded their misery with a public humiliation. He had with him two sticks, one with a brass knob signifying Peace, the other a plain one representing War. Each chief was commanded to step forward separately and choose between the two by touching it, and then 'to kiss the Governor's *foot* in token of absolute submission, and deep humility for their past aggressions upon the colony, and hostility to the British Government.'[121] A second meeting a couple of weeks later, saw further theatrics, with Smith shouting, ripping up treaties and blowing up a wagon loaded with gunpowder.[122]

Once again war had achieved nothing. British Kaffraria was extended right up to the Kei River and most of the chiefs placed under British rule (only Sarhili across the Kei River remained independent).[123] More forts were built to entrench British control. The land from the old Fish River boundary to the Keiskamma, the ceded territory, was divided into districts, some of which were sold off to white farmers. The land north of the Keiskamma to the Buffalo River became 'neutral territory', and the land from the Buffalo to the Kei, 80 kilometres away, was divided between the Ndlambe and Ngqika chiefs, and governed by martial law.[124]

Siwani and Nonibe never again opposed the British: 'We were in the war and we have seen that we were wrong, we fell into a pit – but now we will be true to the government,' they declared, and were informed that if they complied with the colonial authority's terms they would be permitted to live in peace and 'enjoy the protection of a just Government.'[125] When war broke out again in 1850 (the War of Mlanjeni), Siwani and Nonibe kept their word and, like many of the other chiefs who had previously fought against the British, collaborated with the Colony.[126] Siwani's brother Seyolo was one of the few to take up arms again, joining forces with Sandile,[127] Msutu's Great Son. For the first time the Khoi also joined the Xhosa against the British and, although they certainly had many of their own reasons for doing so, there is evidence that they were encouraged by Seyolo. His ardent nationalism won him enormous popular support among the Xhosa, so much so that Siwani struggled to maintain his authority and several of his people left to join Seyolo.[128] The war was bitterly fought and reluctantly conceded. Seyolo surrendered on 9 October 1852 and was 'safely lodged and securely guarded in a strong room'[129] in Grahamstown. He was sentenced to death for sedition and rebellion and held in confinement at Wynberg,[130] but was later reprieved and imprisoned on Robben Island, where his uncle Mhala, Maqoma and other Xhosa leaders soon joined him. Some of the chiefs' children were sent to Cape Town, to be educated as British subjects and Christians at Zonnebloem College. They were not permitted to visit their fathers, but the chiefs were able to smuggle messages home through Seyolo's and Maqoma's wives, who had accompanied their husbands to the island and were permitted to visit Cape Town.[131]

Seyolo's brother Siwani, meanwhile, was rewarded for his neutrality and the authorities promised to extend his territory.[132] There were obvious advantages to being pro-British for the chiefs who 'sat still' during the war – Kama, Pato, Mqayi and Siwani received annual subsidies from the government (Siwani's was £60 per annum)[133] – but for their people as a whole the situation was no better than before.

In October 1852 Nonibe and Siwani met the Governor of the Cape, Sir George Cathcart, near Tamarha Post. Siwani, reported Cathcart, was

> 'as well dressed as any English gentleman could be, with a cloth shooting-jacket, a quiet waistcoat, and some sort of light-coloured trousers, all new, and of the finest materials. His manners and conversation are quite like a gentleman; he is very good-looking, and of a lighter complexion than most Kafirs, Princess Nonebi, his mother, claiming English blood from the traditional descent from one of the two ladies (Miss Campbells, I believe) wrecked on the coast, and about whom there is a romantic story. One, it seems, married the chief of the Amapondas of that day, who was Nonebi's ancestor.'[134]

Communicating through an interpreter they assured him of their continued loyalty and their desire to live in peace.[135] They really had little choice: as the governor himself later remarked, without their Amatola stronghold to fly to ('that great natural citadel' was now in the hands of British troops) they could be controlled easily and, if necessary, crushed.[136] Nevertheless, the governor was very favourably impressed:

> 'the conduct of the Chief Siwani and his tribe, who occupy the greater portion of a broad margin on the left bank of the Keiskamma, is most exemplary, and his fidelity throughout the whole contest gives full confidence not only in his good faith, but in his power to restrain his people from lawless intrusion into the Colony.'[137]

Siwani, said Cathcart, had

> 'sincerely embraced Christianity, and has been doing good service in defence of the northern districts, with his people regularly enrolled as a levy, in which his sons held the rank of officers.'

Before taking his leave of them the governor said that he intended giving

> 'a good bull, well bred, to Siwani, which I have for him, of an Ayrshire breed; and I gave old Nonebi, who is not so very old, by-the-bye, and very arch, a South American "poncha", which I happen to have, of all sorts of colours. She put it on, and, no doubt, rode home with much satisfaction to her kraal.'[138]

Four years later her world imploded.

Chapter Ten

The Seer, the Drunk and the Rapist

The Kei River curves and twists through the southern valleys of the former Transkei like a mighty serpent. Big and broad though it is, there is no bridge spanning the river where it breaks through to the sea, and the coastal road simply stops dead at the water's edge on either side of the mouth, as though it has been bitten through and consumed. The steady stream of rural folk and holidaymakers passing through the scruffy little resort of Kei Mouth, pedestrians and vehicles alike, are obliged to cross its deep brown waters on an old ferry, spilling out onto the opposite bank to resume their journey up the rutted dirt road.

About a kilometre to the north, set well off the road, is a small homestead, a collection of three or four mud and thatch huts, one painted a lurid turquoise. The track my 4x4 is following passes literally within touch of its walls. Beyond the *umzi*, the land falls away in broken planes down to the river and, beyond that, to a lagoon and beautiful beach. The scene is peaceful, the homestead in no way different from all the other homesteads that dot the surrounding hills, except that many years ago, in 1856, a girl named Nongqawuse lived here.

One imagines such a lovely place would bind its people to it tightly, that they would hold this place dear, cling to it and raise their children here, generation after generation, with pride. Yet none of the present occupants are related to Nongqawuse, nor are any of the people living in any of the neighbouring homesteads related to anyone who lived here during her time. They were all wiped out during the Cattle-Killing, even the children – especially the children, in fact – and the people who occupy the land today are descended from others who were brought in to settle the area after the tragedy.

The 4x4s – there are two others besides mine – labour down 'the Staircase' as my guide calls the jagged track, bucking and tilting this way and that until we splash through the Gxara stream at the bottom of the hill in a hollow of enclosing green bush and enter a broad sloping field, at the lower end of which the river loops back and lies in deep, dark, silent pools. The water is strangely motionless, with no flow in the direction of the nearby sea. The banks are overhung with thick bush, the banana-leafed *Strelitzia* casting deep shadows on the almost black water. The only sign of life is a large school of fish drifting close to the surface, presenting me with an uncomfortable reminder that among all this plenty – the fish, the well-watered fields, the fat cattle on the surrounding hills and the extravagant greenery – an entire people once starved to death.

It was at these pools that Nongqawuse first saw the strangers on an autumn day in 1856. She was about fifteen years old and lived at the home of her uncle Mhlakaza. Together with another young girl, she had been sent down to the fields to scare the birds off the crops; a routine enough chore, but one that was to have terrible – unimaginable – ramifications. A winding path took her down to the Gxara in the fold of the hill below the homestead. Even in bright sunlight the spot is shadowy and a little unsettling, but when the mist drifts in off the sea on a dark and cloudy dawn it must be a very disturbing place indeed. Nowadays the mouth of the Gxara forms a blind lagoon, but in those days, before the advent of wattle and other thirsty exotics in the region, the river was probably open to the sea and it may have been the ripple and surge of the incoming tide, disturbing the waters of the deep pools, that triggered Nongqawuse's imagination and was the cause of it all. Or, as the historian Jeff Peires has suggested, it may have been the shadowy forms of dolphins, of which there are plenty along this coast, at play in the river mouth. But however we may try to rationalise it, Nongqawuse was convinced that she saw the forms of three human beings.

Through the mist drifting off the warm water, they called out to her, saying 'Destroy all your cattle, build up your kraals, and you will find all your kraals full of cattle on the eighth day. Throw away all your corn, fill your water vessels....'[1]

Nongqawuse reported their words to her uncle, Mhlakaza: the strangers, she said, had claimed to have risen from the dead, and had told her that if their orders were obeyed then all who were dead, and their chiefs likewise, would arise and return to the land of the living. Initially Mhlakaza chose to disregard his niece's words, but when the strangers appeared to the girl again on the following day, she went to him once more and this time he listened attentively. It was not unusual in Xhosa society for certain individuals to have visions, particularly adolescent girls like Nongqawuse, or menopausal women; Mhlakaza himself is said to have experienced visions from time to time.[2] Those who did were generally perceived as having been 'called' to train as diviners, as mediators between the living and their ancestors who resided in the spirit world, and were treated with respect.[3] It was customary, in periods of crisis, for the Xhosa to appeal to their ancestors for guidance and benign intervention. And at that particular time – the mid-nineteenth century – the Xhosa were faced with a crisis of extreme dimensions.

For over 80 years they had been embroiled in a series of devastating wars, first against the Dutch settlers and then against the British, in the process of which they had lost much of their land, vast numbers of their cattle and countless young men. Before the arrival of the colonists, there had been tracts of unoccupied territory between each of the main Xhosa-speaking peoples, allowing space for hunting, for additional grazing so that the land did not became damaged by overgrazing, or for the establishment of new or breakaway chiefdoms. By the 1850s, however, there was no longer any spare space and the territory into which the Xhosa had been pushed and confined as the Colony expanded could no longer accommodate them. On all fronts they were beset with troubles, overcrowded on overgrazed land, and with their religious and social systems under threat from the missionaries and increasing numbers of converts and refugees. The situation was exacerbated by the appearance of blight in their crops and, at about the same time that Nongqawuse first saw the strangers, a devastating outbreak of lung sickness, brought up from the Cape by trek-oxen.[4] A highly contagious disease, it had swept through the country and by June 1855 had already killed off upwards of 100 000 head of cattle, 'reducing many persons from a state of affluence to one of poverty as when it enters a herd it scarcely leaves a single head behind,' wrote a missionary, from deep in Xhosa territory. He warned that

> '[t]here is every prospect of war breaking out again…. The exciting cause is no doubt the existen[ce] of the Russian War and the [Xhosa] no doubt think that now is their time while the English have enough to do in other directions and the military force is but small.'[5]

But to the leaders of the Xhosa it must have been clear that another war against the British was not the answer. The Xhosa had been driven back too many times and had lost far more than they had gained in the previous wars. Even so, something had to be done if they were to improve their situation. It was obvious that radical action was needed, and when Mhlakaza heard Nongqawuse's words, he must have thought it was the call they had all been waiting for.

A man of great curiosity and intelligence, Mhlakaza had an unusual and somewhat turbulent past. His father, who had been a counsellor to King Sarhili, is said to have killed his mother in a fit of rage.[6] It was perhaps as a result of this tragedy, that Mhlakaza had gone to live in the Colony for some years. There he had learnt to speak Dutch fluently, probably while working on Boer farms, and had become known among the white settlers as Wilhelm Goliath.[7] Later he lived in Grahamstown, where he eagerly set about mastering English too.[8] Like the prophet Makana before him, Mhlakaza embraced Christianity, becoming familiar with all its principles and prophecies, including the story of the Resurrection. He married a Christian woman, an Mfengu named Sarah, and joined the Wesleyan church. Later, in the service of the Archdeacon, Nathaniel Merriman, he began attending the Anglican church and in 1849 became the first black man to receive communion. The following year he was confirmed at Graaff-Reinet.[9] He also learnt to read and write and for a period, starting in October 1850, was in charge of a school for Xhosa children at Southwell.[10]

Mhlakaza's hut in Merriman's garden, Grahamstown, c1850[11]

It was in that same year, 1850, that the War of Mlanjeni began. The war was even more violent than any preceding it: 'Extermination is now the only word and principle to guide us,' stated the British governor,[12] and his troops took him at his word.

As the war escalated the Xhosa took cover in the dense forests of the Waterkloof. The British brought in their heavy artillery to flush them out. The lush yellowwood glades, soaring cliffs and exquisite waterfalls became the backdrop to a most brutal confrontation. Although the Xhosa fought tenaciously, nothing could save them from the terrifying power of the British cannon. One English soldier wrote: '...such a sight I never saw before in all my life. Men, women and children that was killed and wounded by the shot and shell, some with their arms, others with their legs off. It was a terrible sight to see....'[13]

The war had little effect on Mhlakaza's employer: throughout the hostilities Archdeacon Merriman continued to teach, preach and oversee the clergy under his authority. Accompanied by Mhlakaza he travelled almost constantly, throughout the eastern Cape Colony. Merriman occasionally rode a horse, but more often both were on foot. The distances were enormous, the two frequently walking 55–65 kilometres a day in all kinds of weather and on very rough roads. Mhlakaza usually carried both Merriman's possessions and his own and, not surprisingly, often lagged behind his employer, limping into their resting place long after him and well after sunset.[14] He was also expected to provide his own provisions, and while the archdeacon was usually ensured of food at the farmhouses they visited en route, Mhlakaza was not always so fortunate. In all fairness, however, it must be said that Merriman insisted on eating with his manservant, 'sitting cheek by jowl and parting his bread' with him, and when this offended the racist sensibilities of their white hosts he paid them no attention. Nor did he make any attempt to restrain Mhlakaza from arguing against racism with the settlers,[15] which as he spoke both English and Dutch fluently and was familiar with the principles of Christianity, he was able to do rather well.

In 1853 Mhlakaza adopted a young war orphan whose mother and father had been killed by British forces in the Waterkloof. They became so close that the child has been described as practically 'an appendage to [Mhlakaza].'[16]

17

According to the historian Jeff Peires, this was probably his niece Nongqawuse, since she too was an orphan and was living with him when he left Grahamstown and returned to the Gxara River in Sarhili's territory.

Once there, the child's traumatic war experiences – and the atrocities inflicted on the Xhosa as a whole – could not have failed to impact on everyone in the *umzi*, especially on Mhlakaza, the uncle with whom she had bonded so closely:

'Might she have seen her mother shot dead with tens of other Xhosa women by the Colony's black auxiliaries? Might she have seen her father's body suspended on a tree, the blood still trickling from his forehead? Might she have tripped over their bones in a gully or sent their skulls rolling down the pathways as she stumbled out of the living hell of Colonel Eyre's greatest triumph?'[18]

As one of King Sarhili's chief counsellors,[19] Mhlakaza was a man of authority and influence, and once he had accepted the authenticity of his niece's visions the news spread like a veld fire in winter and soon the whole nation knew about the 'new people', 'the strangers' or 'the ancestors', as they were variously referred to. At first the people were stunned: destroying their cattle seemed too great a sacrifice.[20] But when more visions and messages followed the first, some ceased sowing crops and began killing their cattle, depending on the power of the ancestors and retreating into their ancient beliefs, in the hope that the prophecy would be fulfilled.

It was then that Bessie's great-grandson Siwani achieved greatness. It was not the blood-and-thunder greatness of his warrior ancestors, but the stance he chose to take during the Cattle-Killing required tremendous courage nevertheless, and what he was to achieve was nothing less than the preservation of his people.

As word of the prophecy spread, people began travelling to the Gxara to see for themselves, and the stories of the wonderful things they had seen there enchanted and delighted their listeners:

'The horns of oxen were said to be peeping from beneath the rushes which grew around a swampy pool near the village of the seer; and from a subterranean cave were heard the bellowing and knocking of the horns of cattle impatient to rise.'[21]

Some said they had recognised among the ancestors several dead chiefs, heroes of the anti-colonial wars, claiming to have

'actually seen the risen heroes emerge from the Indian Ocean, some on foot, some on horse-back, passing in silent parade before them, then sinking again among the tossings of the restless waves. Sometimes they were seen rushing through the air in the wild chase of old. Then again they were seen marshalled in battle array.'[22]

The 'new people' would drive the colonists into the sea, the believers said, and the land would be restored to its rightful owners. Some of the believers' reports of the wonderful occurrences at the Gxara were truly outlandish – such as the armies seen sailing in umbrellas[23] – and as the stories grew wilder, expectations grew too.

It was even said – this was at the time of the Crimean War – that the Russians would soon be landing to help the ancestors drive out the British. The rumour received an unexpected boost with the debacle of the HMS *Geyser* in November 1856. The vessel had been sent to reconnoitre the mouth of the Kei River, with an eye to sending in troops and supplies at a later stage. The commander, who was drunk and had failed to pick up a pilot at East London, entered the river by the wrong channel and the boat he sent out turned turtle, nearly drowning its occupants, so he upped anchor again and left. The Xhosa, who at the first sight of the ship had sounded the alarm and gathered in huge numbers along the banks, watched with delight as it left. As Kei mouth was just a couple of kilometres from Mhlakaza and Nongqawuse's kraal (and they had no way of knowing that the *Geyser* had only been on a recce) it was obvious to all that the ancestors must have had a hand in driving the British away.[24]

For a modern western mindset the fervour with which the Cattle-Killing was emraced is almost beyond comprehension, but as Jeff Peires has pointed out, '… the Cattle-Killing was a logical and rational response, perhaps even an inevitable response, by a nation driven to desperation by pressures that people today can barely imagine.'[25] To the Xhosa the prophecy was perfectly credible, since it was rooted both in their traditional religious practices – they had always communicated with their ancestors through the sacrifice of cattle – as well as in their ancient creation myths. As the following example from 1807 illustrates, the premises behind the prophecy were neither new nor alien but were closely related to existing beliefs:

> 'In the land in which the sun rises, there was a cavern, from which the first [Xhosa], and in fact All peoples, as also the stock of every kind of animal, came forth. At the same time, the sun and moon came into being, to shed their light, and trees, grass and other plants to provide food for man and cattle.'[26]

The seed of the prophecy may have the originated with Nongqawuse but its subsequent phenomenal growth and spread were possible only because it was what the people themselves wanted, and ultimately the responsibility for what happened as a result of the Cattle-Killing rests not on a fifteen-year-old girl but on her people: they believed because they wanted to believe.

What the ancestors – or rather the believers – were offering the Xhosa was nothing less than salvation. It is no coincidence that the first people to begin visiting the Gxara and to believe most fervently in the prophecy were principally the amaNgqika and amaNdlambe of the Frontier districts,[27] that is, those Xhosa who had been hardest hit by Settler expansionism and who had already lost their loved ones in the wars against the British, and most of their land and cattle. And they believed that by sacrificing their remaining herds they had nothing more to lose but misery and degradation – and everything to gain.[28]

In July 1856 King Sarhili himself visited the Gxara River. Sarhili, as you may recall, was the Great Son of Hintsa, the Xhosa king who had been killed by the British in 1835, and his Great Wife Nomsa, the Bomvana-born granddaughter of a white castaway. By 1856 Sarhili was about 40 years old, and had been king for 21 years. He was by all accounts a modern marketing man's dream, practically made for TV:

> '... [M]ost distinguished looking... tall and well featured... most dignified... pleasant and witty, vivacious... his people drawn to him by personal charm. Handsome he was, second only to his brother Ulindinxowa in that respect. Astute beyond measure....'[29]

Sarhili had all the attributes of an excellent ruler: 'weighty in council, respected and beloved by his people,' he was blessed with strength of character and compassion.[30]

But at the time of his visit to Nongqawuse, Sarhili was under enormous personal strain, weighed down with grief over the recent death of his 12-year-old son. And when his beloved child was 'revealed' to him by the prophetess, the king, in his emotional state, succumbed. Who can blame him? I know I can't: when my dad died in my teens I wanted more than anything for it all to have been just a big mistake and to have him come back, and I think there must be very few recently bereaved people who would not jump at that chance if it was offered to them, especially if – as in Sarhili's case – it dovetailed with their social and religious beliefs.

GXARA MOUTH FROM NONGQAWUSE'S HOMESTEAD.

Convinced that the prophecy was true, Sarhili threw his weight behind the Cattle-Killing and despite the resistance of his mother, Nomsa,[31] ordered his men to begin slaughtering his herds. His subordinate chiefs, with whom he was in constant contact, followed his lead and the movement gained momentum rapidly. Across the land people and dogs gorged themselves on a surfeit of beef[32] and by August the skeletons of thousands of cattle littered the veld.

Against a gruesome backdrop of rotting cattle carcases and untilled fields, an incongruous air of festivity reigned as the believers prepared to celebrate the coming of the new order. Many of the people dressed up in their finest outfits, even 'withered old hags who had discontinued painting and ornaments for years, though tottering with age and want are found covered with red clay and ornaments, hoping soon to have youth restored and an abundance of food.'[33] The date for the Resurrection was set in the middle of the month at the time of the full moon. On that day, it was said, twin suns would rise, collide with one another and darkness would cover the land, the new cattle and resurrected dead would rise from the earth and the English would be driven into the sea. The build-up to the promised day was one long continuous party. No one slept the night before and as the dawn flushed the sky they waited with bated breath. But only one sun rose that morning and nothing else happened. There were no new cattle, no newly arisen loved ones, no returned heroes – nothing. It was the first Disappointment.[34] The believers, however, did not lose faith; the obvious reason the prophecy had not been fulfilled, they argued, was because of the many sceptics who had refused to kill their cattle and continued to till their fields, and pressure began mounting against the unbelievers to do the right thing for the good of the nation.

Sandile[35]

South of the Kei River many amaNgqika commoners had already joined Sarhili's amaGcaleka in supporting the Cattle-Killing movement, but their king, Sandile, had remained neutral. In early October 1856, however, he too began killing his cattle,[36] encouraged by his mother Msutu,[37] whose Great Place, near Burnshill mission station, overlooked the grave of her long-dead husband, Ngqika. Ngqika, as mentioned above, had never wanted to marry Msutu in the first place and had so successfully avoided having anything to do with her that many believed Sandile was not his son. Yet now the elderly woman spent days attempting to smooth her wrinkles and make herself attractive for her soon-to-be resurrected spouse. 'Poor old foolish woman!' remarked the missionary Tiyo Soga, 'She must now be nearly seventy years of age; and I am sure that were Gaika [Ngqika] to rise he would find his wife a perfect fright.'[38]

Bessie's granddaughter Nonibe, her son Siwani, and their people were caught in the centre of the storm. In the heart of amaNdlambe territory, another young prophetess arose, Nonkosi, who was only nine years old. Her prophecies were chillingly similar to those of Nongqawuse, and were fervently believed. Siwani's uncle Mhala, the most powerful chief in British Caffraria after King Sandile, and greatly loved by his people, began openly supporting the Cattle-Killing and ordered that all cultivation cease immediately.[39] Even the unbelievers complied, except, it is said, his nephew Bulungwa.

As the movement gained momentum and the numbers of believers increased, the rate and spread of the killing increased too: cattle were slaughtered faster than they could be consumed, whole carcases were left to putrefy and across the land the stench of death and decay poisoned the air.[40]

In October Mhlakaza began calling on the colonists to kill their cattle too, saying that 'the people who have arrived have not come to make war on the white man, but to bring about a happy state of things to all...,'[41] but there is no evidence that any heeded his call.

As the months passed another date for the Resurrection was set and the believers drove home the need for all remaining cattle to be killed within eight days so that the dead would surely arise. But as before, the prophecy failed.

A young girl from Stokwe's amaMbalu people later described how she and her family joined the crowds to await the new dawn: the night was clear with no moon, and a strong wind was blowing. Large fires were made and the people gathered on the hilltops, eating and dancing until well past midnight. They were awoken by their chiefs in the dark pre-dawn to await the arrival of the new people and their herds, and as they looked out across the hills some among them thought they could see cattle moving about in the bush; 'the men began one and then a nother to say: "Do you see them?" Others would say: "That is them." One could see one thing and another a nother thing.' The girl's father was a firm believer, but she herself was not, which made him sometimes call her 'a mad English girl.' Now as they waited her father scolded her:

> 'Now do you believe it?' he asked, could she not see for herself? 'I said: "See what" "Can you not see the things on the side of that hill?" "No: I can see nothing but thorn bushes." He said that it was not bushes but I thought that the men had eaten too much corn and Meat and drunk to[o] much of [beer] to know what they saw....'[42]

This Disappointment was blamed on the unbelievers, or *amaGogotya*, and the believers turned against them, their anger and hatred increasing with each successive heartbreaking failure.

Among the unbelievers were Bessie's descendants, Nonibe and Siwani. Early in August, prior to the first Disappointment, Siwani had received an urgent missive from the Gqunukhwebe chief Kama, with whom his family had longstanding ties. As a child during the War of 1835, Siwani had lived with Kama;[43] now he received a messenger from the older chief 'to ascertain what course I intended to take in connection with the prevailing excitement and talk about Mhlakaza'. Should he not support the Cattle-Killing and 'throw off the Govt. and take up arms against it,' Kama said; he would be treated as an enemy. The young chief replied respectfully that he thought of Kama 'as my father as he took care of me when I was a child' but, he added, he could not believe in the prophecy, and he would do all in his power to dissuade his people from following the 'foolish predictions.'[44] Not only did he intend remaining loyal to the government, Siwani said, but if necessary he was prepared to take up arms against his own countrymen. The British commissioner had recently made him a present of a plough and he already possessed a wagon and oxen – 'these two things were my support,' he added, 'and a help to my Family – who if I joined in war, would die from hunger and cold.'[45]

On this pragmatic base, the 30-year-old Siwani secured his chieftainship. He not only continued to refuse to kill his own herds but actively encouraged his people to *buy* cattle at rock-bottom prices and thereby increase their herds.[46] Prior to the Cattle-Killing Siwani's imiDushane had been one of the smaller clans that made up the amaNdlambe, weakened by his regent mother's pro-British stance and fragmented by the strife between her and her co-regent, the forceful and anti-British Seyolo. In the ten or twelve years since Siwani had become chief, he had not yet succeeded in rebuilding his following or his people's strength. He had attained neither the fame nor the popularity of his forefathers – his illustrious grandfather Ndlambe, once the most powerful chief in the region, and his courageous father Mdushane, one of the most accomplished military strategists of his time – nor did he enjoy the prominence of his nationalistic half-brother Seyolo, still languishing on Robben Island for his role in the previous war.

But Siwani was not without moral courage, and in the long run his diplomacy and pragmatism were to save more lives than any other chief succeeded in doing. He confronted the believers among his people head-on, punishing those who killed their cattle and forcing them to cultivate their fields – and in so doing incurred their fury. At least one attempt was made on his life. Most of the believers were Seyolo's people who had been placed under Siwani when their chief was imprisoned on Robben Island. Now they began rallying around Seyolo's popular son, Bangayi. Siwani advised them against destroying their property and called for a meeting of all the chiefs to discuss the crisis, but his call went unheeded.[47] As believers turned on the unbelievers, stealing their carefully preserved cattle and food stores and attacking their persons and property, families throughout the land were torn asunder. Many believer women left their unbeliever husbands, refusing to return unless they killed their cattle, and some fathers resorted to killing their unbeliever sons; civil war threatened the nation, but the colonial government, although it was appealed to for help, did little to protect unbelievers. When the chiefs Siwani, Anta and Kama (who, despite his threatening message to Siwani earlier, ended up opposing the Cattle-Killing) moved their people closer to their magistrates, the governor, Sir

George Grey, ordered them to return to their lands, abandoning them to the tender mercies of their neighbours.[48]

With the clarity of hindsight it is obvious that Siwani was right in refusing to participate in the Cattle-Killing, but in the midst of the mass hysteria, enormous peer pressure and the precedents of royalty, resisting as he did required singular courage. Xhosa society set great value on the bonds of kinship[49] and many of Siwani's close relatives and elders were believers. It was also a society in which the elderly were accorded profound respect – as befitted those who were close to attaining reverence as ancestral spirits. Seniority took such precedence that there were incidents of grown men, known to be unbelievers, choosing to kill their cattle (and run the risk of having their wives and children starve to death), rather than show disrespect for their believer fathers. Adding to the tremendous pressure on Siwani to conform were the reports that his dead father Mdushane and grandfather Ndlambe were among the spirits 'seen' at the misty pools on the Gxara, and that knowledge alone must have tempted him to submit to the prophecy, yet he appears to have been unwavering in his refusal. His mother Nonibe's role during this period is unknown, but her pro-colonial sympathies and the fact that both were Christians certainly contributed to his resolve: 'It is astonishing the impression the prevailing prophecies have on the minds of the [people],' he said, '...and I can only view it as a curse of God.'[50]

Siwani's entrepreneurial instincts may have played a role too. The unbelievers were largely those 'who had benefited from the new opportunities offered by the colonial presence'[51] and Siwani's people, as we have seen, had been quick to seize the opportunity to buy up the believers' cattle cheaply, exhibiting, in the words of a contemporary government official, 'a recommendatory spirit to improve themselves and to accumulate property.'[52]

As 1856 drew slowly to a close and the new year dawned, those who had slaughtered their cattle and had no crops to harvest were desperately short of food. Many were starving. As always the most vulnerable members of society, the very young and the very old, suffered the most, and by January 1857 children were dying with terrible frequency, their parents tortured by the knowledge that they themselves had caused their little ones' agony. By February the women had sold all their ornaments to feed their families, and as the months wore on and as more Disappointments followed, the majority of Xhosa found themselves with nothing left to sacrifice, and even the staunchest believers began to doubt the truth of the prophecy. As conditions worsened and their fears grew, the people began demanding of the seers that they receive concrete returns for their sacrifices.

When nothing tangible was forthcoming King Sarhili, whose herds prior to the Cattle-Killing were so vast that it had taken three months to slaughter them all,[53] arranged a special meeting with Nongqawuse and her uncle Mhlakaza, but upon his arrival at their dwelling they were nowhere to be found. Torn by self-doubt and his personal role in his people's suffering,

Sarhili set off for his Great Place in a state of such emotional torment that on the way back he tried to kill himself.[54]

By February, it was reported, the imiDushane believers under Seyolo's son Bangayi were suffering severely for want of food. By March Siwani's erstwhile rival was reduced to working in a road gang.[55] In June 1857, with a tenacity born of despair, the believers set a final date for the Resurrection, but – as one noted bitterly – 'not even a dog rose from the dead.'[56]

Starving and desperate, the believers turned with unprecedented ferocity on the unbelievers, and the colonial government at long last began to establish camps for their protection.[57]

The believers were reduced to gnawing the bark of trees. As the weeks passed and more and more people died, the survivors grew too weak to remove the dead to a safe distance or to bury the corpses, so they threw them instead into their empty granaries – and with macabre irony the new grain pits which had been built to receive the bounty of the prophecy became instead their graves. A few of the survivors, driven insane with hunger, turned to cannibalism. 'The people were eating cats and dogs and women ate their own babies,' recalled a survivor named Sijako.[58] 'I do not even now like to speak about it,' said another survivor, Maseti, a full 50 years later.[59] An English clerk and interpreter at Fort Warden near the Kei River told of riding along a road one day and noticing some smoke coming from a hut:

> 'I looked in and saw an old native roasting the head of another who had died of starvation.... I went on and near a stream found a woman who had a pot on a fire. When I asked what she had in the pot? She replied, "It is my baby". I asked no more: my heart was too full.'[60]

Shockingly emaciated and utterly destitute, the Xhosa were forced – with terrible irony – to turn to their enemy for help. Those who were capable of walking or crawling began making their painful way towards the colonial centres, where they knew there would be food. Villages such as King William's Town and Komgha were inundated by walking skeletons, as if the prophecy had been fulfilled at last, but in the worst and cruellest way possible: 'Day after day, day after day, as these spectres came in crowds and crawled along, one might have imagined that the prophet's prediction had come to pass, and that the dead had indeed risen from their graves.'[61]

Many colonists were moved by the plight of the Xhosa: 'The first sound in the morning,' recalled Mrs Brownlee, a missionary's wife, 'and the last at night was the pitiful endless crying for food.'[62] They helped with relief work, providing soup and sago to the needy, and also dug graves: for many Xhosa help came too late and they died soon after eating their first meal. But other colonists were less sympathetic:

'Some of the [Xhosa] were rendered so daring by hunger that they would come and steal cattle in open day and while we were looking at them. We had to get permission to shoot them, which we did and then they stopped at home and died of starvation.'[63]

Mhala[64]

Siwani's uncle Mhala had been one of most committed of all the chiefs in carrying out Nongqawuse's instructions and the situation amongst his people was especially critical; most of his people were surviving on tree gum and roots, and the plight of the children was particularly sad.[65] In a desperate bid for survival the once-proud chief and his followers became thieves, keeping constantly on the move in order to avoid their pursuers. He was eventually captured by a policeman Mjuza, the only son of Makana, the prophet who had been war doctor to Mhala's father Ndlambe in the attack on Grahamstown in 1819.[66]

Throwing himself on the mercy of his enemies, Mhala begged the colonial government to help his people, but the governor, Sir George Grey, had other plans; labour had always been in short supply in the Colony, and he recognised the crisis as an opportunity to rectify this.

On Grey's orders famine relief was provided only in exchange for manual labour and anyone who tried to remain on and cultivate their own land was refused food. With the aid of colonial police – amongst whom, incidentally, there were many ex-believers – the amaNdlambe magistrate, Major JC Gawler, instituted what has been described as a reign of terror against a defenceless people.[67] Trivial crimes and even unsubstantiated charges were used to force the people off their land and into exile as labourers on white farms. Even children were set to work, some of them apprenticed to masters as far off as Cape Town.[68] In a very short space of time, the Xhosa became a landless and largely unskilled workforce at the mercy of a predatory government and, as a precursor of the hated Pass Laws of apartheid, all who entered the Colony had to be in possession of special passes authorising their presence there.[69]

In justifying its treatment of the Xhosa, the government chose to see the Cattle-Killing not as the last stand of a desperate people but as an act of war. The British authorities were convinced that the two young prophetesses Nongqawuse and Nonkosi had been pawns of the anti-colonial chiefs in an elaborate plot to instigate another outbreak of hostilities against the British, the theory being that the loss of their cattle would free the men from their traditional role of animal husbandry, and that starvation would drive them to fight with greater bravery. This so-called 'Chiefs' Plot' had several flaws, the most obvious being that starving men are generally too weak to fight, a point which was made by both Mhala and the famous strategist and fighter Maqoma, the latter noting wryly that the English had proved stronger than his even when his men had had enough to eat.[70] For Sir George Grey and the colonial administration, however, the 'Plot' constituted the perfect excuse to acquire more land – Mhala's, Phatho's and Maqoma's included[71] – and, having effectively disposed of the inhabitants, to give it to white settlers. Mhala and his fellow chiefs, although they were not British subjects, were tried for treason and joined his nephew Seyolo on the windswept island in faraway Table Bay.[72]

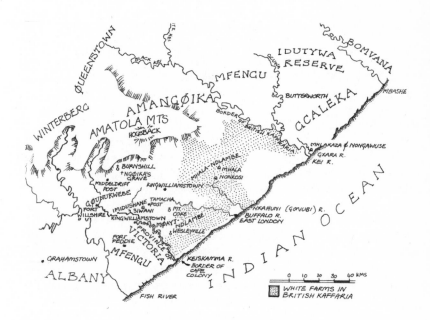

Eastern Frontier 1858–1866[73]

Mhala was released in 1863 or 1864, but his power was broken and he died in the eastern Cape in 1875. Maqoma did not return to the land of his birth alive; he died on Robben Island and was buried there. In the 1980s, Lennox Sebe, the puppet president of the apartheid-created 'homeland' of Ciskei, had Maqoma's remains exhumed and re-interred on Ntaba ka Ndoda, a prominent peak commanding magnificent views of the Amalinde plains and Amatola mountains, some 30 kilometres west of King William's Town. Within a decade Sebe, who was despised by his 'subjects', was ousted and the fascist-style monument he had built nearby was stripped and vandalised by the local people, but Maqoma's grave was left unharmed. His bones still lie there: in an ugly little arrangement, an untended, overgrown plot fenced with sections of pre-cast concrete, its magnificent view blocked by rampant wattle, Ngqika's warrior son rests at last, one hopes, in peace.

In early 1858 the British went after the last of their Xhosa adversaries: troops under Commander Currie crossed the Kei River and swept through Sarhili's territory, and the king, too weak to resist, fled with the remains of his people across the Mbashe into Bomvanaland where he found refuge with chief Moni, his mother's brother.

When Nongqawuse's prophecies had first been heard, Moni had despatched one of his grandsons to investigate her claims. He reported on his return:

> 'I stood on the edge of the pool on the Gxara, and looked into the water to see the forms of those who were to rise and deliver us, as I was bidden. What I saw were the shadows of the leaves of the wild banana trees which overhung the pool, but no forms of men. These shadows moved, but the motion was due to the tide making wavelets – that was all. This talk is all nonsense.'[74]

Moni took heed and consequently the majority of Bomvana had been spared. Only the Great House of the Bomvana, the Nkumba – Nonibe's father's people – had believed the prophecy and had destroyed their cattle.

Like King Sarhili, the two young prophetesses, sixteen-year-old Nongqawuse and the younger, less famous Nonkosi, from Mhala's territory, had sought refuge among the Bomvana.

Four hundred amaNdlambe fighting men were sent from the Colony under WRD Fynn to capture the girls and, with the co-operation of chief Moni, they found the nine-year-old Nonkosi; according to Fynn, Moni was glad to be rid of her because his people were afraid of her.[75] Fynn also located the teenage Nongqawuse, whom he returned to the Colony with the aid of Siwani's cousin, Smith. Getting her back was not easy, either because they had her trussed up too tightly to swim or because she could not:

> 'One or two of the rivers were difficult to cross so with the assistance of my native policeman we gathered logs and tied them together with monkey ropes and made a raft on which I placed Nongqause. We, of course, had to swim and push the raft along. In mid-stream the monkey ropes parted and away went Nongqause shouting for dear life. We caught her up and got her safely across. I took her to King Williams Town and out to Fort Murray,'[76]

where Gawler was waiting to interrogate her.

A photograph in the Cape Archives shows the two young girls seated formally alongside one another. Nonkosi, bare-headed and wearing a simple cloth over the shoulders of her European-style cotton dress, gazes into the camera numbly, looking like nothing more than the traumatised little kid she is. 'My name is Nonkosi,' her testimony to the authorities begins, '[m]y mother and father are dead, as also all my relations. My mother died of sickness, but my father and other relatives died of famine. My father died last moon....'[77]

Nonkosi and Nongqawuse, 1858[78]

Nongqawuse, sits next to her, five or six years older and much taller. Her shoulders are hunched under a plain dark blanket; an elaborate arrangement of beads, brass buttons and decorative chains hangs from her neck. Her expression is hard to read: I have looked at the photo again and again, and every time she seems different, alternately grieving or angry, but there is much more there too, a well of deeper, more complex emotions, well beyond the experience of most girls her age, and probably beyond most modern adults

239

too. Like Nonkosi, Nongqawuse lost practically her whole family in the Cattle-Killing. Only she and one cousin survived out of a family of twenty.[79] Everyone else perished, including her uncle Mhlakaza, who starved to death at his home near the Gxara in December 1857, in the final days of the Great Delusion.[80] He managed to keep faith almost to the very end, but on his deathbed the realisation that all had been in vain could no longer be denied and in his bitterness he struck out at his king, accusing Sarhili of having used him for his own ends.[81]

Nonkosi and Nongqawuse were sent to Cape Town where they were confined to the Pauper's Lodge.[82] Many of the colonists felt that the authorities dealt too leniently with Nongqawuse: 'On arrival in Cape Town, instead of being punished for her part in the disaster she was fussed over and given dresses and shawls…,' one complained.[83]

After several years Nongqawuse was permitted to return to the eastern Cape, but she never returned to the Gxara. She maintained a safe distance from her former home – settling nearly 300 kilometres to the south – and appears to have assumed another name, probably because she feared retribution. She married, though her husband's name, whether or not they had any children, and other details are not known,[84] and quietly lived out her natural days in a simple hut on a farm called 'Glenshaw', at Alexandria between Port Alfred and Port Elizabeth. On her death in 1898 at the age of about 57, a 'katdoring' (*Acacia caffra*) was planted on her grave and it remained her only memorial until 1963, when the farmer who owned the land erected a bronze plaque mounted on a large boulder to mark the spot.

Nongqawuse's gravestone[85]

Her grave lies in a small copse of trees on a gentle slope overlooking a magnificent sweep of countryside – cattle country, ironically, dotted with plump, perpetually grazing herds. It was midsummer when I visited her grave, yet the sky was overcast with the cold-chrome light of midwinter and as dusk fell the land took on a dark and gloomy cast. The place seemed sad and lonely, which could have been just my imagination, but when I look again at the photographs and drawings of that day, I have the same sense of unease I felt then.

It is impossible to grasp the extent of the human suffering caused by the Cattle-Killing. Cold statistics cannot begin to plumb the depths, but they are shocking nonetheless. Sandile alone lost 26 450 of his people. Stokwe lost practically his entire following. Pato's people were utterly destroyed. Some of the smaller clans disappeared altogether. From a total population of 104 721 before the Cattle-Killing, the Xhosa were reduced to 37 229, *a loss of two-thirds of their people* – more than *sixty-eight thousand* souls unaccounted for.[86] A government report[87] issued in 1857 indicates that between January and August of that year, all but one of the Xhosa chiefdoms showed a radical decline in their populations, the sole exception being the imiDushane under chief Siwani.[88] The government supplemented their food with supplies of corn and erected huts to shelter the destitute people who flocked to join them.[89] Siwani's firm stand against the Cattle-Killing had not only saved his people from the famine and disease which devastated the majority of their countrymen but also enabled them to retain their land.

Nongqawuse's grave in the copse of trees, Alexandria

In the aftermath of the Cattle-Killing Siwani and his counsellors were relatively prosperous: they had profited from purchasing the believers' cattle cheaply, and invested their gains in ploughs and other agricultural equipment.[90] Siwani also received a salary,[91] which the British authorities had bestowed on sympathetic chiefs as part of their policy of divide and rule – essentially making them government employees.

Despite her people's relative good fortune, Nonibe had not come through the Cattle-Killing unscathed. Her mother and father's people had been the leading believers among the Bomvana, had slaughtered all their cattle, and had been shattered and impoverished by their participation in the Delusion.[92] Almost all Nonibe's husband's people, the amaNdlambe, had also been believers, including her stepsons, brothers-in-law, uncles and their children. The continual cycle of suffering, exile and death, fighting, feuding and near civil war had taken their toll, tumbling her headlong into the most common solace of South Africa's underclass: Cape Smoke.

Nonibe embraced the local brandy with such complete abandon that less than a year after the Cattle-Killing ended, she was no longer the proud woman she had once been. Now in her mid-fifties, she resided at her son Siwani's Great Place at Tamarha, perched on the hills above the Keiskamma River between King William's Town and Fort Peddie, where a military post and barracks had been built after the War of 1850–53.[93] Nonibe became a regular visitor at the soldiers' canteen, accompanied at all times – as befitted a woman of her stature – by several female companions.[94]

She also began paying frequent visits to the home of the magistrate's young clerk, William Edye. Nonibe does not appear to have been able to speak much English, but her new-found friend, the eldest son of the magistrate at nearby Fort Peddie, had grown up on the Frontier and spoke isiXhosa well enough to act as government interpreter. Unfortunately, he was also a deeply flawed personality, an unsavoury individual who supplied Nonibe and her companions with brandy and – as it later transpired – used his official position to intimidate, abuse and rape her companions.[95]

Rape was almost unheard of in pre-colonial Xhosa society and was considered an extremely grave offence, punishable by a fine of cattle or even death.[96] *Ukuthwala*, the carrying-off of a girl by a young man who wished to marry her, did sometimes occur, but had nothing in common with rape: often the girl's father was informed before the abduction took place, but if not, a boy from the prospective groom's home was sent to inform her family of her whereabouts, and the marriage – and its consummation – went ahead only if they felt it was a suitable match and agreed about *ikhazi*, the bridal cattle.[97]

Incidents of rape became more common only with the arrival of the settlers and increasing numbers of soldiers, but the subject, like venereal disease, is seldom discussed in the literature of the time. Some scattered incidents have, however, slipped through the conspiracy of silence: Coenraad de Buys, for example, the rebel Boer who resided among the amaNgqika in the opening years of the 19th century, is said to have taken chief Langa's wife 'with violence and used her as his own,'[98] and occasional reference is also made of soldiers raping and otherwise abusing Xhosa women during the Frontier wars.[99]

Edye's *modus operandi* at Tamarha was to ply Nonibe and her female companions with alcohol and once they were intoxicated, to separate one of the women from the rest, with the assistance of his policeman, Kohla, and get her alone in his bedroom or office.

Nomkinti, Nonibe's niece, was attacked in exactly that way; she and another woman had gone to Edye's house one afternoon to buy tobacco and been told to wait in the outside kitchen. They were still waiting at sunset when Nonibe and some companions arrived and went into the house, and it was only after dinner that they were finally summoned by Kohla. Inside, Edye gave them brandy.

After some time Nonibe 'complained of feeling drunk and said the liquor had affected her eye.' Together with the rest of the women she then departed, leaving her niece alone with Edye. After drinking some more brandy, the girl also wanted to leave, but was so inebriated that she missed the door and had to ask Edye to show her the way out. He took her instead into his bedroom, and when she refused his advances – 'I said no, I have a young child and my husband has not yet slept with me'[100] – he grabbed her and 'after struggling some time got me on the floor on my back and got between my thighs.'[101]

Out in the kitchen, Nomkinti's friend heard scuffling and heard her scream. She begged Edye's assistant Kohla to go and help her, but the policeman refused saying he 'would not… interfere with his master's work.'[102]

Afterwards Edye gave Nomkinti half a crown. She left the house crying.

Perhaps because Nomkinti – and others who had the same experience – had been drunk and was deeply shamed it took time for news of the attacks to get around. Some of the women did speak out: when Nomadyongolo and Notasi were verbally harassed by Edye, one told her parents about it and the other her father.[103] But there is no indication that any action was taken against the clerk.

Emboldened by his friendship with the chief's mother, Edye became more brazen. One night at his house he ordered Siwani's wife Nomanti to have sex with him and, when she refused, offered her money. Offended she replied: 'I am not a whore although I have drunk brandy….' She reported the incident to her husband, but when Siwani approached Edye the next morning, the clerk simply denied the incident.[104] On another occasion, when he knew Siwani was away for the night, Edye sent a Khoi servant to the chief's favourite wife, Nomvato, ordering her to have sex with him. She too rejected him out of hand.

Edye was 'very very angry' at this.[105] He then approached Siwani's brother, Miti, and suggested he 'lend him' his wife. Miti, who thought the clerk was just joking, replied that 'he might have her.' Even when Edye responded that 'she would not have him …,' implying that he had already tried, Miti does not seem to have realised just how serious the clerk was.[106]

Eventually, however, Edye went too far.

Returning from a visit to King William's Town one night, Siwani and his wife Nomvato were forced to share a tent with the clerk. As they were settling down to sleep, Edye suggested that the chief 'lend' him his wife. Siwani's response, under the circumstances, was extremely restrained: with great dignity but deep contempt he replied, 'are you a child that you should make such a request?'[107] Undeterred, Edye suggested that Nomvato sleep between the two men, but Siwani made his wife lie on the side furthest away from the clerk instead. When the candle was blown out he feigned sleep and even pretended to snore, though he was actually awake and alert. In the darkness he heard Edye begin moving about, and then Nomvato, lying next to him, felt Edye touch her shoulder. She nudged Siwani who shot out his hand and grabbed Edye's, saying 'What do you want?' The clerk claimed he had merely been looking for matches but Siwani was not fooled and gave him a tongue-lashing. The next morning he reported the matter to his counsellors. He did not, however, tell Edye's superior, Major Hawkes, 'as

I did not wish to be hard upon Mr. Edye as he was young and inexperienced and I thought I would wait.'[108]

But Edye did nothing to mend his ways and by November 1858, Siwani had had enough. He confronted the clerk, threatening him with a *sjambok*, a short whip made of rhino hide that is capable of stripping a man's flesh from his bones.[109] Although he did not actually use it, Edye made an official complaint about the incident. Siwani laid counter-charges and at last the whole fiasco was out in the open.

A month later an official commission of inquiry was convened at nearby Fort Murray. The charges against Edye were:

'1. Of having without sufficient reason stripped the pay
   of headmen
2. Of neglect of duty
3. Of injustice and oppression
4. Of immorality.'

The inquiry took almost a month and included the testimony of various petty headmen whom Edye had cheated out of their pay, residents who had been intimidated, and other complainants, but the greater part was taken up by cases of sexual assault. Woman after woman faced the board and gave simple, direct and dignified accounts of their experiences at Edye's hands. Most had never even spoken to the clerk or been to his house prior to being attacked, and afterwards were careful never to go near him or his house again. Very few had ever drunk brandy before he had given it to them, and its effect had been both immediate and incapacitating. Nonibe, who was used to strong spirits, must have known how it would affect her companions and should have warned them about both the brandy and Edye, yet she does not appear to have done so, nor did she in anyway assist them once they were intoxicated or ensure that they were not left alone with him.

The inquiry brought Nonibe's behaviour under the spotlight. In an effort to save face, she lied in her testimony, saying 'we never go to his [Edye's] house when we are drunk.'[110] Whether or not she was a conscious accomplice, Nonibe was certainly a means whereby Edye gained access to his victims. As the mother of their chief, her visits to Edye's home must have assured her companions that they were quite safe in going there, and while Nonibe was seldom in the house when the assaults occurred, on a number of occasions she was quite close by, in the outside kitchen for example, or had only just left. It is inconceivable that she knew nothing about the attacks; as word spread among the women and they became more cautious in their dealings with Edye, Nonibe must at least have heard some of the talk, especially as a number of the rape survivors were members of her own family.

Particularly damning was her behaviour regarding Noyanti. Noyanti, who was pregnant, had accompanied Nonibe to Edye's house one night, where she drank too much, and found herself alone and inebriated with

Edye in his bedroom. He assaulted her but fortunately she managed to escape. In her testimony Nonibe admitted that she had 'heard a noise as of struggling' while Noyanti was in the other room, but protested that she herself was 'so drunk that I do not know what passed.' According to a witness, however, when Noyanti escaped, Nonibe had come out of the house with Edye, who was trouserless, and 'asked where the woman had gone to,' expressing annoyance that she had left.[111]

Was Nonibe really too drunk to realise what was going on, as she claimed, or did she just not care about anything anymore, except not jeopardising her supply of brandy and the oblivion it induced?

It is hard to reconcile the portrait of Nonibe that emerges from the trial with the strong, brave and compassionate woman she had once been, who ruled the imiDushane for more than ten years, who refused to be intimidated by petty officials, who flirted with the governor himself, and who cared enough for others to save the life of an unknown trader. What had become of her? It throws up other questions too. What exactly what her relationship with Edye? Was it because of her that Siwani waited so long before laying charges against Edye? Not once in his statement or in his testimony, incidentally, did Siwani refer to his mother's alcoholism or her visits to Edye's house; in fact he did not mention her at all, which, as she was a central figure, must have taken quite some doing.

Another reason for Siwani's delay in acting against Edye may have been a sense of futility, of his own powerlessness. Instead of the just government they had been promised upon their surrender after the war of 1846, Siwani and his people had been exposed to and were at the mercy of an obviously flawed system. The pages and pages of testimony produced at the inquiry paint a rather sad picture of the imiDushane, of the gradual and widespread impoverishment of the Xhosa as a whole and their transformation into landless and powerless peasants. Although the imiDushane were better off than most after the Cattle-Killing and had retained their land, many struggled to pay the taxes imposed on them and, despite the fact that they had been the allies of the British in all but one of the Frontier wars, it is obvious that the representatives of the government treated them with contempt.

There is no doubt that Siwani knew at least some, if not all of what was going on at Edye's house, but the imbalance of power between the two men is epitomised by the fact that the former, a Xhosa prince and the proud descendant of Mdushane and Ndlambe, could not travel beyond the confines of his own small piece of land or even purchase a drink without the permission of the latter, a lowly government clerk.[112]

When Edye raped Siwani's young niece Notyilo, the chief demanded an explanation from the policeman Kohla, but he did not, it seems, confront Edye himself.[113] When his cousin Nomkinti was raped she told Siwani what had happened to her, but all he said was 'I am waiting.'[114] It's almost the same expression he used in explaining to the Board why he did not inform

Edye's superior officer after the incident with his wife Nomvato: 'I thought I would wait.' He was probably waiting until the evidence against the clerk was so overwhelming that the government would have no choice but to take his complaints seriously.

Siwani's fears – if such they were – were justified by the 'trial'. The Board was anything but impartial. It consisted of two white men, Edye's fellow colonists and government employees, Charles Brownlee and John Ayliff, who openly admitted their partisanship: 'In many cases where a difference of opinion existed… we have willingly received Mr Edye's statements where the shadow of proof has appeared in preference to that of the Natives….'[115] They allowed Edye to interrogate his victims face to face, even Nontyilo who was just a child,[116] and it was his accusers who were vilified in the Board's report rather than himself – Nomkinti's simple and unadorned testimony, for example, was described as 'disgusting.'[117]

The verdict was indicative of how just how powerless the imiDushane were: despite the overwhelming evidence against him, Edye was exonerated on all counts, barring the minor charge of fraud for which he received a small fine. The Board did recommend that he no longer be allowed to work amongst the imiDushane, not because of the suffering he had caused, but because he had 'compromised his own dignity and that of the Government he represents….'[118]

The amaXhosa had become second-class citizens in their own land.

William Bruce Edye remained in the civil service and got married in 1870. The names of his wife, the second daughter of James Praed, a resident of Riebeeck, a village just outside Grahamstown, are most curious since her surname, Couch, is not the same as her father's and her first name, Mahala, is Xhosa. I have not been able to discover anything else about her, barring the fact that a couple of years later she bore a son, who, like his father, was named William Bruce Edye. Edye senior's vocation appears on the baptism notice as 'Superintendant of Natives'.[119] Evidently his career as a rapist had not adversely affected his career in government.

Nonibe seems to have faded from sight after the trial and I have found only one reference to her since then: in 1868, when she was in her mid-60s, she converted to Christianity and joined the Wesleyans – under whose strict supervision, one hopes, she was able to kick her alcohol habit – at Annshaw, a small mission station at Middeldrift in Kama's territory, near today's Fort Hare university.[120] According to Ngubesizwe Siwani, her great-great-great-grandson, she is buried at Nonibe, the small settlement bearing her name, just outside King William's Town.[121]

In the aftermath of the Cattle-Killing, the overall conditions of Siwani's imiDushane continued to deteriorate. Land was in such short supply that it could barely sustain the growing population. By 1863 his territory was so thickly populated that his people were struggling to find pasture for their cattle; 'material and undoubtable inconvenience is already experienced by several of the villages in the location,' wrote a British official.[122] The situation had not improved by late 1877 when Antony Trollope, the English novelist, interviewed Siwani on a fact-finding tour of South Africa.

Siwani was spokesperson for a group of about 20 important chiefs, and he attended the meeting in western-style clothing: '...an old black coat, a flannel shirt, a pair of tweed trousers and a billycock hat,' his conservative outfit offset 'with a watch-key of ordinary appearance ingeniously inserted into his ear as an ornament.' He appears to have spoken no English, communicating with Trollope through an interpreter.

The Xhosa are renowned for their oratorical skills, but Siwani addressed the Englishman in a direct and unembellished manner. Although he had long been a British ally, his words were largely directed against them. He accused the British of not honouring their word. He objected to the fact that Xhosa were languishing in British prisons, pointing out that if a subject committed a crime it was his chief who should be responsible for his punishment, not some distant authority. The Xhosa, he said, 'would be much better off if the English would go away and leave them to their own customs.'

Trollope lamely listed the advantages of British rule: '... trousers for instance, – and I remarked that all the royal princes around me were excellently clad.... "Yes, – by compulsion," he said. "We were told that we must come in and see you, and therefore we put on our trousers. Very uncomfortable they are, and we wish that you and the trousers and the magistrates, but above all the prisons, would go – away out of the country together".'[123]

Siwani appeared older than his fifty years. Life had not been easy, and his experiences had worn him down. The progressive youth of his early years had been supplanted by an embittered and even reactionary man who would not acknowledge the advantages of education and was proud that none of 'his own children had ever gone to school.'[124]

Trollope dismissed him as 'an unmitigated savage,' failing to grasp that this complex and extraordinary man's rejection of all things western had been born of personal disappointment: the 'ample lands' he and his people had been promised had not materialised, the 'support' they had been promised had been given to their abusers, not themselves, and the 'protection of the Colonial Government' which they been promised was noticeable only by its absence.[125]

Despite his obvious dislike of the British, when war broke out again less than a year after Trollope's visit, Siwani once again collaborated with the Colony. His heart may have told him otherwise, but, pragmatist that he was, he must have known that the Xhosa could not hope to win in the long term, and if he and his people were to survive they had to ally themselves with the economic and political force of the future.

Yet Siwani's participation in the war went beyond mere lip-service. As the leader of a Xhosa contingent under Baron Wilhelm Carl von Linsingen, a German immigrant, he scoured the dense bush country of the Keiskamma River valley and the Amatola mountains, hunting down Xhosa dissidents, one of whom was his half-brother Seyolo.[126]

After his release from Robben Island in 1869, Seyolo had returned to the eastern Cape to find his people decimated and scattered; among the foremost believers in the Cattle-Killing, they had also been among its foremost victims.[127] Seyolo's hatred of the British remained undiluted and when war broke out in 1877, despite having spent 14 years in prison and his age (he was over 60), he threw himself into the fray, joining forces with Sandile.

Both men died violently in the war. Sandile was critically wounded by Mfengu soldiers, and holed up in a cave in the Amatola mountains between King William's Town and Hogsback. After his death, the British recovered his body and performed an autopsy, the findings revealing several broken bones, a number of gunshot wounds and bone splinters in the abdomen. Crippled by polio as a youth, overshadowed by his famous warrior brother Maqoma as a leader, and criticised as a weak and indecisive king, Sandile had nevertheless remained true to his beliefs and died in their defence, but it had cost him dearly: the autopsy showed he had taken several days to die and endured terrible suffering.

His ally Seyolo was hardly more fortunate. In April 1878, with at least two of his sons already dead in battle and Siwani's men baying for his blood,[128] Seyolo's forces were routed on the Debe Flats and scattered into the bush, leaving behind many of their wives, who had acted as their supply column. The women were rounded up and, in a gesture calculated to humiliate Seyolo, apprenticed to settlers as domestic servants.[129] Seyolo fought on for a few more months, but early in June Von Linsingen's men tracked him down in the Fish River bush and Seyolo, one of the most famous fighting chiefs of his generation, who had dedicated his life to driving out the British and winning back his people's land and independence, died as he had lived, by the gun.

Siwani followed him a year later, dying on 11 December 1879, at the age of fifty-three. He was survived by three or four wives and several children, and was buried at Menziwe, about three kilometres south of Tamarha, outside King William's Town.[130] With his death the knowledge of Bessie and her strange history seems to have died out among her amaNdlambe descendants.

Although Nonibe had been known as, and exploited the novelty of being the granddaughter of an Englishwoman, Siwani does not seem to have made much of his English ancestry. With him there is a conscious break with the past: he clearly identified himself as Xhosa and nothing else, perceiving the British as distinctly other, as foreign oppressors. The cultural divide between the castaway Bessie's descendants and her countrymen, the English, had become a chasm, the antagonism towards the British which Siwani had expressed to Trollope contrasting sharply with the earlier generation of Bessie's descendants – her son Mdepa and daughter Bessy for example – who had embraced the English with a warmth and trust based on their common ancestry.

Like Siwani, many of Bessie's later descendants were culturally, linguistically and in every other way no different from any of their peers; they were Xhosa first, foremost and exclusively. A few, through circumstances of birth, joined settler society and became whites – 'those whose ears are transparent in the sunlight.'[131] Others occupied a position somewhere in between, marrying people who, like themselves, were of mixed descent, and became known as 'coloureds'.

Siwani's grandson, Gushiphela Siwani c1930[132]

The majority of her descendants have disappeared into the black hole of the past, but the handful who are traceable lived out their lives in vastly diverse circumstances. Their destinies were determined largely by which side of the increasing racial divide they were born on, their lives emphasising both the incredible diversity and, paradoxically, the interconnectness of South Africa's people. The abeLungu and the Tshomane, the Lochenbergs and De Buys, the amaMolo: their stories weave strange and wonderful threads through our social fabric, enlivening and enriching our cultural heritage, but also binding us and linking us all in ways that are perhaps both the simplest and the most profound, through our common genes. Bessie's bloodline, as long and convoluted as the Kei River, with links to many of the major players on the eastern Frontier, the English, Xhosa, Thembu and Afrikaner, the elite, the low-down, righteous, devious, upstanding citizens and downright scumbags of that most critical territory, is probably no less convoluted than many other South Africans'. Blood is the nexus.

Genealogy of imiDushane[133]

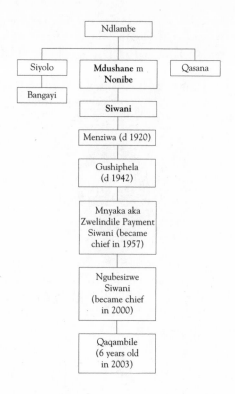

Chapter Eleven

The Wife-beater King and the Trader

'I can't stand the smell of the dressed native,' Sarhili the Xhosa king said; they seldom washed their clothes, he complained, but wore them until they were unbearably dirty and smelly.[1] He himself preferred to dress in the traditional and more hygienic fashion, naked except for a penis sheath, with a *kaross* or leather cloak for cold weather. Despite the spread of Christianity and its emphasis on western apparel, he would not allow his people to wear European-style clothing.[2]

But all that changed with the outbreak of war between his people, the Gcaleka Xhosa, and the abeThembu in 1872. The two main protagonists, Ngangelizwe and Sarhili, were in-laws: Sarhili's daughter Novili was Ngangelizwe's Great Wife and it was his brutal behaviour towards her that caused the war.

Novili had fled to her father 'maimed and covered with wounds.'[3] Sarhili was dismayed and outraged, and the incident was viewed an insult to the Xhosa as a whole. A few of his counsellors advised him to settle the matter quietly, dismissing Ngangelizwe as 'the son of a madman and a madman himself,' but the majority condemned the Thembu king as 'a disgrace to himself and the people,'[4] who deserved to be punished. Sarhili agreed and began preparing for war, whereupon Ngangelizwe hurriedly approached the British for protection, who advised him to pay a fine of cattle by way of compensation. But Sarhili was not satisfied and ordered the invasion of Thembuland.

Ngangelizwe dressed his fighters in western clothing and, not to be outdone, Sarhili ordered his men to do likewise. Within three weeks every trading store in his territory was sold out. Sarhili's forces totally routed the Thembu, winning not only the style war but also the military one: 'babaleka barazuka imisintsila,' the Xhosa said of their enemies, 'they ran so hard they broke their coccyx.'⁵ Ngangelizwe himself reportedly fled in a most undignified fashion, tearing off his trousers so that he could run faster. He sought sanctuary at Clarkebury mission, where he hid out in the kitchen, and offered to cede his whole territory unconditionally to the British in exchange for their protection, but, at the vehement objection of his counsellors, settled for a truce instead.⁶

It was probably in remembrance of this affair that Sarhili named one of his sons Bulukwe ('Trousers'),⁷ and, although he himself still preferred traditional dress, from that time on western clothing became more popular and common among his people.

King Sarhili, son of Nomsa and Hintsa, as an old man.⁸

Ngangelizwe had married Novili in May 1866, a year after her father Sarhili's return from exile in Bomvanaland, where he had fled following the Cattle-Killing.⁹ To all intents and purposes the match was an excellent one, uniting two of the most prominent and independent Xhosa-speaking peoples in the region. Ngangelizwe had been circumcised just three years before and had only recently become king.¹⁰ Traditionally, it was extremely unusual for a ruler of his stature to take his Great Wife so early in life, but there had been an unpleasant prelude to the union that the Thembu elders were eager to put behind them – the botched betrothal of Ngangelizwe to Emma, daughter of Sandile, the amaNgqika king. Emma had grown up in Cape Town, where she had been educated under the auspices of the Anglican church, together with several other children of Xhosa chiefs. The majority of the youngsters' fathers were political prisoners, and were being held at the time on Robben Island, just a few kilometres from the school, though they were not permitted to see them. By educating the chiefs' children at the Cape, the British hoped to raise a generation of western-minded elite amongst the Xhosa, to equip them with the language, religion and literacy necessary for life as British subjects. But all it really did was separate them from their roots and make them outsiders among the very people they were supposed to lead. Emma was the first of these cultural casualties.

Her betrothal to Ngangelizwe had begun well enough. As she wrote to her teacher after meeting him for the first time:

'We both fell in love with each other…. I must tell you that I have seen the young chief, he is a tall fine young man, and I must let you know that the marriage is going to take place. Oh! how I wish you could be here and see him take my hand and kiss it, and I love him to, I am sure you would like him if you were to see him….'[11]

Ngangelizwe was as fond of his bride-to-be as she obviously was of him, and was keen to marry her. But Emma had been baptised during her schooling in Cape Town and she was a committed Christian; both she and the church expected the marriage to be monogamous – which was, of course, in direct conflict with Thembu tradition.

The marriage turned into a political hot potato. Ngangelizwe's people rallied together and in a series of 'large and stormy meetings' voiced their objection to the forthcoming marriage.[12] The Thembu had nothing against Emma herself – they liked the princess very much, they said – but it was imperative that their king have other wives besides her, 'in order to make sure of plenty of the royal seed.'[13]

Ngangelizwe was in a vulnerable position. Having only recently become king, he did not yet have the power to act against the wishes of his people. Had he done so at that point he would have lost not only his supporters but also, probably, his throne. He was forced to submit to their will, and although he was rather miserable about the whole thing and asked for Emma's forgiveness, the upshot of it all was that the marriage never took place. Emma too was forlorn, but although she probably would not have cared to hear it at the time, she had in fact had a very narrow escape – as Novili, who married Ngangelizwe shortly afterwards, was about to discover.

On the surface Ngangelizwe was an extremely attractive man. He stood six feet tall, carried himself well, had a beautifully proportioned body, and was blessed with 'a smooth, pleasant countenance [and] a sweet, charming voice.'[14] His wholesome exterior, unfortunately, was not always matched by his personality: 'usually an easy-going, mild-mannered man, … he was subject to fits of ungovernable temper, when he was prone to commit the most savage acts.'[15] He is said to have ordered regular killings, and is remembered as 'a man of savage disposition.'[16]

His wives seem to have borne the brunt of his brutality. In March 1875 he beat one so badly that she was forced to take refuge with her brother, Daliso, where she subsequently died from her wounds.[17] His assault in 1870 on his Great Wife Novili had left her with severe injuries; a British official who met her shortly afterwards said 'pieces of bone were coming away through a wound in her injured leg.' But she was more concerned about her children than herself: 'Her greatest grief was that according to law she cannot see her children who are bound to reside with the father.'[18] Because of this, Novili returned to her despotic and violent husband.[19] She had a total of five children by him, including Dalindyebo, who, as the eldest son of the Great Wife, was heir to the throne.

A few years after the assault that precipitated the war, Ngangelizwe caused another crisis by assaulting one of his concubines, Nongxokozela, who suffered serious injuries and was killed, on his orders, a few days later.[20] Unfortunately for him, the girl was a niece of Sarhili and secret information about what had happened to her soon reached the Xhosa king. Another war seemed imminent, but the British came to Ngangelizwe's assistance again, and deployed a strong colonial police force to maintain the peace. Consequently Ngangelizwe reopened negotiations with the British and – despite his counsellors' objections – ceded his territory to them in December 1875.[21]

His cruelty has been linked to his humiliation and disappointment at his people's refusal to allow him to marry Emma – at the time he is said to have told his counsellors: 'As you wish me to be a good Kafir, I will be really a Kafir,'[22] but there were also other factors at work, one of which was probably the infamous Cape Smoke.

In 1877 Ngangelizwe paid a visit to some English officials at Idutywa, well beyond the borders of his own territory. His evil reputation by this time extended beyond Thembuland, and the young wife of his English host was expecting the worst. To her surprise she found the king very charming.

> 'While he was eating and drinking I found time to scrutinize our visitor, and could hardly believe the dreadful stories I had heard about this handsome-looking man; there was nothing repulsive in his countenance, and his expression was rather sweet and gentle; beautiful teeth and the smile of a child.'[23]

She noticed, however, that he was very fond of brandy, and drank a full glass in one go. As far as she could ascertain the liquor had no visible effect on him, but Sir Walter Stanford, the Xhosa linguist and legislator, who knew him well, says Ngangelizwe was 'besotted with drink.'[24] Possibly his violent rages were sparked by his alcoholism.

Alcohol abuse had become widespread as the British extended their sphere of influence; Ngangelizwe's father-in-law Sarhili, the last independent Xhosa king, appears to have been one of the few rulers to escape its clutches. Cape Smoke, the potent local brandy, which had brought down such promising leaders as King Ngqika, soon reached the most remote parts of the Wild Coast, brought in and sold by white traders.[25] One of them, a man by the name of John King, was Ngangelizwe's brother-in-law, or rather cousin-in-law, since their wives were cousins, not sisters. Both were great-granddaughters of the castaway Bessie and I was curious to find out more about them.

The first I could put a name to was Nosepisi. The eldest daughter of Cawu, son of Bessie's son Mdepa,[26] she was Ngangelizwe's Right-Hand Wife (second in seniority only to his Great Wife) and bore the king four children.[27] Both the Right-Hand House and the Great House (through Novili's grandmother, Nomsa) of the present Thembu royal family are

therefore descended from white castaways. They also have some San blood:
Ngangelizwe's birth name Qeya, meaning 'Khoisan' and his copper
complexion were the legacy of a San ancestor – his mother and her brother
Matiwana (king of the Mpondomise) having had a 'great great grandma
[who] was a Bushwoman.'[28]

Traditionally Xhosa women's history is inseparable from that of their
men. As the Right-Hand Wife of Ngangelizwe, Nosepisi had been relatively
easy to find out about, because her royal husband's genealogy was an obvious
subject for the traditional oral historians. His in-law John King, however,
was (despite his surname!) a nobody, and finding out about that side of
Bessie's family was to prove much more of a challenge. Which is, I suppose,
what intrigued me – so much of what should be the common currency of
South African history, our diversity and unity as equal parts of a complex
and interesting whole, has yet to be recovered.

In 1883 the government of the Cape set up the Native Law and
Customs Commission to gather information on traditional governance and
society. One of the dignitaries who testified before the commissioners was
Ngangelizwe. The Thembu king was accompanied by two of his counsellors,
namely Silas Pantshwa and a Christian named Xelo. All three men were in
some way connected with Bessie and her fellow castaways. Ngangelizwe was,
as we know, married to Bessie's great-granddaughter, Nosepesi. Silas
Pantshwa was the husband of Nozolo, the daughter whom Bessie's son
Mdepa had fathered when he was 'a very old man, nearly a hundred years
of age.' Xelo's first wife was the descendant of one of the 'black people with
long hair' with whom Bessie had been wrecked all those years ago.[29]

Ngangelizwe's testimony was not particularly informative and, as I suppose
one would expect from a wife-beater, misogynistic: 'In olden times the woman
had no rights… because women are naturally wicked and have no good ways
with them. They are the same now…'[30] His counsellor Xelo's testimony was
far more interesting, however. As a youth he had attended school at Morley
mission where he had known Bessie's son Mdepa well, and he had a fair
amount to say about Bessie and her descendants. And, as both Ngangelizwe
and Silas Pantshwa were present throughout his statement and did not
contradict him, it is safe to assume that they agreed with what he said:

> 'Before I was born an English lady came to this part of Africa…. This
> lady's children were yellow in colour, having long hair and blue eyes.'
> Her second son, Mdepa, 'had a son named Majibana, whose eldest
> son was called Ncani, and who died without male issue. Ncani's sister
> married John King.'[31]

At the same time that the Native Laws and Customs Commission was
gathering its information, William Bazley was gathering information of his
own. Bazley is the old Natal settler mentioned in previous chapters, who
was fascinated by the wreck of the *Grosvenor* and assembled a remarkable

collection of evidence regarding its survivors. He was a spy, a secret agent for the Secretary of Native Affairs in Natal, Sir Theophilus Shepstone[32] (the son, incidentally of the first missionary at Morley), and had an extensive network of informants, which served his hobby well. Travelling throughout Natal and up and down the Wild Coast, he pursued his subject tirelessly, seeking out and questioning the elders among the local people about the castaways and their descendants.

Dynamite fascinated Bazley almost as much as the wreck of the *Grosvenor*. He was notorious for blowing up wrecks, river mouths and cuttings, usually for engineering purposes but sometimes just for the hell of it. His reputation for always having a stick or two of dynamite in his pockets preceded him[33] – and probably scared people into telling him everything they knew, for he was able to assemble a wealth of information, which he jotted down in a couple of notebooks. His notes are random, fragmented and even contradictory, the grammar and punctuation so haphazard that one can sense the speed with which he scribbled them down, translating from Xhosa into English on the spot. Inevitably some of what he learnt about the *Grosvenor* survivors overlapped with or was confused with Bessie's wreck and his notes, consequently, are interspersed with references which are clearly about her descendants, rather than the *Grosvenor*'s. Bazley's notes both confirm and add to Xelo's testimony to the Commission.

Unfortunately, his invaluable notebooks appear to have been lost by the Durban museum to which they were entrusted for safekeeping in the 1940s. I first requested access to the notebooks at the beginning of 2000, but after months of futile pestering they had not been found. I managed to track down Bazley's great-grandson Denzil, and he helped apply pressure on the museum staff. For over two years I phoned in about the missing notebooks on a regular basis, but the answer was always the same: 'We're still looking,' and since this appears still to be the case, I can only conclude that the museum is absolutely enormous.

Fortunately some fragments of Bazley's notes survive in an article written in the 1950s by Professor Kirby of Rhodes university. Several refer to the girl who married John King.

note 22: 'Nchuku, or Patience, died October 1906, aged 87 years. A grand-daughter of Nquma, the white girl found on the beach near Mlambass in East Pondoland.'

note 39: (part): 'John King's wife died 24th Oct, 1906.'

note 30: (part): 'Eliza King got married an Irishman married Conway. Dalasile was a brother of Mrs King.'

note 37: (part): 'Mrs Conway is Mrs J. King's eldest daughter.'

note 23: 'Mrs Conway's eldest daughter's name was Ellen. She is Mrs. Van der Byl, and lives at Libosh. Eliza, Mrs Gale, in Bomvanaland. Annie, a Mrs.van der Byl.'

note 40 (part): 'Harry King's father was married to a Van der Byl,
                   a Portuguese.'[34]

With the help of these fragments I could begin to form a picture of
Bessie's great-granddaughter. If Nochuku/Patience was 87 when she died,
she must have been born in 1819. This was the same year in which Mdushane
attacked Grahamstown, and the Fifth Frontier War broke out, *not* the most
peaceful of times. Neither was Nochuku's early childhood, which coincided
with the Zulu invasions. When she was only four or five years old, Shaka's
invasion of Pondoland drove her family from their ancestral lands at Mngazana.
The Tshomane, as we have seen, were attacked several times and over the
next few years were almost constantly on the move. The continual warfare
and dislocation must have been traumatic for the young child. They certainly
took their toll on the older members of her family; the loss of their herds,
disruption of cultivation and resulting malnourishment left them haggard
and ill-looking, with sunken eyes.[35]

The Tshomane eventually settled in Bomvanaland. Nochuku never
knew her great-grandmother, since Bessie had died about ten years before
she was born, but she certainly knew her grandfather Mdepa because he and
her father Majibana, 'fully 50 years of age, tall and of a copper colour,' were
living within a kilometre of each other in about 1826.[36] Nochuku, who was
about seven, must also have known Bessie's daughter Bessy, since she lived
nearby with her husband, the Bomvana chief Mjikwa.[37]

In 1829, when Nochuku was ten years old, Morley mission station was
built at Matola, and Mdepa, his sons and their families settled close by.
Although the station was burnt down a couple of times, was rebuilt and
even moved, they remained in the vicinity of the mission. When Reverend
Shepstone told them he intended starting a school they promised to send
their children there and Nochuku may have been one of them.[38] The
missionary railed at their pagan upbringing:

> 'When I was at Cetani's [Bessie's grandson, Ngcetane] kraal the other
> day, some of his sons were just about to be introduced to social society,
> by the rite of circumcision, some of whom were nearly white, although
> belonging to the third generation. I could not but reflect, when I saw
> the colour of their skin, "who can tell but some of the ancestors of
> these children, were as eminent for piety, as these are now for
> heathen ignorance?"'[39]

Nochuku, however, almost certainly attended church, and later converted
to Christianity. Her English name, Patience, suggests that she had been
baptised, and, as I later discovered, at least ten of her children were also
baptised, mainly at Morley. Regarding her marriage to John King, however,
I could find nothing. There was no concrete evidence of when she met him,
or who he was.

Historical research is a funny thing. I found it completely absorbing, putting my own life on hold, in a way, to pursue the remnants of others'. By this time I'd been on Bessie's trail for years; I had sold up in Johannesburg, left my work in the film industry and moved my two young sons down to Grahamstown in the Eastern Cape to be closer to the Wild Coast and the research sources I wanted, and had bought and begun renovating a dilapidated old cottage in Artificers' Square, the original Settler quarter of the village, where most of the 1820 immigrants had ended up after fleeing their allotments.

I spent months buried in a mountain of musty-smelling tomes, old documents, crumbling records and fading letters, sifting through the detritus of thousands of lives. It was an eerie experience, and it was the registers of baptisms, marriages and births that really got to me. The life-and-death intimacies of whole families passed before me with each turn of the fragile pages, life after life slipping by in a continuous loop of birth, marriage, reproduction and death, the uniqueness of each – the passion, pleasure and pain of individual human experience – reduced to a line or two of faded ink, so abbreviated that they almost disappeared into thin air. John King was more elusive than most. It was almost as though he had never existed.

I didn't have much to go on, for a start, but his name, which was obviously English. A letter written in 1852 by a missionary based near Morley mission confirmed this: Bessie's grandchildren were 'now about Morley. One is married to an Englishman, John King.'[40]

My guess was that he had been a trader. The Wild Coast in the mid-1800s was a truly remote region with no roads, shops or medical facilities and, barring the occasional mission station, no white settlements or villages for hundreds of kilometres. Englishmen – or any white men for that matter – were few and far between, the only ones being the odd government official, missionary or trader. As John King's name didn't appear on any official lists as far as I could ascertain, it seemed probable he had been the latter. There were certainly traders in and around Morley mission as early as 1834, when Nochuku was fifteen years old and approaching marriageable age, but I couldn't at first establish whether a John King had been among them.[41]

The early English traders on the Wild Coast were either based at Port Natal, to the north, or were members of the 1820 Settler community in the eastern Cape, to the south. There were no John Kings in the original Port Natal party, but among the 1820 Settlers there had been four. Three of them were roughly the same age as Nochuku, including one who had also done some trading up in Natal, and who at first seemed the most likely candidate for Nochuku's husband. This particular John King, the son of Philip and Maria King of Bradshaw's party, was a brother of the famous Dick King.[42] Feted among white Natalians for his 600-mile horse-ride to Grahamstown in 1842 to summon help for the besieged British garrison at Port Natal, the aptly named Dick was just as famous among the Zulus for his womanising – he had, in the words of his (white) son, '… a wonderful way with Natives.'[43] He had his way with Boers too. According to Ndongeni, a

16-year-old Zulu who accompanied Dick on his famous ride, 'Boer girls were fond of Dick. He used to *soma*... with them' (ie have non-penetrative sex).[44]

Dick's trading enterprise sometimes extended into the Wild Coast region; in 1835, for example, he was at Buntingville mission, close to Mdepa's territory,[45] and it seemed possible that John, his brother and partner, would have accompanied him on at least some of these trips.

Almost every Natal trader had Zulu wives and families as well as white wives and children. Dick, for example, 'had an establishment of wives,' whom he 'cast aside' when he married an English woman.[46] So, the fact that his brother John had married a white woman named Mary Jane Hawkins in 1849[47] didn't necessarily disqualify him from also having been Nochuku's husband. What did, however, was the discovery that he had relocated to Kimberley during the diamond rush and remained there until his death in 1901.[48] I crossed him off my list and soon deleted a second John King, the son of Richard King of Baillie's party: within months of the Settlers' arrival in 1820, his father had applied for permission to return to Britain, confessing that he was not the farmer he claimed to be, but 'had passed the great part of his life in a counting house and knew nothing about agriculture.'[49] Scratching a livelihood from the living soil of Africa had been so hard that, in his eagerness to get the hell out of here, he even offered to pay his own passage home.

That left just two John Kings on my list, a father and son of the same name who belonged to Hyman's party.[50] The father was eliminated when I discovered that Nochuku's husband had corresponded with William Bazley in 1907;[51] John King snr, born in 1797, could not possibly have survived that long.

The son, however, was just the right age. Born in 1818, he was just one year older than Nochuku.

Piles of old memoirs, contemporary newspapers and church notices later, however, I still knew almost nothing about him besides his birth date.

A thorough search of the published genealogies of the King family also yielded nothing, although that was hardly surprising. Racial pruning is common in South African family trees, and by marrying a black woman he was practically ensuring that his branch would be lopped off. (Henry Francis Fynn is a case in point; despite having fathered enough children by his Zulu wives to give rise to several clans of Zulu Fynns, there is not a single reference to his mixed offspring, only the white ones, in *Twin Trails*, the otherwise meticulously researched history of the Fynn family.[52])

Generally speaking, a good shake makes all sorts of interesting things fall out of family trees, but the death notices in the Cape Archives turned up nothing; neither did the Natal Archives, nor the Killie Campbell in Durban.

I turned back to John King's parents, and in due course discovered that his father had been a trader. I knew then that I had the right man.

In 1820 John King snr had been unemployed. A victim of the post-Napoleonic War demobilisation, he was a naval pensioner at the ripe old age of 23. Drawn to the African immigration scheme by the promise of a free farm, and the opportunity to rebuild their lives in a new country, he and his wife Eleanor, their infant daughter, Sarah, and two-year-old John King jnr, had joined Hyman's party, a joint-stock party of eleven labourers

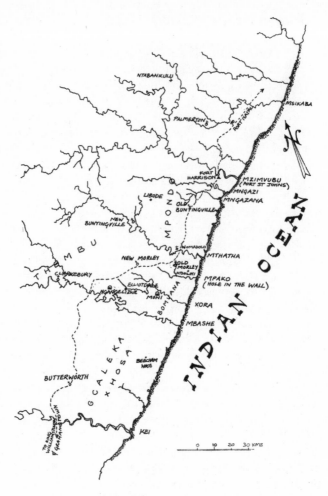

The Wild Coast, 1829–1865

from areas in Britain hardest hit by unemployment, 'persons of irreproachable character, each having some small property and being unwilling to be in actual servitude...' On their arrival in the eastern Cape they were allotted land on a branch of one of the two rivers which form the beautiful twin lagoons of Kleinemonde, near Port Alfred.[53] A tightly knit and mutually supportive unit, the group was one of the few to stay virtually intact under its original leader, but three long years of droughts, floods and rust slowly ground them down. By April 1823 Hyman's party was 'in a truly miserable plight, with scarcely anything to eat.'[54] Its members split up soon afterwards and John King had turned to trade in order to feed his young family.

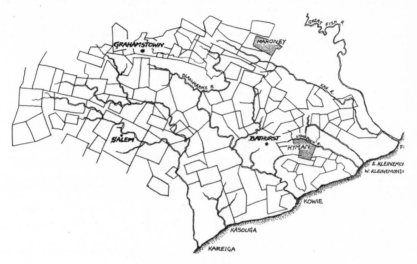

Settler allotments, Albany 1820–22[55]

Since trade with the Xhosa was strictly forbidden, his first customers were probably Boers. Each trip lasted months and covered hundreds of bone-jarring kilometres, but found eager customers. Until the arrival of traders such as King, the Boers, isolated on their vast and far-flung farms in the interior, had worn clothing and shoes made from animal skins.

When trade between the Settlers and the Xhosa was legitimised in 1824, John King was one of the few fortunate enough to obtain a licence for the weekly fairs, which were held at Fort Willshire on the banks of the Keiskamma River, some 50 kilometres north of Grahamstown.[56]

The Settlers who became traders at Fort Willshire came from an astonishing collection of professions, including china painting and piano tuning.[57] Despite their lack of experience, many flourished and the fair grew quickly, particularly as, during the first two years of its existence, the Fort was the only place where the colonists could barter legally with the Xhosa. Towards the end of 1826 a few temporary licences were issued for those wishing to trade beyond the Kei River. The pickings were so rich that within a short time there were at least 20 traders operating beyond the Frontier. In 1830 the border was thrown open, and trade beyond the Kei was legalised. For the first time the people living on the Wild Coast were able legally to exchange their hides, cattle, ivory and later tobacco, grain and wool, for blankets, beads, agricultural implements, knives, horses and firearms,[58] and the Settler traders found a ready market and eager customers.

Within two years there were already 50 cross-border traders, each of whom had an average of four assistants, with stations as far north as Pondoland,[59] where the ivory trade was particularly lucrative. Many made

261

permanent bases there: 'Many of those engaged in regular trade with the Kaffers are not satisfied now with merely visiting the country,' a missionary noted in 1832, 'but they are taking out their families, and becoming residents in it. English Settlers are thus dispersed all over the land, as far as Morley,'[60] the mission station in Mdepa's territory. Nochuku would then have been 13 years old, just a couple of years short of marriageable age.

By the 1840s traders were settling on the Wild Coast in increasing numbers, and there were more than a handful between Morley mission and the Mzimvubu valley. Although the elephant population was steadily declining, the hippopotami, which had given the mighty Mzimvubu its name (it means the home of the hippo) still abounded and were favoured for their ivory and their hides.[61]

A multiple drowning on the river in 1847 gives some insight into these traders, all of whom appear to have been of 1820 Settler stock. In January of that year two small boats belonging to Messrs Ford and Jeffery, who had a trading station about 29 kilometres upriver, overturned in the river mouth, drowning most of their occupants. Among the traders who helped search for the bodies east of the river was John King, who had a trading station a little upstream from the mouth.[62] The first few bodies were found on the fifth day. William Fynn, British agent with the Pondo, wrote:

> 'Messrs. King, Mortimer, Dicks, Vice, Calverley, and Hottentots brought the bodies up to King's last night in the surf boat. I assure you these poor fellows had a hard time of it, and no brothers could have done more than they have to give proof of their respect.'

The War of the Axe, which had broken out in the Colony the previous year and was still in progress, had caused a number of traders to the south of the river to retreat to the Mzimvubu for safety. Reverend Gladwin, the missionary at Buntingville mission between the Mzimvubu and Morley, where the bodies were sent for burial, calls the traders 'the English refugees.' Whether the John King mentioned above was the Nochuku's husband or his father is not certain – the younger John King would then have been 29 years old and the elder 50 but it was probably the former. Nochuku's husband did, at one stage, have a dwelling or trading station on the Mzimvubu,[63] though, as the register of baptisms and marriages for Morley makes clear, his *permanent* base was much closer to the mission station.

Scratchily penned into the battered and rather fragile old book are the fading names of John and Nochuku's children:[64]

Thomas, born on 7 September 1842, had been baptised at Morley on 29 April 1857 when he was already 14 years old;

John, born 25 October 1845, baptised at Morley on 11 August 1850 along with his younger siblings William and Eliza;

William, born 19 October 1847;

Eliza, born 4 December 1849;

Henry, born 15 April 1851, baptised at Mqanduli 15 April 1852;

Ellen Sarah, an infant baptised on 19 June 1858 at Tshinini (probably Ntshilini);

Frederick, baptised at Morley on 1 August 1859;

Elizabeth, an infant baptised on 7 July 1861 at Tshinini;

James, baptised on 24 July 1863 at Tshinini; and

Joseph, baptised on 1 September1864, also at Tshinini.

By modern western standards it's a huge family. I had done John King a great injustice in assuming that like Dick King, Henry Francis Fynn and some other traders, he may have abandoned his wife and children of colour in favour of a white wife. He and Nochuku had not only remained together, they had child after child together over a period of more than 20 years. When Nochuku died at the age of 87 in 1906, the couple had been married for at least 64 years but probably longer, since the average Mpondo girl married in her mid-teens. Nochuku's eldest son Thomas, who was born when she was already 23 years old, may have been not her first-born but her eldest surviving child; she may have had others before him, who did not survive infancy.

The only medical facilities on the Wild Coast in the mid-1800s were at the mission stations, which were few and far between – and they were very basic. Judging by the missionaries themselves, almost all of whom lost one or more of their children at an early age, infant mortality was high, and may also account for the gap of six years between the birth of Nochuku's son Henry and her daughter Ellen Sarah.

The territory, underdeveloped even today, was extremely remote in the 1850s and 60s. The only roads were wagon tracks. 'You have no conception of travelling in the wilds of this country,' wrote a missionary so agitatedly that he entirely forgot his punctuation, 'what with the bad roads accidents happening things getting lost etc it is indeed labour.'[65]

Life was harsh and the bush held many dangers, including wild animals and poisonous snakes. The traders faced other hazards too. There was always the possibility of another war breaking out, as well as localised feuds and skirmishes. At a time (1858) when the residents of Grahamstown were being urged to come and buy 'Great Bargains in Straw Hats!!!… Girls', Maids' and Ladies' Straw Hats, in the most fashionable styles and shapes,' an article in the *Grahamstown Journal* reported 'Another Englishman' murdered near the Mzimvubu, and warned all British subjects 'who are residing among native tribes or whose business calls them to journey through them,' to be on their guard.[66] Under the circumstances, it's amazing that Nochuku and John King were not only able to raise ten children, but to survive to such ripe old ages themselves.

On 24 October 1865, according to the Old Morley marriage register, Nochuku and John's eldest daughter Eliza got married, at the age of 15, to a man called Andrew John Conway, at Morley. The young couple settled at 'Tshinini', probably Ntshilini, a little east of Morley on the other side of the

Mtata River and about five kilometres from the coast, where the bride's father and mother also lived. Their first child, Sarah Jane, was born 8 June 1867, followed two years later, to the day, by a son, Michael.[67]

Bazley's notes, jumbled as they were – 'Eliza King got married an Irishman married Conway' – had been right.

Like his father-in-law and the other traders who had been active in the Mzimvubu valley in the 1840s, Conway was descended from the British Settlers of 1820.

His grandparents, Andrew and Ann Conway, were part of an obstreperous group of Irish labourers recruited in London by the equally obstreperous Thomas Mahoney, a Westminster-based builder and architect. The voyage out to South Africa was enlivened by constant brawling, both amongst themselves and with the ship's officers, and several ended up in irons. 'Mr Mahoney always very troublesome,' wrote Sophia Pigot, a member of a well-to-do English party aboard the same ship, and his men were no better: 'Disturbances with some one almost every day – very troublesome Irish people,' she noted a few days later. And later still: 'Great disturbance with the Irish people, sharpening both sides of their knives.'[68] The other passengers were so concerned they formed a Committee of Public Safety.

Andrew Conway was a mason, contracted to work for Mahoney for three years, during which time he would be fed, clothed and paid £10 a year, and at the end of which he would be given 35 acres of land and a two-roomed house. He was 35 years old in 1820 and his wife 30; they had two children, Eliza, nine, and Michael, who was six. On their arrival in the eastern Cape, Mahoney's party was allotted land at the Clay Pits, in the elephant-infested wilderness of the Fish River valley. The following account, written by a neighbouring Settler, the alphabetically challenged Jeremiah Goldswain, gives some idea of their location:

> 'On 23rd Decr. [1820] I mounted a pack Ox and road over to Mr. Mahonys at the Clay pites a bout 10 Miles having heard that he was in want of Sawers. I had not gon more them four or five miles wehn I lost my way: I had got into an Eelephents path wich went in a quit opersite direction: at last I got on an ight hill and saw the place but how to git thear I did not know: thear ware a verey deep Crance [*krans*] and a verey Long range of Cloffs bush and rocks.'

The elements were as hostile as the terrain – violent thunderstorms, hail and torrential rain, followed by scorching droughts – and the displaced Xhosa even more so.

The Clay Pits were right on the frontline, the place where the amaNdlambe traditionally obtained their supplies of ochre and the source of an almost immediate and rapidly growing friction between themselves and the Settlers – Mahoney himself was killed there by the Xhosa some years later, the feather mattress on his wagon slashed along with his throat so that the surrounding *veld* was a surreal snowstorm of tiny white feathers,[69] but by then the Conways were long gone. Their party was one of the first to break up; Mahoney's ill-treatment sparked a mutiny among his labourers and they were released from service. They dispersed rapidly and by May 1822, less than two years after his arrival in South Africa, Andrew Conway was already well established in Grahamstown, with a plot about 100 metres up the road from where I write this in Artificers' Square.[70]

Grahamstown in 1822

In order to survive Conway had turned to trading and, like John King snr, obtained a licence to trade at the Fort Willshire fairs.[71] In January 1828, he applied for a licence to trade privately with the Thembu, on the basis that the beads and other goods he had in hand were unsuitable for disposal at Fort Willshire.[72] When the cross-border trade was legalised in 1830 he was among the first to seize the opportunity to expand into the Wild Coast region.

Trade in liquor and firearms was strictly prohibited and licences were supposedly issued only to persons of good character,[73] but the Settler traders were not all honourable men, of course, and a roaring trade in illicit articles was conducted. Their underhand dealings with the Xhosa were cited as one of the causes of the war that broke out in 1835; traders were singled out for retribution and at least nine were killed and the majority of their stores were torched. There was a brief decline in trade immediately after the war and fewer licences were issued,[74] but the traders soon resumed and even expanded their operations.

It is not hard to see why some traders inspired hostility. Besides cheating their customers, many also became involved in local power struggles and feuds, which did not in fact concern them. Andrew Conway is a case in point: soon after the border was opened he was involved in the murder of Sonyangwe, chief of the amaBhaca refugees who had settled in Pondoland. The attack, instigated by one Mbazo, took place at Ntabankulu about 70 kilometres inland from Lambasi Bay. Conway and two fellow traders, Kew and Malie, surrounded Sonyangwe's *umzi* at dawn and burnt him in his home. His people mounted a counter-attack; Conway and Kew managed to get away, but left Peter Malie behind. He was caught and killed.[75]

Like Conway, Malie (or Meley, as it is spelt on his trader's licence), was a resident of Grahamstown and a Fort Willshire trader.[76] So was Patrick Kew (or Keogh), who had come out to South Africa at the age of 25 in 1820, aboard the *Weymouth* – the same Settler ship that had brought out John King. Kew's son Henry attended school in 1824 with Conway's son Michael, who was then 10 or 11 years old. The school was tiny, with a total of just 42 children, most of whose Settler parents were so poor that their fees were paid in cheese, butter or even benches. When harvesting or household chores called, the pupils simply took a holiday.[77]

By 1837 Michael Conway was 23 years old. In October of that year he married Magee Maria Coetser, a girl of Dutch descent.[78] The couple had two daughters and, on 3 March 1841, Nochuku's future son-in-law was born, Andrew Johannes[79] (his Irish-Boer name calculated to cover his parents with both sets of *their* parents). Five years later, the War of the Axe broke out. Michael Conway became Captain of the Mfengu levy at Fort Peddie and, as mentioned in an earlier chapter, saw action against the amaNdlambe – an enemy that included Nonibe and Siwani, Bessie's granddaughter and great-grandson.

After the war Conway returned to trading. By 1851 he was travelling regularly between Grahamstown and Mdepa's territory.[80] He became so familiar with the people, language and terrain of the region that he served as scout and interpreter for the British military and, during the Cattle-Killing of 1856–57, as an informant to the Cape government.[81]

The cross-border trade continued to flourish; many Xhosa-speakers and colonists became dependent on it for their livelihood, as did the latter's suppliers and associates back in the eastern Cape and, consequently, a substantial proportion of the Colony's economy. By the 1860s trading stores up and down the Wild Coast contained practically everything that could be found in the shops of Grahamstown, including such luxuries as watches, dinner services, furniture and clothing of every description.[82] The illegal arms trade grew apace and became so widespread that it began to impact on the balance of power and succession of chiefs throughout the Wild Coast region; by the 1880s the amaMpondo alone had established five major gunpowder-manufacturing centres. The traffic in bootleg liquor flourished, at astronomical prices – a bottle of Cape Smoke could be traded for an ox – and drunkenness increased alarmingly, particularly among the chiefs and elders, effectively contributing to the disintegration of traditional society.[83]

In many ways the traders became more efficient agents of change than the missionaries. The introduction of ploughs, for example, disrupted the traditional division of labour. Up until then agriculture had been the sole domain of the women; all breaking of ground, hoeing, planting, weeding and harvesting was done exclusively by them. Ploughs, which could do the work of many women in half the time, were appreciated immediately for their efficiency and efficacy and, since they were drawn by oxen and women were forbidden to handle cattle, men became involved in agriculture for the first time.[84]

It is possible Conway was in partnership with John King and others, whom he had known as far back as Fort Willshire and who had based themselves on the Wild Coast, bringing in supplies of trade goods from Grahamstown and taking their bartered hides and ivory back to the Colony to sell.

For itinerant traders like Conway, life was far from easy (though the profits were high). Besides the dangerous wildlife, flooding rivers, backbreaking wagon trails, occasional murders and outbreaks of war, there were other annoyances to be dealt with. Theft was one: in November 1858, for example, unknown men made a daring and partly successful attempt to steal the oxen from one of Conway's wagons.[85] Another problem was red tape: contrary to popular belief, bureaucracy in the old days was almost as pernicious as today. Traders were granted licences only on condition that they could produce two sureties, 'being persons possessed of immovable property situate within this colony, to the value of one hundred pounds at the least.' Each licence had to be renewed annually, at £3 a shot. The authorities reserved the right to search a trader's goods and wagons at any time for such illegal items as firearms and liquor.[86] All wagons had to have license plates, with the owner's name and surname 'painted in one or more straight line or lines upon some conspicuous part on the right or offside of his wagon or cart.' There were even laws against road rage, or 'furious driving' as it was called.[87]

For the traders who had settled on the Wild Coast, such as Conway's son Andrew John and John King, life was probably a lot easier in many ways. The majority gravitated towards the missions, establishing their stores on mission land or on sites granted by the local chiefs, who derived revenue by taxing their business, and where they 'could build huts, break fields and graze stock in much the same way as members of an established homestead.'[88] One trader, when asked why he preferred such an isolated life to the comforts of a town, replied that he would much rather live like a king in the country than like a mouse in town.[89]

Most of the traders were young bachelors. Many married black women and produced large families, binding them closer to the communities they served. Frank Guthrie, an old Pondoland magistrate, claimed that the traders' predilection for marrying local women owed much to 'the fondness the Pondos had for setting fire to the establishment of anyone they did not like.' The traders, he says,

> 'found that when they pressed for the payment of debts their stores burnt down. They therefore married (according to native custom) a daughter of the local chief, who at once put his new son-in-law under his wing.'[90]

Marriage as fire insurance, if you like, but the reality was naturally more complex; one trader, for example, took as his common-law wife a spouse of the Bhaca chief Makaula[91] – a move hardly guaranteed to *discourage* arson. And one of the reigning amaBhaca chiefs in the 1870s had a white wife, 'a lady who, upon receiving her considerable inheritance from England, had to have everything explained clearly as she could neither read nor write, and her family in another part of the country refused all acknowledgement of her and wanted no contact with her at all.'[92]

This kind of prejudice was not limited to whites. Catherine Dunn, first wife of the Natal Settler John Dunn and herself a woman of mixed ancestry (she was the great-granddaughter of a *Grosvenor* castaway),[93] would not associate with her husband's Zulu wives (of whom there were 49). As South African officialdom became increasingly racist and separatist in its policies mixed marriages become noticeably less 'acceptable'. One white trader used to shoo his black wife and children into the bush whenever other whites came to visit. 'Edotyeni! Edotyeni! "To the long grass",' he would shout, 'whereupon his family would run and hide, till his white visitors were gone.'[94] This particular story dates from the 20th century, but from an even earlier date the white population in general seem to have frowned upon mixed marriages and the children they produced. A variety of names distinguished people of mixed ancestry, most of them derogatory: 'Hottentots, Bastaards, Half-castes, and Bruinmenschen or brown people, the last a name of their own selecting....'[95]

Some of Bessie's descendants, as we have seen, were absorbed into the amaTshomane – regardless of how pale their complexions were, they regarded themselves as black – others may have been absorbed into white society, but some, Nochuku and John King's children among them, belonged to neither the former nor the latter. They were Coloured people, a name that is still used in South Africa today and very loosely at that. It is an umbrella term which includes English and Afrikaans speakers, Muslims and Christians, peasants and city-dwellers, of pale and dark complexion, the descendants of such diverse peoples as the Malays, Malagasy, Irish, Chinese, Dutch, Indian and English, their common denominator being some degree of mixed ancestry.

Long before apartheid, racism infected the national psyche, and for some reason people of mixed blood were singled out for particular abuse. Thomas Philipps, an otherwise relatively liberal English settler, probably summed up the attitude of contemporary Settler society when he wrote in 1827: 'Bastaards... like the half-castes in all countries, are cunning and presuming.'[96] It was common throughout the Colony to consider them 'as under a legal obligation to be under *contract of servitude*....'[97] Economic discrimination added insult to injury: the wages of white or 'European' labourers and house servants in the eastern Cape, for example, were more than double the wages of their 'free coloured' peers.[98] Nor was it only the economically disadvantaged who were discriminated against. In 1821 the poet Thomas Pringle described the deliberate exclusion from a German settler's funeral of his coloured dependants, many of whom possessed considerable property, including wagons and vast herds, but who, because of their mixed ancestry, were not allowed at his wake and tolerated at his funeral only if they remained 'at a humble distance,' even though they were the old man's 'only real mourners.'[99] Some were the sons of another old German called Groepe, who as field-cornet of Zwagershoek had once been a man of importance, 'but who (now in extreme old age) was considered to have *lost caste*, from his associating with his own children by a Hottentot woman.'[100]

Yet even in the heart of the Colony there were some marriages between whites and people of colour, which did not raise an eyebrow. In 1833, for example, Lieutenant Thomas Henry Duthie, an English officer of the 72nd Highlanders, married Caroline, the daughter of George Rex of Knysna (who was widely believed to be the illegitimate son of George the Third of England[101]) and his wife Carolina, a 'negress' ex-slave.[102] In 1838 Caroline's brother, Frederick, the surveyor who laid out Fort Beaufort and other eastern Cape towns, married the daughter of Andrew Geddes Bain, a high-profile engineer renowned for his spectacular road-building feats.[103] A visitor to the Rex home in Knysna in about 1832 wrote that 'several of the family partake strongly of the dark tinge and features,'[104] especially Caroline and Frederick's brother, John. (Sophy Gray, wife of the first Bishop of Cape Town, remarked how astonished her servants were when he visited her at Bishop's Court in Cape Town.[105]) Yet none of the contemporary documents I have come across refer negatively to either marriage – either because their authors didn't know or because they couldn't have cared less.

Racial prejudice was a legacy of the slave-based economy of the Cape, complicated by British imperial attitudes (read superiority complex) and the feudal relationships that grew up between a black peasantry, increasingly dispossessed of their land, and the white settlers into whose hands it passed. In time 'Bastaard' was ditched for obvious reasons and the term 'Coloured' was adopted, by whites to distinguish them from themselves, and by mixed-race people to distinguish themselves from black Africans, thus subscribing to and perpetuating the very same racial prejudices that discriminated against themselves. One missionary reported that a colleague 'found the half-castes in his circuit so fastidious on this subject, many of them as to race desiring to be called Dutch, and as to colour white, that to keep a clear conscience himself, and yet not offend their vanity, he spoke of them under the high-sounding title of 'De Hollandsch-spreekende Gemeente' (the Dutch-speaking community),' though behind their backs he called them 'De Ongebleekten', or Unbleached.[106] 'They are inclined to be arrogant,' he added in a sweeping generalisation, '… affecting a vast superiority over the Kafirs, upon whom they pretend to look down.' This eagerness to deny one half of one's ancestry in favour of the other should have been funny, but was actually very serious, since in South Africa one's skin colour was tied to survival. Coloured people were oppressed, but black people were even more so. It was all a question of colour.

As the 19th century progressed, South African society seems to have regressed; marriages between black and white became less tolerated and even discouraged. The changing racial attitudes are reflected in legislation passed by the Natal Executive Council in the late 1850s which prohibited coloured people from owning or being in possession of guns, gunpowder or even an assegai, unless they had the written permission of the lieutenant-governor. Coloured chiefs were permitted to own one horse each, as were five of their counsellors, but no other coloureds were allowed to do so unless they lived in a 'European'-style house, had only one wife, and had a permit from the resident magistrate.[107] In an economy based on hunting and trading this effectively emasculated the coloured community. And the really creepy thing is that the settlers responsible for this oppressive legislation were the same white men who had married Zulu women and fathered lots of coloured children. The hypocrisy is breathtaking.

But to get back to Nochuku and John. There are a number of Kings still living in and around Port St Johns, the busy little town at the mouth of the Mzimvubu River, and in Bomvana territory, near Old Morley. Some undoubtedly are Bessie's descendants, but there is little indication that her story has been preserved among them. Much had already been lost 100 years ago, when the indefatigable William Bazley, the dynamite and *Grosvenor* connoisseur, enlisted the help of Eliza Conway, eldest daughter of Nochuku and John King, in an effort to uncover her family's unique past.

Fear of the increasing racial divide may well have played a role in hampering Eliza's attempt to learn more about her white ancestor. The same fear may also have motivated the unknown hand that censored Eliza's subsequent letter to Bazley. I came across a copy in the Cory Library in Grahamstown, and almost chewed the furniture in frustration when I read it.

> 'Elliotdale 18:3:07
> Dear Mr. Bazley
> Dear Sir, – I have the opportunity to write these few lines according to my promise; but I nearly [needed?] a long time through trying a chance to find out some particulars. So I must say I sent my brother over to one fellow name of Falilanga. Well, Falilanga says "The servant girl and the lady what was married to Sango; that servant girl gets married to one of Sango's big counsellors. And [words torn out] say thats about all [words torn out] this Lady Sango's [words torn out]. And about the others [words torn out] Falilanga says she [words torn out] married to another petty chief, but the name of that petty chief I don't know for I am unable to go about myself. I had to do it very gradually, for the natives getting frightened to tell me about this [words torn out) any more. They say the [word torn out] people will take them [words torn out]." And I am sorry I delayed you so long. This man Falilanga himself grandchild of servant girl.... He knows

all. So if you come down again we can try to see him for I am only by myself. Yrs E. Conway.'[108]

White South Africans as a group probably have a lot more black ancestors than is generally realised, especially the old Afrikaans families, since sex across the so-called colour line was a popular South African tradition right from the start of the Colony in 1652. Based on personal experience one settler graded his preference as follows: 'First the *Madagascar* women, who are the blackest and best; next to these the *Malabars*, then the *Bugunese* or *Malays*, after these the Hottentots, and last and worst of all, the white Dutch women.'[109] A 1685 investigation names 58 slave children under the age of 12 who had Dutch or German fathers, while a 1693 census lists 370 adult slaves of partial European descent in the Company slave lodge alone.[110] Some remained slaves and were not assimilated into settler society, but a large number were: in fact, from 1685 all female slaves of mixed descent in the Company slave lodge were encouraged to marry Dutch settlers and the practice became so commonplace that, as these women were entitled to manumission and the Company had to obtain compensation from the groom, a scale of payments had to be drawn up: marriage to a 22-year old mulatto slave woman, for example, cost 150 guilders in 1685.[111] Female slaves who were privately owned also contracted marriages with settler men, usually after having been first baptised and then freed. For example, the Basson family of South Africa is descended from an Indian slave woman called Angela of Bengal. She originally belonged to the commander, Jan van Riebeeck, but later married the settler Arnoldus Willemsz Basson in 1669 and bore him seven children, from whom all future Bassons were descended,[112] including such luminaries as Dr Wouter Basson, recently in court on charges including killing opponents of the apartheid government.

Like its people the Afrikaans language is a blend, and was in fact first written in Arabic script.[113] The Dutch colonists brought slaves of all nationalities to the Cape; Malagasys, Mozambicans, Indians,[114] Malays,[115] Angolans, etc, and the Afrikaans language evolved from a kind of kitchen Dutch blended with elements of all of these other disparate languages, as well as that of the Khoi 'apprentices',[116] in an attempt to find a common means of communication.[117] Archbishop Merriman, writing in 1848 refers to the 'Africanders, a mixture of Dutch and black blood,'[118] and although he was probably referring to a particular clan in the eastern Cape, the description is true to some extent of modern Afrikaners too. An academic study conducted by a respected Afrikaans historian in the 1970s–1980s concluded that roughly 8% of Afrikaner ancestry was black (causing such a furore, I seem to recall, that he was literally tarred and feathered by conservative whites.) In researching this book, I have come to believe that the same is probably true (in mirror image) of black South Africans. Many more of us than we will ever know have European and Asian ancestry, especially amongst the Zulu- and Xhosa-speaking peoples of the east coast where castaways and traders all made their contribution. Many well-known black South Africans have mixed genes, the veteran anti-apartheid activist Walter Sisulu, for example, was born in the Transkei to a white father and a black mother, and Winnie Madikizela-Mandela's mother, Gertrude, had long red hair, blue eyes and a very pale complexion.[119] Gertrude came from Bizana, in eastern Pondoland, not far from Gun Drift, on the KwaZulu–Natal border, where some of Nicolaas and Sarah Lochenberg's descendants resided.[120] Perhaps she was related to the old renegade, though she is more likely to have been the daughter of a white trader since, as a resident missionary noted in 1912, practically every white trader in the Bizana district had a black wife.[121]

In 1961, shortly before being sentenced to life imprisonment and interred – like Makana, Seyolo, Maqoma, and so many others before him – on Robben Island, Gertrude's son-in-law made the following speech in court:

> 'I hate all race discrimination, and in my hatred I am sustained by the fact that the overwhelming majority of people, here and abroad, hate it equally. I hate the systematic inculcation in children of colour prejudice and I am sustained in that hatred by the fact that the overwhelming majority of people, here and abroad, are with me in that. I hate the racial arrogance which decrees that the good things of life shall be retained as the exclusive right of a minority of the population, which reduces the majority of the population to a position of subservience and inferiority, and maintains them as voteless chattels to work where they are told and behave as they are told by the ruling minority. I am sustained in that hatred by the fact that the overwhelming majority of people both in this country and abroad are with me. I have done my duty to my people and to South Africa. I have no doubt that posterity will pronounce that I was innocent and that the criminals who should have been brought before this court are the members of this government.'[122]

Bizana, where Gertrude was born, is only about 50 kilometres from Lambasi Bay, where both Bessie and the *Grosvenor* were wrecked. There's the slimmest of chances – but nice to consider, nevertheless – of a distant link between Nelson Mandela's mother-in-law and Bessie.

Genealogy of Ngangelizwe[123]

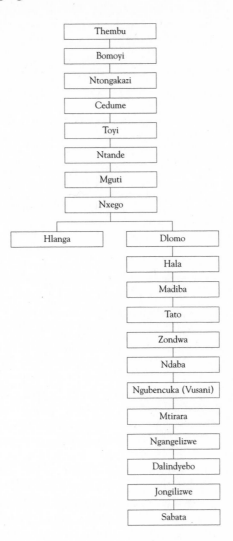

Genealogy of Novili, Great Wife of Ngangelizwe

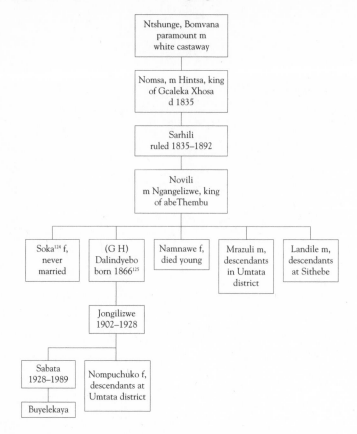

Genealogy of Nosepisi, Right-Hand Wife of Ngangelizwe

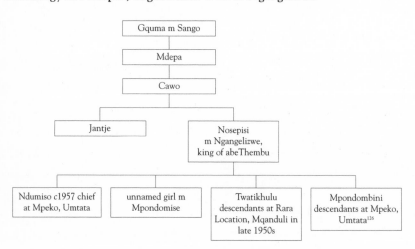

Genealogy of Mdepa and Bessy

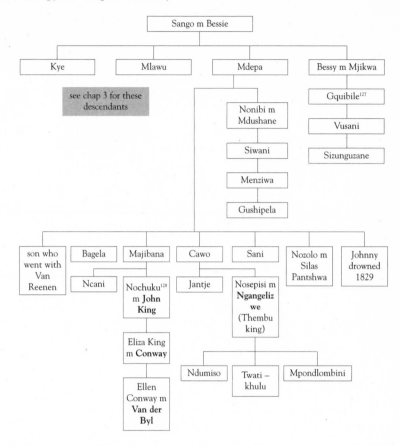

Genealogy of the Kings

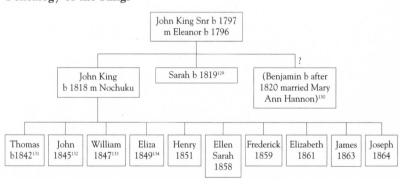

Genealogy of the Conways

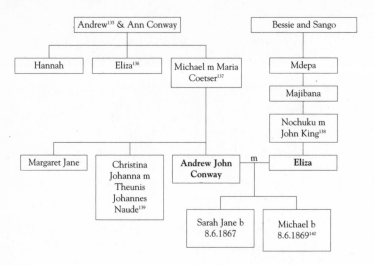

Chapter Twelve

The Castaway Revised

In the 1880s a trader by the name of Sidney Turner blew up the site of Bessie's wreck, blasting the reef at Lambasi with dynamite in pursuit of the legendary treasure of the *Grosvenor*. He didn't find the fabulous trove he had been hoping for, but he did recover some 800 coins, including silver Indian rupees and gold 'mohurs':

> '[N]o one knows but myself what I went through to recover the coins in diving for them in a place swarming with large cuttle-fish and sharks, as I had to dive with the charges of dynamite lighted, at least the fuses were, to blow up the rocks under water ...'[1]

No one will ever know, either, how much vital evidence he destroyed in the process: any relics or remains of the *Grosvenor* within range of the explosions must have been blown to pieces, and its remains must literally have fused with those of Bessie's wreck.

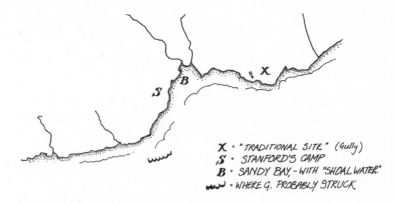

Sketch map of Lambasi Bay, 1955, speculating on the Grosvenor *wrecksite*[2]

Although the oral traditions of the amaMpondo clearly stated that the *Grosvenor* was wrecked at Lambasi, and although the written accounts of traders who had visited the Bay within a generation of the tragedy concurred, and the discoveries of treasure hunters such as Turner added weight to their claim, for more than 200 years there was no tangible proof that the Indiaman had actually gone aground there. It was only in 1999 that that proof was finally obtained. A salvage team working under the auspices of the East London Museum combed the gully at Lambasi and recovered a brass plate inscribed with the name 'Colonel Edward James'. James was an elderly English army officer who, together with his wife Sophia, was a passenger aboard the *Grosvenor* on its fateful last voyage, and the discovery of his name plate confirmed beyond all doubt that Lambasi was the site of the wreck. Among the other relics recovered during the salvage operation were gold and silver coins, dating from about 1759–1777.[3]

The reef at Lambasi – and the pulverised remains of the *Grosvenor* – lies on the surf-line, a shifting seabed of sand and rock churned up by the incoming swells, which for most of the year are big and rough.[4] Any artefacts from Bessie's wreck that may have survived the constant pounding of the waves and the passage of time, not to mention Sydney Turner, would be distinguishable from those of the *Grosvenor* only by the fact that they date from a slightly earlier period. The majority of the rupees recovered by Turner appear to have come from the reign of Shah Alam II, 1759 to 1806[5] and are therefore too late to have been on Bessie's vessel, but five other silver coins recovered at the site are thought to have come from a much earlier period (to the reign of the first Shah Alam, in the 12th century, according to one estimate, or to the reign of Akbar-Shah, c1556–1605, according to another).[6] Turner also found a number of coins which, he thought, may have been Spanish; he could not date them conclusively, but estimated them to be 'either about the year 1740 or 1770'[7] – roughly the same period as the coins recovered in 1999, although the earlier date does not preclude Bessie's wreck.

George Cato, a Natal trader and later a mayor of Durban, who visited Lambasi in the 1850s, also found several gold coins at the site, 'thin and worn but bearing devices apparently of popish origin,' the design and appearance of which convinced him belonged not to the *Grosvenor*, but 'to a catastrophe of an earlier date.' He also met 'the grandchild descended from the survivors of this wreck... now a man of 50 or 60 years old,' adding that 'his grandmother (Betsy) was a child when wrecked.'[8]

That Bessie should have been wrecked at exactly the same place as the *Grosvenor*, the wreck with which her own story is so often confused, may seem an unlikely coincidence, but all the evidence points to it being true. Her own son stated quite clearly that '[t]he vessel in which she was wrecked was cast ashore at the mouth of the Lauwambaz, a small river some miles to the eastward of the Zimvooboo'[9] and other, independent, sources concur. Reverend Thomas, who served at Morley in the 1850s and made extensive enquiries about Bessie, concluded 'there cannot be a doubt' that Lambasi was 'the spot from whence Dapa's mother came.' Her ship, he wrote, 'cannot have been the *Grosvenor*, East Indiaman, for Dapa's mother was married and had children when the Boers [under Van Reenen] came in search of that wreck....'[10] William Bazley in the late 1800s also placed Bessie's wreck 'on the beach near Mlambass in East Pondoland.'[11] So did Pondo oral historians

in the 1920s: the site of her wreck was 'in the neighbourhood of the
Lwambaso river… some miles N.E. of the Umzimvubu, or St John's River,'[12]
they told JH Soga; 'at the mouth of the Lwambasu river in the Eastern
Pondoland beyond the St John's', said old Zali, one of the oldest living
abeLungu, in 1953.[13] Other members of the abeLungu in the 1950s also
maintained that it was 'at Lambazo,' 'at the mouth of the Lwambazo' and
'at the Lambazo.'[14] Professor Kirby of Rhodes University, who established
himself in the 1940s and 50s as the foremost authority on the *Grosvenor*,
stated that there was 'clear and incontrovertible evidence' that the vessel

> 'whose name is unknown, which brought the tragic little figure of
> the English girl "Bess" to the shores of Pondoland… was wrecked at
> precisely the same place as the *Grosvenor*, for Bess's own half-caste
> daughter informed various Europeans that the vessel in which her
> mother arrived in Africa ran aground at *Lauwambaz* which was, of
> course, our familiar *Lambasi*….'[15]

There is concrete evidence, too, that the *Grosvenor* was not the only
wreck at the site: an East Indiaman of its size normally carried an armament
of 26 guns, yet a salvage team working on the site in the 1950s counted
more than 30 – and that is excluding the near-dozen which had already
been removed from the spot.[16]

Like the *Grosvenor*, Bessie's ship appears to have been English.

Henry Francis Fynn, who visited Pondoland in the mid-1820s and was
one of the first white men to interview Bessie's children, reported that she
was 'an English lady,' and the travellers and missionaries who followed him as
well as Bessie's descendants all said the same.[17] 'Bessie', as mentioned before,
was almost certainly a diminutive of Elizabeth, which was one of the most
popular girls' names in England at the time. Reverend William Shaw
remarked after meeting Bessie's son in 1828: 'It is highly probable that the
European ancestors of the mixed race under Depa were English… from the
names by which the three Europeans mentioned by his family were called.'[18]
At least one of Bessie's grandsons, Johnny, also had an English name – well
before the arrival of English traders and missionaries in the region.[19]

While I've not yet established the name of Bessie's vessel, there are some
clues to its identity. Only a handful of English East Indiamen went missing
at about the time of Bessie's wreck: the *Derby* in 1735, the *Devonshire* in
1736, the *Pelham* in 1737, the *Sussex* in 1738, and the *Normanton* in 1739;
two others 'disappeared' somewhat later: the *Expedition* in 1756 and the
Grantham in 1758.[20] At least two of these were taken by pirates, which
leaves the fate of just five unknown, and if Bessie's ship was among them,
a core of teak recovered during salvage operations at Lambasi might offer a
clue to its identity. The *Grosvenor* was constructed of oak, but, owing to an
acute shortage of timber in Britain, many other English East Indiamen in the

1700s were built in Indian shipyards, using the superior hardwood teak.[21] If any of the five ships unaccounted for were built in India, it would narrow down the list of possibilities considerably.

There is a strong possibility that her ship was homeward-bound from Malacca when it went aground. According to Jacob van Reenen, shortly after leaving Bessie's village on their way to Lambasi Bay, he and his men were informed of another castaway, who had come from the same wreck as she, and whom they found at the Mzimvubu a few kilometres away. Because the river was in flood, Van Reenen could not cross it, but he was able to call to the man on the other side, and it was apparent that he spoke good Dutch, though the breadth and noise of the river made it difficult to communicate. When the waters subsided the following day, however, the Boers met him face to face and his story corroborates the claims of Bessie's descendants that 'she had come from the eastward.'[22] The castaway stated quite clearly that he had sailed 'with the English from Malakka.' Nothing remained of the wreck, he said, except the cannon and ballast, adding 'that all the English were dead, some having been killed by the natives, and that the others had starved from hunger and want.'[23]

At least one translation of Van Reenen's journal has presumed that this wreck was the *Grosvenor*,[24] but the Mpondo clearly maintained that the castaway had come off the same wreck as Bessie,[25] and as he was black (he told the Boers he was 'a freeman', probably to douse the glint in the bounty-

The Straits of Malacca[26]

hunter Jacob Joubert's eye) it is possible that he was Bomboss or Paneya, one of the two black men who, according to Bessie's grandson Ngcetane, were wrecked with her. Because he spoke good Dutch, Van Reenen presumed he was a runaway slave from the Cape. 'Malakka' though, was a Dutch colony. In fact, there were two Dutch colonies of the same name at the time. The Spice Islands, situated between Celebes and New Guinea[27] and famous for their cloves and cinnamon, were sometimes referred to as the Molucca Islands, but 'Malakka' was more commonly used to denote the Malay peninsula and the important settlement on its western shore, about 160 kilometres north-west of Singapore.

The City of Malacca in 1726[28]

The city of Malacca had been founded in 1252 at the mouth of the Malacca River. It was taken by the Portuguese in 1511, by the Dutch in 1641 and by the English in 1795, but at the time of Bessie's wreck it was still a Dutch possession.[29] It was an important strategic centre, separated from the island of Sumatra by the Strait of Malacca[30] and controlling the passage between the Indian Ocean and the South China Sea, in other words the trade route between India and China.[31] By the mid-1700s, when Bessie was wrecked, some twenty to thirty English ships, many of which were engaged in the tea trade with China, were India-bound each year. The pleasures of tea drinking, to which the English had recently been introduced, had created a demand which grew so rapidly that the value of tea purchased by the English East India Company from China had quickly outstripped the value of the goods it exported to that country. By 1750 the Company was handling almost two and a half million pounds of tea a year,[32] an amount that could have resulted in a crippling adverse trade balance. What saved it was the opium trade, and it is no exaggeration to say that practically every cup of tea enjoyed in the British Isles was paid for in opium. The East India Company monopolised the production of Indian opium, auctioning it off in Calcutta to locally based British and Parsee firms, which shipped it to

China. The millions of silver dollars generated in profits were used by the Company against bills on London, freeing it – in the days before banks – from the dangers of shipping bullion and allowing the Company to purchase as much tea as it wished without bothering about its balance of trade.[33]

The English factory in Bengal played a major role in the trade between India and China;[34] even the Indiamen engaged in the opium and tea trade with Canton usually returned to Europe via the subcontinent. This route naturally took them through the straits and past the town of Malacca. Valentyn, who visited it in 1726, described it as a handsome settlement of fine stone buildings in the Portuguese style, with spacious though unpaved streets. Surrounding the settlement were lush plantations of coconut palms, occupied chiefly by Malays, and beyond them dense forests in which lurked elephants, crocodiles and tigers. The wildlife, said Valentyn, was a serious threat to the inhabitants of the town but apparently there were ways and means of dealing with them: '[T]he Malacca tigers of the middle of the sixteenth century,' an early Portuguese explorer wrote, 'were dealt with by excommunication.'[35]

The prevailing religion of Malacca – the Catholic bent of its tiger population notwithstanding – was Islam.[36] So it was with some interest that I learnt that the names of some of Bessie's fellow castaways, her 'brothers' Paneya and Bomboss, and 'sisters' Noqualekiza and Colaz, were of Arabic or Persian origin. If so, they were probably Muslim.[37] Islam had been brought to Malacca and other parts of the East Indies from India, where it had been introduced by Persian invaders many centuries before. The Mughal emperors of India were all Muslim and, by the mid-1700s, when Bessie's wreck occurred, Muslims comprised one-quarter of the population of India. For some reason, probably because of the influence and dominance of the Arab maritime trade network, which extended from east Africa to China, the percentage was much higher among Asian seamen, and the majority of Lascars were Muslims. (Most Lascars came from the Indian subcontinent, predominantly from eastern Bengal, especially the Chittagong area,[38] and spoke Urdu, a Persianised or Arabic version of Hindustani, the most important or widespread of the Indian languages.[39])

Indian seamen were common on all European vessels involved in the eastern trade. Employed as replacements for European crew who had been lost through desertion, disease and especially scurvy on the long voyage from Europe and in and around the East, by the end of the 18th century their numbers were so great that they often comprised more than half of the sailors aboard European ships calling at the Cape.[40] Like their European counterparts, disease took its toll on the Lascars, but it was the European climate that proved the most lethal to them: when the *Seurat Castle*, for example, put in at the Cape after a voyage from England in 1800, 120 of its crew – of which four-fifths were Lascars – had died, 'not able to bear the severity of the Cold and bad weather upon the outset of the Passage.'[41] Since Lascars were common on both homeward and outward-bound European vessels, their presence aboard Bessie's ship is no indication of which way she was headed when it was wrecked. However, the castaway's statement that he had sailed 'with the English from Malakka' and, as we shall see below, Bessie's age and the fact that she was attended by a Lascar woman who remained with her until she died,[42] strongly suggests that her ship was homeward-bound for Europe.

By 1740, around the time Bessie was wrecked, India was Britain's sole possession in the East.[43] So even if her ship had come via Malacca, my guess is that Bessie boarded the vessel somewhat later in the voyage, at an English port on the eastern seaboard of India, either Calcutta or Madras.

The English had entered the Eastern trade late. The Honourable East India Company was established only on the last day of the 16th century, over a century after the Portuguese had pioneered the sea route to the East, and it was another eight years before their first ship landed at Seurat, 267 kilometres north of Bombay (today's Mumbai),[44] but what they had lost in time they more than made up in energy and initiative, coupled with political intrigue and bribery, increasing military and maritime expertise – and greed. Blessed with a potent mix of luck, mercenaries and a profitable share of the opium trade, and despite competition from other nations such as the Dutch, Danish and French,[45] by the end of the 1600s the English had ousted the Portuguese from most of their possessions and established themselves as the dominant foreign power in India. To their chagrin, though, for many years after consolidating their power the English were referred to by Indians as 'Portuguese' – testimony to the enormous impact the latter had had on Indian trade.[46]

To maintain its position in India the English East India Company built up its own private armies, one of which was stationed at each of its three main factories (trading posts) at Bombay on the west coast, Madras on the east and Calcutta in the Gulf of Bengal. From at least 1662, when Sir Abraham Shipman was sent out with 400 soldiers to take possession of Bombay from the Portuguese and become governor,[47] the British army also had troops in India, and by the beginning of the 1700s the interests of the Company and the British state had become inseparable.[48] As its territory and political leverage grew, the Company pulled out all the stops to maintain its monopoly of the Indian trade, in one year alone paying out £100 000 in bribes to scuttle a British parliamentary proposal to end it.[49] With corruption practically Company policy, many of its employees did not hesitate to make it their own and were able to assemble vast private fortunes. As long as their activities did not threaten its own interests, the so-called Honourable Company turned a blind eye to those who

> 'tended to live in style on the proceeds of private trading and use their position to extract gifts; increasingly, because of their military and financial success, they came to look on themselves as a superior race.'[50]

India was a much older and more sophisticated culture than the West, but by the 18th century the Mughal Empire was past the summit of its power and, like a plump turkey at Christmas, ready to be plucked. The English East India Company was only too keen to take advantage of the political vacuum promised by its imminent collapse. When Aurangzeb Alamgir, the last great Indian emperor, died in 1707 and the Empire began to disintegrate, the Company seized the advantage, and by the time Bessie's ship was wrecked, India was 'the pot of gold at the end of the rainbow', Britain's most important and lucrative trading partner.

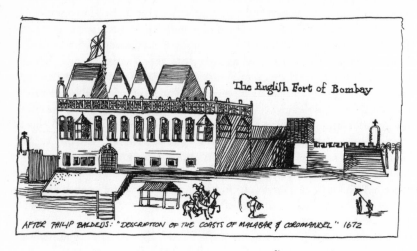

The English Fort at Bombay, 1672[51]

In the India of Bessie's childhood, typhoid, smallpox, malaria and other diseases were rife; even the drinking water could be lethal, and the mortality rate among Europeans was extremely high. It was said that 'at Bombay a man's life did not exceed two monsoons.'[52] Particularly at risk were the children.

It became common practice among the well-to-do British in India to send their children off to be schooled in Britain as soon as they were old enough to survive the hazards of the long voyage. It is no coincidence that the majority of children aboard the homeward-bound *Grosvenor*, Tom Chambers, Robert Sanders, Thomas Law and Mary Wilmot, were about seven years old,[53] – the same age as Bessie when she was wrecked.

> 'Year after year weeping mothers took their children down to the great trading ports of Calcutta, Madras and Bombay, and handed them over to the care of friends or nurses to be taken 'Home' and brought up by relatives, or in many cases... by strangers.'[54]

Most of the children were destined not to see their parents until twelve or thirteen years later, and grew up hardly knowing them, but as difficult as the separation must have been for the youngsters, for their mothers it must have been emotionally devastating: each and every one of the children they bore either died in infancy or was sent away. The practice continued well into the 20th century, with little contact between parent and child except by mail: when the post arrived, one latter-day mother recalled, 'You would race back to your bungalow and there would be those longed-for letters from home, possibly photographs of a four-year-old on an English beach. You lived for that letter day.'[55]

Parenting in Bessie's day was even more by remote control, even for those children who had not yet been sent 'home'. Practically every well-to-do British child was raised by an 'ayah' or Indian nursemaid, who was often more of a mother than the biological one, and it was common practice, when the time came, for her to accompany her charge on the voyage to England. Occasionally the childminders were male – seven-year-old Thomas Law of the *Grosvenor*, for example, was attended by a manservant, Reynel – but more commonly they were women, like the Indian maid called Mary who accompanied three-year-old Eleanor Dennis aboard the same vessel, or the slave woman wrecked with her charges, two little English girls aged eight and nine, aboard the *Orange* in Table Bay in 1692.[56] The archetypal ayah was renowned not only for her gentleness but also for her elaborate jewellery, often wearing so many nose-rings, ankle bands and bangles, 'that when she was moving about you could hear her a mile off.'[57] It may have been from one of these women, perhaps the Lascar woman who was Bessie's lifelong companion, that she acquired her love of bangles and bracelets.[58]

For some of the children, as we have already seen, the homeward voyage could be as much of a health hazard as staying in India.

The biggest danger was a late departure: any homeward-bound vessel leaving Indian shores later than February/March was forced to pass through South African waters during winter, when the most fearsome seas and violent storms raged. The *Grosvenor* is a case in point: although it had sailed from Bengal suitably early in 1782, the ship left Sri Lanka only on 13 June, at the height of the southern winter. Six weeks later it lay in pieces at the bottom of Lambasi Bay. A traveller who visited the site of the wreck in the winter of 1851 was appalled by the wildness of the sea, remarking that he had '[n]ever witnessed such a terrible surf.'[59]

Driven ashore at the same spot, Bessie's vessel, also apparently homeward-bound, probably fell victim to the same seasonal currents and weather conditions. Like the *Grosvenor*, it may have begun its voyage as part of a convoy but, as we've seen, there was no guarantee that the fleet would remain together for the entire voyage. Apart from the terrifying hurricanes and freak waves that stalk the Wild Coast, there was also scurvy, and an array of other shipboard diseases, which could render a crew so weak they could not keep up with the rest of the convoy. And it was not only the forces of nature which conspired against their safety but also inaccurate charts, leaking bilges and faulty navigation – not to mention the additional hazard of piracy.

Indiamen were the largest merchantmen afloat, built specifically for trade.[60] Fully loaded for the homeward voyage, they were tempting targets for the predators that roamed the Indian Ocean: the French corsairs prowling the Coromandel coast, Indian pirates patrolling the Malabar coast, and the American, English and French pirates lurking about Madagascar, preying on

Arab vessels as well as European. The business of piracy was well organised and all nations participated, the merchant houses of Europe and America facilitating the distribution of loot and partaking of its profits as much, if not more, than the merchants of Zanzibar. American pirates and their middlemen were particularly successful; one of the most notorious fences was the Phillips Bros Company, which had grown so fat off Caribbean piracy that it expanded into the Indian Ocean. New York was practically built on piracy, its shops and streets so awash in Eastern merchandise that at times they resembled an Arabian market.[61]

At least two of the seven English East Indiamen that 'disappeared' around the time of Bessie's wreck were victims of piracy. The 480-ton *Derby* was seized by pirates in 1735 and held at Suvarnadrug.[62] The 499-ton *Grantham*, thought to have been lost near the Cape in 1759,[63] was also taken by pirates, captured by a French corsair in 1758 and sunk in Port Louis harbour, Mauritius.[64] There is no information regarding the passengers of either vessel – Indiamen always carried passengers as well as goods – but the females among them had little chance of making it home. Some were raped and killed.[65] Others were absorbed by pirate society and, to all intents and purposes, disappeared, like the 100 young girls aged between 12 and 18 years old, taken by English pirates in the early 1700s from a ship belonging to the Great Mogul. The girls were accompanying their parents on a pilgrimage to Mecca when the pirates attacked. The pirate captain, a notorious Englishman by the name of Tew, was so moved by the distress of the girls and their parents that he wanted to let them all go, but 'as they wanted women' his men overruled him.[66]

By comparison, the two little English girls and slave woman who were wrecked in Table Bay in 1692[67] were extremely fortunate. So were the girls' parents, since the children not only survived the wreck but even made it safely back to Europe. Other parents were not as lucky: Bessie's parents, for example, probably believed until the end of their days that she had been drowned at sea. And it may even have been a comfort to them to think so, since drowning was better than being taken by pirates. It is sad that they had no way of knowing that she not only survived but lived a long and fruitful life.

When the trader-salvager Sidney Turner dynamited the rocks at Lambasi in the 1880s, among the more minor odds and ends that he blasted out were a copper plate bearing the name 'Buttall', and a gold clasp or plate which appeared to have come from a purse and bore the initials 'J.S.C'.[68] Neither appear to have come from the *Grosvenor*: there was no one on board named Buttall and only one whose initials were JC, viz the Captain John Coxon, but he had no middle name.[69] There is a chance, however, that they came from Bessie's wreck.

The gold clasp is particularly interesting, the initial 'C' bringing to mind the widespread and enduring rumour that Bessie's granddaughter Nonibe was descended from a shipwrecked family named Campbell (see chapter 9). According to Buck Adams, a private who served in the 7th Dragoons during the War of 1846,

> 'This woman was the granddaughter of General Campbell, who, with his three daughters, was wrecked off the Coast but succeeded in reaching the shore, when they were made prisoners by the Kaffirs. The youngest daughter became the wife of a Chief and had several children of which only one survived, who eventually became the wife of Seyola, the present Chief. Her name was Nunnoobee, but she was sometimes called Nebudoo. Miss Campbell, – her mother –, had been dead some years. It was not known what had become of the General and his two eldest daughters. One of them was reported to have become the wife of Umtikaka, another Chief, but I believe this was never authenticated.'[70]

Nonibe, of course, was the wife of Mdushane, not his son Seyolo, but Adams' reference to 'Umtikaka' is interesting. This could be either Mtirara, a son of the Xhosa king Hintsa, whose Great Wife Nomsa was the granddaughter of a white female castaway,[71] or the Thembu King Ngangelizwe,[72] two of whose wives were descended from white female castaways and whose clan-name was Mtirara.[73] Perhaps there is truth in Nonibe's supposed relationship to the Campbells too.

Adams was not the only one to mention the Campbell connection: Harriet Ward, whose husband had served as a captain in the 91st Regiment, and was deployed against Nonibe's people in 1846–47, wrote that Nonibe's mother 'was the daughter of a Miss Campbell, one of the General's unhappy daughters, who had been seized and retained by a Kaffir chief as his "great wife".'[74]

Elsewhere she writes:

'General Campbell and his three daughters being wrecked off the Coast of Africa, in the *Grosvenor* East Indiaman, the unfortunate ladies were allotted as wives to the Kaffir chiefs. Nunnube's [Nonibe's] grandmother was one of these....'[75]

Napier, the British cavalry officer who participated in the attack on Nonibe's *umzi* in November 1846, also refers to the Campbell rumour: among the *Grosvenor's* female passengers, he says, there were

'two daughters of a General Campbell, who, it is said, became the wives of a Kaffir chief; and from one of the latter, her T'Slambie majesty, Queen Nonube – whose "capital" we so ungallantly destroyed – is said to be able to trace a lineal descent.'[76]

Captain Garden of the 45th Regiment also knew the story; on a visit to Lambasi Bay in the 1850s, he wrote in his diary: 'As to the fate of the unfortunate daughters of General Campbell supposed to have been in the *Grosvenor* when she was lost, nothing positive is known.'[77]

One of the more prominent of the British settlers who came out to the eastern Cape in 1820 was a Major-General Charles Colin Campbell, whose family had close ties with India. His father Colonel Charles Campbell, born 1723, had joined the British East India Company in 1749, about the same time that Bessie was wrecked on the Wild Coast, and had married at Madras in 1750. His third son, baptised at Madras in 1762, also joined the service and rose to major-general, before emigrating to South Africa in 1820.[78] The major-general was married three times and, on his death in 1822 at Barville Park, his estate near Grahamstown, was survived by eight sons and five daughters. If the *Grosvenor*-Campbell story had come from them, it could hardly have had better credentials.

Except for one thing: there were no passengers named Campbell on the *Grosvenor* when it was wrecked.[79]

Since Bessie's ship and the *Grosvenor* are so often confused with one another, though, there is a possibility that Nonibe's reputed grandmother (the castaway Campbell) and her real grandmother (the castaway Bessie) were one and the same.

Fortified by the old 'no-smoke' cliche, I set out to discover if there had been any Campbells in the East Indies, focusing on India in particular because of its primacy – both territorial and commercial – in Britain's eastern empire around the time Bessie was shipwrecked.

I knew that looking for a General Campbell who might have been Bessie's father was a long shot, but several of my earlier hunches had paid off, and at first glance the quest didn't look too difficult. Despite the Company's rapid expansion, the number of British in India before the establishment of the Raj in the 19th century was small. Out of a population of 250 000 in and around Madras in 1740, for example, only 100 were British,[80] the majority of whom were employed by the East India Company. The latter's monopoly was so absolute that no one could proceed to India without its permission; it rarely issued licences to civilians other than merchants, lawyers and, from the beginning of the 1700s, when the standard five-year contract was extended to allow for lifelong employment in India, women destined for the marriage market.[81]

Unfortunately the records dating back to the period of Bessie's birth, being among the earliest available, contain the least information. All are bare one-liners. For example:

'Colin Campbell (Madras). Lieutenant of Captain John Campbell's Company. Buried at Madras, 26th Sept. 1748. (No further information regarding this officer has been found.)'

His commanding officer's record is no more helpful:

'John Campbell. (Madras). Captain of a Company in 1748. (Nothing further regarding this officer has been discovered....)'[82]

Working on the assumption that any Campbell who had been a general had to have been a member of the gentry – there was little chance of rising through the ranks in those days and commissions had to be purchased – I concentrated on the Campbell elite. The House of Campbell was an immensely powerful family, with extensive and far-flung interests. In the mid-1700s, its head was the third Duke of Argyll, one of whose ancestors had been a founder of the English East India Company.[83]

For the British aristocracy India was a godsend, the place where they sent their reprobate offspring when all other options had been exhausted – 'the last resource of ruined profligates' according to William Hickey, who was himself sent there and for similar reasons.[84] With its own private army at each trading post and corruption the order of the day, the East India Company was fertile ground for ambitious and adventurous young Brits, particularly ones with good contacts, who were unable or unwilling to conduct themselves like gentlemen and whose moral values were flexible.[85] And judging by the vast numbers of Campbells who served in India, the clan had more than its fair share of black sheep: between 1600 and 1858 no less than 250 Campbells served in the Honourable East India Company.[86]

Compounding the problem of numerical overload was the fact that the Campbells favoured a very limited number of Christian names. Apparently it was a Scottish custom to name the eldest son after his father's father, the

next son after his mother's father, and the third after his father; daughters
were named in similar fashion, that is, the first after her mother's mother,
the second after her father's mother, and the third after her own mother.[87]
But the Campbells outdid everyone, repeating the same names over and
over again from generation to generation in what is almost a parody of the
already conservative tendencies of British nomenclature. For twenty
generations – from the 14th to the 19th century – all the chiefs of Clan
Campbell were called Archibald, Colin or John, with an occasional
Duncan thrown in.[88]

Trying to trace a specific individual can be an exercise in absurdity. Upper-
class-twit tomes such as *Burke's Peerage* or *Burke's Landed Gentry* are dotted with
such gems as John Campbell, an army captain who married Mary Campbell, a
daughter of John Campbell, and produced a daughter, Mary Campbell, who
married Colonel John Campbell.[89] Since the Campbells also had a predilection
for marrying amongst themselves, including their first cousins, Bessie's children's
exotic genes would have been a beneficial addition to the family gene pool!

Looking into the history of the Clan Campbell I found that, despite the
obvious differences, there were surprising similarities between them and
Bessie's adoptive people: if Bessie was indeed Scottish she could hardly have
chosen anyone more compatible than the amaMpondo.

Both societies were based on the clan system,[90] with several minor chiefs
emerging from the stock of a senior male chief while maintaining their
ancestral identity. Rather like the Gcaleka/Rharhabe split that tore the
amaXhosa in two in the 18th century, during that same period there were two
Campbell territorial empires, the cause of the latter rooted, like the former, in
the clan system. As one historian says,

> '...like most political structures with a strong kinship element in them,
> Highland clans had a built-in tendency to fission once they expanded
> beyond a certain size and it became difficult to maintain the immediacy
> of the relationship between the chiefly house and the all-important
> cadet branches. This can be seen in the case of the Clan Campbell
> in 1715.'[91]

The terms the Highlanders used to describe themselves are the same
used by the amaMpondo: the Duke of Argyll, for example, was the head of
the *House* of Campbell, and was known as Mac Chailein Mor, which is
Gaelic for the *Great Son* of Colin.[92] The Scots also spoke of themselves as
Highland *clans*, 'a race of *warrior herdsmen*', led by '*chiefs*',[93] and so on.
Foreigners also used similar terminology: 'savages', the King of France's
cosmographer said of the Highlanders in 1583.

Both social systems regarded women pretty much as minors regardless of
their age or social position. Both Scottish and Mpondo genealogies betray
this in the dearth of information regarding the female descendants of their
chiefs. Belief in witchcraft was widespread both among the Scots and the

Xhosa – in *Burke's Landed Gentry* there is at least one Campbell woman who, like Bessie's granddaughter Nonibe, was accused of witchcraft.

There is also an amusing similarity in the clothes they wore. The *brecan feille*, or big tartan skirt, which came into general use among the Highland clans in 1600, was not unlike the leather *kaross* of the Xhosa-speaking peoples and served the same purpose of keeping its wearer warm. Totalling about 7–8 metres in length, it was much larger than the small kilt with which we are now familiar (and which in those days was worn only by the poorer Scots); the lower part was wrapped around the waist, while the upper part was worn about the shoulders as a cloak and was ideal for campaigning as it could also serve as a blanket at night.[94]

And there's more. The Scots did not exactly wear Mpondo-style penis sheaths but what they did wear was close enough, as the following description of Highland dress in 1688 shows: 'their thighs were bare, with heavy muscles.... What should be concealed is hid by a large shot-pouch, on each side of which hangs a pistol and a dagger, as if they found it necessary to keep those parts well protected.'[95]

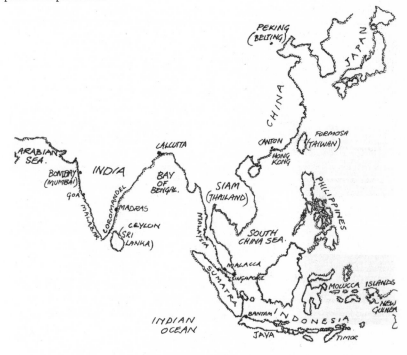

The East Indies[96]

The House of Campbell was renowned for its fierce spirit and naked ambition: 'The policies of the Argyll family led them to employ every means for the acquisition of property and the extension of the clan.'[97] In this they were so successful that by the time Bessie was born the Campbells were the most powerful of all the clans in Scotland. Their climb to dominance was in many instances utterly ruthless, unmitigated even by the blood that bound them together. One early Campbell chief, the 1st Earl of Argyll, overcame the dynastic ambitions of a rival named Angus Og by imprisoning his pregnant wife – who happened to be the Earl's own daughter. And, as if that wasn't bad enough, following the birth of his grandson, he kept him prisoner too – for the first 19 years of his life.[98]

The Campbell feistiness carried over into the clan members who headed for the East. Many had very distinguished careers and became pillars of the British establishment. The governors of Fort George (Madras) in the mid-1700s and towards the end of the century were both Campbells.[99]

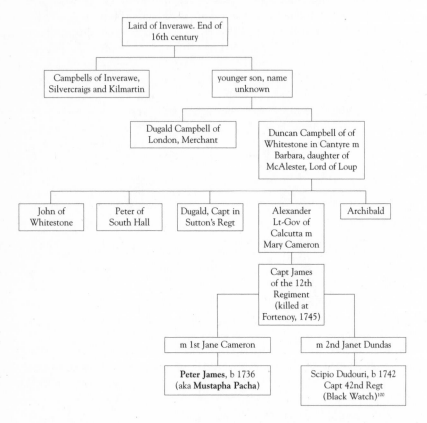

Other Campbells rejected the establishment, along with everything else they had been born to, even the church: Peter James Campbell, left Calcutta for Constantinople, where he tutored the Sultan's son, converted to Islam and became known as Mustapha Pacha. (When his former pupil became Sultan he was appointed Grand Vizier, and later fought against Napoleon in Egypt.) Born in 1736, he was Bessie's exact contemporary and could almost have been her brother, especially as he was the grandson of Alexander Campbell who, rather interestingly, had been Lieutenant-Governor of Calcutta[101] shortly before Bessie was wrecked.

I realised that, like most oral history, Nonibe's Campbell rumour should not be taken too literally: Bessie could as easily have been the granddaughter of a Lieutenant-Governor Campbell as the granddaughter of a General Campbell. And then again she might have been neither: the records to which I had access in South Africa were simply not detailed enough to know.

Looking for Campbells who had been lost at sea was not the obvious short-cut it should have been. Neither the websites I have visited nor *Burke's Peerage* and *Landed Gentry*, nor the early *Dictionaries of National Biography* to which I have had access listed any Campbell females as having been lost at sea during the period when Bessie was wrecked – but, then again, only one mentioned the loss of Thomas Chambers, the seven-year-old son of Sir Robert Chambers, Chief Justice of Bengal, in the famous wreck of the *Grosvenor* in 1782.[102]

I did discover, however, that in about 1804 a Major-General Nixon was lost with the *Prince of Wales* off the South African coast,[103] along with two of his daughters and a number of his grandchildren, and that in 1808 Olympia, a daughter of Lieutenant-General Sir Alexander Campbell, was drowned off the coast of Africa with her husband.[104] Perhaps the rumour that Nonibe's grandmother was a Campbell arose from a fusion and confusion of these two incidents.

That is just one conclusion of course; Bessie could really have been almost anyone. Said to have come 'from a cold place,'[105] she almost certainly came from one of the hottest; said to have been English, she was quite possibly a Scot; born in the Indies and raised in Africa, she died an Mpondo. Born into a world that excluded women from politics and adopted by a society that did likewise, she became a politician of note. Widely admired for her compassion, she was accused by her daughter of neglecting her spiritual needs. Admired for her wisdom, she wore enough bangles and baubles to win the title of First Kugel on the Coast. 'Enigmatic' doesn't even begin to describe her.

For a researcher based in Britain it should not be impossible to find out which of the handful of East Indiamen that went missing at around the time of Bessie's wreck were built in the East (of teak) and were homeward-bound – probably from China via the Strait of Malacca and Bengal. For committed genealogists, the Scottish connection may yet yield valuable information and fill in some parts of the puzzle.

DNA analysis could also provide an interesting pointer regarding Bessie's genetic contribution to many present-day Xhosa, Thembu, Bomvana and Mpondo royal families. But for me at least the search is over. I think I have reached a point where I no longer expect to know everything but am, to quote Noni Jabavu, 'capable of uncertainties.'[106]

It has been a long journey. I've followed Bessie across the length and breadth of South Africa, selling up and moving kids, cat, lock, stock, and assorted barrels to the Eastern Cape to complete my research and write it all up. It was crazy but it was fun, and we had some interesting experiences and met some wonderful people. Towards the end of it all I went to meet Bessie's great-great-etc grandson, Ngubesizwe Siwani, the direct descendant of Siwani, Great Son of Bessie's granddaughter Nonibe and her husband Mdushane. I should have met him ages before and had in fact tried to, but for various reasons managed to do so only after I had pretty much put this book to bed and had already left the Eastern Cape again. He sounded a bit anxious on the phone when I asked if I could come and visit him, explaining that I had been writing about his ancestors: could I come when his counsellors would be there, he suggested, as he was rather young himself. He had become chief only in 2000, following the death of his father, and did not know much about his people's history, he said, though he had a good book if I was interested.[107] At my request, though, it was a very informal meeting, just him and me, and lasted only a couple of hours.

Chief Siwani's Great Place is at Tamarha, a small hilltop settlement of scattered homesteads and browsing cattle, a few kilometres outside King William's Town. As the main road winds uphill from Peddie and the Keiskamma River valley, the countryside is badly eroded, the grass patchy and the cattle thin. Anticipating that the community was pretty poor, I warned my sons Kash and Ky that the people we were going to see might be humble folk and that they were to be especially respectful – no smart-ass city-kid stuff, please. As it turned out the Siwanis were very well off, either because of the chief's mother's entrepreneurial skills (she runs a butchery in a nearby town) or because his father had been a collaborator in Lennox Sebe's government (Minister of Justice, I think). On my best behaviour, I didn't ask any awkward questions about this – Sebe's Ciskei was a puppet 'homeland' set up by the apartheid government to facilitate its 'separate development' policy – as I did not want to embarrass Chief Siwani. I was there just to touch sides, say hello and ask if he would accept a copy of the book when it came out. It was nice meeting him; he was kind and hospitable and, although he was busy, took time off to show me the graves of his father and of Menziwe, Siwane's Great Son.

As the sun sank on the horizon, the boys and I said goodbye – we had a fair way to go as we were staying down on the coast – and shook hands and then I completely embarrassed the chief by giving him a huge hug. As I drove off, I thought, Why did I do that? – we hardly knew each other after all, and he was obviously startled. And then, winding down towards the coast through the fine and lovely hills with the sun setting gloriously behind me, I knew. It wasn't only him I was saying goodbye to. It was Bessie.

END

Appendix I

The Black Whites

The abeLungu, or the Whites, are a black, Xhosa-speaking clan whose origins can be traced back to the three English castaways, Jekwa, Hatu and Badi.

The abeLungu take pride in their unusual history, but, as time goes by, it is slowly being lost. This was already evident in the 1950s, when Reverend Holt interviewed elderly members of the amaTshomane and abeLungu. His informants were noticeably more confused about their history and the names and sequence of their progenitors than earlier generations had been; individual names and unique stories were beginning to blend into a *potpourri* of castaways and wrecks along the Wild Coast. As a man called Mantuhamba told Holt:

> 'Long ago a wreck occurred between the Cape and Algoa Bay. There were a great many people but many of them were drowned. The survivors afterwards left in boats in which they sailed up the coast. At Lwambaso there came ashore four men and two women. Their names were Bhuku and his daughter; Bhayi and his wife, Nozisali; uMbhetha; and uMera.'[1]

It is a muddled amalgamation of at least three different parties of castaways – Bhayi and Mera, the Indian progenitors of the amaMolo clan; Bhuku, a descendant of the white man Jekwa; and John Bryan (uMbhetha) of the *Grosvenor*. And when I met members of the abeLungu nearly 50 years after Holt, the situation had declined further, exacerbated by the fragmentation of traditional life under the combined onslaught of the migrant labour system and westernisation.

The youth in particular have been drawn to the cities, yet many abeLungu can still be found in Bomvanaland today, the greatest concentration among Bessie's Tshomane, between the Kwaaiman Cuttings and the sources of the Mapuzi River in the district of Mqanduli. Between them and the sea are the Tshezi,[2] the line from which Gambushe, his granddaughter Nomsa and her son, the last independent Xhosa king, Sarhili, were descended.

Another portion of the abeLungu live on the coast at Xora mouth,[3] a fitting home for the descendants of castaways since it is known for its shipwrecks.

One of the vessels wrecked near Xora mouth was a Norwegian vessel, the *Circassia*, which ran aground in the 1890s. Largely through the efforts and bravery of a member of the abeLungu, no lives were lost.[4]

Arthur Stanford heard the story on a holiday trip to the area some time after the wreck.

Stanford was relaxing on the shore one day when an abeLungu man joined him and told him how Gasela's bravery had saved the officers and men: 'The vessel was on the rocks, with the waves breaking over her, and there was no means of communication with the shore.' The sea was wild, but Gasela, who was a fine swimmer, had plunged in, using the current of the river to take him out to the wreck, and then swum back to shore with a light line. A substantial rope was attached, and every soul on board brought safely to shore. A Thembu man who had joined Stanford and his companion was amazed on hearing this:

> "But," he asked, "why should Gasela do all this of which you tell us? The people on board the ship were no concern of his. They were just strangers. It was their risk." "Ah," came the answer, "you do not understand about us. We are the abeLungu; our forefathers were white men. Gasela swam to save his own people".'[5]

A century after Stanford's visit, I heard much the same sentiment from the abeLungu at Xora:

> 'We are not lost. We are Xhosas as you think we are. We are not lost, we know where we are coming from – overseas.'

The speaker, Dennis Nameko, also had a shipwreck story to tell: he was descended from a white man wrecked in 1856. His ship had been an American vessel, said Dennis, *isitimela samanzi* (literally, a steam engine of the water), and had given its name to part of the coast where it was wrecked. Two white men had come out of the vessel, and a girl. They had swum over to the shore and been taken to the paramount chief: 'the chief chose to marry this white girl,' said Dennis, and in return his sister married one of the white men:

> 'That was the beginning, and they were continuously increasing their population, and also were searching for the name of their clan.... The white male side immediately protested that they are the white clan.... We are different, as we are abeLungu....'[6]

Some of this story sounded very Bessie-ish, especially as Dennis maintained that, like hers, this wreck had occurred at Lambasi Bay, but there were clearly more modern elements woven into its fabric so when I got back to Jo'burg I did a little digging around and turned up a good half-dozen American vessels which had been wrecked on the Wild Coast. The closest match was the *Calcutta*. It was, as Dennis had said, a steamship. In 1881, en route from the Phillipines to Boston, it was wrecked a little south of Xora mouth. The site of the wreck was subsequently known as The Twine, because of the cargo of Manila hemp or twine that washed ashore there.[7] As Dennis had said, the wreck had given its name to part of the coast.

Only three of the *Calcutta's* crew were saved, which may account for Dennis' confusion with Bessie's story, yet he was quite specific in naming his ancestors, and his praises include the cows of Mbombashe, or 'Bombass' the black man with whom Bessie was wrecked, and who has also been linked to the white castaways Jekwa, Hatu and Badi.[8] It is possible, therefore, that the next part of Dennis' account offers an explanation (if somewhat opaque) for the disappearance of Bessie's 'father', Badi, shortly after her marriage to Sango. In any case Dennis considered it important enough to mention twice, and I offer both accounts for what they are worth: 'As they reached the shore, one man realised that his £20 is left in that ship. He returned back to the water, swimming towards the sinking ship and also drowned there, never came back;' 'Out here one man said, "Oh my £20. I have forgotten my £20 in that ship." He went back to the sea and swam. He reached the sinking ship and he drowned while he was trying to get his £20. He never came back, that was the end.'[9]

That Badi might have drowned while salvaging, robbing or perhaps even assisting the survivors of a wreck, is not improbable. The wreck of Jekwa, Hatu and Bati's ship some years before 1736, Bessie's wreck in the 1740s, Dennis' ancestor's in about 1856, the *Calcutta* in 1881 and the *Circassia* in the 1890s, are just a few of the wrecks associated with the abeLungu. While Jekwa, Hatu and Badi are cited as the progenitors of the abeLungu, they were not the only foreigners from whom the clan is descended. This is confirmed by the abeLungu themselves:

> *Interpreter to abeLungu:* 'Let me get this point before you sit down, sir. As you arrived here by ship as whites, how many were you?'
> *Gwaxaza kaLugaga:* 'Oh… they never recorded the number, as it was not only one ship that was broken [it was] one after another.'[10]

Clearly other shipwreck survivors added to the clan's store of castaway ancestors. I don't know how they found the time, in between being wrecked, foraging for food, overlanding for help, being rescued by expeditions, trading ivory, etc etc, but evidently enough of the survivors of assorted shipwrecks over the centuries were also able to make vital contributions to the local gene-pool. One can only admire their commitment.

Appendix II

The amaMolo

Just as the abeLungu identify their progenitors as having been white castaways, the amaMolo identify theirs as black castaways. Castaways such as Bhayi and his companions were just a handful among hundreds if not thousands of Indian seamen, who formed a sizeable part of the crews, wrecked in our waters. Many of the coastal inhabitants of South Africa – Zulu- and Xhosa-speakers as well as Khoikhoi – must have Indian and East Indian ancestors. In the case of the amaMolo, some of these castaways can actually be named and they are said to have come off the same wreck. But like the abeLungu, the amaMolo's foreign ancestors were probably more diverse.

The origins of the amaMolo girl called Minna, for example, remains something of a mystery. Even her name was probably not her original one, since there is a strong probability that she was one of the child survivors of the *Grosvenor*, Mary Wilmot, who was seven when the East Indiaman was wrecked.

In 1907 the *Natal Witness* published a report by the *Grosvenor*-obsessed William Bazley. In it Bazley describes how, after the women and children were abandoned by Captain Coxon and his officers, one little girl, whom he calls Minna, was carried across the Mzimvubu River by a Lascar man. Bazley's informants told him that 'she and the lascar were picked up on the beach between the Umtata and the Bashee,'[1] and that

> 'Minna was... taken up to Willem Lochenberg's place where she grew up and got married to a soldier who had deserted from the Cape. She had some children by this husband before he died.'[2]

Willem Lochenberg was the brother of Nicolaas Lochenberg, the old Boer who guided the first missionaries to Bessie's son Mdepa in 1827.

As the *Grosvenor* was wrecked in 1782 and the Lochenberg brothers do not seem to have settled in Xhosa territory until 1797,[3] when Mary Wilmot would have been 22 years old, she must have grown up elsewhere. Since Bazley calls her 'maMolo'[4] she was probably raised by the amaMolo, and joined Lochenberg's party only on her marriage to the deserter. Several renegade soldiers from the Cape Garrison are known to have been associated with the rebel Boers – some were German and at least four were Englishmen (John Madder, Thomas Bentley, Harry Obry and Coves Bork) – and Minna's husband was surely one of them.[5] By 1799 the Boers were based at King Ngqika's Great Place on the Keiskamma River, which is somewhat south of the Mbashe River, but their leader, Coenraad de Buys, and several others frequently travelled to Thembuland and beyond, and one of them, perhaps William Lochenberg or the soldier himself, could have brought Minna (or Minnie as Bazley sometimes calls her) back with them.[6]

After the death of Minna's first husband, says Bazley, she was married 'to an escaped slave, or most probably one of the Lascars, survived from the *Grosvenor*,' whom he calls Domosi.[7] The name could be a corruption of 'Damin', since a runaway Bengalese slave of that name, who spoke Dutch and acted as Ngqika's mother's interpreter, is known to lived alongside the Boers. Towards the end of 1799, he began attending scripture classes with the missionary, Van der Kemp, who was also resident at Ngqika's Great Place and taught Damin, whom he describes as a 'Mahometan Hindoo' (!), to read and write.[8] Another of Van der Kemp's pupils was the Khoi woman Sarah, who later married Nicolaas Lochenberg and a 'Heathen' woman called Mary, who had at first objected to Sarah's conversion to Christianity, but later began attending scripture classes herself. As Minna, like Sarah, eventually settled at Butterworth mission station,[9] it seems likely that Minna the child survivor of the *Grosvenor* and Christian convert, Mary the convert and Mary Wilmot the seven-year-old *Grosvenor* survivor, were all one and the same person.

Van der Kemp's Mary was a grown woman in 1800; Mary Wilmot would have been 25 years old. Dressed in traditional skins, exposed to the southern sun for two decades, having spoken nothing but Xhosa since the age of seven, and without Bessie's giveaway sky-blue eyes, it is not surprising Van der Kemp did not realise she was 'white'.[10]

According to Bazley, the castaway Minna was married twice, once to a soldier and once to a runaway slave. But there is a strong possibility that Minna may have been married a third time, to another ex-slave. On 14 December 1828 the Reverend Shrewsbury of Butterworth solemnised the marriage of Simon Xila and a woman called Mina. Xila was nearly 70 years of age, and a runaway slave. He was also known as April – probably his slave-name, since slaves were commonly named after the month in which their ships arrived at the Cape (hence the proliferation of surnames such as September, October and February, in South Africa today). Born in Batavia, he had been brought as a young man to the Cape, where he remained for a time and was cruelly treated. Eventually he fled to the Xhosa of the east coast, where, like so many others, he found refuge and 'a willing protection'. Xila had at least one child, a daughter. By 1828 he had been living among Hintsa's people for upwards of thirty years, ie since about 1798, the same time that the Lochenbergs arrived in the area. He was a member of Reverend Shrewsbury's congregation and was baptised by him on 22 June 1828.[11]

Reverend Shrewsbury describes Xila's wife Mina as 'one of Matiwana's people.' Matiwana was an Mpondomise chief of San descent,[12] suggesting Minna was also of mixed descent. Minna-the-castaway is also known to have settled at Butterworth mission. And she already knew Xila. In fact, in

1828 when she was about 53 years old, she had known Xila for at least 29 of them: in 1799 a 'Zila' had acted as Van der Kemp's interpreter at Ngqika's Great Place.[13] According to Willem Lochenberg, eldest son of old Nicolaas Lochenberg, Xila and Zila were the same man: 'now a member of this station' he was 'formerly one of my father's people,' but had left Lochenberg when Butterworth was established.[14]

Minna and her second husband, the ex-slave, had several children. One was a son, May Jong, whose name hints at his father's eastern origin; he is said to have lived for many years at the Ibisi in East Griqualand, 'and died at a good old age there.'[15] At least two of Minna's daughters married white

men, says Bazley; one became 'Mrs Toughy', and the second 'married a man called Piarse, and a daughter by this union became Mrs John Dunn.' (This is Catherine Dunn: see chap 11.) A third daughter, Lydia, married Poswa, an Mfengu of 'the Mashlati or Langalati tribe,' and had several children, the youngest of whom was Elizabeth, who Bazley mistakenly says became the 'wife of Mr Carson.'[16]

Elizabeth's husband's name was really Charles Canham, a white trader with a rather dodgy reputation – at least one official described him as 'a rascal.' Canham had lived on the Wild Coast since at least 1856, in which year he had written a letter on behalf of the Thembu chief to the colonial governor regarding the murder of Reverend Thomas of Beecham Wood mission, a crime in which some of Bessie's descendants were involved. The missionary had apparently been caught up inadvertently in a squabble between 'the Morley people', Canham's close friend, Mathew Ben Shaw, son of Reverend William Shaw, co-founder of Morley mission, and the amaMpondo. The feud included an attack on the latter by several armed and mounted men led by Shaw. Four men were killed. Witnesses described the clothes of the protagonists in great detail – probably in order to identify them, but the report, as a result, reads like a bizarre fashion spread: mounted on a bay horse called Fly, Shaw was dressed entirely in black, with a white shirt and a white hat nicely finished off with a black band.[17]

When Sir Walter Stanford, a colonial official, met the Canhams in the 1880s, they were living in the vicinity of today's village of Lusikisiki, a little inland from Lambasi Bay where Bessie was shipwrecked. Elizabeth, says Stanford, was 'a light-coloured woman of civilised habits and ways…'[18] and, perhaps because of their proximity to Lambasi Bay, he assumed that she was descended from Bessie, or as he put it 'one of the three old women seen by

Jacob van Reenen at Umgazi on his expedition in search of survivors of the *Grosvenor.*' Elizabeth's death notice in the Cape Archives proves, however, that she was really Minna's granddaughter.[19]

Genealogy of Minna of the amaMolo

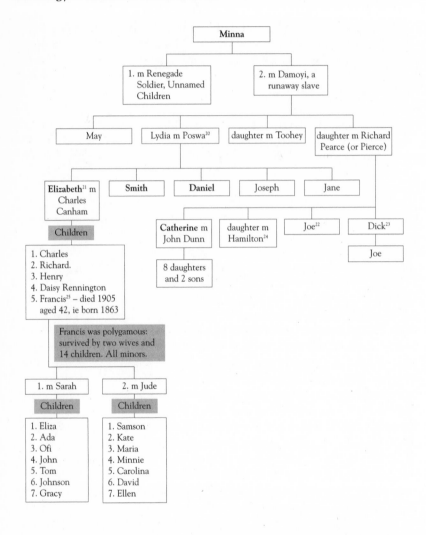

The cultural diversity/convergence of Minna/Mary Wilmot's offspring rivals that of Bessie, and even a superficial glimpse illustrates the marvellous complexity of South Africa's make-up. Her grandson Smith Poswa, the son of a coloured man,[26] was a Xhosa chief. He was literate, promoted education, and petitioned the granting of individual title deeds, which directly opposed the traditional communal use of the land. He was a Christian, condemned initiation dances, complaining 'of being kept awake at night by the dancing going on,' and was opposed to *ukulobola* and polygamy.[27]

His nephew was the exact opposite. Francis Canham, the son of a white man, was a polygamist with two Pondo wives and appears to have been illiterate.[28]

Minna's female descendants were just as diverse. One of her daughters married 'Toughy', probably DC Toohey, a ship's cook who liked to be addressed as 'Doctor', who arrived at Port Natal early in 1835 aboard the *Circe*.[29] Within four years he had established himself as the acknowledged chief of around 2 000 Zulu refugees and, along with another English settler, Henry Ogle, was master of a territory that extended a considerable distance down the coast from the Mgeni River.[30] He worked as a trader for a Grahamstown firm, travelling up and down the country with two other traders, Robert Biggar and John Cane.[31] He had at least one son, Tshali (the Zulu version of Toohey's name, Charles), by a Zulu woman who lived at the Thukela.[32]

Another of Minna's daughters married a white man called 'Piarse' or Pierce.

The Pierces first arrived in South Africa as 1820 Settlers aboard *La Belle Alliance*. Richard Pierce, a 41-year-old baker, his wife Ann and three sons were members of Willson's party.[33] The eldest son, Dick, who was then eleven, grew up to marry a woman 'of Cape Malay origin,'[34] the daughter (name unknown) of the castaway Minna and the runaway slave.

Dick Pierce and his wife worked in Port Elizabeth as servants to Robert Newton Dunn, also an immigrant of 1820. When Robert Dunn moved his family in the 1830s to Port Natal[35] where his father-in-law Alexander Biggar was a leading figure in the fledgling settler community, with – like most of the other Englishmen there – a son by a Zulu woman,[36] the Pierces went with them.[37] Dunn settled at South Coast Junction, imposing his authority over several hundred Zulu and coloured clients. His son John was born in about 1835, followed three years later by the Pierces' daughter Catherine. The two children grew up together. When John was about 14 his father was trampled to death by an elephant. His mother died a few years later and the household broke up. The orphaned John, in his own words, 'took to a wandering existence, having always been fond of my gun and a solitary life.'[38] He disappeared for a few years, taking Minna's granddaughter Catherine with him. The teenagers lived off the land – 'Dunn was a regular white kaffir and used as a boy to go about in native dress,'[39] said one old settler – surviving by hunting and ivory trading. They were 'found' by a trader named Walmsley. While hunting in the wilds of Zululand near the Thukela River, he glimpsed a young boy who was apparently white, but dressed exactly like a Zulu. Walmsley, who 'was always catching something or somebody,' captured the elusive youth, took him under his wing and educated him. John Dunn stayed with the trader for six years,[40] marrying his childhood companion Catherine Pierce in 1853. John was about 18; she was just 15 years old.

By the 1860s John Dunn was well established as a gunrunner, conducting an extensive trade in firearms, for which the Zulu King Cetshwayo was a leading customer. Dunn became his friend and confidant and was awarded some land near the eMatikulu River. He became a man of power and adopted Zulu customs, one of which was polygamy. Eight years after his marriage to Catherine he took a Zulu woman by the name of Macebose Mhlongo as his second wife, then another and another, securing marital ties with clans living in his district, as well as many beyond his jurisdiction. Despite his first wife Catherine's violent protests, Dunn eventually clocked up a total of 49 Zulu wives. He was careful to respect traditional marriage rituals, paying *lobolo* of nine to fifteen head of cattle for each and every one of them. Many of the unions were probably politically expedient: wives, land, livestock and clients were vitally important in gaining power in the Zulu political economy, and 'Dunn accumulated an abundance of all four of these essential resources.'[41]

Zulu homestead in the hill country

During the Anglo-Zulu War Dunn sided with the British and betrayed Cetswayo. When hostilities ceased, the vanquished kingdom was divided into 13 chiefdoms and Dunn was rewarded with the largest portion, the southern region stretching from the coast to the Buffalo River.[42]

John Dunn was described in 1880 as

> 'a handsome, well-built man about five feet eight in height, with a good forehead, regular features, and keen grey eyes; a closely cut iron-grey beard hides the lower half of his bronzed, weather-tanned countenance, and a look of determination and shrewdness is discernable in every lineament....'[43]

He was frequently visited by whites – important officials from the colony of Natal, hunters and travellers – but neither his wives nor his children were allowed to socialise with them.[44] Nor did Dunn ever take any of his black wives with him to Natal, and in this way their existence could be politely ignored and socially awkward situations avoided.[45] His son Dominic acknowledged that

'… there was a kind of segregation practised. But it did not have that name. My father kept to his whiteness in social matters, and his friends whom he entertained were usually white people of high position – we, the children, as coloureds, lived separately from the natives.'[46]

They were not encouraged to establish relationships with the Zulus. Catherine remained very much opposed to his marriages to Zulu women, and despite the fact that she was herself of mixed descent, she 'aspired to being as "European" as possible and condemned Dunn for his "degenerate" social behaviour.'[47]

But one of her stepsons had this to say – in 1954, at the height of apartheid, which institutionalised racial discrimination and segregation, officially turning Dunn's descendants into second-class citizens:

Catherine Dunn[48]

'I want to say this now, that I have no fault to find with my father and mother for bringing me into this world of colour discrimination and segregation and where I am grilled and drilled as if I was an intruder in my own country. I excuse and forgive my parents for I am also the means of bringing other men and women into the world. And while the thought is with me I want to say that it is my earnest desire that none of my children, in the face of God, will ever be led to the deceitful belief that they are inferior to any other creatures in this world. God has created all and it has pleased him to have different colours in people. The blood that flows in my veins from an English-man and an honest Zulu woman is no disgrace to me, nor should it be a disgrace to my children.'[49]

Dunn died on 5 August 1895, aged 60. He was survived by 33 sons, 46 daughters, and 23 wives, including Catherine. Two years after his death, the rinderpest epidemic destroyed 90 percent of the Dunn's cattle and his dependants and descendants were reduced to extreme poverty. The government of the colony of Natal set aside a piece of land for the occupation of Dunn's descendants, but many were forced to leave Zululand to seek employment and today they are to be found all over the world, including Britain, America, Canada and Australia.[50]

Catherine died on 27 January 1905, aged about 70. She left no buildings or land to her surviving children; the ones she lived in reverted at her death to her husband's will, which stated that they were 'to be shared amongst all members of his family.' Described as a 'housewife' in her estate papers, she was survived by several children, listed as Anne Agnes (41), Sarah Amy (39), Mary Rose (38), Alice Lilly and Lizzy Edith (both 35), Catherine Louise (34) and Sunny Dunn (26).[51]

Appendix III

Coenraad de Buys

' ... [A] ruffian, utterly devoid of morality, a giant of great physical strength, considerable ability, eloquent, energetic and a popular leader of other wandering rebels in exile,'[1] Coenraad de Buys deserves more than a passing reference.

His great-grandfather was a Frenchman, Jean du Buis of Calais, who arrived at the Cape in 1688 aboard the *Oosterland*, part of a group of Huguenot refugees fleeing religious persecution in Europe.

By 1712 Jean was settled on the farm 'Knolle Vallei', on the Palmiet River, across False Bay from Cape Town, and was married to Sara Jacob, the daughter of another Huguenot. Their son, also Jean, was baptised in 1709 and in 1730 married Elsie Hofman, daughter of Maria Louisz, 'van der Kaap', a Cape-born slave woman. The eldest of their seven children was Johannes, Coenraad's father.[2]

Coenraad was born near Cape Town in 1761,[3] the second youngest of five children. When he was eight years old his father Johannes died and his mother Christina remarried, leaving the boy in the care of relatives who abused him, used him as their servant, and neglected his formal education.[4] He found an escape from this unhappy situation by retreating into the veld to hunt, and quickly acquired practical knowledge of the bush, which was to stand him in good stead later. As he grew, so did his renown as a hunter – and Coenraad was destined to be a giant of a man.[5]

By the time he was in his early twenties, he stood over two metres tall, was powerfully built, and had a reputation to match. He was more African than French, had forgotten the spelling of his original surname and had drifted well to the east of his birthplace, to a farm in the newly established district of Graaff-Reinet. He acquired a second farm in the Zuurveld in the eastern Cape and, by 1790, had a third called 'Boschfontein', between the Bushman's and Sundays rivers. This was right on the Frontier. It was here that the eastward drift of renegades, wanderers, traders and farmers of mostly Dutch descent, first came into contact with the amaXhosa. The Xhosa and the Boers were both cattle farmers, both were expansionist and both sought the same resources, land for grazing, water, and freedom of movement – competition for which led to increasing hostilities between the two.

Coenraad de Buys had his first run-in with the authorities when he failed to pay the taxes on his three loan-farms. This was not unusual – life as a frontier farmer was precarious and difficult – but it did signify the beginning of his troubles. As the cross-border conflict escalated Coenraad's farm was plundered and his livelihood destroyed, 'the buildings on his farm and all his goods burned, all his cattle stolen.' De Buys was left destitute, 'wandering in poverty.'[6]

Losing everything seems to have freed him from the constraints of civilised behaviour and from this point on De Buys became more and more unruly and antisocial, even depraved, in his actions. The charges against him began to pile up: he was guilty, it was reported, of forgery, freebooting and the violent abduction of another man's wife.[7] When the British invaded the Cape in 1795 and ended Dutch rule, he joined an uprising against the liberal *landdrost* Maynier,[8] but even after everything had died down, De Buys remained a thorn in the side of the authorities, constantly in trouble, accused of everything from harbouring cattle thieves to instigating unrest amongst the Xhosa. He was ordered to appear in Graaff-Reinet to account for his actions, but failed to do so and in 1797 was declared an outlaw and banished from the Cape Colony.

His brother Johannes had had a farm beyond the Bushmans River as early as 1784,[9] but De Buys went further afield, crossing the Fish River frontier and seeking refuge amongst the Xhosa. He returned to the Colony in January 1799, when the infamous Commandant Van Jaarsveld[10] was arrested for fraud and the Boers rebelled again. Together with Martinus Prinsloo, De Buys signed a letter calling the Boers to arms and was soon the leader of about 180 of these tempestuous men as well as 'a great number of Hottentots and slaves likewise armed with muskets and ammunition.'[11] The British responded by sending two detachments of troops to the area, and within a short time most of the rebels had surrendered, but De Buys was not among them. He had crossed the Fish River again and hidden out among the amaXhosa. The rebellion fizzled out and, although a £200 reward was posted 'for the capture, dead or alive, of Coenraad Buys,'[12] it was never claimed and he remained at large.

In due course a number of his fellow rebels joined him in Xhosa territory. When the missionary, Van der Kemp, arrived at the Xhosa king's Great Place on the Tyumie River in September 1799,[13] he found De Buys well established as Ngqika's advisor and interpreter. Now in his early forties,

De Buys was a handsome giant of a man, as the following contemporary account illustrates:

> 'His uncommon height, for he measured nearly seven feet, the strength, yet admirable proportion of his limbs, his excellent courage, his firm countenance, his high forehead, his whole mien and a certain dignity in his movements, made altogether a most pleasing impression.'[14]

De Buys' party consisted of a very mixed bag of followers, rebels and outlawed Boers with their wives and concubines, some white, some black, their children, deserters from the Cape garrison, Khoi servants, runaway slaves and even the odd castaway.[15] The Boers included Frederik and Cornelius Bezuidenhout, Jan Knoetzen, Gert Oosthuisen, Piet (or Jan) Steenkamp, Frans Krieger, and Christoffel and Jan Botha. The latter had only one arm and no education, which he made up for in extraordinary courage.[16] There were also the brothers Willem and Nicolaas Lochenberg and Cornelius Faber, who acted as schoolmaster to the children, many of whom were De Buyses.[17] With him in exile was De Buys' wife, Maria van der Ros, 'a light-coloured bastard woman' (in the words of her stepson Michael) descended from slaves.[18]

At first De Buys had wielded a strong influence over Ngqika, but the Xhosa king resisted De Buys' exhortations to attack the newly established British authorities in the Colony,[19] and as time went by he became increasingly suspicious of the Boer; when the missionary Van der Kemp left Ngqika's territory in December 1800 to return to the Colony, De Buys and his mixed bag of deserters, renegades, women and children, fifty-eight people in all, decided to leave too. Tensions on the Frontier were running high:

> 'the familiar easy interchange of one society and culture for another, of being able to move casually and naturally between white world and black, was finished. On that frontier such shifting attachments had become too dangerous, mistrusted by both sides....'[20]

De Buys' party travelled north towards the Kei River and then swung west, reaching the Colony four months after setting out, in April 1800.[21] According to De Buys' son Michael, before entering the Colony

> 'they went to Natal and to the old place of the "Kaalkaffers" of which he did not know the name. There his father took the sister of Moselikatse and they were married in the colony. Her children were Doris, Gabriel, Jan, Baba and Michael himself.'[22]

Michael's account was recorded in his old age, 40 or 50 years after the events he described, and he may have been confused about 'Moselikatse'. This has been taken to mean Mzilikazi, the ruthless and deeply feared general who later broke away from Shaka and led his people north-westwards from Zululand, wreaking havoc across the Highveld before settling around Bulawayo (in modern Zimbabwe) in the early 1840s. But De Buys is unlikely to have been able to get his whole party as far as Zululand from the eastern Cape and back to the Tarka district in the Colony in just four months. Logic dictates that Michael's mother must therefore have belonged to a much closer people, living along the Wild Coast, which in those days was also known as Natal.

When De Buys entered the Colony in April 1800 he had with him, besides his two wives, a 'Mambookis' girl, from 'the second nation' beyond the Xhosa:

> 'This girl he caused to be well educated , when he discarded his Hottentot and Caffre wives and married her.'[23]

The 'Mambookis' were probably the Bomvana who lived beyond the 'Tambookies' or Thembu. Coenraad is known to have paid several visits to the Thembu and others beyond them from mid-1799 on, and it was at about this time that the Bomvana and abeLungu moved south from Mngazi and settled at Matola. Among them was Bessie's daughter Bessy, whose husband Mjikwa was Bomvana. There is no hard evidence that De Buys met Bessy or her descendants but, as Mjikwa was an important chief and member of the royal family, it seems likely. De Buys certainly knew of their existence: in 1803 he told a party of visiting Dutch officials 'that north of the [Thembu] there lived a yellow-skinned nation with long hair, named Matola.'[24]

By mid-1803 De Buys was back at Ngqika's Great Place, where he immersed himself in local intrigues and conspired with the king against his uncle Ndlambe.[25] In that same year, 1803, Batavian rule replaced British rule at the Cape and all previous political offences were treated leniently.[26] De Buys was offered amnesty by the Dutch officials, on condition that he moved back to the Colony and behaved himself, which he agreed to do.[27] No longer an outlaw, De Buys settled on a farm near the orderly village of Swellendam, his legal status remaining unchanged even after the British retook the Cape in 1806. It was a period of relative calm for Coenraad de Buys and he took advantage of the proximity of the church to have his brood baptised. Some had been born to Maria van der Ros, the woman of slave descent who appears to have been his first wife. Their daughter Maria Magdalena was baptised in 1807;[28] Johannes, born 1794, was also baptised in 1807, along with Georg Frederik. Another child Eliza, born in 1805, was baptised in 1809, and Aletta, born in 1795, was baptised the following year.

De Buys also baptised at least two daughters named Elizabeth, one in 1810 and another in December 1812 along with her brother Petrus (born 1798).[29] Two days after their baptism their father married again, taking as his wife Elizabeth, born in the land of the 'Makinas' beyond the Thembu, and possibly the 'Mambookis girl' referred to above.[30] (With an Eliza and three

Elizabeths it must have been a very confusing household. And the fact that Coenraad had a son, also called Coenraad, could not have helped.)

De Buys already had at least two children by Elizabeth, both born before the marriage was formalised, one in 1808 and Michael, born early in 1812. Their siblings, Doris, Gabriel and Baba were probably born later.[31]

De Buys was an enthusiastic polygamist. Maria and Elizabeth were not his only wives. Others included women of Khoi or San origin, some Xhosa, and at least one Thembu.[32] His liaisons produced numerous children, many of whose names and births were not recorded.[33] He also had several concubines and lovers, the most notable – and powerful – of whom was Yese, the mother of Ngqika.[34] His use and abuse of women included abduction and rape, and he was not above using his own flesh and blood to forge political alliances, at one stage offering his 15-year-old daughter to Ngqika as a bride.

For several years after his return to the Colony De Buys lived a fairly quiet existence, but slowly complaints against him began mounting; his friends are said to have despised his black wife, but it was probably his openly polygamous behaviour that most offended them. In about 1814, 'he left the colony in disgust' and, at the age of about 53, returned to roaming, and what has been termed 'the most lawless period of his career.'[35]

The turbulent Boer and his family headed for Transorangia, beyond the Orange River, where he had established himself as a quasi-chieftain of the San, infecting them with his restlessness and rebelliousness, and urging them to resist and expel the missionaries who sought to convert them.[36] This was at least twenty years before the Voortrekkers' Great Trek into the hinterland and only a few Boers and small parties of Xhosa had penetrated the area. One of the latter was led by Ndlambe's half-brother, Nzwane, better known as Danster. As early as 1805 Danster and his followers, each with his gun and his horse, had established themselves north of the Orange, where they lived as hunters and cattle raiders. De Buys joined forces with them for a while in 1815,[37] supplying them with firearms and rapidly becoming one of the most powerful of the raiders.[38] His activities contributed to the social and political instability of the region, to the general displacement of the territory's people and, in a small way, to the subsequent and widespread devastation known as the *Mfecane*. He formed a formidable partnership with a runaway slave named Joseph Arend and together the two embarked on a highly successful career in elephant hunting and cattle raiding.[39]

De Buys' wanderings soon took him deeper into the interior, and the Marico became his hunting ground, his men fighting and looting among the Barolong and Kwena peoples.

Inevitably, De Buys' gun-running and cattle raiding attracted the attention of the colonial authorities and in 1818 they launched an attack on his camp about 150 kilometres north of Griquatown. The attack failed, and, with another reward on his head, De Buys severed his trade links with the south and led his motley party still further from the Cape, 'beyond all possible contact with authority.'[40] They spent some time with Chief Moroko at Kunwana, in today's North-West Province of South Africa, and in June 1819 De Buys headed east, trekking into the far-flung mountains of Vendaland, attacking a number of black chiefdoms he found in his way, offering his services as a mercenary to some, and setting himself up as the chief of others.

He had run out of ammunition and firearms, and was reduced to fighting and hunting with bows and arrows, but was able to form a strong alliance with the baPedi, who had strong trade links with the Portuguese of Mozambique. By July 1819 he was within two days' travel of the Portuguese settlement of Delagoa[41] (now Maputo), and was probably able to replenish his supply of weapons.

In 1820 he was back west again, north of the Molopo River, in modern Botswana. Here fortune failed him and the enemies he had made began closing in. Makaba, chief of the baNgwaketse, seized De Buys and his party and kept them virtually prisoner for a while.[42] A colonial official reported:

> 'He is quite worn out by the restless life he has been obliged to lead; hunted from one tribe to another after his ammunition was exhausted, exposed to the inclemency of the weather and extreme fatigue, without a single horse.'

De Buys' rough life and age were also taking their toll. He appears to have suffered a stroke, for he is said to have 'lost the use of one side and is really wretched.'[43] The loss of his legendary strength must have been a devastating blow to a man whose life had been defined by his enormous physical prowess and fearlessness.[44] He was also without a single horse, and without the speed and mobility essential in such rough and expansive terrain. Maimed and pathetically reduced in circumstance, De Buys' spirit remained fierce. He slept little, fearing attack, and taught his wife to load his three guns so he could concentrate on shooting if they were attacked.[45]

That he had survived such a tempestuous career in such wild and dangerous territory for so long is testimony to De Buys' courage, intelligence, resourcefulness and the luck of the devil. The historian Noel Mostert has said that Coenraad de Buys' life epitomised the Africanisation of the early European immigrants. The restless, roughshod Boers, who were descended from the Huguenots, embraced an Africa that lay beyond the wide oak-lined avenues and wine farms of their *bourgeois* ancestors:

> 'Jean du Buis could hardly have supposed that such a... man would be among his posterity: dressed in animal skins, more at home in hut than house, more familiar with the temper of a charging bull elephant than with church or school.'[46]

It was not only De Buys' genteel ancestors, though, who shuddered to claim kinship with this striking and unscrupulous man. The Afrikaners who came after him also cold-shouldered him, ignoring his extraordinary deeds and his remarkably extensive penetration of the unknown hinterland, and failed to celebrate his memory. In any other nation, such a pioneering spirit, such courage and independence, would have ensured his status as a folk hero, but De Buys' liaisons with black and coloured women and his many half-caste children made him an untouchable, unmentioned and unmentionable in the racially pure annals of Afrikaner nationalism.

By the late 1820s De Buys was still accompanied by various hangers-on and several of his children, but his once-extensive harem was reduced to one – Elizabeth, the Bomvana woman to whom he had been married since 1812.

He was still on the move, though. According to one observer, De Buys may even have penetrated beyond Bulawayo in Zimbabwe: Thomas Baines describes a 'halfcaste wagon driver Toris [Doris?] who died of fever near Hartley Hill' in about 1870, near which were the ruins of a house occupied by a white man 45–50 years earlier, ie c1820–25.[47] This incidentally was not far from Inyathi, where Mzilikazi built his Great Place, though that was only after De Buys' death. Nevertheless, as his son Michael claimed, De Buys may well have taken one of Mzilikazi's sisters to wife; there were a number of times when the two men might have met: in Pedi territory in 1822–23, along the Vaal from 1823–27 and south of the Magaliesberg, where Pretoria stands today, in 1827.[48] De Buys and Mzilikazi shared several common traits: they were both ruthless, ambitious, prone to cattle raiding and violent behaviour, and neither would have missed an opportunity to forge alliances, be they military or marital, in order to enhance or consolidate their power. It is speculative, but possible, that if such an alliance did exist, De Buys' ill-treatment at the hands of – and intimate knowledge of – the cattle-rich baNgwaketse may have been behind Mzilikazi's attack on them in 1828.

It is also not impossible that De Buys and his family and hangers-on did go well north of the Limpopo and deep into Zimbabwe. According to Michael they wandered about a lot, before finally making what seems to have been another attempt to reach Delagoa Bay, probably to open up trade with the Portuguese.[49]

Leaving K'ghadi, they turned east and followed the Limpopo; after five days Elizabeth became ill with fever, probably malaria, and died. De Buys, who was now nearly seventy, appears to have been heartbroken with grief. He said a solemn goodbye to his children, entrusting them to the care of God. In the words of his son Michael:

> 'Hy (myn vader) was zeer bedroefd over het verlies van onze moeder, en sprak ons in zyne droefheid aan, dat hy ons daar zou laten, wij moesten niet verder het land ingaan, en ook niet terug. Hy zeide nog dat de blanken naderhand zouden komen. De Heer zou voor ons zorgen. De volgende morgen vonden wy hem niet, hy was dien nacht vertrokken.'[50]

The gist of this is:

> 'My father was distraught about our mother's death, and told us he
> would be leaving us.... "Don't go deeper into the wilderness, don't go
> back either. The whites will soon come. God will look after you." The
> next morning we could not find him, he had left during the night.'

They never saw him again.

A period of immense hardship followed for De Buys' children. Eventually
they settled near the western end of the great pan that gives the Soutpansberg
its name, and there ended their near-endless wanderings. In 1888, at the
request of De Buys' son Michael, the government of the South African
Republic set aside land in the district for the occupation of Buys' descendants
in recognition of services rendered 'in some native wars.' Individual title was
held, not by the Buysvolk, but in trust by the government 'in the same way as
land is reserved for the use of natives.' Coenraad de Buys' lifelong flight from
the restraints of petty laws and authorities had come full circle, and his sins
against the system were visited upon his descendants: as people of colour they
were regarded by the government 'as members of the native races' (read 'as
children') and it would continue 'to administer them under Pass, Tax and
other laws relating to natives.'[51]

De Buys' descendants became part of the same weird world as Bessie
and Minna's offspring. Coenraad's son, Coenraad Willem, and daughter
Elizabeth, whose mother had been Coloured married whites and raised their
children as whites.[52] His descendants who settled in the Soutpansberg after
his disappearance, 'the Buysvolk', married whites and Venda people. In time
a split developed within the community as to who was or was not a Buys,
one faction contending that all children 'born to a Buys man or woman by
any sort of union' qualified, while the other held that only children born of
a Buys and a white person, could qualify and that those born of a Buys and
black person could not. As the 'Suiwer' ('Pure') Buyses were increasingly
outnumbered by the 'Nie-suiwers' ('Impure'), the more conservative
members of the community lobbied for legislation to prevent Buyses
marrying blacks.[53] This bizarre racial discrimination by a people whose very
existence was the result of unbiased racial mixing of all kinds owed a lot to
the increasingly racial inequities of South African society. By emphasising
their white heritage, and at the same time distancing themselves as much
as possible from their black heritage, the paler Buyses hoped to win the
privileges and rights enjoyed by whites but denied to blacks, such as the
freedom to purchase liquor, own land and not carry the passes by which
every move they made was restricted and monitored.

Coenraad de Buys' descendants had not only forgotten the tenets by
which he had lived his life, they had forgotten him too: by the 1930s, in a
classic illustration of the compressive effects of oral history, the Buysvolk

believed that Michael, rather than Coenraad himself, was their forefather. A government commission in 1937, just over a century after De Buys' death, was told that Michael had come

> 'originally from Beaufort West District in the Cape. There he seems to have got into trouble with the authorities, and somewhere about the middle of last century Michael was outlawed from the Colony and fled northwards. He took to wife a sister of Moselikatsi, the king of the Matabele, and eventually settled in the Zoutpansberg.'[54]

Appendix IV

The *Grosvenor* Diamonds

In the 1920s, an elderly German named John Boch lived on a farm at the mouth of the Kei River some 200 kilometres, as the crow flies, south of the *Grosvenor* wreck. He was not a wealthy man – before settling down on the Kei he had had a rather chequered career and held a variety of different jobs – and his land was more of a smallholding than a farm.

Boch is long gone, but his house still stands, close to the beach. As you take the ferry across the river at Kei Mouth with the small resort village behind you, on your right you can see the waves breaking on the sandbank in the mouth. Ahead are the flat tidal flood plains, beyond which a solitary dirt road rises into rolling hills dotted with mud and thatch homesteads, small fields and footpaths. Close to the riverbank to the left, on a slight rise, is the farmhouse where Boch and his family lived.

Boch's son found the first diamond. He picked up the pretty stone on a cattle path and gave it to his father.

Boch did not at once realise what his son had found. It was only some time later, when the bright pebble had been lost or mislaid, that the elderly farmer realised it may have been a diamond. Perhaps by then he had found a couple more stones himself. At any rate, he got himself a prospecting licence and began a thorough search of the farm. His efforts were rewarded and he soon had a haul of diamonds, all found lying around on the surface, so he staked out a claim and began digging. The diamonds were small, the largest just under 4 carats, but there were a lot of them and easily recovered, on or just under the surface of the ground. Within a fortnight he had over 300 diamonds, and in due course had unearthed over a thousand of the gems.

The news spread fast. South Africa is rich in mineral wealth, with some of the biggest gold and diamond mines in the world, so Boch's find sparked huge and immediate interest and diggers flooded in to peg their claims. Boch floated a company and sold shares. At the age of 73, it seemed that the humble farmer suddenly had it made.

Then, just as suddenly as his luck had turned, it turned again. Boch's diamonds were evidently not indigenous to the site and he was arrested and charged with salting his claims. Boch protested his innocence vigorously, but to no avail.

The trial opened in Butterworth in March 1928. Experts agreed unanimously that the geological formation of the Kei was not diamond-bearing. A Dr Brink testified that the stones were not even South African in origin,[1] and must therefore have been placed at the site artificially, put in the sea sand by human hands, presumably Boch's. There was great excitement when a bottle containing the offending gems was knocked over and everyone in the court scrabbled about on the floor looking for them.

In his client's defence, Boch's advocate pointed out that the Wild Coast where his farm was situated, was notorious for its shipwrecks and argued that it was from one of the most famous, the *Grosvenor*, that the diamonds had come. The rumours of the fabulous treasure reputed to have been on board the ship were well known, and he speculated that one of its survivors could have carried the diamonds as far as the Kei mouth, and have died on Boch's land alongside the river, where the diamonds had remained undetected for a century and a half.

The prosecution, however, was able to show that there was no mention of diamonds in the *Grosvenor's* manifest. The case for the defence floundered. Boch was found guilty of fraud and, despite his advanced age, was sentenced to three years' hard labour. As he stood and heard the sentence passed against him, the old man broke down and cried.

Boch served out and survived his sentence. Afterwards he moved inland, some 200 kilometres away from his farm at the mouth of the Kei River. He died at King William's Town a couple of years later.

It was only in 1960 that Professor Kirby, an academic at Rhodes University and acknowledged expert on the wreck of the *Grosvenor*, was able to give substance to Boch's defence. Kirby was able to prove that there had indeed been diamonds aboard the famous ship; a lot of diamonds – worth over £10 000 at the time of the wreck. The captain, John Coxon, had had twelve parcels of diamonds in his possession. One of the passengers, William Hosea, the wealthy 'Chief' of Murshidabad, Bengal, was also carrying diamonds, at an estimated worth of 70 000 rupees.[2] Like the diamonds found by Boch, they were uncut.

Neither Coxon nor Hosea reached the Cape, and they may not even have got as far south as Boch's farm. Both were still at least 100 kilometres short of the Kei mouth when last seen alive. But if they did not personally carry the diamonds there, others may have, with as little luck as their original owners.

The first expedition sent out from the Cape to find survivors of the *Grosvenor*, under Heligert Muller in 1783, found 'five skeletons of people with some men's torn clothing....' It was on the north bank of the Kei, the same side as Bock's smallholding, close to the river mouth.[3]

Boch's trial was almost certainly a miscarriage of justice, but he seems to have got off more lightly that the diamonds' previous owners. At least he lived, if only for a while and in not particularly comfortable circumstances.

When I visited Kei mouth in 2000, I heard that Boch's descendants were seeking his posthumous pardon. Boch's diamonds have disappeared: they should have been held at Kimberley, the diamond centre of South Africa, for further study after the trial, but all trace of them has been lost.

Appendix V

Makana

When the missionary Van der Kemp left Ngqika's territory and established Bethelsdorp in 1801, Makana's father Balala was one of the Xhosa who moved there with him. Balala died while Makana was young, and his mother took him to live among Ndlambe's people. She is said to have neglected the infant, leaving him alone in a hut and only approaching to suckle him. As he grew, the lad continued to spend much of his time alone; solitary and mysterious, he seems to have inherited his father's interest in Christianity.[1] After he was circumcised and became a man, Makana went to live in the newly established British military headquarters of Grahamstown, at the home of the Cape Regiment's chaplain. By the time he returned to Xhosa territory, around 1816,[2] settling near the Wesleyville mission station near Peddie, he had not only acquired an understanding of Christian principles but was enough of a believer to reprimand the powerful chief Ndlambe for practising polygamy.

Over the next couple of years, Makana's consciousness became more political, and his theology adapted accordingly. He embraced Xhosa tradition and became a polygamist himself, abandoned the Judeo-Christian concept of a single divine being, declaring the existence of two gods, one for Englishmen and one for the Xhosa, and began to speak of driving the colonists off the lands which they had seized from the amaNdlambe. He called for the destruction of all dun-coloured cattle – the symbolism is obvious – and, in a theme later to recur in the prophecy of Nongqawuse and the Cattle-Killing movement, claimed that they would be replaced by vast herds which would rise from the sea, accompanied by the Xhosa ancestors armed and ready to do battle against the British.[3] His sermons were a persuasive mix of Christian resurrection dogma and traditional Xhosa beliefs, which held that all men and all animals had originated in a vast underground cavern.[4] As his speech became more warlike and the destruction of the whites became a recurrent theme, he began to attract a considerable following.

Makana formed alliances with many Xhosa clans, but his main support was among his own people, the amaNdlambe. In preparation for Mdushane's attack on Grahamstown in 1819, spies were sent into the village to gather information, and the amaNdlambe received advice and some training in firearms from renegade British soldiers, deserters from the notorious Royal Africa Corps – a unit comprising mainly foreign mercenaries, criminals and other wayward individuals who had 'volunteered' for military service rather than serve time in prison – and who had 'discharged' themselves as soon as they arrived on the Frontier.[5]

Despite Mdushane's experience and pragmatism the attack, as we have seen, was a failure and the decimation of the amaNdlambe was due, in part, to their over-confidence in Makana's mystical powers.

In the aftershock, while the British gathered their forces to pursue the retreating Xhosa, the amaNdlambe withdrew to the safety of the dense Fish River bush. The British adopted a scorched earth policy, burning, shooting and destroying as they went, which resulted in widespread famine among the fugitives. Eventually, in order to alleviate his people's suffering and end the war, Makana decided to offer himself up as a hostage. 'People say that I have occasioned the war,' Makana said. 'Let me see whether my delivering myself up to the conquerors will restore peace to my country.'[6] In an act of incredible bravery he strolled unarmed and alone into the camp of Stockenstrom, an officer in the British forces.

Makana was taken under escort to Grahamstown. Mdushane and Ndlambe petitioned the British authorities, offering to surrender if he was set free. But it was too late: under heavy guard, Makana had already been sent to Algoa Bay (now Port Elizabeth), where he was put aboard a Navy sloop and taken to Cape Town. He was sentenced to life imprisonment on Robben Island, in the middle of Table Bay, a few kilometres off Cape Town. He drowned in 1820, about a month after his arrival on the island, while trying to escape to the mainland in a whaleboat with about 20 other prisoners, including Stuurman, a Khoi rebel, who ended up in Australia, and possibly Jacob Simbiti, or Hlambamanzi, who later became interpreter and advisor to Shaka, king of the Zulus.

The closest point on the mainland to Robben Island is probably Big Bay, near Blaauwberg, and it's likely that it was there that Makana met his death: the boat is known to have reached the mainland, but it overturned in the surf. Makana was either badly injured or did not know how to swim; instead of making for the shore 'he clung for some time to a rock and "his deep sonorous voice was heard loudly cheering on those who were struggling with the billows" until he was swept away and drowned.'[7]

Despite his failings, Makana's reputation remained strong, even after his death. He is viewed as one of the first resistance leaders, and his name was immortalised in his place of exile and death: Robben Island is also known as the Isle of Makana.

Appendix VI

The Death of Hintsa, King of the amaXhosa

The Great Son of Kawuta and his Great Wife Nobuto, and grandson of Gcaleka, Hintsa spent his early years as a herdboy in charge of the royal herds. He was just entering manhood when his father died,[1] making him king. He was still a young man when he allied himself with Ndlambe's forces against Ngqika, at the Battle of Amalinde in 1818.

When the colonial forces attacked after the amaNdlambe assault on Grahamstown, Hintsa withdrew to the Mbashe River. His marriage to his Great Wife Nomsa, daughter of Gambushe, chief of the amaBomvana,[2] may have taken place around this time, since it appears that their Great Son Sarhili was born shortly before the arrival of the 1820 British settlers.[3]

During the War of 1835, although Hintsa had taken a neutral stance, the Governor of the Cape, Sir Benjamin D'Urban, invaded his territory and declared war. Simultaneously attacked by the Thembu and the Basotho and unprepared for war, Hintsa's people lost 15 000 head of cattle to the colonial invaders.[4] What happened next was a tragedy, which could surely have been averted.

According to the colonial version Hintsa offered himself up as hostage.

According to the Xhosa, however, Hintsa had merely gone in to parley with Sir Harry Smith when the latter suddenly arrested him and held him prisoner.[5] Hintsa sent a message to his people, saying he was being held against his will, and advising his brother chiefs to look out for themselves.[6]

Sir Benjamin D'Urban, Governor of the Cape, gave his personal assurance of the king's safety, but shortly afterwards, in a supposed escape attempt, Hintsa was shot dead and his body mutilated.

The British had demanded that Hintsa hand over 25 000 head of cattle, 500 horses and all the guns in his possession within five days,[7] and he had set off on horseback to facilitate their collection, under an armed guard led by Colonel Harry Smith. Near the Nqabara River (just south of the Mbashe River) Hintsa's horse forged ahead of the others. He may have been trying to escape or Harry Smith may have panicked and just thought he was, but in any case he tried to shoot Hintsa. His pistols misfired so he threw them at the king instead, hitting him under the ear and knocking him off his horse.

If Hintsa had not been attempting to escape before, he certainly had reason to do so now, and he got up and ran. Smith's aide-de camp, Lieutenant Balfour and George Southey gave chase and caught up with the king down in a river bed. Southey got there first. According to him, Hintsa lifted an assegai, so he shot him through the head – killing him – and gave three hoorays.[8]

When the rest of Smith's men reached the scene, Southey and another man cut off Hintsa's ears and the skin of his chin, another tried to dig out his teeth with a bayonet, and a third, Lieutenant Nourse, 'cut out the emblems of his manhood.'[9] They did not bury Hintsa – Smith later said he did not have the tools to do so – but left the body lying on the ground near the river.[10]

Southey's claim that he killed Hintsa in self-defence was an attempt to justify the unjustifiable. It's highly unlikely that Hintsa would have had an assegai to throw, or been able to do so even if he had. By the time he reached the river, Hintsa had been knocked off a galloping horse, had been shot in his left leg by Southey, 'just under the calf and close to the bones,' had fallen again and scrambled down a hill, had been seriously wounded again by Southey, the ball passing through his body just under the ribs and shattering his right wrist (he was right-handed), fallen again, rolled over and run down another hill, through bush and down a 5–7 metre bank.[11]

In all probability Southey shot Hintsa in cold blood. As Balfour himself acknowledged (and he was the only other person at the river besides Southey and Hintsa)[12] the king *called out for mercy several times,* before Southey shot him.[13] Edward Driver, next on the scene, also heard the king calling out for mercy: 'but,' he said later, 'you know Southey had much to revenge.'[14]

Even more tellingly, the fatal shot was fired into the back of Hintsa's head, almost certainly from behind his left ear, execution style.[15]

Unfortunately the main witnesses to Hintsa's killing were his killers and – in the outcry that followed – they had their reputations to protect and their skins to save. More than one of them lied before the subsequent Commission of Enquiry, their answers in court blatantly contradicting their private statements. The inquest was a farce:

> 'Did you see those ears? – I did see ears, but I do not know if they were Hintsa's.
> In whose possession were those ears? – I cannot say, they were lying on the ground.'[16]

Justice was not done. Not even a semblance of justice was done, and even Hintsa's enemies were shocked. As one colonial officer wrote with dismay, 'Altho' the Governor knew well how the body of Hintza had been mutilated by our people, instead of censuring they were praised by him in General Orders.'[17]

The betrayal, slaughter and mutilation of their king, along with the official cover-up that followed, strengthened the amaXhosa's suspicion and hatred of the British and, for generations to come, Hintsa was a symbol of their struggle against British imperialism

Hintsa lies buried on the eastern bank of the Nqabara River, the boundary of his territory, about four or five kilometres from Mbongo Hill, just off the road to the old Mbhangcolo trading station.[18]

Glossary, Notes,
Punctuation and Spelling

GLOSSARY

Abbreviations. **Af** = Afrikaans; **Kh** = Khoekhoe; **M** = Malay;
Xh = isiXhosa; **Z** = isiZulu

abakwetha (Xh) – boys undergoing circumcision and initiation rites.
amaGogotya (Xh) – unbelievers; those people who did not accept the
  prophecy of Nongqawuse in the Cattle-Killing of 1856/57.
amaphakathi, pl of iphakathi (Xh) – counsellors, whom the chief was
  expected to consult on all important matters.
daga/dagha (from udaka – mud Xh, Z) – a mixture of clay and cattle dung.
dagga (Kh) – marijuana, cannabis.
donga (from Xh 'udonga') – eroded or washed-out gully.
drift (from Af 'drif') – ford across a river.
Fingo – see Mfengu
Fitcani – see Mfengu
Great Wife – the senior wife, mother of the chief's official heir.
Great Son – eldest son of the Great Wife; the official heir.
Great House – the senior line of the Chief's family for purposes of authority
  and inheritance.
ibandla (Xh) – gathering of the people, a mass gathering to make decisions
  affecting the whole community.
intonjane (Xh) – a girl initiate, a girl who has reached puberty and undergoes
  female initiation rites. (There is no genital mutilation of any kind.)
igqirha (Xh) – traditional healer, diviner.
ikhazi (Xh) – bridal cattle, cattle given by the groom/the groom's family to
  the bride's family.
impi (Z) – army (Plural izimpi – armies).
iphaca (Xh) – penis sheath (according to Monica Hunter – *see*
Bibliography). *See also* isidhla.
iqadi (Xh) – junior wife appointed as a support to the Great House, to bear
  the Great Son in the name of the Great Wife should the latter prove barren.
isidhla (Xh) – penis sheath (according to BJF Laubscher – *see* Bibliography).
ixiba (Xh) – son of a junior house, or important but unrelated individual,
  appointed as head of an important house which no longer has a male
  head, to provide descendants and ensure that it does not die out.
kaross (Af, from Kh) – cloak or sleeveless coat like a blanket made of
  animal skins.
kleintjie (Af) – little one.

322

kloof (Af) –gorge, ravine.

kop/koppie, *also* kopje (Af) – a small hill.

kraal (Af) – cattle corral, sometimes 'settlement' or 'homestead'.

krans (Af) – cliff or precipice.

laat-lammetjie (Af) – a child born well after its siblings, generally when the mother is advanced in years.

landdrost (Af) – magistrate

Mfecane – the wide-spread wars, famine and dislocation of people that peaked in the 1820s

Mfengu – destitute wanderers, refugees who began entering Xhosa territory from about 1822, mainly from the region now known as KwaZulu-Natal.

mielies – non-indigenous maize.

pan – depression, shallow basin.

Right-Hand House – the second in seniority to the Great House.

sjambok (Af from M) – short whip, usually made of hippopotamus hide.

soma (Z) – non-penetrative sex.

sloot (Af) – gully, ditch.

taal (Af) – language.

toyi-toyi – rousing dance-chant, performed at political rallies.[1]

trek (Af) – to pull, journey or migrate.

ukuhlonipha (Xh) – to speak respectfully using substitute words to avoid verbal taboos

ukulega (Xh) – to race oxen.

ukulobola (Xh) – to give cattle to the bride's family.

ukumetsha (Xh) – 'sweethearting', to have non-penetrative sex.

Umkhonto weSizwe – 'the Spear of the Nation', military wing of the ANC in the struggle against apartheid.

umsul'udaka (Xh) – a young man's first wife; literally 'she who wipes away the clay'(of the initiation ceremonies).

umzi (Xh) – homestead. (Plural imizi)

upondo – horn, tusk

veld (Af) – field, grasslands.

vlakte (Af) – flat plains.

voorloper (Af) – one who walks ahead of, and leads, a team of oxen.

NOTES

Kaffir, Khoi, San, Bastard and Boer

South African history, unfortunately, is full of derogatory words.

The word 'kaffir', in particular, is highly offensive to modern people. It derives from Arabic and originally meant 'infidel', or non-believer. As far back as the 1860s many black people regarded it 'as a term of reproach,'[2] while its use today is downright racist. Unfortunately it appears in practically every document, record and book predating the 20th century and not a few after. In nineteenth-century South Africa, it was used to refer particularly to the amaXhosa and/or Xhosa-speakers, and although I have tried to avoid using the word wherever possible, in the context of some quotations it has been unavoidable.

'**Khoi**' – originally meant 'angry men', so-called by their San opponents, but nowadays the word is perceived as less derogatory than the Dutch slang 'Hottentot'.

'**San**' – was originally a derogatory term used by the Khoi, meaning rascal or robber,[3] but now appears to enjoy more popularity than the old colonial term 'Bushman'.

'**Bastard**' – originally used to denote people of mixed race.

'**Boer**' – literally Dutch for 'farmer'; the term was used during the latter years of the 20th century by members of the anti-apartheid movement to denote white agents of the racist regime, but appears to have slowly recovered its original meaning.

PRONUNCIATION

isiXhosa is a very beautiful language, soft, sibilant and lilting, peppered with clicks, of which there are three: 'q', 'x' and 'c'.

Q – hard palatal click made when the tongue is pulled away sharply away from the palate, eg Gquma: *click-ooma* (the g is almost unheard, ie it is not 'g-click-ooma')

X – neither hard nor soft, tongue snapped against side teeth. It is like the click made when urging a horse forward, eg Xhosa: *click-orsa*, without pausing between the 2 syllables. The 'h' is silent.

C – soft dental click, tip of tongue against the front upper teeth, rather like a sympathetic tut-tutting, eg Cha!: *click-uh*, without a pause. The 'h' is silent.[4]

> **R** – pronounced like the 'gh' in 'urgh!'
> **Th** – the 'h' is almost silent, eg 'Thembu': tem-boo.
> **Ph** – the 'h' is almost silent, eg Phalo: par-loh.
> **hl** – as in ukuhlonipha - is a soft slur, rather like the Welsh 'll'.
> **dl** – as in Ndlambe- is a harder sound, made with the front-side of
>   the tongue against the lower teeth, left or right of centre in the
>   mouth, literally running 'd ' straight into 'l'.

SPELLING

The book is full of quotes from many different centuries (including a time before spelling was standardised), from many different languages and from people of different nations, not all of whom were perfectly literate. As a result there are many spelling and grammatical mistakes, so many that to have acknowledged every single one of them with the standard 'sic', would have made this work almost unreadable. As long as the meaning is clear, and the person or place referred to is not obscured, I have left the quoted texts in their original forms.

Both the colonials and the Xhosa-speaking peoples – when they were not further complicating matters with the use of nicknames – tended to pronounce foreign names in whichever way was easiest for them. Xhosa modifications of English names include:

'Tshalisi' for Charles Brownlee, 'u-Hagile' for Hargreaves, and 'Bisi' for Colonel Bisset.[5] There was also 'Komeni' for Cumming, 'Gana' for Garner and 'Lili' for Leary.[6]

Colonial modifications often took more than one form: for example, Rharhabe the Xhosa king into whose line one of Bessie's granddaughters married, and whose name probably sounded to the uninitiated like the clearing of a sore throat, was variously referred to in colonial writing as Gagabie, Chacha-bea, Hahabee and even Kahabe.[7] It may require some stretch of the imagination to accept that these all refer to the same person, but they do.

Below is a list of absolute worsts:

'Oom Louw' - Mlawu[8]
'Api' – Ncaphayi[9]
'Chief Kitti Lellaty' – Mzilikazi[10]
'Ochacho' – Tshatshu[11]
'Tcachoo' – Tshatshu[12]
'Timbuctoo' – Mzimvubu[13]
'Umsenphubo' – Mzimvubu[14]
'Sinwoewoe' – Mzimvubu[15]
'Om sin colo' – Mzimvubu[16]
'Bosjie' – Mbashe[17]
'Jurrij Mijer Evens' – Jeremiah Evans[18]
'Bonny Larij' – Barney Leary.[19]
'Hammafondos' – amaMpondo[20]
'Class Logenberk' – Nicolaas Lochenberg[21]
'Class Rickenburg' – Nicolaas Lochenberg[22]
'Catoe the Revolter' – Nqeto[23]
'Gachabi' – Rharhabe[24]
'Sambeh' – Ndlambe[25]

Timeline

Some comparative dates from the time of the Portuguese discoveries to the death of Siwani.

1488 – Bartholomew Dias sails round the Cape of Good Hope (without realising it, at first). Leaves black woman slave alone on beach near today's city of Port Elizabeth to gather information about the country.

1492 – Christopher Columbus 'discovers' America.

1496 – Jews are expelled from Portugal.

1497 – Vasco da Gama spends Christmas off the Wild Coast and names it Natal. His men catch a shark there and upon opening its stomach discover, to their amazement, 'a pewter plate, a gimlet, and a shoe'.

1498 – Vasco da Gama reaches India.

1500 – Bartholomew Dias drowns off the Cape of Good Hope.
     – Madagascar is 'discovered' by the Portuguese, Diego Dias.

1502 – Spanish Muslims have to 'choose' between converting to Christianity or exile.

1503 – Antonio de Saldanha explores Table Bay.

1505 – first recorded Portuguese shipwreck, the 'Soares Wreck', near Mossel Bay.

1509 – Henry VIII becomes King of England, part of a small island off the west coast of Europe.

1510 – Khoikhoi defeat Almeida's Portuguese at the Cape.
     – the first slaves from Guinea arrive in Haiti.

1519 – Magellan begins his voyage around the world.
     – Cortez conquers Mexico.

1512 – Selim I, The Grim, becomes Ottoman Sultan.

1520 – Luther is excommunicated.

1521 – Joao I becomes King of Portugal.

1529 – Vienna besieged by Turks.

c1530 – 4 000 to 5 000 slaves are shipped annually from the Congo.

1536 – The Inquisition is established in Portugal.

1547 – Edward VI crowned King of England.

1551 – wreck of the *Sao Joao de Bescoinho*, at Ponta do Ouro.
     – one tenth of the population of Lisbon are African slaves.

1552 – wreck of the *Sao Joao*, at Port Edward.
     – wreck of the *Sao Jeronymo*, possibly at Richard's Bay.

1554 – wreck of the *Sao Bento*, probably at mouth of Msikaba River.

1558 – Elizabeth I becomes Queen of England

1564 – birth of William Shakespeare.
     – birth of Galileo.

1576 – there are 40 000 African slaves in Spanish America.
1577 – Sir Francis Drake begins his voyage around the world.
1588 – Spanish Armada sails for England.
1593 – wreck of the *Santo Alberto*, probably at Mtata River mouth.
1595 – first official Dutch trading voyage to the East.
1601 – English East India Company established.
     – first English East India fleet visits the Cape.
     – Table Bay renamed (previously known as Aguada de Saldanha).
1602 – Dutch East India Company established.
1604 – French East India Company established.
1608 – wreck of the *Santo Espirito*, near Haga-Haga.
1610 – Galileo invents the telescope.
1611 – King James Bible published.
1613 – Xhore is kidnapped at the Cape and taken to England.
1614 – Xhore returns to the Cape.
1615 – English convicts 'settle' at the Cape.
     – William Harvey discovers the circulatory system.
1616 – Danish East India Company established.
     – death of William Shakespeare.
     – English 'settlement' at the Cape is abandoned.
1619 – first recorded Danish shipwreck on coast of Africa
       (the *Jaeger*, in Table Bay).
1620 – the *Mayflower* sets sail for North America.
1621 – Philip IV becomes King of Spain and Portugal.
1622 – wreck of the *Sao Joao Baptista*, near Port Elizabeth.
1624 – Dutch found New Amsterdam, later known as New York.
1625 – Charles I becomes King of England.
c1625 – Wambu Kalunga becomes ruler of the Kingdom of Huambo.
c1627 – Xhore is hanged at the Cape by the Dutch.
1630 – wreck of the *Sao Goncalo*, at Plettenberg Bay.
1644 – beginning of the 'Ching' dynasty in China.
1649 – Charles I of England is beheaded.
1652 – Dutch occupation of the Cape, led by Jan van Riebeeck.
1653 – first slave arrives at the Cape.
1655 – first slave escapes at the Cape.
1672 – Turks attack Poland.
1682 – Newton discovers the Law of Gravity.
1685 – wreck of the *Good Hope*, probably at Mzimvubu River mouth.
1686 – wreck of the *Stavenisse*, probably near Mngazi or Mngazana
       River mouth.
     – wreck of the *Bonaventura*, on Pondoland coast.
1688 – the first Huguenots (French religious refugees) begin arriving at
       the Cape.
1689 – a Cape Dutch expedition meets amaXhosa near Algoa Bay and
       kills several
     – the Irish revolt against William III.

1690–6 – Captain Rogers makes several visits to the Mzimvubu to trade for ivory.

1699 – Captain Stadis of the *Fidele* leaves three Englishmen at the Mzimvubu River to trade for ivory.

1702 – a Cape Dutch expedition meets amaXhosa near the Great Fish River and kills several.

– King Tshiwo of the amaXhosa dies and his son Phalo is born.

1713 – wreck of the *Bennebroek* near Mtana River mouth.

–· Smallpox epidemic at the Cape decimates Khoi

1714 – the *Clapham Galley* visits the Wild Coast to trade in ivory.

1716 – green tea first used in Britain.

1736 – Hubner traders are killed at Phalo's Great Place.

c1740 – Bessie is shipwrecked.

1743 – war breaks out between Britain and France.

1752 – Beutler's expedition to Xhosa territory.

1755 – wreck of the *Doddington,* on Bird Island near Port Elizabeth.

c1755 – Bessie's son Mdepa born.

1757 – Dutch crew of the *Naastigheid* meet black sailor chief on the Wijde River.

1760 – the slave population of Maryland totals about 200 000.

c1760 – Rharhabe moves west of the Kei.

1761 – Coenraad de Buys is born.

c1766 – Bessie's daughter Bessy is born.

1775 – death of Phalo, king of the Xhosa.

1776 – America declares independence from Britain.

1778 – death of Gcaleka, king of the Xhosa.

– the Fish River becomes the eastern boundary of the Cape Colony.

1779 – the First Frontier War.

1782 – wreck of the *Grosvenor,* at Lambasi Bay.

1783 – Muller's expedition to find *Grosvenor* survivors.

1787 – death of Rharhabe.

1789 – the Second Frontier War.

– the French Revolution begins.

– Hintsa, future Xhosa king, is born.

1790 – Van Reenen's expedition meets Bessie.

1792 – Bessie's husband Sango dies.

1793 – Louis XVI executed.

1795 – end of French Revolution.

– first British occupation of the Cape.

1796 – *Hercules* wrecked near Begha River mouth.

1799 – the Third Frontier War begins.

– missionary Van der Kemp arrives in amaNgqika territory.

1800 – Van der Kemp returns to the Colony.

– Coenraad de Buys goes with him.

1803 – Dutch reoccupy the Cape.

1806 – second British annexation of the Cape.
1807 – Cowan overland expedition leaves Cape for Delagoa Bay.
c1808 – amaBomvana move to Hintsa's territory.
    – Bessie dies at Mngazana.
1811 – the Fourth Frontier War.
1812 – Ndlambe expelled from the Zuurveld.
    – Coenraad de Buys marries Elizabeth, 'born in the land of the Makinas'.
1818 – Ngqika defeated by Mdushane and Hintsa at Amalinde.
    – Fifth Frontier War begins.
1819 – Mdushane attacks Grahamstown.
1820 – Makana drowns off Robben Island.
    – English settlers arrive in eastern Cape.
1824 – Shaka attacks amaMpondo.
    – amaTshomane leave Mngazana, flee south.
    – English traders settle at Port Natal.
1826 – Siwane, Great Son of Mdushane and Bessy, is born.
    – Gambushe, chief of the Bomvana, dies.
1828 – Ndlambe dies.
1828 – Shaka attacks amaMpondo again.
    – Wesleyan missionaries meet Bessie's son and daughter.
    – Shaka assassinated.
    – amaTshomane attacked by Matiwane.
    – Matiwane defeated at Mbholompo.
1829 – Morley mission is established among amaTshomane.
    – death of Ngqika
    – Nicolaas Lochenberg killed
    – Morley destroyed by Nqeto
    – death of Mdushane
    – Faku defeats amaQwabe.
c1830 – Elizabeth, wife of Coenraad de Buys, dies.
    – Coenraad de Buys abandons his children and disappears.
1834 – emancipation of Cape slaves; four-year 'apprenticeship' period begins.
c1834 – Mdepa dies.
Dec 1834 – Sixth Frontier War begins.
1835 – King Hintsa is killed.
1836 – Great Trek of the Boers begins.
1837 – Victoria becomes ruler of the British Empire.
1838 – full emancipation of Cape slaves becomes effective.
1846 – Seventh Frontier War (the War of the Axe) begins.
1850 – Eighth Frontier War begins.
1854 – the Crimean War begins.
1856–7 – the Cattle-Killing.
1858 – Siwani lays charges against Edye, clerk at Tamarha.

1863 – the first London Underground is built.
1866 – Ngangelizwe, king of the Thembu, marries Sarhili's daughter Novili.
     – the Ku Klux Klan is founded in the USA.
1867 – Faku, king of amaMpondo dies.
c1870 – Nonibe dies.
1870 – Ngangelizwe assaults his Great Wife Novili.
1872 – Sarhili declares war on Ngangelizwe.
1875 – annexation of Transkei to Cape.
1877 – Ninth Frontier War begins.
1878 – death of Sandile, king of amaNgqika.
     – death of Seyolo, brother of Siwani.
     – Edison invents the phonograph and Bell the telephone.
1879 – Edison and Swann make the first electric light bulb.
     – Bessie's great-grandson, Siwani, dies.

Bibliography

Adams, Buck: *Buck Adams' Narrative*, ed by A Gordon-Brown, Cape Town, Van Riebeeck Society, 1941.

Alberti, Ludwig: *Account of the Tribal Life and Customs of the Xhosa in 1807*, Trans by Dr William Fehr Cape Town, AA Balkema, 1968.

Alexander, JE: *Narrative of a Voyage of Observation Among the Colonies of Western Africa...and of a Campaign in Kafir-Land...* London, Henry Colburn, 1837.

Allen, Geoffrey & David: *Clive's Lost Treasure*, London, Robin Garton, 1978.

Allen, Geoffrey & David: *The Guns of Sacramento*. London, Robin Garton, 1978.

Appleyard, JW: *The War of the Axe and the Xhosa Bible. The Journal of the Reverend JW Appleyard*, ed by John Frye, Cape Town, Struik, 1971.

Atkinson, CT (ed): *Supplementary Report On the Manuscripts of Robert Graham Esq of Fintry*. Historical Manuscripts Commission 81, London, His Majesty's Stationery Office, 1942.

Austen, HCM: *Sea Fights and Corsairs of the Indian Ocean*, Port Louis, Mauritius, Government Printer, 1935.

Axelson, E: *Dias and His Successors*, Saayman & Weber, 1988.

Axelson, E: *Portuguese South-East Africa 1600–1700*, Johannesburg, Witwatersrand University Press, 1969.

Axelson, E: *South-East Africa 1488–1530*, London, Longmans, Green, 1940.

Axelson, E: Vasco da Gama: *The Diary of His Travels*, Stephan Phillips (Pty) Ltd, 1998.

Ayliff, Reverend John: *The Journal of 'Harry Hastings' – Albany Settler*, Grahamstown, Grocott & Sherry, 1963.

Ayliff, Reverend John: *The Journal of John Ayliff 1821–1830*, ed by Peter Hinchliff (The Graham's Town Series), Cape Town, AA Balkema, 1971.

Ballard, Charles: *John Dunn: The White Chief of Zululand*, Johannesburg, Ad Donker, 1985.

Bannister, Saxe: *Humane Policy; or Justice to the Aborigines of New Settlements*, Underwood, 1830.

Barnard, Lady Anne: *South Africa a Century Ago. Letters*, ed by WH Wilkins, Cape Town, Maskew Miller, 1913.

Barnard, Lady Anne: *South Africa a Century Ago. Letters and Journal Extracts*, ed by HJ Anderson. Cape Town, Maskew Miller, 1924.

Barrow, John: *Travels into the Interior of South Africa in the Years 1797 and 1798*, London, 1801.

Bazley, Denzil: *Nil Desperandum: The Bazley Story*, Kloof, The Royle Trust, 2000.

Beck, R: *The Legalisation and Development of Trade on the Cape Frontier, 1817–1830*, Ann Arbor, Michigan, Umi Dissertation Information Service, 1987.

Becker, Peter: *The Pathfinders. The Saga of Exploration in Southern Africa*, Penguin, 1987.

Beddy, Arthur J Rex: *Genealogy of the Rex Family*, Cape Town, AA Balkema, 1971.

Beinart, William: *The Political Economy of Pondoland 1860–1930*, Cambridge, Cambridge University Press, 1982.

Bender, Colin: *Who Saved Natal?* Durban, 1988.

Bergh, JS & Bergh, AP: *Tribes and Kingdoms*, Cape Town, Don Nelson, 1984.

Bergh, JS & Visagie, JC: *The Eastern Cape Frontier Zone*, Durban, Butterworths, 1985.

Bisset, Major-General: *Sport and War, or Recollections of Fighting and Hunting in South Africa from the Years 1834 to 1867*, London, John Murray, 1875.

Boeseken, AJ: *Slaves and Free Blacks at the Cape 1658–1700*, Cape Town, Tafelberg, 1977.

Bowker, John Mitford: *Speeches, Letters and Selections*, Grahamstown, Godlonton and Richards, 1864.

Bradlow, Edna and Frank, (Eds): *Henry Somerville's Narrative of his Journeys to The Eastern Cape Frontier and to Lattakoe 1799–1802*. Cape Town, Van Riebeeck Society, 1979.

Branch, George & Branch, Margo: *The Living Shores of South Africa*, Cape Town, C Struik, 1983.

Brigg, Arthur: *'Sunny Fountains' and 'Golden Sand': Pictures of Missionary Life in South Africa*, London, T Woolmer, 1888.

Brookes, EH & Webb, C de B: *A History of Natal*, Pietermaritzburg, University of Natal Press, 1987.

Broster, Joan A & Bourn, Herbert C: *AmaGqirha. Religion, Magic and Medicine in Transkei*, Cape Town, Via Afrika, 1981.

Brownlee, Charles Pacalt: *Reminiscences of Kafir Life and History*, Reprint ed by Christopher Saunders, Durban, Killie Campbell Africana Library, 1977.

Brownlee, Frank: *The Transkeian Native Territories: Historical Records*, Westport, Connecticut, Negro Universities Press, 1970.

Brownlee, WT: *Reminiscences of a Transkeian*, Pietermaritzburg, Shuter and Shooter, 1975.

Bryer, Lynne & Hunt, Keith S: *The 1820 Settlers*, Cape Town, Don Nelson, 1984.

Bryer, Lynne & Theron, Francois: *The Huguenot Heritage*, Cape Town, Chameleon Press, 1987.

Buckland, CE: Dictionary of Indian Biography. Lim, Swan Sonnenschein, 1906.

Bulpin, TV: *Islands in a Forgotten Sea*, Cape Town, Howard Timmins, nd.

Bulpin, TV: *Lost Trails of the Transvaal*, Cape Town, Books of Africa, 1989.

Bulpin, TV: *Natal and the Zulu Country*, Cape Town, Books of Africa, 1966.

Burman, Jose: *Strange Shipwrecks of the Southern Seas*, Cape Town, Struik, 1968.

Burton, AW: *The Highlands of Kaffraria*, Cape Town, Struik, 1969.

Butler, Guy (ed): *The 1820 Settlers*, Cape Town, Human and Rousseau, 1984.

Callaway, Godfrey: *Pioneers in Pondoland*, Lovedale Lovedale Press, nd.

Campbell, Margaret: *Merchant Campbell 1769–1846*, Oxford University Press, 1965.

Campbell, Sir Duncan: *Records of Clan Campbell in the HEIC 1600–1858*. London, Longmans, Green, 1925.

Carter, George: *The Wreck of the Grosvenor*, Cape Town, Van Riebeeck Society, 1927.

Cathcart, Sir George: *Correspondence… Relative to His Military Operations in South Africa*, London, John Murray, 1856.

Caton-Thompson, G: *The Zimbabwe Culture: Ruins and Reactions*, Oxford, The Clarendon Press, 1931.

Chalmers, John A: *Tiyo Soga: A Page of South African Mission Work*, Edinburgh, 1878.

Chase, John Centlivres: *History of the Colony of the Cape of Good Hope*, Cape Town, 1869.

Chase, John Centlivres: *The Natal Papers*, Cape Town, Struik, 1968.

Chatterton, E Keble: *The Old East Indiamen*, London, T Werner Laurie Ltd, 1914.

Child, Daphne (ed): *Portrait of a Pioneer, The Letters of Sidney Turner*, Johannesburg, Macmillan, 1980.

Chilvers, A Hedley: *The Seven Lost Trails of Africa*. London, Cassell, Ltd, 1931.

Cook, PA: *Social Organisation and Ceremonial Institutions of the Bomvana*, Cape Town, Juta, 1932.

Cope, John: *King of the Hottentots*, Cape Town, Howard Timmins, 1967.

Cory, GE: *The Historical 'Conversations' of Sir George Cory*, ed by Michael J Berning, (The Graham's Town Series), Cape Town, Maskew Miller Longman, 1989.

Cory, GE: *The Rise of South Africa*. London, Longmans, 1910.

Coulter, Jean: *They Lived in Africa*, Port Elizabeth, Express Litho, 1988.

Crealock, John: *The Frontier War Journal of Major John Crealock 1878*, ed by Chris Hummel, Cape Town, Van Riebeeck Society, 1989.

Cross, Colin: *The British Empire*. London, Hamlyn, 1972.

Crowhurst, Patrick: *The Defence of British Trade, 1689–1815*, Folkestone, Dawson & Sons, 1977.

Cullinan, Patrick: *Robert Jacob Gordon 1743–1795: The Man and his Travels at the Cape*, Cape Town, Struik Winchester, 1992.

Davidson, Basil: *Old Africa Rediscovered*. London, Victor Gollancz, 1959.

Davies, C Collin: *An Historical Atlas of the Indian Peninsula*, Oxford, Oxford University Press, 1959.

Deacon, Harriet (ed.): *The Island*, Cape Town, Mayibuye Books & David Philip, 1996.

De Kock, Victor: *By Strength of Heart*, Cape Town, Howard Timmins, 1953.

De Kock, Victor: *Those in Bondage*, London, George Allen & Unwin, 1950.

Delegorgue, Adulphe: *Travels in Southern Africa*, 2 vols, trans by Fleur Webb, Durban, Killie Campbell Africana Library, 1990 & 1997.

De Mist, Augusta Uitenhage: *Diary of a Journey to the Cape of Good Hope and the Interior of Africa in 1802 and 1803*, Cape Town, Amsterdam, AA Balkema, 1954.

De Villiers, CC & Pama, C: *Genealogies of Old South African Families*, 2 vols, Cape Town, Rotterdam, A A Balkema, 1981.

Dickson, Patricia: *Red John of the Battles*, London, Sidgwick & Jackson, 1973.

Donaldson, ME: *The Council of Advice at The Cape of Good Hope 1825–1834* (Doctoral Thesis), Grahamstown, Rhodes University, 1974.

Duggan-Cronin, AM: *The Bantu Tribes of South Africa*, Kimberley, Deighton, Bell, 1939.

Dugmore, Reverend Henry Hare: *The Reminiscences of an Albany Settler*, Grahamstown, Grocott & Sherry, 1958.

Duminy, Andrew, & Guest, Bill (eds): *Natal and Zululand from Earliest Times to 1910*, Pietermaritzburg, University of Natal Press/Shuter & Shooter, 1989.

Dunn, John: *Cetywayo and the Three Generals*, ed by Duncan Campbell Moodie, Natal Printing and Publishing Co, 1886.

Elphick, Richard & Giliomee, Hermann (eds): *The Shaping of South African Society 1652–1820*, Cape Town, Johannesburg, Longman Penguin, 1979.

Enklaar, Ido H: *Life and Work of Dr J Th Van der Kemp*, Capetown, AA Balkema, 1988.

Fairbridge, Dorothea: *Historic Houses of South Africa*, Oxford, Oxford University Press, 1922.

Featherstone, Donald: *Victorian Colonial Warfare: Africa*, Bok Books International, 1992.

Feely, JM: *The Early Farmers of Transkei, Southern Africa, Before AD 1870*, Cambridge, Monographs in African Archeology, Bar International Series, 1987.

Field, DM: *Tracing Your Ancestors*, Treasure Press, 1998.

Fleming, Reverend Francis: *Kaffraria, and Its Inhabitants*, London, Smith, Elder, 1853.

Forbes, Vernon S: *Pioneer Travellers in South Africa*. Cape Town, Amsterdam, AA Balkema, 1965.

Fortescue, JW: *A History of the British Army*, London, Macmillan, 1910.

Fraser, Antonia: *Plain Tales from the Raj*, ed by Charles Allen, London, Futura Publications, 1977.

Fritsch, Gustav: *Die Eingeboren Sud-Afrika's. Atlas & Text*, Breslau, Ferdinand Hirt, 1872.

Fynn, Henry Francis: *The Diary of Henry Francis Fynn*, ed by James Stuart & D McK Malcolm, Pietermaritzburg, Shuter and Shooter, 1950.

Gardiner, RN: *Narrative of a Journey to the Zoolu Country in South Africa*, London, William Crofts, 1836.

Gardner, Brian: *The East India Company*, London, Rupert Hart-Davis, 1971.

Gilbey, Emma: *The Lady. The Life and Times of Winnie Mandela*. London, Vintage, 1994.

Godlonton, R: *The Irruption of the Kaffir Hordes* (facsimile reprint), Cape Town, Struik, 1965.

Godlonton, R & Irving, Edward: *Narrative of the Kaffir War 1850–52* (facsimile reprint), C Struik, Cape Town, 1962.

Godee-Molsbergen, Dr EC & Joh Visscher: *South-African History Told in Pictures*, Amsterdam, SL Van Looy, 1913.

Goldswain, Jeremiah: *The Chronicle of Jeremiah Goldswain*, 2 vols, ed by by Una Long, Cape Town, Van Riebeeck Society, 1946.

Gordon-Brown, A: *Pictorial Africana*, Cape Town, Rotterdam, AA Balkema, 1975.

Gordon, RE: *Shepstone – Family History 1820–1900*, Cape Town, AA Balkema, 1968.

Graham, Alistair & Beard, Peter: *Eyelids of Morning*, San Francisco, Chronicle Books,1990.

Grey, Stephen (ed): *The Natal Papers of 'John Ross'*, Durban, Killie Campbell Africana Library, and Pietermaritzburg, University of Natal Press, 1992.

Guthrie, Frank: *Frontier Magistrate*, Cape Town, Stewart, nd.

Halford, SJ: *The Griquas of Griqualand*, Cape Town, Juta, nd.

Hall, Martin: *The Changing Past: Farmers, Kings and Traders in Southern Africa, 200–1860*. Cape Town & Johannesburg, David Philip, 1987.

Hall, Richard: *Empires of the Monsoon*, London, Harper-Collins, 1998.

Hamilton, Carolyn: *Terrible Majesty: The Powers of Shaka Zulu and the Limits of Historical Intervention*, Cape Town and Johannesburg, David Philip, 1998.

Hamilton, Carolyn (ed): *The Mfecane Aftermath*, Johannesburg, Witwatersrand University Press, Pietermaritzburg, University of Natal Press, 1995.

Hammond-Tooke, David: *The Roots of Black South Africa*, Johannesburg, Jonathan Ball, 1993.

Hammond-Tooke, WD: *The Tribes of King William's Town District*, Pretoria, The Government Printer, 1958.

Hammond-Tooke, WD: *The Tribes of Mount Frere District*, Pretoria, The Government Printer, 1955.

Hammond-Tooke, WD: *The Tribes of the Willowvale District*, Pretoria, The Government Printer, 1956–1957.

Hammond-Tooke, WD: *The Tribes of Umtata District*, Pretoria, The Government Printer, 1956–1957.

Hammond-Tooke, WD: (ed): *The Bantu-Speaking Peoples of Southern Africa*, London & Boston, Routledge & Kegan Paul, 1974.

Hattersley, Alan F: *The British Settlement of Natal*, Cambridge University Press, 1950.

Hattersley, Alan F (ed): *John Sheden Dobie, South African Journal, 1862–66*, Cape Town, Van Riebeeck Society, 1945.

Heese, JA & Lombard, RTJ: *South African Genealogies*, Pretoria, Human Sciences Research Council, 1968.

Hickey William: *Memoirs of William Hickey*, ed by Alfred Spencer, London, Hurst & Blackett, Ltd, nd.

Hinchliff, P: *Calendar of Cape Missionary Correspondence 1880–50*, Grahamstown, Rhodes University, 1967.

Hodgeson, Janet: *Princess Emma*, Johannesburg, Ad Donker, 1987.

Holden, Reverend W Clifford: *History of Methodism and of Methodist Missions in South Africa*, London, Wesleyan Methodist Book Room, 1887.

Holleman, Helen (ed): *Grahamstown – The Untold Story*, Black Sash, 1997.

Holt, Basil: *Greatheart of the Border*, King William's Town, SA Missionary Museum, 1976.

Holt, Basil: *They Came Our Way*, Cape Town, Howard Timmins, 1974.

Holt, Basil: *Where Rainbirds Call: A Record of the Transkei*, Cape Town, Howard Timmins, 1972.

Hook, Major DB: *With Sword and Statute*, Cape Town, JC Juta, 1906.

Hunter, Monica: *Reaction to Conquest*, Oxford, Oxford University Press, 1936.

Isaacs, Nathaniel: *Travels and Adventure in Eastern Africa*, ed by Louis Herman and Percival R Kirby, Cape Town, C Struik, 1970.

Jabavu, Noni: *The Ochre People*, London, John Murray, 1963.

Johnson, Captain Charles: *A General History of the Robberies and Murders of the Most Notorious Pirates…*, ed by Arthur L Hayward, London, George Routledge & Sons, 1926.

Johnston, A Keith: *A General Dictionary of Geography…*, London, Longmans, Green, 1882.

Kay, MM (ed): *The Golden Calm: An English Lady's Life in Moghul Delhi*, London, Viking Press, 1980.

Kay, Stephen: *Travels and Researches in Caffraria…*, Harper & Brothers, 1834.

Kayser, Reverend FG: *Journals and Letters*, ed by Chris Hummel (The Graham's Town Series), Cape Town, Maskew Miller Longman, 1990.

Keay, John: *The Honourable Company: A History of the English East India Company*, London, Harper Collins, 1991.

Kennedy, RF: *Johannesburg Africana Museum Catalogue of Pictures* (7 vols), 1967.

Kirby, Donald, et al: *Peddie – Settlers' Outpost*, Grahamstown, Grocott & Sherry, 1960.

Kirby, Percival R: *A Source Book on the Wreck of the Grosvenor East Indiaman*, Cape Town, Van Riebeeck Society, 1953.

Kirby, Percival R: *Andrew Smith and Natal*, Cape Town, The Van Riebeeck Society, 1955.

Kirby, Percival R: *Jacob van Reenen and the 'Grosvenor' Expedition of 1790–1791*, Johannesburg, Witwatersrand University Press, 1958.

Kirby, Percival R: *New Light On the 'Grosvenor' East Indiaman, 1782*, Africana Society, 1945.

Kirby, Percival R: *Sir Andrew Smith 1797–1850*, Cape Town, AA Balkema, Amsterdam, 1965.

Kirby, Percival R: *The True Story of the Grosvenor East Indiaman*. Oxford, Oxford University Press, 1960.

Krige, Susan: *The Frontier*, Creative History Series, Johannesburg, History/Education Dept, University of the Witwatersrand, 2001.

Kuttel, M: *Quadrilles and Konfyt: The Life and Journal of Hildagonda Duckitt*, Cape Town, Maskew Miller Ltd, 1954.

Laidler, PW. & Gelfand, M: *South Africa: Its Medical History*, Cape Town, Struik, 1971.

Laubscher, BJF: *Sex, Custom and Psychopathology: A Study of South African Pagan Natives*, London, George Routledge & Sons Ltd, 1937.

Le Cordeur, Basil & Saunders, Christopher: *The War of the Axe, 1847*, Johannesburg, Brenthurst Press, 1981.

Lenman, Bruce: *The Jacobite Risings in Britain 1689–1746*, London, Eyre Methuen, 1980.

Leibrandt, HCV: *Precis of the Archives of the Cape of Good Hope*, Cape Town, South African Library, 1988.

Leibrandt, HCV: *Rambles Through The Archives of the Colony of the Cape of Good Hope 1688–1700*, Cape Town, JC Juta, 1887.

Leverton, Dr BJT (ed): *Records of Natal*, vols 1–3, Pretoria, The Government Printer, 1989.

Lichtenstein, Henry: *Travels in Southern Africa in the Years 1803, 1804, 1805 &1806*, 2 vols, Cape Town, Van Riebeeck Society, 1928.

Lister, Margaret Hermina (ed): *The Journals of Andrew Geddes Bain*, Cape Town, Van Riebeeck Society, 1949.

Lucas, TJ: *Camp Life and Sport in South Africa*, Johannesburg, Africana Reprint Library, 1975.

Lugg, HC: *A Natal Family Looks Back*, Durban, TW Griggs, 1970.

Mackeurtan, Graham: *The Cradle Days of Natal*, London, Longmans, Green, 1931.

Maclean, Colonel: *A Compendium of Kafir Laws and Customs*, Pretoria, The State Library, 1968.

Maclennan, Ben: *A Proper Degree of Terror – John Graham and the Cape's Eastern Frontier*, Johannesburg, Ravan Press, 1986.

Mandela, Nelson: *Long Walk to Freedom*, Randburg, Macdonald Purnell, 1994.

Marshal, Michael W: *Ocean Traders from the Portuguese Discoveries to the Present Day*, London, BT Batsford, 1989.

Mason, Philip: *The Men Who Ruled India*, London, Jonathan Cape, 1985.

McCulloch, JR: *A Dictionary, Geographical, Statistical, Historical…*, 2 vols, London, Longmans, 1843.

Meinties, Johannes: *Sandile: The Fall of the Xhosa Nation*, Cape Town, TV Bulpin, 1971.

Meiring, Jane: *The Truth in Masquerade: The Adventures of Francois Le Vaillant*, Cape Town, Juta, nd.

Metrowich, FC: *Assegai over the Hills*, Cape Town, Howard B. Timmins, 1953.

Metrowich, FC: *Frontier Flames*, Cape Town, Books of Africa, 1968.

Milton, John: *The Edges of War*, Cape Town, Juta, 1983.

Molema, SM: *The Bantu Past and Present*, C Struik, Cape Town, 1963.

Moodie, Donald: *The Record, or a Series of Official Papers Relative to the Condition and Treatment of the Native Tribes of South Africa*, pts I, II & V, Cape Town, AA Balkema, 1960.

Moodie, Duncan Campbell: *The History of the Battles and Adventures of the British, The Boers, and the Zulus, etc, in Southern Africa*, 2 vols, Cape Town, Murray & St Leger, 1888.

Morse-Jones, E: *Roll of the British Settlers in South Africa*, Part 1: Up to 1826, Cape Town, AA Balkema, 1969.

Mossop, Dr EE (ed): *Journals of the Expeditions of Bergh (1682 & 1683) and Schrijver (1689)*, Cape Town, Van Riebeeck Society, 1931.

Mostert, Noel: *Frontiers*, London, Jonathan Cape, 1992.

Naidoo, Jay: *Tracking Down Historical Myths*, Johannesburg, Ad Donker, 1989.

Napier, EE: *Excursions in Southern Africa*, 2 vols, London, William Shobel, 1849.

Nash, MD: *Bailie's Party of 1820 Settlers*, Cape Town, A.A. Balkema, 1982.

Nash, MD: *The Settler Handbook*, Chameleon Press, 1987.

Norwich, Oscar I: *Maps of Southern Africa*, Johannesburg, Ad Donker & Jonathan Ball, 1993.

Paravicini Di Capelli, WBE: *Reize in De Binnen-Landen Van Zuid-Africa*, ed by Dr WJ de Kock, Kaapstad, Van Riebeeckvereniging, 1965.

Paver, Richard: *The Reminiscences of Richard Paver*, ed by AH Duminy with LJG Adcock (The Graham's Town Series), Cape Town, AA Balkema, 1979.

Peires, JB: *The Dead Will Arise: Nongqawuse and the Great Cattle-Killing Movement of 1856–7*, Johannesburg, Ravan Press, 1989.

Peires, JB: *The House of Phalo: A History of the Xhosa People in the Days of Their Independence*, Johannesburg, Ravan Press, 1987.

Perestrelo, Manuel de Mesquita: *'Roteiro' of the South and South-East Africa, From The Cape of Good Hope to Cape Corrientes (1576)*, ed by A Fontoura da Costa, Lisboa, Agencia Geral Das Colonias, 1939.

Philipps, Thomas: *Philipps, 1820 Settler*, ed by A Keppel-Jones, Pietermaritzburg, Shuter and Shooter, 1960.

Pigot, Sophia: *The Journals of Sophia Pigot*, ed by Margaret Rainier (The Graham's Town Series), Cape Town, AA Balkema, 1974.

Pinnock, Patricia Schonstein: *Xhosa, A Cultural Grammar For Beginners*, Cape Town, African Sun Press, 1994.

Pringle, Thomas: *Narrative of a Residence in South Africa*, Cape Town, C Struik, 1966.

Prior, James: *Voyage Along The Eastern Coast of Africa...*, London, Sir Richard Phillips, 1819.

Pritchard, Helen M: *Friends and Foes in the Transkei*, London, Sampson, Low, 1880.

Raper, PE: *Dictionary of Southern African Place Names*, Johannesburg, Lowry Publishers, 1987.

Raven-Hart, Major R: *Before Van Riebeeck*, Cape Town, C Struik, 1967.

Raynal, Abbe': A *Philosophical and Political History of the Settlements and Trade of the Europeans in the East and West Indies*, 6 vols, London, 1798.

Rennie, James Alan: *The Scottish People: Their Clans, Families and Origins*, London, Hutchinson, 1960.

Reynolds, Rex and Barbara: *Grahamstown: From Cottage to Villa*, Cape Town, David Philip, 1974.

Robinson, John (ed): *Notes On Natal*, Pretoria, The State Library, 1967.

Rock, Lyle M: *Hearts of Oak*, Pietermaritzburg, 1974.

Rose, Cowper: *Four Years in Southern Africa*, London, Henry Colburn & Richard Bentley, 1829.

Rosenthal, Eric: *Cutlass and Yardarm*, Cape Town, Howard Timmins, 1954.

Ross, Robert: *Cape of Torments: Slavery and Resistance in South Africa*, London, Routledge & Kegan Paul, 1983.

Rousseau, Leon: *The Dark Stream*, Johannesburg, Jonathan Ball, 1999.

Saunders, Christopher & Derricourt, Robin (eds): *Beyond The Cape Frontier*, London, Longman, 1974.

Scallan, Joyce: *Dick King, Feats Family Fame*, Port Elizabeth, Killarney Downs, 1987.

Schoeman, Agatha Elizabeth: *Coenraad de Buys, The First Transvaler*, Pretoria, JH de Bussy, 1938.

Schoeman, Karel: *The Face of the Country*, Cape Town, Human & Rousseau, 1996.

Scott, JM: *The Tea Story*, London, Heinemann, 1964.

Scully, WC: *Transkei Stories*, Cape Town, Afrikasouth Paperbacks, David Philip, 1984.

Semple, Robert: *Walks and Sketches at the Cape of Good Hope 1805*, Cape Town & Amsterdam, AA Balkema, 1968.

Seymour, Wilfred Massingham: *Native Law and Customs...*, Cape Town, Juta, 1911.

Shaw, William: *The Journal of William Shaw*, ed by WD Hammond-Tooke (The Graham's Town Series), Cape Town, AA Balkema, 1972.

Shaw, William: *The Story of My Mission in South-Eastern Africa...*, London, Hamilton, Adams, 1860.

Shaw, EM & Van Warmelo, NJ: 'The material culture of the Cape Nguni', pts 1–3, Cape Town, *Annals of the South African Museum*, 1972–1980.

Shell, Robert C-H: *Children of Bondage. A Social History of the Slave Society at The Cape of Good Hope, 1652–1838*, Johannesburg, Witwatersrand University Press, 1994.

Shrewsbury, W: *The Journal and and Selected Letters of Reverend William J Shrewsbury 1826–1835*, ed by Hildegard H Fast (The Graham's Town Series), Johannesburg, Witwatersrand University Press, 1994.

Shrewsbury, W: *The Memorials of the Reverend William J Shrewsbury*, ed by JVB Shrewsbury, London, Hamilton Adams, 1869.

Sleigh, Dan: *Jan Compagnie: The World of the Dutch East India Company*, Cape Town, Tafelberg, 1980.

Smith, Sir Harry: *The Autobiography of Lieutenant-General Sir Harry Smith, GCB*, 2 vols, ed by GC Moore Smith, London, John Murray, 1901.

Soga, JH: *The South-Eastern Bantu*, Johannesburg, Witwatersrand University Press, 1930.

Soga, JH: *The Ama-Xosa: Life and Customs*, Lovedale, Lovedale Press, 1931.

Soga, Tiyo: *The Journal and Selected Writings of the Reverend Tiyo Soga*, ed by Donovan Williams (The Graham's Town Series), Cape Town, AA Balkema, 1983.

Southey, George: *The Shooting of Hintza*, Appendix L in *The Life and Times of Sir Richard Southey* by Alex Wilmot, London, Sampson, Low, Marsten & Co, nd.

Spaarman, Anders: *A Voyage to the Cape of Good Hope... and to the Country of the Hottentots and the Caffres from the Year 1772–1776*, 2 vols, ed by Prof VS Forbes. Cape Town, Van Riebeeck Society, 1975.

Spencer, Shelagh O'Byrne: *British Settlers in Natal 1824–57*, Pietermaritzburg, University of Natal, 5 vols so far, Work in Progress.

Stanford, Sir Walter: *Stanford's Reminiscences*, ed by JW Macquarrie, Cape Town, Van Riebeeck Society, 1958.

Stapleton, Timothy: *Faku: Rulership and Colonialism in the Mpondo Kingdom (c1780–1867)*, Waterloo, Ontario, Wilfrid Laurier University Press, 2001.

Stapleton, Timothy: *Maqoma: Xhosa Resistance to Colonial Advance*, Johannesburg, Jonathan Ball, 1994.

Steedman, Andrew: *Wanderings and Adventures in the Interior of Southern Africa*, London, Longman, 1835.

Stephen, Leslie (ed): *Dictionary of National Biography*, London, Smith, Elder, 1886.

Stockenstrom, Sir Andries: *The Autobiography of the Late Sir Andries Stockenstrom...*, ed by CW Hutton, Cape Town, JC Juta, 1887.

Storrar, Patricia: *Drama At Ponta Delgada*, Lowry, 1988.

Stout, Benjamin: *Narrative of the Loss of the Ship Hercules... on the Coast of Caffraria... 1796*, Reprint ed by A Porter, Port Elizabeth, Historical Society of Port Elizabeth, 1975.

Stretch, Charles Lennox: *The Journal of Charles Lennox Stretch*, ed by Basil A le Cordeur (The Graham's Town Series), Cape Town, Maskew Miller Longman, 1988.

Stubbs, Thomas: *The Reminiscences of Thomas Stubbs*, ed by WA Maxwell and RT McGeogh (The Graham's Town Series), Cape Town, AA Balkema, 1978.

Swettenham, Sir Frank: *British Malaya*, London, The Bodley Head, 1907.

Taylor, Reverend William: *Christian Adventures in South Africa*, London, Hodder and Stoughton, 1867.

Theal, George Macall: *Documents Relating to the Kaffir War of 1835*, London, Government of the Union of South Africa, 1912.

Theal, George Macall: *History and Ethnography of Africa South of the Zambezi*, London, Swan Sonnenschein, 1910.

Theal, George Macall: *History of South Africa*, London, Swan Sonnenschein, 1897.

Theal, George Macall: *History of South Africa Since 1795*, Reprint, Cape Town, Struik, 1964.

Theal, George Macall: *Records of South-Eastern Africa*, Cape Town, Struik, 1964.

Theal, George Macall: *Records of the Cape Colony*, London, William Clowes and Sons, 1897.

Thunberg, Carl Peter: *Travels at the Cape of Good Hope 1772–1775*, ed by Prof VS Forbes, Cape Town, Van Riebeeck Society, 1986.

Thompson, George: *Travels and Adventure in Southern Africa*, ed by Vernon S Forbes. Cape Town, Van Riebeeck Society, 1967.

Trevelyan, GM: *English Social History*, Harmondsworth, Pelican Books, 1980.

Trollope, Antony: *South Africa*, ed by JH Davidson, Cape Town, AA Balkema, 1973.

Turner, Malcolm: *Shipwrecks and Salvage in South Africa – 1505 to the Present*, Cape Town, Struik, 1988.

Turpin, Eric: *Basket Work Harbour*, Cape Town, Howard Timmins, 1964.

Unstead, RJ: *Emerging Empire (1689–1763)*, London, Macdonald, 1975.

Uys, Ian: *Survivors of Africa's Oceans*, Fortress Publishers, 1993.

Valentyn, Francois: *Description of the Cape of Good Hope...*, Cape Town, Van Riebeeck Society, 1971.

Van Reenen, DG: *Dirk Gysbert Van Reenen se Joernaal*, ed by Blommaert and Wiid, trans by Franken and Murray, Cape Town, Van Riebeeck Society, 1937.

Van Reenen, Jacob: *Journal of a Journey...* See *The Wreck of the Grosvenor*, Cape Town, Van Riebeeck Society, 1937.

Van Warmelo, NJ: *A Preliminary Survey of the Bantu Tribes of South Africa*, The Government Printer, Pretoria, 1935.

Van Warmelo, NJ: *History of Matiwane and the Amangwane Tribe*, The Government Printer, Pretoria, 1938.

Varley, DH & Matthew, HM (eds): *The Cape Journals of Archdeacon NJ Merriman*, Cape Town, The Van Riebeeck Society, 1957.

Veloso, Gaspar (1512): 'Notes made by Gaspar Veloso, clerk at the factory of Mozambique, and sent to the King', in *Documents on the Portuguese in Mozambique and Central Africa 1497–1840*, vol III *(1511–1514)*, Salisbury, National Archives of Rhodesia and Nyasaland and Lisbon, Centro de Estudos Historicos Ultramarinos, 1964.

Vigne, Randolph (ed): *Guillaume Chenu De Chalezac, The 'French Boy'*, Cape Town, Van Riebeeck Society, 1993.

Vincent, William: *The Commerce and Navigation of the Ancients in the Indian Ocean*, 2 vols, London, 1807.

Ward, Harriet: *Five Years in Kaffirland*, 2 vols, London, Henry Colburn, Publisher, 1848.

Ward, Harriet: *The Cape and the Kaffirs: a Diary of Five Years Residence...*, London, Henry G Bohn, 1851.

Wallis, JPR: *Thomas Baines*, Cape Town, Rotterdam, AA Balkema, 1976.

Wannenburgh, Alf: *Forgotten Frontiersmen*, Cape Town, Howard Timmins, 1980.

Webb, C de B & Wright, JB (eds): *The James Stuart Archive*, vols 1–5,
Pietermaritzburg, University of Natal Press, & Durban, Killie Campbell Africana
Library, 1976–1986.

Whiteside, Reverend J: *History of the Wesleyan Methodist Church of South Africa*,
Cape Town, Juta, 1906.

Willcox, AR: *Footprints on a Southern Land*, Drakensberg Publications, 1988.

Willcox, AR: *Shipwreck and Survival on the South-East Coast of Africa*, Drakensberg
Publications, 1984.

Willson, Beckles: *Ledger and Sword, or The Honourable Company of Merchants of
England Trading to the East Indies (1599–1874)*, London, Longmans, Green, 1903.

Wilmot and Chase: *History of the Colony of the Cape of Good Hope*, Cape Town, 1869.

Wilson, Monica & Thompson, Leonard (eds): *A History of South Africa to 1870*,
Cape Town, David Philip, 1986.

Worden, Nigel & Rais, Clifton (eds): *Breaking the Chains*, Johannesburg,
Witwatersrand University Press, 1994.

Wylie, Dan: *Savage Delight*. Pietermaritzburg, University of Natal Press, 2000. Young,
Samuel: *A Missionary Narrative of the Triumphs of Grace*, London, John Mason, 1842.

WORKS ALSO CONSULTED

Annual Register, or A View of the History, Politics, and Literature For the Year
1786, London, 1788 (also 1782–87, 1789–90 and 1759).

Burke's Landed Gentry, ed by H Pipie-Gordon, London, Shaw Publishing Co, Ltd,
1906 and Centenary Edition, 1937.

Burke's Peerage and Baronetage, Fifty-Eighth Edition, London, 1927.

Collecteana vol 1, Cape Town, The Van Riebeeck Society, 1924.

Collection of Voyages and Travels..., vols II & III, London, 1765.

The Cambridge History of India, ed by Professor EJ Rapson.

Dictionary of South African Bibliography, National Council for Social Research.

Directory and Guide For Eastern Province, 1880, 1881, 1883.

Dutch-Asiatic Shipping: Homeward Voyages, The Hague, 1979.

East London and Frontier Red Book 1906 & 1907.

Ezakwantu: Beadwork from The Eastern Cape. Exhibition Catalogue, Cape Town,
South African National Gallery, 1993.

General Gazetteer; or, Compendious Geographical Dictionary, compiled by R Brookes
and revised by AG Findlay, London, William Tegg, 1851.

Methodist Missionary Notices, several volumes, but esp vol 4, 1829–31, London.

*Papers Relating to the Ships and Voyages of the Company of Scotland Trading to
Africa and the Indies 1696–1707* ed by George Pratt, Edinburgh, The Scottish
Historical Society, 1924.

Public Documents Showing The Character of Sir Benjamin D'Urban's Administration,
Cape Town, Gazette Office, 1838.

Records of the Natal Executive Council, 1856–59, ed by VR Fourie & LJ Wyman, Cape Town, 1964.

Report and Proceedings… of the Government Commission On Native Laws and Customs, Cape Town, Government Printers, 1883.

Report of Commission of Enquiry Regarding Cape Coloured Population of the Union, Pretoria, Government Printer, 1937.

Selected Articles from The Cape Monthly Magazine (New Series 1870–76), ed by AM Lewin Robinson, Cape Town, Van Riebeeck Society, 1978.

Societies of Southern Africa in the 19th and 20th Centuries, vol 7: 'Economic Change in Pondoland in the Nineteenth Century' by William Beinart, 1977.

Statute Law of the Cape of Good Hope…, Cape Town, Solomon, 1862.

Transactions of the London Missionary Society, vol 1, 1795–1802, London, T Williams, 1804.

JOURNALS

Africana Notes and News, Johannesburg, Africana Society, Africana Museum:

vol 3:   Eastern Province History in Sketches, by FT Ions.

vol 5:   The Cape Coloured Regular Regiments, 1793–1870, by Major G Tylden. The Grosvenor as a Literary Theme, Comments by M Kannemeyer.

vol 7:   A further note on the Wreck of the Grosvenor, by S A Rochlin.

vol 9:   Major-General Sir Thomas Willshire, GCB, and the Attack on Grahamstown on 22nd April, 1819, by G Tylden.

vol 11:   On the Track of the 'Grosvenor' by Basil Holt.
Where Was Port Grosvenor?, by Percival R Kirby.
A Visitor's Impressions of Port Grosvenor, by Basil Holt.
Old Forts of the Transkei, by Basil Holt.

vol 12:   Fort Brown (Hermanus Kraal), by Percival R Kirby.
'Grosvenor' Discoveries, by Percival R. Kirby.
The Grosvenor Treasure: Turner's Discoveries, by Basil Holt.
Mr GC Cato, by Killie Campbell.
Notes on the Original Text of Jacob van Reenen's Journal…, by JML Franken.
The Old Cemetery of Morley, by B Holt.
Discovery of a Manuscript Written by Jacob van Reenen…, by M Kuttel.
Who Was Hermanus Hubner? by Dr J Doge.

vol 15:   Professor Kirby and the 'Grosvenor', by AHS.
Native and Malay Studies, by JW Bell, Duff and Others, by RF Kennedy.

vol 28:   The Mass Grave of Viceroy D'Almeida and His Men in Hout Bay, by Ronald G Shuttleworth.

vol 29:   Where Was the Aguada de Saldanha? by Eric Axelson.

African Studies Quarterly, Johannesburg, Wits University Press:

vol 13(1), 1954: Gquma, Mdepha and the Amatshomane Clan: A By-Way of
Miscegenation in South Africa, by Percival R.Kirby.

vol 15: Letter on Lochenberg, by Mr Rochlin.
Professor Kirby and the 'Grosvenor', by AHS.

vol 18(4), 1959: The Early History of the Transkei and Ciskei,
by Monica Wilson.

vol 35, 1976: Early European Travellers in the Transkei and Ciskei,
by Robin M Derricourt.

The Kaffarian Museum Xhosa History Series:

vol 1, January 1986: 'A quarrel between half-brothers' by Manton M Hirst.

Coelacanth:

vol 20(2), 1982 & Vol 21(1), 1983: A brief maritime history of the coast
between the Kei and Fish rivers, Parts 1 & 2,
by Graham Bell-Cross.

vol 25(1), 1987: Oriental blue and white porcelain sherds at shipwreck sites
between the Fish and Kei rivers, by Gillian Vernon.
The Occurrence of Cornelian and Agate Beads at Shipwreck Sites
on the Southern African Coast, by Graham Bell-Cross.

vol 32(1), 1994: A Portuguese Shipwreck Site at Bonza Bay: Is it the Santa
Maria Madre De Deus of 1643? by Gillian Vernon.

vol 32(2), 1994: Bennebroek, by Graham Bell-Cross and Gillian Vernon.

vol 37(1), 1999: Coffee Bay in the Early Twenties, by Roy Altenkirch.

vol 38(1), 2000: The 'Grosvenor': Finding the Real Treasure, by Gill Vernon.

Journal of Natal and Zulu History:

vol V, 1982: Natal 1824-1844: The Frontier Interregnum, by Charles Ballard.

NEWSPAPERS

Dates of editions specified in footnotes:
The Natal Witness, Pietermaritzburg.
The Natal Mercury, Durban.
The Grahamstown Journal, Grahamstown.

CORY LIBRARY FOR HISTORICAL RESEARCH, GRAHAMSTOWN

Findlay, George: *Miscegenation – A Study of the Biological Sources of Inheritance of the South African European Population*, South African Pamphlets vol 60, Pretoria, The Pretoria News and Printing Works, 1936.

PR 804: 'Early Footsteps by the 'Mthatha River', by Reverend Basil Holt, *Territorial News*, Umtata, 5 August 1954.

PR 848: 'A Great Transkeian Pioneer', by Basil Holt, *Territorial News* Aug 1959.

PR 906: Clippings From *Territorial News*, Umtata, January 1957, 'The First Transkeians', a series of articles by Basil Holt.

PR 1294: Clipping from *The Cape Argus*, Cape Town, 27 October 1928: 'Shipwrecks on the coast of Pondoland', by Sir W Stanford.

PR 2363: Boesak...the Hottentot who saved Grahamstown, *Eastern Province Herald*, 29 July 1965, by Eric Turpin.

PR 3665/3: *Genealogy of the Tshezi* by EW Pearce.

PR 8246: *History of the District of Alfred* by BE Camp, c1973.

Unpublished Manuscripts, etc:

MS 14600: 13 notebooks by Dr AW Burton relevant to history of the Transkeian Territories.

MS 14886.

MS 14886/10.

MS 15011: The Reverend Thomas Jenkins, private papers, compiled by Dr CJ Uys, Pietermaritzburg 1935.

MS 15711 (D): EJ Barrett's Genealogical Notes, Eastern and Western Pondoland Chiefs.

MS 1714: Letter From Reverend Shepstone to Col Somerset, 16 October 1829, including letter From John Cane.

MS 17202: Vernon Forbes' clippings, 19 folders.

MS 17038: Notebooks of George Cory (15 vols).

MS 1831 & 1832: Two letters from William Bazley to Eliza Conway and John King, March 1907.

MS 1833: Two letters from Eliza Conway to William Bazley, March 1907.

MS 2106: Unsigned & undated testimony, Shipwrecks on the Pondoland Coast, presented by JG Maker.

MS 6212: Letter from Reverend JS Thomas, 20 April 1846, Morley.

MS 6214: Letter From Reverend JS Thomas, 3 June 1855, Clarkebury.

MS 7391: Hancock's Drift, by FW Powell, 1958.

Church Registers

MS 14 878/4: St Michael's & St George's baptisms, 1869–1964.

MS 15015: Clarkebury baptisms.

MS 15223: Morley Mission, baptisms and marriages 1833–1866.

MS 15897: Register of baptisms for Mount Coke and Tamacha, October 1898–August 1907.

MS 17 236: Fort Peddie baptisms April 1841–May 1857.

PR 3516: Umtata and Buntingville Circuits, register of baptisms, 1837–1881.

Killie Campbell Africana Library, Durban

MS 65608 File 3 & 5: Capt Garden's Diary: (Photocopy Transcript. Original in Natal Society Library, Pietermaritzburg).

KCM 5803 Files 26 & 27: Killie Campbell Correspondence, Early 1954.

MS 1025: Letter From Mary Holmes née King, 19th December 1941.

MS 1026a: Memories of My Father, Dick King, by Richard Phillip Henry King, 1942.

MS 1027: Letter from Burton, 1942.

Natal Archives, Pietermaritzburg

Death Notices & Estates 1848–1972.

H F Fynn Papers: 1/1/7/7 A1382 vol 16.

The Bird Papers: A79 vol 5–7.

Estates: MSCE 1184/1908 (Duka Fynn).
    MSCE 22/168 (Catherine Dunn (née Pierce)).

Cape Archives, Cape Town

BK 14 (? New Number Bk 24 No 97, 8 Pages): Examination of Prophetess 'Nonqause', 27 April 1858.

BK 15: Gaika Commissioner1855–58.

BK 16: Gaika Commissioner 1859–60.

BK 74: Ndlambe Commissioner 1849–1852.

BK 80: Agent With Sewani 1856-1866.

BK 89:

BK 90, 92 Missions.

BK 91 Missions 1857–1860.

CAD1/2/14, Vol No. 11/11 A14: Report by Order of His Excellency Maurits De Chavonnes, Councillor Extraordinary of India and Governor of the Cape of Good Hope, Made by Ferdinandus Marchand of Gravenhage, Corporal in the Army, Frederick Jansz of Amsterdam, Gerrit van der Pijpen, Both Sailors, All in the Service of the Hon Company, On Board the Return Ship Bennebroek.

CMK 2/108 Misc Letters.

GH 8/45

GH 8/50

GH 23/8

VC 94, No.8: Extract From The Logbook of the Centaur, February 1688.

VC 20: Dag Register Kaap De Goede Hoop 1711–14.

Assorted Cape Death Notices in the Cape Archives, Cape Town.

LIBRARIES

The South African Library, Cape Town

Cape of Good Hope Government Gazette 06.02.1819–25.05.1822. 003154
Mp 1247

Parlimentary Papers: G 5 – Examination of Nonkosi by JC Gawler and John
Maclean, 1857.

The Wesleyan-Methodist Magazine, vol 12, 1833, & vol 13, 1834.

Pocock Photo

Photo of Nonkosi and Nongqawuse

Strange Library, Johannesburg

Account of the Hubner Massacre by Hendrick De Vries De Jonge and Hendrick
Scheefer De Jonge, English Translation, Store No S, Store 968.601t 1736 Hub.

Private Papers of Percival R Kirby.

EAST LONDON MUSEUM

The Survivors' Story by Graham Bell-Cross, Unpublished Paper, Courtesy of the
Author and Mrs Jill Vernon.

INTERNET

www.ships.clara.net/ships/1shpntro.html
www.truth.org.za/decisions/1999/ac990249.htm

Endnotes

Chapter 1

1. 'Gquma' is pronounced by putting the tip of your tongue against the roof of your mouth and then snapping it away suddenly to produce a sharp and distinctive click, flowing immediately into 'ooo-ma'.
2. Theal (1897) *Records of the Cape Colony* II: 19–20.
3. Extracts from Capt' Garden's Diary, 28 July 1851 and letter from Reverend Jenkins to Garden, 14 May 1852 (Kirby papers in Strange Library Jhb).
4. He was assassinated by apartheid agents in Swaziland in 1987. Rest in peace, Comrade Cas.
5. WC Scully, reprinted in *Transkei Stories* (Africa South Paperbacks, David Philip) 1984). My thanks to Marie Philips for permission to reproduce extracts from it.
6. Soga *SE Bantu* 380–1.
7. Tapes in author's possession, barring one lost in a robbery at the translator's house.
8. Beinart (1982) 14.
9. Scully 61.
10. Soga *SE Bantu* 379; for Mpondo sub-chiefdoms see Beinart *Societies of Southern Africa* vol 7: 33.
11. Cook 117.
12. Alberti 54.
13. Scully 61.
14. Holt *Territorial News* 17 Jan 1957; Cory PR 906.
15. Shaw & Van Warmelo pt 2: 197.
16. G Caton-Thompson (1931) 262; Veloso 'Notes' (1512) 185.
17. My thanks to James Duthie of Dubai, according to whom '… 'imali' is very close to amwali and Mali which means 'my money' in Arabic (the first one plural, second one singular)' (e-mail, 1 April 2001).
18. Holt PR 907. Although some historians believe the red beads found on the Wild Coast came from later Portuguese ships engaged in trade with India, they were first used on the south-east African coast by Arab and Indian traders. 'Alaquequas', as the Portuguese called these beads, derives from Arabic, *al aqiq*. (Bell-Cross *Coelacanth* vol 25(1): 20, 22).
19. Evidence of Francisco Vaz D'Almada *Records of SE Africa* vol VIII: 90, 95, 99.
20. *Records of SE Africa* vol VIII: 103.
21. The *Santo Alberto*, 1593, under the wise leadership of Nuno Velho Pereira (*Records of SE Africa* vol II: 283–346).
22. Scully 61–2.
23. Scully 62.
24. Hammond-Tooke *Roots of Black South Africa* 12; Pinnock 35.
25. Scully 62.
26. Kay 303.
27. Evidence of Ngcetane (Kay 303).
28. Soga *SE Bantu* 379.
29. Kay 303.
30. William Bazley's notes (nos 29 and 31), quoted by Kirby *African Studies* vol 13(1): 18.
31. Evidence of Xelo 1883 Native Laws and Customs Commission Report 432.
32. Soga *SE Bantu* 379. John Henderson Soga (1860–1941) was the second son of the first black South African missionary, Tiyo Soga, son of Jotelo, councillor to King Ngqika, and a Scotswoman, Janet Burnside. JH Soga was educated in Glasgow and at the University of Edinburgh, was ordained and served as a missionary in the Transkei. His two works on Xhosa history, *The South-Eastern Bantu* and *The ama-Xosa: Life and Customs*, both of which were originally written in isiXhosa, are invaluable sources of information.
33. Soga *The ama-Xosa* 332.
34. Soga *SE Bantu* 379.
35. Kay 74.
36. Evidence of Mdepa, Bessie's son, 1828 (Shaw *The Story of My Mission* 494).
37. Scully 65. According to Reverend Thomas she may have been slightly older, 'about 10 or 12 years of age'. (extract from Capt Garden's papers, Killie Campbell to Kirby, 24 October 1956, Kirby papers, Strange Library).
38. Evidence of Mdepa (Kay 303).
39. Scully 62.
40. Xelo, friend of Bessie's son Mdepa, at the 1883 Native Laws and Customs Commission 432.
41. Xelo, 1883 Native Laws and Customs Commission 432. Shaw *Journal* 29 June 1828: 133. See also Scully 65.
42. Scully 64.
43. Reverend Kay's Journal (*Methodist Missionary Notices* vol IV: 71).
44. Kay 307.
45. Fynn 112.
46. Letter dated 13 March 1829, in Bannister *Humane Policy*, lxx; Shaw *The Story of my Mission* 499, Kirby *African Studies* p 1 - 23
47. Shaw *The Story of my Mission* 499.
48. Xelo, 1883 Native Laws and Customs Commission 432.
49. Kay (who met the Tshomane in 1829) 304.
50. Xelo, 1883 Laws and Customs Commission 432.
51. Scully's description of this beach, which he says 'stretched for miles to the north from the reef on which the ship had been wrecked…,' is more descriptive of Mngazana, where Bessie lived as an adult, than Lambasi Bay where she was wrecked as a child.
52. Scully 67.
53. Scully 65.
54. Scully 66–8.
55. EW Pearce, Native Commissioner, in a letter to Kirby, 1953 (Kirby's personal papers, Strange Library Jhb).
56. Scully 66. Although it was not permitted for a girl or woman to inherit immovable property, it was possible for her to own or earn stock (Hunter 117).
57. Because they were sometimes extensive, shipwrecked Europeans mistakenly called them villages.
58. Shaw & Van Warmelo pt 1: 31.
59. Hunter 15.
60. Hunter 22.
61. Delagorgue 76–7. Although he was referring specifically to the Zulu-speaking Northern Nguni, his words are as true of the Xhosa-speaking Southern Nguni.
62. This is true even today.
63. Soga *SE Bantu* 379, 332.
64. Cory MS 14600 vol 11: 65 – 'The father of Tshomane resided near Lwambaso River'.
65. Soga *SE Bantu* 108; see also 381.
66. *The ama-Xosa* 57.
67. Maclean 12–13.
68. Hunter 180.
69. Hunter 186.
70. Hunter 182–3.
71. Hunter 101.
72. Laubscher 76.
73. Alberti (1807) 31.
74. Hunter 222.
75. Hunter 223.
76. Fynn 112.
77. Callaway 108.
78. William Bazley, in Kirby *African Studies* vol 13: 19.
79. Scully 67; Fynn *Diary* 112.
80. Hunter 20, 165–74.
81. Hunter 170.
82. Fynn 112.
83. Wilson *African Studies* vol 18: 173–4. See also Soga *SE Bantu* 301.

84. Wilson *African Studies* vol 18: 173–5; Derricourt *Beyond the Cape Frontier* 39–82 and Feely *Early Farmers* 14, 42–7.
85. Hunter 186. Date based on Van Reenen, who met Bessie in 1790 and estimated that she was then about 60 (Barnard 213). The Mpondo married a little later than their Dutch counterparts in Cape Town, where most girls were already married or mothers by then, and where 'ten, twelve, and even eighteen children [were] not uncommonly the product of one marriage' (Semple 50).
86. Shaw *Journal* 166.
87. *House of Phalo* 29.
88. Maclean 24–6.
89. Statement by old Zali 1889, letter from Pearce to Kirby, 8 June 1953 (Kirby's private papers, Strange Library, Jhb).

Chapter 2
1. Annual Register... for the Year 1786: 38.
2. There was also the odd abduction, but it was frowned upon: 'It is disgusting as it is nobody's wish as a parent. In our custom, you are supposed to ask this girl to marry you, and she must be brought to you by her family accordingly. If you abduct her it means you are forcing her, you are stealing her.' (Interview with abeLungu, 1989. Tapes in author's possession.)
3. Hunter 187.
4. Maclean 19.
5. Hunter 32.
6. Seymour 106; Hammond-Tooke *Tribes of Willowvale* 54.
7. Maclean 27. See also Cook 75.
8. Mostert *Frontiers* 566.
9. Soga *SE Bantu* 302–3.
10. Hunter 187.
11. Cook 73.
12. Cook 82-3.
13. Hunter 192-3. Although the custom of lobola has survived into the present, its spiritual significance has largely diminished due to the frequent substitution of money for cattle.
14. Maclean 55.
15. Hunter 194.
16. Hunter 194–5.
17. Interview with abeLungu, Xora mouth, 1989. In modern times the girl is wrapped in a blanket.
18. Hunter 196–7.
19. Maclean 53.
20. Soga *The ama-Xosa* 238.
21. Interview with abeLungu, Xora Mouth, 1989.
22. Soga *SE Bantu* 367, 381.
23. Evidence of Tomsoni kaGojwela, *Where Rainbirds Call* 21.
24. Hunter 198–9.
25. Soga *SE Bantu* 380.
26. Hunter 533.
27. Hunter 44.
28. Hunter 38.
29. Soga *The ama-Xosa* 208; Hunter 35, 51.
30. Shaw & Van Warmelo pt 3: 256, also 253.
31. Hunter 191.
32. Soga *SE Bantu* 381.
33. Evidence of Nathaniel Umhala, 1883 Native Laws and Customs Commission 257.
34. Henry Francis Fynn , Natal Archives A1382 vol 16: 46–7.
35. Maclean 55.
36. Soga *SE Bantu* 380.
37. Hunter 191; Cook 73.
38. Kay 304.
39. Bazley note 29; Kirby *African Studies* 18.
40. Kay (who met Bessie's son Mdepa) 304.
41. Fynn published diary 112.
42. Eg the Xhosa King Gcaleka's mother (Maclean 15), or Ngqungqushe's wife (Stapleton *Faku* 11, 13, 14).
43. Cook 36.

44. Kay 128–35.
45. Delegorgue 76–7.
46. After Shaw & Van Warmelo, also sketches on 32 & 38.
47. Alberti (1807) 82–3.
48. Cook 17.
49. Kay 304.
50. See Shaw's journal (*Methodist Missionary Notices* vol IV: 200).
51. Soga *SE Bantu* 379 fn 331. The first was probably a family name and the second a royal title.
52. Shaw, May 1829, excerpts from his journal (*Methodist Missionary Notices* vol IV: 200).
53. Kay 304, quoting Bessie's grandson Ngcetane.
54. Scully 68.
55. Shaw's journal, May 1829 (*Methodist Missionary Notices* vol IV: 200). Kay 304 also refers to him as Tshomane's brother.
56. Cook 31.
57. Hunter 211.
58. Hunter 211.
59. *SE Bantu* 379.
60. Evidence of Nathaniel Umhala, 1883 Native Laws and Customs Commission 257.
61. Scully 68.
62. Kay 304, as told by Bessie's grandson.
63. Kay 304.
64. Kay 304, 307.
65. Hunter 25.
66. Letter from Dutch official, 16 April 1689, quoted by Shell 26.
67. Xelo, friend of Bessie's son Mdepa, 1883 Native Laws and Customs Commission 432.
68. Xelo, 1883 Native Laws and Customs Commission 432; Kay 304.
69. Soga *The ama-Xosa* 294.
70. About 16 when the *Grosvenor* was wrecked in 1782, she was 'considerably younger' than Mdepa (Kay 307.)
71. Xelo, 1883 Native Laws and Customs Commission 432. Shaw *Journal*, 29 June 1828: 133. See also Scully 65.
72. Bazley *African Studies* vol 13: 18 notes 29, 31.
73. According to Bessie's son Mdepa, she 'lived and died near the little Umgazi River', ie Mngazana (Kay 305).
74. Feely *Preferred Locations* 41–2.
75. For more see the Truth and Reconciliation website: http://www.truth.org.za/decisons/1999/ac990249.htm.
76. Private communication with Bryan Haynes, August 1999.
77. Kirby *Sourcebook on the Wreck of the Grosvenor* 43, 85.
78. Morse *Roll of the British Settlers* 17, 24–5.
79. *SE Bantu* 382.
80. Beinart *Societies of Southern Africa* vol 7: 33.
81. *History of SA* vol II: 204. EW Pearce came to the same conclusion – see his notes on the abeLungu in Cory PR 3665: 4.
82. Based largely on Soga *SE Bantu*.
83. Hunter 399.
84. According to Shaw (1829 *Methodist Missionary Notices* vol 4: 200) Mlawu was the Great Son, who inherited the Chieftainship on Sango's death, rather than Gela, as Soga claimed. As Prof Kirby quite rightly noted, Soga 'does not seem certain of the early relationships. He certainly never consulted Shaw's Journal in the *Wes. Meth. Mag.* for 1829' (Kirby's annotated copy of Soga's *South-Eastern Bantu* in my possession.) See Pearce (Cory PR 3665: 4) and Shaw (*Journal* 172).
85. Based largely on Soga *SE Bantu* 380.
86. Gela may actually have been Bessie's grandson, Begela, son of Mdepa.
87. Xelo, 1883 Native Laws and Customs Commission 432.
88. Dudumayo was 'a tall handsome man' of 'high character' (Cory PR 1294).
89. Evidence of Zali of the abeLungu, from Kirby's private papers, Strange Africana Library, Johannesburg.
90. Kay (303) says he was black. See fn 92.
91. According to Soga (*SE Bantu* 381) Badi was childless,

but at least one of the abeLungu interviewed by Holt in the 1950s, Putsu kaGamtshe, claimed to be Badi's descendant (Holt *Where Rainbirds Call* 22–3).

92. Soga's genealogy for Jekwa seems confused: Mbomboshe [Bomboss], for example, was not Jekwa's biological son, but a black man said to have been cast away with Bessie.

93. Soga's informant appears to have joined the descendants of two of Jekwa's sons into one long line. As we shall see in chap 9, by 1810 Nogaya was a grown man, whose son Gaqelo was also fully grown. Assuming Nogaya was 50 at the time and applying 30 years per generation gives Jekwa a birth date of around 1610, impossible for a man who was one of Bessie's protectors 140 odd years later.

Chapter 3

1. Chatterton *The Old East Indiamen* 10.
2. Lichtenstein vol 1: 296.
3. Hall *Empires of the Monsoon* 263–4.
4. Gardner *The East India Company* 25.
5. Edward Terry, 1616 (Raven-Hart *Before Van Riebeeck* 81–2). For 'tigers' and 'wolves' read leopards and hyenas.
6. Edward Terry, 1616 (*Before Van Riebeeck* 81–2).
7. Table Bay takes its name from the huge flat-topped mountain that looms over it, sometimes covered with a 'table-cloth' of soft white cloud, which tumbles down the face of the rock, disappearing as it reaches the lower slopes and magically re-forming at the top. It was first known as Saldanha Bay, but was renamed Table Bay by Joris van Spilbergen in 1601; thereafter 'Saldanha' was applied to the bay further north that still bears the name today (*Before Van Riebeeck* 25–7).
8. Hall 202–6.
9. Hall 213.
10. Castanheda (*Records of SE Africa* vol 5: 399).
11. Cornelius de Houtman, 1595; Jacob Pieterszoon van Enkhuisen, 1604 and Sir Edward Michaelbourne, 1605 (Raven-Hart *Before Van Riebeeck* 18, 29 and 33 respectively).
12. Thomas Best, 1612 (*Before Van Riebeeck* 58).
13. Halford 2.
14. Castanheda (*Records of SE Africa* vol 5: 400).
15. Valentyn vol 2: 137; Castanheda (*Records of SE Africa* vol 5: 401).
16. De Barros (*Records of SE Africa* vol 6: 299).
17. De Barros (*Records of SE Africa* vol 6: 300).
18. De Barros (*Records of SE Africa* vol 6: 303; Hall 202; Mostert 85–6; Gordon-Brown 4; De Kock (1953) 30).
19. Castanheda (*Records of SE Africa* vol 5: 404).
20. Manuel de Mesquita Perestrello, survivor of the *Sao Bento*, 1554 (*Records of SE Africa* vol 1: 226).
21. Gardner *The East India Company* 18.
22. Gardner *The East India Company* 18.
23. Davies *Historical Atlas of the Indian Peninsula* 16.
24. De Kock (1953) 63.
25. Cope 87–8.
26. Thomas Elkington, 1614 (Raven-Hart *Before Van Riebeeck* 67).
27. Cope 106.
28. Walter Peyton, 1615 and Edward Dodsworth, also 1615 (Raven-Hart *Before Van Riebeeck* 72, 67).
29. Cope 113–17; De Kock (1953) 58–9.
30. Edward Terry, 1616 (Cope 113).
31. Edward Dodsworth, captain of the *Hope* , 1615 and John Milward, 1614 (*Before Van Riebeeck* 68, 70).
32. Edward Dodsworth, 1615 (*Before Van Riebeeck* 68).
33. Cope 130.
34. The first version is reported by Martin Pring, 1616 (Raven-Hart *Before Van Riebeeck* 69–70), the second by Edward Terry, 1616 (Cope 126–7).
35. John Jourdain, 1617 (*Before Van Riebeeck* 88).
36. De Kock (1953) 65.
37. De Kock (1953) 92.
38. De Kock (1953) 92.
39. Burton 49–50.
40. Van Riebeeck, quoted in Norwich 21.
41. Hall *Empires of the Monsoon* 295.

42. For Valentyn's lyrical description of the Gardens see *Description of the Cape of Good Hope* vol 1 chap 2.
43. Valentyn vol 2: 161.
44. Theal *History of SA 1652–1795* vol 1: 427.
45. Valentyn vol 1: 218–19.
46. Valentyn vol 1: 219. As labour became scarce, the price of slaves rocketed and only cash transactions were acceptable (Shell *Children of Bondage* 108).
47. Journal of Ensign Isaq Schryver, Jan-April 1689 (*The Record* pt I: 433–40).
48. Placaaten were issued in 1677, 1727, 1739, 1770, 1774 and 1786 (Beck (1987) 45) but were largely ignored (see eg the string of colonists reported for illegal trading in Moodie *The Record* pt III).
49. Literally 'farmers'.
50. See Schryver's journal in Mossop 207–end.
51. Cory *Rise of SA* vol 1: 20.
52. Mostert *Frontiers* 154.
53. 'An account of what took place on an expedition to the country of the Caffers, undertaken, inter alia, for the purpose of shooting elephant, related, in accordance with the order of His Excellency the Governor and the Honourable Council of Justice, by the burgers Hendrick de Vries de Jonge and Hendrick Scheefer de Jonge.' Copy in the Strange Library, S.Store 968.601 1736 HUB.
54. Adams *Buck Adams' Narrative* 29.
55. De Mist 44.
56. De Mist 45.
57. This was the route taken by Beutler 16 years later, in 1752 (see Forbes 9–10).
58. De Mist 45.
59. ' An Account…'; Cullinan 50–1; Spaarman vol 2: 15.
60. Kirby *Africana Notes and News* vol 12(1): 10.
61. In 1835 a fort was built on the site and its name changed to Fort Brown: it still exists, a cluster of low buildings on the banks of the Fish River, about 30 kilometres outside Grahamstown on the Fort Beaufort road. For more see Kirby *Africana Notes and News* vol 12(1): 10.
62. Report of Landdrosts and Heemraden, 7 February 1770 (Moodie *The Record* pt III: 2-3).
63. Forbes 10, 13.
64. Theal *History of SA* (1897 ed) vol 2: 130.
65. Lichtenstein vol 1: 309. See also Alberti (1807) 20–1.
66. 'An Account…'
67. 'An Account…'
68. 'An Account…'
69. Theal *History of SA* vol 2: 22.
70. Derricourt's map in *Beyond the Cape Frontier* 75.
71. Axelson *Dias and His Successors* 69–76.
72. DG van Reenen 175.
73. Other examples of Xhosa-ised English names are 'Bisi' for Colonel Bisset, who fought in the Frontier wars; 'Tshalisi' for the missionary Charles Brownlee, and 'Hagile' for the Reverend Hargreaves (Soga *SE Bantu* 214–15).
74. A1382 vol 16: 48. Apparently Biale left a son called 'Jugugaler', but if he was indeed Badi's son, he was not of the Great House – see abeLungu genealogy, chap 2.
75. Shaw *Journal* 133.
76. A British officer in the 1850 war estimated that a Cape wagon could carry 'some two or three tons dead weight' (Lucas 44), while Basil Mills, a resident of Grahamstown and one of only a handful of men who can still yoke and drive a team, estimates the carrying capacity at 7 tons (conversation with author, 9 May 2001).
77. Alexander 366. 'Upondo' means horn, or tusk of an elephant (Shaw & Van Warmelo pt 2: 185).
78. 'There is evidence that, by 1593, mercantile trade, presumed to have come from Delagoa Bay, had penetrated as far south as the Transkei…' (Tim Maggs *Natal and Zululand* 42). See also Collins (1809), who says that the peoples to the north of the Xhosa traded ivory for iron and copper for ivory etc (Moodie *The Record* pt V: 43).
79. Alberti 33. See also Hunter 95.
80. Hubberley in Kirby *Source Book* 82. For a history of beads in the Eastern Cape see Kaufmann 'Ezakwantu' 48-50.

81. Tim Maggs *Natal and Zululand* 43; Beinart *Societies of Southern Africa* vol 7: 27.
82. 'An Account…'
    (Strange Library, Jhb).
83. 'An Account…'
84. It was not uncommon for the people of the Wild Coast to travel about in this way. There was a constant trade in cattle and goods and a corresponding movement of people from homestead to homestead and well-trodden paths linking them. Beinart (1982) 21; Saunders & Derricourt *Beyond the Cape Frontier* 70.
85. 'An Account…'
86. Theal *Records of the Cape Colony* vol II: 399; DG van Reenen 164–5; Elphick & Giliomee (1979) 350.
87. Tshomane territory lay some 1 000 kilometres from Delagoa Bay. The crew estimated they had travelled about '180 Duitsche mylen', that is about 1300 kilometres (1 German mile = 7,4 kilometres).
88. Mackeurtan 84–5.
89. Theal *Records of SE Africa* vol 6: 481 (kindly translated by Biula van de Kaa, 31 July 2000).
90. Putsu kaGamtshe, an elderly member of the abeLungu, to the Reverend Holt in the late 1950s (Holt *Where Rainbirds Call* 23).
91. Mackeurtan *Cradle Days of Natal* 84; Raper 233.
92. Introduction to *Elvira: Or The Eagle's Nest* (author unknown, published by JA Guest, Port Alfred, 1887).
93. See Rosenthal *Cutlass and Yardarm* 62.
94. Johnson, 1725; Bulpin *Islands in a Forgotten Sea* 120, also 127.
95. *Islands in a Forgotten Sea* 129.
96. 'An Account…'
    (Strange Library, Jhb).
97. Soga *SE Bantu* 121; Peires *House of Phalo* 45–6.
98. Soga *SE Bantu* 121. The Hubner traders called him Faro.
99. Lichtenstein vol 1: 18.
100. 'An Account…'
    (Strange Library, Jhb).
101. 'An Account…'
102. Hermanus and Frederik Hubner were the sons of Catherina Potgieter and Pieter Hubner, a Dutch East India Company soldier who became a Cape burgher and farmed at Paarl. The younger brother, Frederik, was married to Catherina Hoffman, daughter of Johannes Hoffman and Maria Louisz, a woman of slave descent. Frederik's daughter, also called Catherina, was baptised in 1736, the year of her father's death. Hermanus was unmarried. (De Villiers & Pama, vol 1: 334. See also 'Who was Hermanus Hubner?' *Africana Notes & News*, vol 12: 149).
    Antony Lotze was also known as Antonie Potje. He was the youngest of five children born to Jacob Potje and Catharina Potgieter, who married in 1705.
    Phillipus Simon Constant was married to Catharina Heylon of Mauritius in 1705. His death left her with eight children, the youngest of whom was three years old.
    Jan Andries Esterhuijsen was the third of five children born to Christoffel Estrreux of Esterhuysen who had arrived at the Cape in 1692 and married Elizabeth Beyers.
    Gerrit van Vooren or Vuuren (the spelling of surnames was standardised only much later) was named after his father Jan's father, who had arrived at the Cape in 1691 with his wife, Susannah Jacobs. He was in his early twenties, married with one daughter (all from De Villiers & Pama).
103. Kirby *Source Book* 156.
104. Soga *SE Bantu* 123.
105. 'An Account…'
    (Strange Library, Jhb).
106. The man is an enigma. The Cloetes were an extremely close-knit and wealthy Cape family (the old adage has it that the Van der Byls, another well-to-do Cape family, spoke only to the Cloetes, and the Cloetes spoke only

to God). Their extensive properties included the famous estate of Groot Constantia, built by an early Governor of the Cape, Simon van der Stel. Since there is not a single person named Louis in the Cloete genealogy of the period, Louis' surname was probably incorrectly transcribed. He was probably Louis Cortje, eldest of 12 children born to Phillipus Cortje and Elisabeth Malherbe. Baptised in 1716, Louis would have been about 20 years old at the time of the expedition. (For the Cloete and Cortje genealogies see De Villiers & Pama 142 and vol 1:158.)
107. 'An Account…'
108. 'An Account….' The Hubner massacre had a tragic sequel.. In 1761 Coenraad Scheffer, now aged 47 and a lowly *knegt* [servant] employed by Hendrik Hop, accompanied the latter on an exploratory expedition to the Orange river, far to the north of the Cape of Good Hope. The party consisted of 17 whites and 68 'half-breed Hottentots'. Hop seems to have wanted a show of strength and mustered as much firepower as he could. He was probably not looking for trouble so much as preparing for all eventualities, but when the trouble did come, it was from within his own ranks – from his own *knegt*. And Scheffer's behaviour in the wastes of Namaqualand may have been a direct result of his traumatic experiences on the Hubner expedition 25 years before.
    The journey north was slow but smooth, Namaqualand is a dry, sandy land without any perennial rivers. The Nama, who inhabited the land, lived in great poverty, continually harassed by the San and rogue trader/farmers from the Cape, who raided their stock and sometimes took their lives as well. After crossing the desolate sand flats of the Koa Valley, the expedition reached the Orange on about 19 September. They crossed the river 10 days later, their route taking them to the west of the Karas Mountains, and in due course they reached the 26th parallel. The climate appeared healthy, the cattle sleek and abundant. But all was not well: the inhabitants north of the river fled at their approach, leaving only the weak and elderly behind. It was a land torn by strife, its population living in fear of their lives and their property.
    As summer advanced, the land lay numb in the sweltering heat, the already-sparse grazing withered and water became increasingly scarce. In about the first week of December the party turned back to the Cape. Then followed a two-week gap in which no entries were made in Hop's diary. In the middle of this inexplicable silence, on the evening of 14 January 1762, Coenraad Scheffer went off the rails: left in charge of some cattle and Khoi attendants on the north bank of the Orange, he ordered Ruyter, a Khoi servant, to fetch water from the river, but Ruyter seems to have objected and a struggle ensued in which Scheffer stabbed him twice. Ruyter ran away chased by Scheffer. Later than same night when the camp was asleep, Scheffer shot and wounded Ruyter; he died two days later, after making a statement to the expedition leaders which, together with eyewitness reports, were later used in court as evidence against Scheffer.
    Depositions made at his trial agree that he was 'suspicious, childish and wrong-headed' and that 'everyone, yea, the slaves included, considered Scheffer mad'. As there is no indication that he was anything but normal in his early 20s, when he joined the Hubner expedition, Scheffer's experiences must have disturbed him severely. His mental instability was a mitigating factor in his trial and he was sentenced to banishment for life on Robben Island, several kilometres offshore in Table Bay. There he remained for about 19 years, until July 1782, when he escaped to the mainland, at the same time as an English fleet under Commodore Johnstone seized a Dutch convoy in Saldanha Bay. Six French convicts also escaped, as well as five slaves, one

of whom made his way to Saldanha where he was shot dead by the English. Some of the other escapees may also have headed there, including perhaps the 67-year-old Scheffer. Nothing more is known of him (Mossop (1947) esp 117–18).

109. Baines *Journal* vol 1: 52.
110. 'An Account…'
(Strange Library, Jhb).
111. *History of SA 1652–1795* vol 2: 13.
112. *History of SA 1652–1795* vol 2: 13.
113. Thunberg 254.
114. Collins, 1809 (*The Record* pt V: 9).
115. Isaacs 87–9. The traders lives were spared only when they agreed to act as mercenaries against one of Shaka's enemies.
116. 'An Account…'
(Strange Library, Jhb).
117. 'The boys are occupied in attending the cattle – *nor are they admitted to the chase with the men*, neither are they allowed to mix with them in Society…' (Somerville, 1799–1802: 32 – my italics).
118. Hunter (at 165, 527) says Mpondo circumcision took place between the ages of 17 and 20, while Reverend Shaw says Xhosa initiates were 12–15 (*The Story of my Mission* 456).
119. This is compatible with the *Naastigheid* report. If Badi and his companions were, say, 25–30 years old in 1713, by 1736 they were 48–53, and when Badi disappeared in about 1750, 62–67. By the time of the *Naastigheid* crew's visit in 1757 they would have been 69–74 or – as the chief claimed – dead.
120. See for example, the crew of the *Hercules* when it was wrecked in 1796: although the ship was American, the majority of the sailors were Lascars, but included Danes, Swedes, Dutch, American and Portuguese. Most were recruited in India (Stout 23).

Chapter 4
1. John Gribble, marine geologist at the South African Heritage Resources Agency, estimates there are some 2 200 wrecks along our coasts (*New African* April 2001: 45).
2. George and Margo Branch *Living Shores of SA* (1983) 15.
3. *The Star*, Johannesburg 15 July 1999: 1; *The Sunday Times* 14 January 2001. See also Uys *Survivors of Africa's Oceans* 32–8.
4. The date was 4 August, the same day on which the *Grosvenor* had sunk 209 years before, on the same coast.
5. Turpin *Basket Work Harbour* 10, 80, 134; Bulpin *Natal and the Zulu Country* 57, 88, 438.
6. Stout 23.
7. Spaarman vol 1: 315.
8. Spaarman vol 1: 315 fn 110.
9. 'South African Sailing Directions' in Axelson *Vasco da Gama* 70.
10. Unsigned letter to Killie Campbell, 19 Feb 1954, KCM 5852.
11. Davidson *Old Africa Rediscovered* 149.
12. Hall *The Changing Past* 78.
13. From Fra Mauro's map, AD 1459, quoted by Vincent (1807) vol II: 672–3.
14. Manuscript of Al Edrisi, from Vincent *Commerce and Navigation* vol 2: 563.
15. Basil Davidson 152; Hall 101.
16. 'An account of the wreck of the ships *Sacramento* and *Nossa Senhora da Atalaya*… 1647' (Theal *Records of SE Africa* vol 8: 352).
17. *Records of SE Africa* vol 8: 99.
18. 'An account of the wreck of the ships *Sacramento* and *Nossa Senhora da Atalaya*… 1647' (*Records of SE Africa* vol 8: 308).
19. *Records of SE Africa* vol 8: 312.
20. Valentyn vol 2: 139.
21. The boy was 10 or 11 years old. Weakened by hunger, he had been left behind somewhere in the care of the slave who had carried him on his shoulders (*Records of SE Africa* vol 1: 137).

22. 'Narrative of the wreck of the great galleon Saint John… 1552' (*Records of SE Africa* vol 1: 146–7).
23. Theal *History of SA 1652–1795* vol 1: 442–3; Theal *History and Ethnography* vol 3: 13.
24. De Kock (1953) 33.
25. *Annals of Natal* vol 1: 24–5; Willcox 34.
26. Axelson *Da Gama* 76.
27. Perestrelo 47. Until the end of the 1600s a league was somewhat less than the 3,4 miles it came to signify later (Axelson *Da Gama* 54 fn 3). I have calculated it at 3,2 miles, ie 5,12 kilometres
28. For more see Da Costa in Perestrelo 85 and Joao de Lisboa (1514) in *Da Gama* 75.
29. *Da Gama* 69–76. See Prior: 'The country, called *Natal*, from being discovered on Christmas-day *succeeds* to the colonial territory…' James Prior (1819) 23–4 – my italics. Thanks to Dan Wylie for drawing my attention to this.
30. *Annals of Natal* vol 1: 34; Moodie *History of the Battles* 28.
31. *The Record* pt II: 419.
32. 'Extracts from the Journal of Commander Simon van der Stel', March 7, 1687, *Annals of Natal* vol 1: 34.
33. 'Extracts from the Journal of Commander Simon van der Stel', March 7, 1687, *Annals of Natal* vol 1: 34.
34. Moodie *History of the Battles* 28.
35. Evidence of the sailmaker (Valentyn, quoted in Vigne (ed) *The French Boy* 93; Moodie *History of the Battles* 26).
36. *Annals of Natal* vol 1: 27; *History of the Battles* 26–7.
37. *The French Boy* 83, 85.
38. 'Extracts from a Despatch from Commander Simon van der Stel…' *Annals of Natal* vol 1: 45.
39. Vigne (ed) *The French Boy* 65.
40. Statement of Jansz Kind and others (*The French Boy* 85).
41. *The Record* pt I: 427.
42. *The Record* pt I: 424.
43. *Annals of Natal* vol 1: 29.
44. *The Record* pt I: 417; *Annals of Natal* vol 1: 31. The surgeon eventually died of his injuries; the boatswain's mate was crushed by an elephant.
45. *Annals of Natal* vol 1: 29.
46. Moodie *History of the Battles* 29.
47. *Annals of Natal* vol 1: 33. The wrecksite could be somewhere between Port Shepstone and Durban. The survivors claimed to have been wrecked 'in the bay 'Piscada'. According to Perestrelo's survey of the coastline: 'Point Pescaria' lies 12 leagues (about 60 kilometres) beyond the Last Point of Natal [Mtamvuna River] (Perestrelo 49, 51).
48. *History of the Battles* 30. See also *The Record* pt I: 417–18.
49. Moodie *History of the Battles* 32–5; the *Centaur's* logbook (*Annals of Natal* vol 1: 37–9).
50. The Dutch terrestrial *myl* was 3 890 metres (*African Studies* vol 35: 278). Soga is one of the few to maintain that the *Stavenisse* was wrecked on the Pondoland coast (*SE Bantu* 101).
51. Cape Archives VC 94 no 8, entry for Wednesday, 11 February 1688 (my translation). Cf Lichtenstein vol 1: 367.
52. Peires *House of Phalo* 42.
53. Monica Wilson (1959) 'The early history of the Transkei and Ciskei' *African Studies* vol 18(4). Mackeurtan suggested that the 'Semboos' referred to the abaMbo of present-day Natal , but Zulu oral history describes the latter as 'quite recent arrivals in Natal' (Mackeurtan 64; James Stuart Archives vol 4: 42).
54. Mpondo kings: at least eight generations of kings before Faku, who was born in 1780, are buried between the Mzimvubu and Mtamvuna rivers.
Mpondomise chiefs: the graves of the early Pondomise chiefs are at the sources of the Mzimvubu; later ones were buried at Latana near Shawbury and in the Tina river.
Xhosa kings: Ngcwangu, who ruled about 1635, is buried near Port St Johns; Sikhomo, ruled c 1660, buried at Cumgce, Buntingville, Pondoland; Togu, died c 1695, buried at Qokoma, Ngqeleni district, Pondoland ; Ngconde, buried near Buntingville, Pondoland ; Tshiwo, died c 1702, buried at Ngcwanguba, near Hole in the

Wall; Phalo, died 1775, buried near Butterworth (Soga
SE Bantu 102, 111, 113, 114, 120, 125). Even if the main
body of the Xhosa were located between Brazen Head
and the Mtata River when the *Stavenisse* was wrecked
in 1686, independent clans were spread further afield.
In 1702 just 16 years after the wreck, a group of Dutch
colonists encountered amaXhosa as far south as today's
city of Port Elizabeth.

55. *The Record* pt I: 419, 441.
56. Cory MS 14600 vol 3: 14; Axelson *Da Gama* 69,
Dias and His Successors 38 fn 75.
57. Supplement to vol 2, Dampier's Voyages, from *Collecteana*
128–9, Van Riebeeck Society 1924.
58. Cory MS 14600 vol 3: 14.
59. Shaw *The Story of My Mission* 402. The Mzimvubu may
be the Bay of Natal, to the south of the *Grosvenor* wreck,
on Pisani's map of 1793. (reproduced in Norwich 78–9).
60. Delegorgue vol 1: 48.
61. Evidence of John Shepstone, son of the missionary
at Morley (*James Stuart Archive* vol 5: 301).
62. *The Record* pt I: 442 fn 2; Dalrymple's report on the
Grosvenor (Kirby *Source Book* 31).
63. *The Record* pt I: 441, 446. Of the 18 survivors, only
4 reached the Cape.
64. *The Record* pt I: 429.
65. Mossop 49.
66. Axelson *The Portuguese in SE Africa 1600–1700* 207–8.
67. Mossop 45–59.
68. Mossop believes they got just beyond Aberdeen, but
some of Schryver's entries indicate that they were
substantially further east: five days from the coast, on
the banks of the Kariega River (which enters the sea
at today's resort of Kenton-on-Sea, just south of
Grahamstown) they met people of mixed Xhosa and
Khoi blood who lived in clay huts. The countryside
was not dry and studded with fynbos as it is around
Aberdeen, but was covered with good grassland and its
inhabitants were cattle-farmers (see Mossop 231–3).
69. Theal *History of South Africa 1652–1795* vol 1: 393.
70. *History of South Africa 1652–1795* vol 1: 393.
71. The Naval Museum at Den Hage in the Netherlands has
records of the outward-bound journey of the *Bennebroek*,
but the vessel spent about three years in the East before
heading back to Holland, and it was on this return trip
that it sank. I was unable to get crew records from the
relevant authorities in Sri Lanka.
72. There are various translations: '57 Europeans and 20
blacks were saved, convicts and slaves' (Leibbrandt's
Precis 261); '57 Europeans and about 20 blacks, mostly
slaves, and criminals' (Bell-Cross, 'The Survivors' Story'
(unpublished paper) 2 or '57 Europeans and 20 Blacks,
the latter consisting of slaves and convicts'
(CAD 1/2/14).
73. Multinational crews were common. See chap 5 for the
Asian and Italian sailors aboard the English *Grosvenor*,
for instance.
74. Mackeurtan *Cradle Days of Natal* 74; Willcox *Shipwreck
and Survival* 34.
75. Turner 51.
76. Bell-Cross 'The Survivors' Story' 5 (Courtesy of the
author and Mrs Jill Vernon of the East London Museum).
77. Leibbrandt's *Precis*, 4 Sept 1714 (CAD 1/2/14).
78. Leibbrandt's *Precis*, 4 Sept 1714. 'Die benaming "Tierra di
Natal" slaan nie op die hedendaagse Natal nie maar op
Pondoland en Transkei. (Inligting van prof E Axelson.)'
Valentyn vol 2: 34 fn 88.
79. CAD 1/2/14.
80. Unstead 48.
81. 'The Survivors' Story' 3; Valentyn vol 2: 105–6;
Burman *Strange Shipwrecks* 52.
82. Letter from Frank Brownlee to C Graham Botha of
the Cape Archives, 26 August 1926 (CAD 1/2/14
11/11A14).
83. Feely 19. For more detail see *Records of
SE Africa* pt 1: 128.

84. Feely 19. Feely based this on marine archaeological
evidence in conjunction with survivors' accounts.
Opinions differ widely: 'in a gully on the seaward side
of the island off the Mzikaba River mouth' (*Annals of the
Natal Museum* vol 25(1): 1–39); 'off the Bashe River
mouth' (Storrar *Ponta Delgada* 20); 'at the mouth of the
Keiskamma' (Axelson *Da Gama* 59). The navigator
Perestrelo, a survivor of the wreck, however, placed it
at the mouth of the River Infante, the Great Fish
(Perestrelo 45–6 and notes at 85).
85. Theal *Records of SE Africa* vol 1: 235–8, 251.
86. Mackeurtan 29. Graham Bell-Cross (*Coelacanth* vol
20(2)) and Turner 121 place it near East London,
Willcox at Mazeppa Bay (*Shipwreck and Survival* 43), but
from the evidence of D'Almada of the *Sao Joao Baptista*,
who met some of its survivors 29 years later, I would say
Mackeurtan's claim for the Mtata is the most accurate
(*Records of SE Africa* vol 8: 102).
87. Gillian Vernon (*Coelacanth* vol 32(1)).
88. Feely 19.
89. Axelson *Portuguese in SE Africa 1600–1700* 199.
90. Feely 19.
91. Theal *Records of SE Africa* vol 8: 217, 220.
92. Gillian Vernon (1994) *Coelacanth* vol 32(1).
93. Theal *Records of SE Africa* vol 8: 313, 328, 338.
94. Turner 121.
95. Theal *Records of SE Africa* vol 8: 235–360.
96. See my argument above.
97. See above.
98. *Annals of Natal* vol 1: 27–53.
99. CAD 1/2/14. He was about eighty, French by birth, and
had been the ship's cook. He remembered the captain
was David Appleman, but could no longer recall the
name of the vessel. It had sailed from Holland in 1683
and, like the *Bennebroek*, spent some time in the East
before being wrecked on its homeward voyage. He lived
quite well, although, said the *Bennebroek* survivors,
'Whether it was from disposition or birth... [the Xhosa]
were more civil towards us than towards this old man'.
100. Bell-Cross 'The Survivors' Story'; Gillian Vernon
(*Coelacanth* vol 32(2)). Items salvaged from the
Bennebroek in January 1984 were on display in the
'Victoria', a replica of an 18th-century ship that used to
be moored at the V&A Waterfront in Cape Town, but
now stands in the courtyard of a casino in Goodwood.
101. The captain of the *Doddington* was certain that the
Dolphin, which 'disappeared' whilst it was outward-
bound for Bengal, was wrecked at exactly the same spot
as his own (Allen & Allen *Clive's Lost Treasure* 21).
102. Turner 123.
103. *Clive's Lost Treasure* 40.
104. Kirby (1957) *African Studies* vol 12(5): 181.
105. See chap 5.
106. Introduction to Stout *Loss of the Hercules*.
107. Turner 124.
108. *Transactions of the LMS* vol 1: 428. When a rebel Boer,
Coenraad de Buys, also resident in King Ngqika's
territory, admonished him for the murder of the
castaways, 'the king was astonished, and defended the
fact, saying, that it was well done, as they, being
strangers, had nothing to do in the country any more
than the wolves' (*Transactions of the LMS* vol 1: 467).
Although the incident is similar to the experience of
Hubberly and two other castaways from the *Grosvenor*
on the Fish River in 1782 (see next chapter), they
could not have been one and the same, or Van der
Kemp's fresh coffee beans would have been 18 years old,
and unusable.
109. Alberti (1807) 72.
110. Barrow 196.
111. Axelson *Dias and His Successors* 49.
112. Cory MS 17202, folder 3.
113. Theal *History of SA 1652–1795* vol 2: 127, 129.
114. Theal *History and Ethnography* vol 2: 451.
115. Theal *History and Ethnography* vol 3: 158.

116. De Kock (1953) 50.
117. Theal *Records of SE Africa* vol 2: 318.
118. Evidence of Eric Strachan in the 1950s (Holt 25); Soga *SE Bantu* 489.
119. Soga *SE Bantu* 490.
120. Evidence of Mqhunywa ka Makaleni and Mantuhamba (Holt *Where Rainbirds Call* 19, 21).
121. Evidence of Oswald Strachan (Holt 25).
122. According to Mqhunywa ka Makaleni, this is where Bhayi first 'emerged from the sea' (*Where Rainbirds Call* 21).
123. *Where Rainbirds Call* 25.
124. Soga *SE Bantu* 489.
125. Bazley notebooks, note 35, quoted in *African Studies* vol 13: 19.
126. Kirby *African Studies* vol 13: 10. Holt, however, says the name derives from Mholo, son of Bhayi, who is said to have lived a good long life (*Where Rainbirds Call* 25) . According to Soga, Molo was Bhayi's father (*SE Bantu* 384).
127. My thanks to Nidhi Raina for her translation and interest.
128. Monica Hunter *African Studies* vol 18(4): 174–5. This is based on the fact that approximately 210 years separated the death (c1692) of Togu, king of the Xhosa, from that of his seventh successor, Sarhili, in 1902.
129. Evidence of Hubberley (Kirby *Source Book* 79, also 130 fn 52): 'Doubtless a number of these remained behind in Pondoland'.
130. See list of ship's company and passengers (Kirby *Source Book* 200).
131. Two of the other maids, Betty and Hoakim, who had accompanied Mrs Logie and Mrs Hosea, did reach the Cape (Kirby *Source Book* 200; Kirby *True Story* 93).
132. See Holt (Cory PR906).
133. Information from *SE Bantu* opp 490. For more on the amaMolo see Appendix 1.

Chapter 5
1. Hosea to Lady Chambers, 9 November 1781 (*Africana Notes & News* vol 2: 116–17); Kirby *True Story* 35.
2. William Hickey vol 2: 127.
3. Kirby *True Story* 35.
4. Rochlin, *Africana Notes and News* vol 3: 54.
5. *True Story* 36.
6. Crowhurst *The Defence of British Trade* 88.
7. Kirby *Source Book* 3–4.
8. Carter *The Wreck of the Grosvenor* 2.
9. Kirby *Source Book* 60–1.
10. Kirby *Source Book* 61–2.
11. Carter 5.
12. Kirby *True Story* 48–50.
13. Cory PR 1294. Elderly Mpondo to Capt Sidney Turner, c1867.
14. As told by two unnamed amaMpondo to Zacky Bowles, who visited the wreck site in 1856. The two men, about 50 years old, 'gave us details as they had learned them from their fathers who were boys of about 12 when the wreck happened' (*Rock Hearts of Oak* 95–6).
15. Carter 6, 9.
16. Evidence of Hubberly (*Source Book* 71, 197–201).
17. Scully 6.
18. Rock *Hearts of Oak* 95–6.
19. Carter 11; Kirby *Source Book* 68–9.
20. Evidence of unnamed Mpondo (*Hearts of Oak* 95–6).
21. Evidence of John Hynes (Carter 13).
22. Cory PR 1294. Elderly Mpondo to Capt Sidney Turner, c1867 near Bunting, at the *umzi* of Ndamase, whose grandfather Ngqungqushe was the Pondo king at the time of the wreck.
23. W Warner *Evening Post* 23 July 1955; Cory MS 17202, folder 5.
24. Hubberly, in Kirby *Source Book* 71.
25. Evidence of Hubberly (Kirby *Source Book* 71, 76); Carter 22.
26. Chilvers 61–2.

27. Ben Dekker of Port St Johns, private correspondence, August 2000.
28. Carter 17; Kirby *Source Book* 52 fn 36.
29. Carter 18–19.
30. See chap 1.
31. Alberti (1807) 23.
32. Carter 72.
33. Carter 29.
34. Birkby (c1954): 86.
35. Son of Thomas Saunders, Governor of Fort St David at Cuddalore on the east coast of India in 1751, 'a cold, austere and silent man', also described as 'one of the most formidable Englishmen' in India at that time and the man behind Clive's military success at Arcot in 1751 (Gardner 60–1; Willson *Ledger and Sword* chap 4).
36. Hubberly's evidence (Kirby *Source Book* 77–81; Kirby *True Story* 45).
37. *Source Book* 126; *True Story* 47).
38. Kirby *New Light on the Grosvenor East Indiaman* 34.
39. William Bazley, letter to *The Natal Witness* (1905), quoted by Denzil Bazley *Nil Desperandum* 146.
40. Bazley *The Natal Witness*, 4 March 1907.
41. Bazley *The Natal Witness*, 4 March 1907.
42. Bazley *The Natal Witness*, 4 March 1907.
43. Chilvers 62. Bungana's brother's name, Nomedola, is interesting because variations of it crop up repeatedly in connection with castaways in the years to come. In 1803, for example, it was reported 'that north of the Tamboekies [Thembu] there lived a yellow-skinned nation with long hair, named Matola…' (Dirk Gysbert van Reenen 167). The site of the mission station in Bessie's son's territory was known as Nomadalo. (Holt *Africana Notes & News* vol 12: 279–80). In 1850 a Mrs Simpson told the artist Thomas Baines that she had 'lived some time at Amadoli, this side the Umzimvoobo, where she saw the son of a white woman, wrecked in the *Grosvenor*. He was a little copper-coloured fellow with long white hair, but his father was a tall, athletic Kaffir' (Baines vol 2: 3).
44. The party had just crossed the Ntafufu River, within 20 kilometres of the Mlambomkulu River (evidence of Hubberly (Kirby *Source Book* 77–8 fn 45, 48; 130)).
45. Shaw *Journal* 133.
46. Shaw 498–9. The then king of the Mpondo was Ngqungqushe. In January 1998 Jeanette Deacon of the then Monuments Commission told me that one of his descendants, a son of Sigcau who claimed also to be descended from one of the women of the *Grosvenor* and whose name was, I think, Gordon Ball, was then engaged in a hunt to find the legendary *Grosvenor* treasure.
47. Cory MS 2106.
48. Evidence of William Bazley (1907) (*James Stuart Archives* vol 1: 62. See also Denzil Bazley *Nil Desperandum* 146.
49. *James Stuart Archives* vol 2: 115, 135 fn 3.
50. 'Lambasi', incidentally, is derived from the Xhosa word for mussels.
51. Evidence of Mahaya ka Nongqabana (*James Stuart Archives* vol 2: 115). The fact that the girl ate eggs was notable because they were taboo for females (see chap 2).
52. Evidence of Mahaya's son Nzunzu *James Stuart Archives* vol 2: 115.
53. Evidence of Mahaya *James Stuart Archives* vol 2: 113, 115.
54. Evidence of Mahaya *James Stuart Archives* vol 2: 113, 115, 127. I have applied 25 years between the male members and 20 between the female members, working backwards from Mahaya's birthdate.
55. Mendu, Mahaya's maternal uncle was one of a party of amaMpondo present when King Shaka of the Zulus was assassinated in 1828 (*James Stuart Archives* vol 2: 111, 135 fn 9).
56. Carter 58.
57. Probably the same men whom an unnamed Mpondo later described as having 'got safely as far as Umtata, except that some of them died from eating poisonous roots' (Rock *Hearts of Oak* 95–6).
58. Carter 47, 53.

59. Carter 68.
60. Carter 58.
61. Kirby *Source Book* 123–4.
62. Kirby *Source Book* 123.
63. Carter 93, 95.
64. Carter 48.
65. Evidence of Wormington to Dalrymple (1783) in Moodie *History of the Battles* vol 1: 95.
66. Evidence of Price (Moodie *History of the Battles* vol 1: 98). .
67. Evidence of Leary (Moodie *History of the Battles* vol 1: 95).
68. Kirby *Source Book* 36, 38, 72.
69. Kirby *True Story* 42; *Source Book* 72.
70. Hubberly (Kirby *Source Book* 81).
71. Hubberly (Kirby *Source Book* 82).
72. William Bazley, Natal pioneer and traveller, quoted in *African Studies* vol 13: 19.
73. Shrewsbury 82.
74. Carter 65.
75. Van Jaarsveld's ' Report on the expulsion of the Kafirs'. The incident occurred on the Little Fish River, near Botma's farm (Moodie *The Record* pt III: 110; also Peires *House of Phalo* 50).
76. Kirby *Source Book* 103–5.
77. *Source Book* 107.
78. *Source Book* 110, 133 fn 117.
79. *Source Book* 112.
80. See Van der Kemp's diary, *Transactions of the LMS* vol 1: 467.
81. Kirby *Source Book* 124; Carter 97–8.
82. Carter 98.
83. Carter 98.
84. Metrowich *Frontier Flames* 271.
85. Carter 100.
86. Evidence of Price (Moodie *History of the Battles* vol 1: 100; Carter 101–5).
87. Carter 105.
88. Carter 111.
89. Kirby *Source Book* 165.
90. *Source Book* 173.
91. Muller's Report (*Source Book* 175). According to Kirby, Anton had been living at the mouth of the Jujura River for six years and was probably the 'black Portuguese' who reportedly gave some of the survivors food (*Source Book* 96, 132 fn 85) He was tied to a wagon, but fortunately escaped during the night (evidence of Lewis in Moodie *History of the Battles* vol 1: 97).
92. For a full report of the Muller expedition, see *Source Book* 159–191.
93. Letter from Governor van Plettenberg to the Governor of Bengal (Kirby *Van Reenen's Journal* 19).
94. Kirby *True Story* 112–14.
95. The term originated during the 1713 epidemic, which was brought to the Cape by infected children on a ship (Valentyn vol 1: 217). Letter from Veld-Commandant David Schalk van der Merwe to Governor van Plettenberg (Kirby *Van Reenen's Journal* 16, 111).
96. Theal *History and Ethnography* vol 3: 92.
97. Lichtenstein vol 1: 310. See also Paravicini 42–3: 'Some years ago small-pox which is otherwise rare among these [people] was spread amongst them, probably by the crew of a stranded vessel and according to their accounts, many people perished at the time.'
98. *The Morning Chronicle and London Advertiser* 25 April 1783; Kirby *Source Book* 10.
99. 'The "Grosvenor" as a Literary Theme' *Africana Notes and News* vol 5: 100–1.
100. As Captain Bligh, of *Bounty* notoriety, who spent some time at the Cape noted: 'Dutch farmers are fond of making expeditions into the country, that they may have opportunities of taking away cattle' (Kirby *Van Reenen's Journal* 11).

Chapter 6

1. Barnard 210.
2. Kuttel *Africana Notes and News* vol 12(4): 135.
3. Lichtenstein vol 1: 32.
4. Ignatius Muller to Lichtenstein (Lichtenstein vol 1: 279).
5. Van Reenen 4. The names of the Khoi were not recorded. The colonists were Jan Holtshausen and his son Philip, Jacob van Reenen, Hillegard Muller, who had been leader of the earlier rescue attempt, Cornelius and Ignatius Muller, Tjaart and Pieter van der Walt, Lodewyk Prins, Pieter Lombard, Stephanus Scheepers, Hendrick van Rensberg and Jacob Joubert (Theal *History of SA, 1652–1795* vol 2: 203).
6. Van Reenen 97.
7. Kirby *Source Book* 179; Van Reenen 100.
8. Van Reenen 101.
9. Carter 159.
10. Moodie *History of the Battles* vol 1: 73. Carter (at 160) mistakenly spells it 'Oemtonoue', but Kirby, who examined the original Dutch document confirmed 'Oemtonone' to be the correct spelling (Van Reenen 73).
11. Carter 160.
12. Peter Lombard, one of the expedition members, to Thompson in 1822 (Thompson vol 1: 171).
13. Kay 305. See also evidence of Johannes Lochenberg (Cory PR 1294).
14. Carter 160.
15. Van Reenen 101.
16. Evidence of Ngcetane, Bessie's grandson (Kay 303).
17. Gambushe, chief of the amaBomvana (Carter 160–1).
18. Van Reenen 102.
19. Van Reenen's Journal, 17 November 1790 (Carter 167).
20. Van Reenen's Journal, entries for 8, 14 and 21 November 1790 (Carter 162, 165, 169). Various individuals reported finding coins in the vicinity of the wreck in the 1800s; Captain Sidney Turner, who conducted salvage operations on the site a century after Van Reenen's visit, recognised the pit Van Reenen mentions 'as being between woods' on the banks of the Tezana stream and says that 'the little rising ground' yielded to him a good deal of coins and other small items (Turner to Stanford, Cory PR 1294. See also Holt *Africana Notes & News* vol 11: 88 and vol 12: 131–4).
21. Van Reenen 104.
22. Songomela, 'a man of intelligence', to Henry Francis Fynn (Fynn 100).
23. Van Reenen's Journal, 21 November 1790 (Moodie *History of the Battles* vol 1: 77).
24. Van Reenen's Journal, Friday 26 November 1790 (see also Moodie *History of the Battles* vol 1: 78).
25. See chap 1.
26. Muller to Captain Vaillant, c1792 (*African Studies* vol 13(1), (4); Van Reenen 92).
27. Kay 303.
28. Eliza Conway to William Bazley, 13 and 18 March 1907 (Cory MS 1907).
29. William Bazley, notes 29, 31 (*African Studies* vol 13: 18).
30. Evidence of Xelo, 1883 Native Laws and Customs Commission 432.
31. Evidence of Silas Pantshwa, 1883 Native Laws and Customs Commission 432.
32. Kay 306.
33. Bazley *The Natal Witness* 4 March 1907. In an apparent reference to the same boy, Bazley asks in a letter to John King, a white man who married one of Mdepa's daughters, 'Do you think it possible to get me the letter that Umdepa's brother [sic] wrote from Cape Town asking about his people?' (Bazley to King, 18 March 1907 (Cory MS 1831)).
34. Kirby *Source Book* 188.
35. Near the Nqabara River in Thembu territory (Van Reenen 115 fn 73).
36. Letter from the Landdrost of Swellendam to Governor Plettenberg, 4 December 1777 (Moodie *The Record* vol 3: 73).

37. Reproduced in Van Reenen 38.
38. Van Reenen 123.
39. Barnard 207–8.
40. Delegorgue 116.
41. Barnard 213. She is mistaken, of course, in saying that Bessie's sons' status depended on the colour of her skin – it was because she was the chief's Great Wife.
42. Carter 171.
43. Based on Kay 305 and Shrewsbury, quoted in *African Studies* vol 13: 7, who give her age as about 80 c1810.
44. For *ukuhlonipha*, see chap 2.
45. Evidence of Xelo, 1883 Native Laws and Customs Commission 432.
46. Van Reenen 58. The date should read 1782, not 1781.
47. Carter 160.
48. Tim Maggs *Natal and Zululand* 42; Beinart *Societies in Southern Africa* vol 7: 27. A missionary who met Bessie's son in the 1820s noted that he was growing sweet-potatoes (which come from South America), although none of his neighbours were (Kay 306).
49. Tim Maggs *Natal and Zululand* 58.
50. Van Reenen 101 ('eenige van geele slaaven en Bengaalders').
51. Fynn, published diary 113.
52. Fynn 113. See also his original diary (Natal Archives A1382 vol 16: 47–8).
53. See Bomvana genealogy opp 360 in Soga *SE Bantu*. John Cane, another Natal trader, thought they were survivors of the *Grosvenor* (*Records of Natal* vol 1: 18); but neither Jeffrey nor Mornegal (Michael?) appear in the East Indiaman's crewlist (See Kirby *Source Book* 197–201).
54. Fynn's original diary has 'Jantjie Lapoole', perhaps the slave Lapoot who had accompanied two Uitenhage brothers, Jan and Stephanus Cronje, on hunting/trading expedition into Xhosa territory in 1777–78 (Moodie *The Record* pt III: 73; Cronje genealogy in De Villiers & Pama).
55. Fynn's original diary vol 16: 48.
56. Fynn published diary 111 (original diary has 'Umbate' at 47).
57. Fynn 111.
58. See for example Moodie *The Record* pt V: 39, 41; Lichtenstein vol 1: 273–4.
59. Moodie *The Record* pt III 72–3.
60. Fynn's original diary, vol 16 48, Natal Archives A1382.
61. Moodie *The Record* pt I: 384.
62. Entry for September 1714 (Leibrandt *Precis of the Archives of the Cape of Good Hope* 260).
63. Journal of DG van Reenen 167.
64. Du Buis genealogy (De Villiers & Pama 116).
65. Lichtenstein vol 1: 368.
66. Bazley to *The Natal Witness*, 4 March 1907.
67. Kirby *New Light on the Grosvenor East Indiaman* 31; *Africana Notes and News* vol 2: 105. See also Forbes *Pioneer Travellers* 110.
68. *The Record* pt III: 48.
69. Evidence of the Mullers to Captain Vaillant. (*African Studies* vol 13(1): 4).
70. Hunter *Reaction to Conquest* 234–5, 266.
71. Alberti (1807) 93–4.
72. Charles Brownlee 245.
73. Hunter *Reaction to Conquest* 119.
74. Alberti (1807) 96.
75. Alberti (1807) 95–6.
76. 'When a chief dies, a new kraal is always made, but is frequently not more than six or seven hundred yards from the old site, and it may be nearer, if there should be a favourable spot' (Maclean, quoted by Shaw & Van Warmelo pt 1: 27).
77. Extract from Reverend Shaw's journal dated May 1829 (*Methodist Missionary Notices* vol 4: 200).
78. Soga *SE Bantu* 381, Bomvana genealogy opp 360; Pearce 3 (Cory PR 3665/3).
79. *SE Bantu* 364–5, Bomvana genealogy opp 360.
80. *SE Bantu* 363.
81. Soga *SE Bantu* 367–70, genealogy 381. Bluebuck skins

were a favourite and costly component of women's headdresses (Beinart *Societies of Southern Africa* vol 7: 28).
82. On the Inhlonyane River, about eight kilometres north of the Mbashe River (*SE Bantu* 372, 382; Cook 5).
83. Scully 68. He got her age all wrong though, saying she died 18 years after her marriage, whereas she actually died about 18 years after her second husband's death.
84. Evidence of her son Mdepa in 1829 (Kay 303).
85. Reverend Shrewsbury wrote in 1827 that she had 'died at a very advanced age, twelve or fourteen years ago', while Reverend Kay, writing two years later, said she had gone 'down to the grave full of days, twenty-two or three years ago' (Kay (1829) 305; Shrewsbury, 30 September 1827, quoted by Kirby *African Studies* vol 13(1): 7).
86. Scully 68–9. He says that Bessie asked for her little daughter to be at her side, but is mistaken in this as Bessy was not only fully grown but in her early 40s when her mother died.
87. Kay 294. Based on the funeral of the wife of an amaMolo chief.
88. Kay 294; Hunter 229; Cook 111.
89. Note from Rochlin, *African Studies* vol 15: 36.
90. Evidence of Xelo, 1883 Native Laws and Customs Commission 432.
91. Evidence of Hans Lochenberg to Sidney Turner (Cory PR 1294); Van Reenen 116 fn 93. See also Reverend Jenkins to Garden, 29 April 1852 (Kirby Papers, Strange Library, Jhb).
92. Prospero, in Shakespeare's 'The Tempest', Act IV, Scene 1.
93. Bessie's grandson to Reverend Kay (Kay 304).
94. Kay 304–5.
95. Scully 60.
96. 'Cattle raiding from neighbouring tribes was a usual and honourable pastime' (Hunter 132).
97. Alberti 90–2; Scully 66.
98. Scully 69.
99. Soga *SE Bantu* 383.
100. Kay 307
101. Extract from Palmer's journal, June 1834 (*Methodist Missionary Notices* vol 5: 422, vol 6: 597–8).
102. See chapters 9 and 10.
103. *SE Bantu* opp 360.

Chapter 7
1. Merriman (1853) 205.
2. Evidence of Xelo, 1883 Native Laws and Customs Commission 432.
3. Dan Wylie 24.
4. Bergh & Bergh 30; Hamilton (ed) *The Mfecane Aftermath*.
5. After Fritsch *Atlas* xxiii.
6. Beck (1987) 32; Wannenburgh *Forgotten Frontiersmen* 46.
7. Beck (1987) 35–6; Hamilton (ed) *Mfecane Aftermath* 63.
8. Lichtenstein vol 2: 283–5. Danster (or Nzwane) was a brother of Ndlambe, whose son later married Bessie's granddaughter (see chap 8). His people moved to the Orange River in about 1805–6, flourished on the northwest frontier and by 1826 had become a large, stable community possessed of large herds of cattle, sheep and goats, they were on excellent terms with the local colonists and kept a check on the raiding activities of neighbouring bands of San (Bannister 169; Beck (1987) 240–1).
9. Hall 129–31, 127.
10. Captain Moorsam to Commodore Christian, 1825 (Leverton (ed) *Records of Natal* vol 1: 64). In 1825 Thomas Pringle, the English settler and poet, reported that refugees as far south as the Kei River, near the Cape Frontier, 'had come from a country lying considerably to the North East, that they had been driven from their own land by a people of yellow complexion with black beards and long hair and who were armed with swords. This long-haired people must certainly be the Portuguese' (Thomas Pringle, letter dated 29 May 1825: *Records of Natal* vol 1: 61).
11. After Godee-Molsbergen 69.

12. Hall 136. Although the Zulus traded with the Portuguese, they despised and did not participate in their slaving activities (Fynn 179).

13. Map based on Elphick & Giliomee *Shaping of SA Society* 42, 249; Wannenburgh *Forgotten Frontiersmen* endpapers; Somerville 175–6, 215–17; Hall 127–31; Bergh & Bergh 17.

14. Lieut Rogers to Major Forbes, 27 May 1825 (Leverton (ed) *Records of Natal* I: 59).

15. *Records of Natal* II: 133; Shaw *Story of My Mission* 511; Kay 307; Beinart *Societies of Southern Africa* 7: 26.

16. Fynn 119.

17. Fynn 61–3.

18. Evidence of Henry Francis Fynn before Native Commission, 1852 (Bird 103).

19. Fynn 110.

20. Fynn 92–3. Charles Brownlee estimated that, of the 1 million people living between the Thukela and Mzimvubu rivers at the beginning of 1800, not more than 500 were left when he visited the area in 1836 (*Reminiscences* 78).

21. Although he goes on a bit about civilising the locals and bettering himself, Fynn's real objective 'was to open a trade in ivory' (Fynn 93, 103).

22. Evidence of John Shepstone *James Stuart Archives* vol 5: 301.

23. Fynn's mistaken use of 'Dawa' is probably due to the fact that his diary was written years after the events recorded here. (The original diary, wrapped in an elephant's ear, was lost when it was accidentally buried with his brother Frank; according to Zulu custom the deceased's possessions were interred with the corpse, and as the diary was in his possession at the time of his death it was thought to be his.) In the very next line Fynn mentions his host, the 'son of Mbethi, the blacksmith of the *Grosvenor*'; later historians have suggested that 'Mbethi' comes from the word meaning 'to beat', but to me it seems more likely to have meant 'Betty' or Bessie, and that Fynn had muddled her name with the blacksmith's. Ndawa means to fall down, and the blacksmith, John Bryan, was lame – that's why he had stayed behind at the wreck. (My thanks to Andiswa Vinolia Mbane for helping me here.)

24. See eg Thomas Philips, letter 13 June 1828 (Philips 337).

25. Evidence of Henry Francis Fynn before Native Commission, 1852 (Bird 103).

26. '… [T]he circumstance of his being descended from the English by his mother… may perhaps operate as one powerful motive in his mind' (Shaw *Journal*, 15 October 1827).

27. Shepstone 25.

28. Shrewsbury's letters 58.

29. *Transactions of the LMS* vol 1: 372, 376.

30. *Transactions of the LMS* vol 1: 424, 426; Enklaar (1988) 101.

31. *Transactions of the LMS* vol 1: 425. My thanks to Dr Julie Wells of Rhodes University for lending me her copy.

32. According to the census of 1904, 87,53 % of all 'Other races than European or white' were illiterate. (Karel Schoeman (1996) 95).

33. Heese & Lombard vol 5: 150–1.

34. Shaw *Story of My Mission* 492.

35. Stockenstrom (1887) 43; Collins (*The Record* pt V: 41).

36. Collins (*The Record* pt V: 41); Stockenstrom (1887) 43.

37. He was baptised in 1781, the son of Nicolaas van Lochenberg and his wife Gesina Vortman who farmed at Stellenbosch. (De Villiers & Pama).

38. *Thomas Baines' African Journal* vol 2: 275.

39. Fynn 196.

40. Kay 261.

41. Shrewsbury's letters 60.

42. Quoted by Thomas Philips, 19 March 1828 (Philips 333).

43. Shrewsbury's letters 60.

44. Shrewsbury's letters 60–1.

45. Shrewsbury letters 194 fn 46.

46. Shrewsbury 68–9.

47. Nathaniel Isaacs 155.

48. Shaka's nephew, sketched from a lithograph by GF Angas in Bergh & Bergh.

49. Butler 226–7.

50. Leverton (ed) *Records of Natal* vol 1: 272, 273.

51. Shrewsbury letters 82, 30 June 1828.

52. Fynn 130.

53. Evidence of Maziyana (*James Stuart Archives* vol 2: 274).

54. Ballard *Journal of Natal and Zulu History* vol 5: 50–1.

55. Extract from Major Dundas' report, 15 August 1828 (Leverton (ed) *Records of Natal* vol 2: 107).

56. GH 23\8 Cape Archives. Report Bourke to the Governor, 26 August 1828. Fynn's fellow Natal trader Henry Ogle ('Wohlo' in Zulu) also accompanied Shaka's forces – evidence of his son John Ogle (*James Stuart Archives* vol 5: 218).

57. Bell, letter to Lt-Col Somerset, 5 February 1829 (Leverton (ed) *Records of Natal* vol 2: 97).

58. From a photo in Butler 227

59. Evidence of Bazley (*James Stuart Archives* vol 1: 58); Leverton (ed) *Records of Natal* vol 2: 75, 78, 96; Stapleton *Faku* 84 and Dan Wylie *Savage Delight* 93–4.

60. Lieut Rogers to Major Forbes, 27 May 1825 (*Records of Natal* vol 1: 59).

61. Van Warmelo *History of Matiwane* 5.

62. *History of Matiwane* 44, 47.

63. Shrewsbury letters, 82.

64. Shaw *Journal* 130–1.

65. Shrewsbury 82.

66. Shaw *Journal* 131–2; extract from his letter of 13 August 1828 (*Methodist Missionary Notices* vol 4: 21).

67. Extract from Shaw's letter dated 13 August 1828 in *Methodist Missionary Notices* vol 4: 21.

68. Shaw *Journal* 132.

69. Reverend Shepstone, 26 and 31 May 1829 (*Methodist Missionary Notices* vol 4: 184).

70. Afrikaans: literally 'look-theres' (gawking sightseers).

71. Shaw *Journal* 131.

72. Shaw *Story of My Mission* 494.

73. Shaw *Journal* 131.

74. Evidence of Reverend Davies, Campbell to Bell, 11 July 1828 (Leverton (ed) *Records of Natal* vol 1: 215).

75. Shaw *Journal* 133; Shrewsbury's letters 61; Cory MS 14600 vol 8: 73.

76. Shaw *Story of My Mission* 498; Shrewsbury 82.

77. Shaw *Story of My Mission* 499.

78. Shrewsbury's letters 134, 136; Thomas Philips 242.

79. Cory PR 804; Kay (*Methodist Missionary Notices* vol 4: 71); Shrewsbury to Lt-Col Somerset, 12 June 1828; Campbell to Bell, 11 July 1828 (Leverton (ed) *Records of Natal* vol 1: 173, 215).

80. Cory PR 804; Dundas to Somerset, 14 July 1828 (*Records of Natal* vol 1: 236); Major Dundas' Report, 15 August 1828 (*Records of Natal* vol 1: 274).

81. Frank Brownlee *Transkeian Native Territories* 65; Bowker (Cory MS 14600 vol 8: 74).

82. Shaw *Journal* 166; Letter from Reverend Boyce, 11 May 1830 (*Methodist Missionary Notices* vol 4: 359).

83. Major Dundas' Report, 15 August 1828 (Leverton (ed) *Records of Natal* vol 1: 273).

84. Lt-Col Somerset to Bouke, 23 August 1828 (*Records of Natal* vol 1: 265–6); Extract from Bowker's diary (Cory MS 14600 vol 8: 74).

85. 'Advice of Council' 11 August 1828; Dundas to Somerset, 1 August 1828 (*Records of Natal* vol 1: 257, 259). Ngubencuka is also known as Vusani, which was his family name (Soga *SE Bantu* 477).

86. Excerpt from Ellenberger's 'History of the Basotho' in *History of Matiwane* 55.

87. Shaw *Journal* 199 fn 153, 142. Shaka was killed while meeting a delegation of Mpondo sent by Faku (*James Stuart Archives*).

88. Thomas Philips 277.

89. See Fynn 175–6.

90. Reverend W Eveleigh, quoted in Shepstone 28.

91. Kay 301.

92. Shaw *Journal* 159.
93. Shaw says he was the son of the Right-hand Wife (extract from Shaw's journal (*Methodist Missionary Notices* vol 4: 200), and he was therefore probably Sango's younger brother.
94. Letter from Reverend Boyce (*Methodist Missionary Notices* vol 4: 359), who identifies the original site of Morley as 'Amandola'. See also Reverend Basil Holt (*Africana Notes and News* vol 12: 280), who says the original site was on the Pondoland side of the Mtata River, 'at a place still called Nomadalo'.
95. Extract from Shaw's journal, (*Methodist Missionary Notices* vol 4: 204); Shaw *Journal* 131.
96. Shepstone, 4 June 1829 (*Methodist Missionary Notices* vol 4: 184).
97. Shepstone, 26, 31 May 1829 (*Methodist Missionary Notices* vol 4: 184); Shaw *Journal* 174, extract from Shaw's journal (*Methodist Missionary Notices* vol 4: 204–5): Reverend Shepstone, 21 Oct 1829 (*Methodist Missionary Notices* vol 4: 242).
98. Saunders & Derricourt *Beyond the Cape Frontier* 202.
99. Kay 284.
100. Shrewsbury's letters 75.
101. Kay 243.
102. Shrewsbury's letters 129.
103. This was Jumba, eldest son of the Right-hand House of Ndaba, king of the Thembu. (Stanford vol 1: 56–7).
104. Shepstone, 4 June 1829 (*Methodist Missionary Notices* vol 4: 184).
105. Soga *SE Bantu* 311. 'He refused to be ruled by Dingana as he said he was [Chaka's] equal.' (Evidence of Mbovu ka Mtshumayeli (*James Stuart Archives* vol 3: 31).)
106. Evidence of Mbovu ka Mtshumayeli (*James Stuart Archives* vol 3: 31).
107. Kay 326.
108. Evidence of William Lochenberg, his son, as told to the missionary Kay (Kay 326).
109. Kay 245. See also Holt *Where Rainbirds Call* 31. After his death, his wife Sara moved permanently to the mission station at Butterworth (Reverend Ayliffe, 17 July 1831 (*Methodist Missionary Notices* vol 5: 9–10)).
110. Kay 327.
111. Shaw *Journal* 163.
112. Kay 329; Reverend Shepstone, 21 October 1829 (*Methodist Missionary Notices* vol 4: 242).
113. Farewell to Campbell, 25 September 1829, Morley (Leverton (ed) *Records of Natal* vol 2: 141).
114. Reverend Shepstone, 21 October 1829 (*Methodist Missionary Notices* vol 4: 243).
115. Soga *SE Bantu* 313.
116. Stapleton *Faku* 25.
117. Isaacs 170.
118. Stubbs *The Reminiscences of Thomas Stubbs* 211.
119. Shepstone (*Methodist Missionary Notices* vol 4: 243).
120. Kay 330. Not undercover, but over-cover!
121. Shaw *Story of My Mission* 505.
122. Kay 332.
123. Shepstone (*Methodist Missionary Notices* vol 4: 247).
124. Stapleton *Faku* 27; Kay 333; Shrewsbury's letters 121.
125. Soga *SE Bantu* 314.
126. Kay 301.
127. Kay 294.
128. Kay 294–5.
129. Kay 319.
130. Kay 301–2, 307. Mdepa gave the missionary a spear, which he had often used in battle, as a gift to his mother's countryman as he termed it. Kay sent it to London to the Wesleyan Museum, but it can no longer be traced (*African Studies* vol 13: 10).
131. Kay 302.
132. Kay 307.
133. Letter from Reverend Shepstone at Morley, 4 April 1830 (*Methodist Missionary Notices* vol 4: 551–2).
134. Shaw *Story of My Mission* 506.
135. Extract from Reverend Boyce's letter dated 11 May 1830 (*Methodist Missionary Notices* vol 4: 358); Kay 286; Shepstone (*Methodist Missionary Notices* vol 4: 406, 552–3; vol 5: 74).
136. Evidence of WRD Fynn, 1883 Native Laws and Customs Commission 282. For more on the people who attended the missions see Chalmers *Tiyo Soga* 22–4; at Chumie they included a leper, a victim of narcolepsy, a lunatic, a cripple and a blind woman.
137. Palmer, 10 June 1833 (*Methodist Missionary Notices* vol 5: 421); Evidence of Xelo, 1883 Native Laws and Customs Commission 432.
138. Kay 307.
139. Kirby quoting Reverend Palmer (*African Studies* vol 13: 18).
140. Palmer (*Methodist Missionary Notices* vol 5: 422.
141. Lichtenstein vol 1: 327.
142. Palmer (*Methodist Missionary Notices* vol 5: 422); Whiteside (1906) 189.
143. Sketched from photo in Kirby (*African Studies* vol 13: opp 16). The picture was taken by the Natal settler George Cato, who made several journeys along the Wild Coast, penetrating as far south as the Mtata River in amaTshomane territory (*The Natal Witness*, 28 January 1853), and supplied to Kirby by the pioneer Africana collector and curator Killie Campbell: 'A Mrs. Andrews, aged 92 in 1924, who had known Cato well, handed me the photo, given to her by Cato, of Betsy's grandson, a descendant of an earlier wreck than the Grosvenor on the Pondoland coast...' ('Mr GC Cato' 1957 *Africana Notes and News* vol 12: 168).
144. Palmer's journal, 24 June 1834 (*Methodist Missionary Notices* vol 5: 598).
145. Reverend Boyce, 18 April 1831 (*Methodist Missionary Notices* vol 5: 39–41).
146. Letter from Satchel, 14 October 1834 (*Methodist Missionary Notices* vol 6: 73).
147. Palmer, 24 June 1834 (*Methodist Missionary Notices* 1832–1834: 593).
148. Evidence of Xelo, 1883 Native Laws and Customs Commission 432.
149. Evidence of Tomsomi kaGojwela (Holt *Where Rainbirds Call* 20).
150. Letter from Palmer, 28 May 1835 (*Methodist Missionary Notices* vol 6: 130).
151. Letter from Palmer, 16 May 1836 (*Methodist Missionary Notices* vol 6: 347); Gardiner *Narrative of a Journey to the Zoolu Country* 374.
152. Holt, *Africana Notes and News* vol 12: 282.
153. Taylor *Christian Adventures in South Africa* 323–4.
154. See chap 8.
155. Born c1777.
156. Bagela or Gela's descendants listed from Soga (*SE Bantu* 301), who mistakenly lists him as Bessie's son. He was actually her grandson – see chap 2, fn 59 above.
157. Baptised 1727; became a Stellenbosch burgher (De Villiers & Pama vol 1: 481).
158. Baptised 1781 (De Villiers & Pama vol 1: 481. No children listed, but Heese and Lombard give at least one, Gertruyda Margaretha, a daughter born to his first wife Alberta Maria Joubert van de Kaap, and baptised in 1802 (Heese & Lombard vol 5: 150).
159. Baptised 1784 (De Villiers & Pama vol 1: 481).
160. Baptised at Beecham Wood Mission, 7 November 1841 (MS 15223).
161. Baptised at Beecham Wood Mission, 17 July 1845 (MS 15223).
162. Cory MS 15223. Robert Sanders may have been descended from the *Grosvenor* survivor of the same name, who was seven years old at the time of the wreck. Kirby reports that in Pondoland in 1936 there was a coloured man called Robert Saunders, who was 'emphatic that his grandfather's name was Robert Sanders too, and that he had been wrecked near Port St Johns 150 years ago', ie at about the time of the *Grosvenor*. He himself had been born in 1903, and his

father Arthur in 1865, he said. The *Grosvenor* survivor
Robert Sanders would have been 81years old by then
and while it is just possible that he was Arthur's father –
Mdepa, after all, fathered a child when he was nearly
100 – it is more likely that there was another generation
between them (Kirby *Africana Notes and News* vol 15:
p 258), probably the Robert Sanders who married
Martha Lochenberg, granddaughter of old Nicolaas
and Sarah Lochenberg.

163. Cory PR 3516.
164. Cory MS 15223.
165. Bulpin *Natal and the Zulu Country* 78–9.
166. Cory PR 3516. The Reverend Charles White performed
the ceremony. Neither bride nor groom were literate,
both signing their names with an X. Old Sarah
Lochenberg's name had been passed on to her
granddaughter's generation, as had her Christianity, but
not her hard-won ability to read and write.

Chapter 8

1. Kay *Travels and Researches in Caffraria* 309. His use of
'unhappy' is a reference to their paganism, not to any
general misery!
2. Mouth of the Mapuzi River, Bomvanaland.
3. Alexander *Narrative of a Voyage of Observation* vol 2: 225.
4. Stanford (Cory PR 1294).
5. Kay 307, Dugmore *Reminiscences of an Albany Settler* 73,
Stanford (Cory PR 1294).
6. Whiteside (1906) 181–2.
7. Kay 307; Dugmore 73.
8. Private communication with Chief Siwani, his direct
descendant, at Tamarha, July 2000. Soga is more
ambivalent: 'Concerning Mdushane, some regard him as
Ndlambe's eldest son, others say Mhala, others again
Mgayi' (*SE Bantu* 150).
9. Hirst 'A quarrel between half-brothers' Kaffarian Museum
Xhosa History Series vol 1: 10, 13.
10. Soga *SE Bantu* 128.
11. Collins, 1809 (Moodie *The Record* pt V: 9); Soga *SE
Bantu* 129–30.
12. e.g. the imiDonge, amaMbalu and amaGqunu Khwebe.
13. General Report of Commandant Opperman (Moodie
The Record pt III: 67).
14. Spaarman vol 1: 239.
15. Drawn from Samuel Daniel (1803).
16. Cullinan 34–5.
17. One old colonist told Collins in 1809 that he had been
responsible for the death and enslavement of 3 200 San in
six years; another had killed 2 700 (Moodie *The Record*
pt V: 7). The Boers were not the only ones waging a war
of extermination against the San: Rharhabe pursued
them with such ferocity that at his death few were left in
his territory (Charles Brownlee 182).
18. Report of Field Sergeant Charl Marais (Moodie
The Record pt III: 81).
19. Collins, 1809 (Moodie *The Record* pt V: 23).
20. While the San were wiped out ruthlessly, the Khoi
suffered more of a cultural genocide; decimated by
imported diseases and deprived of their land, many were
absorbed into settler society as menial labourers, and as
early as 1820 many full-blooded Khoi had forgotten their
own language and could speak only Dutch.
21. Spelling and grammar as per original: Report of Field
Sergeant David van der Merwe to Commandant
Opperman (Moodie *The Record* pt I: 63).
22. Theal *History of SA 1652–1795* vol 2: 127.
23. Cory *Rise of SA* 31; Elphick & Giliomee *Shaping of
SA Society* 303.
24. Pinnock 9. It was the name given to one of their earliest
chiefs (see Soga *SE Bantu* 88). Despite intermarriage
between the two peoples, the Khoi and the amaXhosa
had a history of bloody strife. As far back as 1714, the
Bennebroek survivors had noted that the amaXhosa were
'in endless war with the lighter coloured Hottentots'
(Leibrandt's *Precis* 262).
25. *SE Bantu* 129–30.

26. Moodie *The Record* vol 5: 51.
27. Soga *The ama-Xosa* 25; Elphick & Giliomee *Shaping
of SA Society* 305; Milton *Edges of War* 34.
28. Sketched from a reproduction in *The Daily Dispatch*
5 December 2001.
29. Interview with Mdandala (Cory *Conversations* 111).
30. Peires *House of Phalo* 53; Alberti 99.
31. Lichtenstein vol 1: 407; *House of Phalo* 55. See also
Elphick & Giliomee *Shaping of SA Society* 313, 315.
32. Collins, 1809 (Moodie *The Record* pt V: 10). See also
Shaping of SA Society 308.
33. *Transactions of the LMS* vol 1: 396.
34. Paravicini 147.
35. Mostert 272–3.
36. Paravicini 248.
37. Soga *SE Bantu* 155.
38. Charles Brownlee 184.
39. Peires *House of Phalo* 59. Ngqika, says Soga scathingly,
'lacked the principles which govern honourable conduct'
(*SE Bantu* 155).
40. Elphick & Giliomee *Shaping of SA Society* 313.
41. Hart, quoted in Maclennan 118.
42. Elphick & Giliomee *Shaping of SA Society* 315.
43. Peires *House of Phalo* 66.
44. Atkinson (ed) *Supplementary Report on the Manuscripts
of Robert Graham* 89.
45. Thompson (1824) vol 2: 195; *House of Phalo* 65–6.
See also Maclennan 103, 107.
46. Pringle 275.
47. Graham to Lt-Col Reynell, 26 February 1812
(*Supplementary Report on the Manuscripts of Robert
Graham* 108.)
48. Campbell of the London Missionary Society (1813),
quoted in Maclennan 126.
49. Maclennan 125.
50. Beck (1987) 26.
51. Pringle 278.
52. Robert Hart, quoted in MacLennan 158.
53. After a watercolour by Paravicini (Bergh & Bergh 10).
54. Samuel Edward Krune Mqhayi (1875–1845), quoted in
Peires *House of Phalo* 177.
55. Burton's Notebooks, vol 8. (Cory MS 14600).
56. As Jeff Peires wrote, in his widely quoted passage: 'He
purchased it, danced for it, sold his wives for it, begged
for it, and ultimately died for it' (*House of Phalo* 82).
57. *House of Phalo* 79.
58. Eugene Marais, in Rousseau *The Dark Stream* 360–1.
A morphine addict, Marais had an intimate grasp of
substance abuse.
59. Meintjies 53.
60. There was about a five-year difference in age between the
two boys (Paravicini 248, fn 63). The homestead was
located where Burnshill mission station was later
established, about 12 kilometres from Middledrift on the
road to Keiskammahoek (Hammond-Tooke *Tribes of King
William's Town District* 73).
61. Soga *SE Bantu* 150.
62. *Tribes of King William's Town District* 73–4.
63. Maclean 19–20.
64. Thompson vol 2: 195–7; Kay 222.
65. Hammond-Tooke *Tribes of the Willowvale District* 37–8;
Shaw *Story of my Mission* 320.
66. Mackeurtan 87.
67. See for example Harriet Ward *Five Years in Kaffirland*, EE
Napier *Excursions in Southern Africa* and J E Alexander
Narrative of a Voyage of Observation....
68. *Autobiography of Sir Harry Smith* appendix II: 368.
69. Evidence of Mdandala (1910) Cory *Conversations* 111.
Soga refers to Nomsa as Gambushe's daughter, perhaps
because the elderly – and more famous – Gambushe
resided at Ntshunge's umzi (Sóga *SE Bantu* 371).
70. WRD Fynn to Hook, 11 March 1907, reproduced in
Hook *With Sword and Statute* 221–2. 'Nutshunci' is
Ntshunqe.
71. Theal *Blue Book on Native Affairs* (1885), from Brownlee
Transkeian Native Territories 34.

72. Tiyo Soga *Journal* 108.
73. Evidence of WRD Fynn, 1883 Native Laws and Customs Commission 269.
74. Soga *SE Bantu* opp 360.
75. See Appendix 2.
76. 1883 Native Laws and Customs Commission 432; Kay 304.
77. Letters to John King and Eliza Conway in March 1907 (Cory MS 1831, 1832). For more on Nochuku and her daughter Eliza Conway, see chap 11.
78. Stanford (Cory PR 1294).
79. Stanford (Cory PR 1294). Strachan had a grant of land stretching from the Mnenu to the Mthakatye mouth and inland for about 12 kilometres (*Where Rainbirds Call* 85).
80. The Mnenu enters the sea just south of Rame Head between Mngazi, when Gambushe lived prior to 1810, and the Mtata, where he afterwards relocated.
81. Fynn, letter in Hook 222.
82. Soga *SE Bantu*, genealogy of the Bomvana opp 360.
83. Evidence of Brown Nombida (Cory MS 15711(d) 4).
84. 'The Chiefs in those days always married Tembus as they wanted to have royal blood on both sides. The Xosas could not marry among one another as they were all related. Hintsa, however, did not marry a Tembu, he married a Bomvana…. Her name was Nomsa…' (evidence of Mdandala, Cory *Conversations* 111).
85. Evidence of Xelo, 1883 Native Laws and Customs Commission 432.
86. Soga *SE Bantu*, Genealogy of the amaBomvana opp 360.
87. Evidence of Mdandala, 1910 (Cory *Conversations* 111).
88. *Tribes of the Willowvale District* 31.
89. *Tribes of the Willowvale District* 49.
90. Soga *SE Bantu*, Xhosa genealogy opp 81.
91. Installed 2 June 1933. *Tribes of the Willowvale District* 27.
92. *Tribes of the Willowvale District* 51.
93. Soga *The ama-Xosa* 73.
94. Thompson vol 2: 198; Soga *SE Bantu* 164–6.
95. Peires *House of Phalo* 63.
96. Kay says it was in a beautiful little valley called 'Koogwala' (Kay 79).
97. Kay 224.
98. Lichtenstein vol 1: 341; Maclennan 190.
99. Willshire, quoted in Maclennan 191.
100. From a sketch by Thomas Phillips (1841), in *The Journals of Sophia Pigot*, after 94; Bryer and Hunt 14.
101. Willshire to Moodie (*History of the Battles* vol 1: 199).
102. Moodie *History of the Battles* vol 1: 199.
103. Soga *SE Bantu* 150; Fraser to Graham, 23 April 1819 (Cory *Rise of SA* vol 1: 391). Also Maclennan 190; Tylden *Africana Notes and News* vol 9: 137.
104. Kay 224.
105. Maclennan 174.
106. Based on Moodie, who knew the commanding officer, Willshire, personally. There were 100 men of the 38th and Major Frazer, who were at the Fish River during the battle, together with another 350 'European soldiers' who remained in Grahamstown, 'and a small detachment of mounted hottentots' under Sgt-Major Blakeway, which, according to an authority on the Cape Coloured Regular Regiments, numbered 121. (See Tylden *Africana Notes and News* vols 5 and 9, and Moodie *History of the Battles* vol 1: 198–9.)
107. Moodie *History of the Battles* vol 1: 198; Cory *Rise of SA* vol 1: 389, 391; Maclennan 190.
108. Holleman (ed) *Grahamstown – The Untold Story* 20. Visagie & Bergh 23 map 5, place his Great Place further south, closer to Alexandria. When Graham founded the town in 1812 Church Square was occupied by the burnt-out remains of a Boer farmhouse. They were rebuilt, to become the British Officers' mess. (Stockenstrom (1887) 63). The farm, De Rietfontein, had belonged to Lucas Meyer, and was named for the spring said still to exist somewhere under the Cathedral.
109. Tylden *Africana Notes & News* vol 9: 136.
110. Evidence of Tanco (Cory *Conversations* 124); Maclean

87. Makana was also known as Nxele and Lynx, a corruption of the Afrikaans 'links', in reference to his left-handedness. (For more see Appendix 5.)
111. Maclennan 187, 92; Peires *House of Phalo* 66–9.
112. Moodie *History of the Battles* vol 1: 197; Tylden *Africana Notes & News* vol 9: 136.
113. Maclennan 199.
114. Cory *Rise of SA* vol 1: 389.
115. There is a pronounced tendency in contemporary reports to downplay the size of the British force while overstating the number of Xhosa. Governor Somerset, for example, claimed that there were only 331 British and up to 15 000 Xhosa (Somerset to Torrens, 22 May 1819 (*Records of the Cape Colony* vol XII: 202–3).
116. Moodie *History of the Battles*, vol 1: 198; Pringle 283.
117. Pringle 283. A Khoi leader of the same name had been killed by Ndlambe's people in 1799 despite the fact that he was their ally and 'not withstanding… the many services he had rendered them' (Collins (1809) *The Record* pt V: 14). If this was Boesak's father, he certainly avenged his death. At the time of the battle Boesak was based near Theopolis, but later moved to the Katberg where he died sometime before 1834 (Kay 411).
118. Cory *Rise of SA* vol 1: 390, 387–8.
119. Moodie *History of the Battles* vol 1: 197.
120. John Patross to Reverend Shrewsbury (Shrewsbury's letters 79).
121. Maclennan 194.
122. See Cory *Rise of SA* vol 1: 390; Maclennan 197. Mdushane's spy Nquka was amongst the dead, captured and shot out of hand by a British soldier (Moodie *History of the Battles* vol 1: 198).
123. Cory *Rise of SA* vol 1: 390.
124. Kay 87.
125. Letter from Major Fraser to Col Graham, 23 April 1819 (Cory *Rise of SA* vol 1: 391).
126. Evidence of Mdandala (Cory *Conversations* 112). For more on Makana see Appendix 5.
127. Dugmore *Reminiscences of an Albany Settler* 73; Kay 86; Thompson vol 2: 199.
128. Peires *House of Phalo* 69.
129. See for example Lord Somerset to Sir Henry Torrens, 22 May 1819 (*Records of the Cape Colony* vol XII: 203).
130. Shrewsbury *Memorials*.
131. Pringle 283.
132. Stockenstrom (1887) 153–5. The amaNdlambe were accompanied by several white men – whom Stockenstrom (156–7) refers to as 'deserters' from the British military.
133. *Government Gazette* August–October 1819.
134. Moodie *History of the Battles* vol 1: 199; Pringle 284.
135. Maclennan 212; Moodie *History of the Battles* vol 1: 199–200.
136. *Government Gazette* 16 and 23 October 1819. See also Maclennan 216.
137. Thompson vol 2: 200.
138. *Journal of Harry Hastings* 52.
139. Shaw *Story of my Mission* 57.
140. Reynolds *Grahamstown From Cottage to Villa* 37.
141. Cory *Rise of SA* vol 1: 13.
142. Bryer & Hunt 41.
143. *Dompas* – the official pass notorious during the apartheid era, without which black South Africans were arrested and imprisoned. In 1809 laws had been promulgated obliging the Khoi of the eastern Cape to have a pass (Maclennan 57, see also Thomas Stubbs 70–1).
144. See Somerset to Dundas, 26 Jan 1828, which contained a pass for 'Chief Dusani' (Beck (1987) 137. The quote is from Jabavu 129.
145. The diary of young Sophia Pigot, for example, barely mentions them (Rainier (ed) *The Journals of Sophia Pigot*).
146. Kay 22.
147. Shaw (1860) 372.
148. Kay 78–9; Maclennan 220.

149. Hammond-Tooke *Tribes of King William's Town District* 71; Cory *Rise of SA* vol 1: 26.
150. Kay 73–4; Bergh & Visagie 41.
151. Besides Siwani she had at least two other children, both daughters, one of whom was called Nongogo (BK80 53 Evidence of Nomanti).
152. Shaw *The Story of My Mission* 456; Kay 74.
153. Kay 75. Without circumcision the Xhosa male would have remained a boy in the eyes of his people regardless of how old he was – unable to participate in battle, unable to marry, unable to inherit anything and unable to participate fully in the life of his community.
154. Cory *Rise of SA* vol 3: 179.
155. Huntley, letter to the Commissioners of Enquiry, 17 January 1826 (Stockenstrom *Autobiography* 254–5).
156. Extract from his journal, December 1825 (*Philipps, 1820 Settler* 288).
157. Kay 48; extract from Thomas Philipps' journal, December 1825 (Philipps 287).
158. Rose *Four Years in Southern Africa* 94.
159. Penis-sheath.
160. Kay 48.
161. Peires *House of Phalo* 84.
162. Kay 78, 86.
163. Shaw *The Story of My Mission* 383.
164. Kay 87–8.
165. Rose 55.
166. Rose 56.
167. Shrewsbury 347; Shaw *Story of My Mission* 429; Kay 70; evidence of Somana (Cory *Conversations* 124; Burton's Notebooks, MS 14600 vol 1: 22).
168. Peires *House of Phalo* 82.
169. Hammond-Tooke *Tribes of King William's Town District* 94. For more see Soga *SE Bantu* 151; Shaw *Story of My Mission*.
170. Kay 163, 169. See especially *House of Phalo* 84.
171. Laidler & Gelfand 118, 149, 217, 346. My thanks to Dr Murray Gainsford of Grahamstown for information on the disease (private communication, July–August 2001).

Chapter 9
1. Harriet Ward (1848) vol 1: 235.
2. Charles Brownlee *Reminiscences* 245.
3. Broster and Bourn 84.
4. Reverend Dugmore, quoted in Shaw *Journal* 186 fn 66.
5. Charles Brownlee 245.
6. Broster and Bourn 78 & 84.
7. Based on Butler *The 1820 Settlers* 60.
8. Peires *House of Phalo* 54. See also Thomas Philipps 158.
9. Elphick & Giliomee *Shaping of SA* 307.
10. Stockenstrom 124.
11. Stockenstrom 252–3; Philipps 298.
12. Dugmore 73.
13. Based on his age of about 20 in 1847. Pottinger to Grey, March 1847 (Le Cordeur & Saunders *The War of the Axe* 31).
14. Broster and Bourn 22–3.
15. Based on a contemporary 'smelling-out' at Chief Pato's Great Place (Shaw *Journal* 106–8).
16. Tortures included being smeared with honey and bound to a nest of angry ants or tied down and covered with hot stones (Lichtenstein vol 1: 316).
17. Kay 78.
18. Appleyard 73 fn 42; Hammond-Tooke *Tribes of King William's Town District* 75.
19. Seyolo was about a decade older than Siwani – see Pottinger to Grey, March 1847 (Le Cordeur & Saunders *The War of the Axe* 31; Dugmore 72). It was probably his group of *abakwetha* Reverend Kay had seen in 1825 – 'all fine, active, and interesting lads; one of whom was Dushani's son' (Kay 75).
20. Ayliff, 14 July 1836 (*Methodist Missionary Notices* vol 6: 382).
21. Young 53.
22. Shaw *Journal* 143; *Tribes of King William's Town District* 74; Young 47–9, 56.
23. The amaXhosa had been using horses for many years and their use was now widespread.
24. Shrewsbury's letters 122–3.
25. Shaw *Journal* 143.
26. Charles Brownlee *Reminiscences* 174.
27. Dugmore 72.
28. Alexander *Narrative of a Voyage* vol 2: 222. He gives her age as almost 40 in 1835. Both concur roughly with Cathcart who says she was in her early fifties in 1852 (see below).
29. Lichtenstein vol 1: 338.
30. Shaw *Journal* 143–4.
31. Alexander *Narrative of a Voyage* vol 2: 222–3.
32. Lichtenstein vol 1: 259; Mostert 272–3; Hammond-Tooke *Tribes of the Willowvale District* 55, 61.
33. Fleming 17.
34. Charles Brownlee *Reminiscences* 302.
35. Chief John Tzatzoe (Peires *House of Phalo* 93).
36. Goldswain vol 1: 82.
37. Alexander vol 1: 357.
38. Dugmore *Reminiscences of an Albany Settler* 73.
39. Van Warmelo *History of Matiwane* 241; Whiteside 199; Dugmore *Reminiscences of an Albany Settler* 67, 74.
40. From an etching by Pons (Featherstone 88).
41. Dugmore *Reminiscences of an Albany Settler* 72.
42. Dugmore *Reminiscences of an Albany Settler* (72–4) calls him 'R.B.' of Clumber, a village on the Torrens River settled by the Nottinghamshire group led by Thomas Calton. Richard Bradfield is the only member of the party whose initials & age fit. (Morse-Jones *Roll of the British Settlers* 12; Nash *The Settler Handbook* 52–4).
43. Napier *Excursions in SA* (1849) vol 2: 303
44. Adams *Buck Adams' Narrative* 246.
45. Godlonton *The Irruption of the Kaffir Hordes* pt II & III 202.
46. Alexander vol 1: 121; vol 2: 223.
47. Alexander vol 1: 366.
48. Sir Benjamin D'Urban, letter to the Earl of Aberdeen, 19 June 1835.
49. Harriet Ward, *Five Years in Kaffirland* vol 2: (?) 54; vol 1: 262 .
50. Dugmore *Reminiscences of an Albany Settler* 73–4.
51. Steedman vol 2: appendix IV 340; Whiteside 199.
52. *Autobiography of Harry Smith* vol 1: 68–77.
53. *Autobiography of Harry Smith* vol 2: 376–7 appendix II.
54. *Autobiography of Harry Smith* vol 1: 77; vol 2: 65.
55. Meintjies 59–60.
56. Cory *Rise of SA* vol 2: 396.
57. Alexander vol 2: 184. Her pale complexion may have been the legacy of a Khoi ancestor. (Stretch 71) and there is no evidence that Msutu was linked to Bessie, though the Thembu royal family, to which she belonged, did have links with the Tshomane. In the second half of the 17th century Hlanga, son of the Thembu King Nxego, was deposed by his brother Dlomo and driven across the Mbashe, where he married Nobeta,

> 'the daughter of a chief of the Tshomane, the former royal house of the Mpondo, also in exile. This woman was so attractive and so energetic, that in the praise-verses (*izibongo*) of her husband's people, she became the central figure, and in time the clan came to be called the Qiya, after her father'

(Bennie in Duggan-Cronin vol 3: 38; see also Soga *SE Bantu* 466, genealogy of the abeThembu).
58. Alexander vol 2: 31.
59. Stretch 177 fn 42; Meintjies 193.
60. After a drawing by Charles Bell, Bergh & Bergh 44.
61. Stretch 46, 61.
62. Alexander vol 2: 71.
63. Cory *Rise of SA* vol 3: 238.
64. *Autobiography of Harry Smith* 76, 449.
65. Stretch 86.

66. From an engraving by CC Michell (Bergh & Bergh 41).
67. Letter from Reverend Ayliff, 14 July 1836 (*Methodist Missionary Notices* vol 6: 382).
68. Alexander vol 2: 129; Saxe Bannister xci.
69. Goldswain vol 1: 101.
70. *Autobiography of Harry Smith* vol 2: 374.
71. D'Urban to Smith, 10 May 1835 (*The Irruption of the Kaffir Hordes*, Narrative 163).
72. For more see Naidoo 65–81 and Sir Harry Smith's account in his *Autobiography*.
73. Naidoo 67.
74. George Wood to 1883 Native Laws and Customs Commission 161.
75. Drawn from a photo in Butler *The 1820 Settlers* 272.
76. Hook 223.
77. *Autobiography of Harry Smith* vol 2: 368 appendix II.
78. Alexander vol 2: 222–3; 'Public Documents… of Sir Benjamin D'Urban' 108.
79. *Autobiography of Harry Smith* vol 2: 76–7; *The Grahamstown Journal* 6.8.1835. Pop psychology would probably excuse George Southey on the grounds of his troubled childhood: Richard, George and William were the sons of the leader of the Southey party of 1820 Settlers, an abusive (and later indigent) parent against whom they laid an official complaint in 1827 (Cory MS 17038 vol 4: 591). The recent past had not been kind either: in the 1835 war the brothers were members of the Corps of Scouts, made up entirely of settlers whose homes had been destroyed by the Xhosa; George was particularly hard hit and virtually bankrupted. (Naidoo 167 fn 75).
80. Peires *House of Phalo* 84, 223 fn 42.
81. Bisset 116.
82. Interview with Old Maseti (Cory *Conversations* 108); Cory MS 14600 vol 1: 19; Meintjies 141; Charles Brownlee 310.
83. Appleyard 87; Thomas Philipps 258.
84. Mostert 874, 883. One of the very few chiefs to side with the British was Mqayi, the Ndlambe chief who resided near Fort Peddie (Appleyard 50, 55, 57).
85. Italics as per original, D'Urban to Cox, 12 May 1835 (Theal *Documents of 1835* 157–8).
86. Appleyard 47–8, 54, 58ff.
87. Adams *Buck Adams' Narrative* 181.
88. Peires *House of Phalo* 94, 118.
89. Interview with Lindinxiwa (Cory *Conversations* 101; Cory MS 17038 vol 4: 606–7).
90. Mostert 876.
91. Adams *Buck Adams' Narrative* 126.
92. Thomas Philipps, who employed some of them, said although they could not at first speak a word of English or Dutch, 'they are so quick and so desirous of doing everything we wish, that they really do very well already…' Some were traumatised by their refugee experiences: a little girl who had been stabbed twice on the side of her head with an assegai refused a gift of a sixpence, saying ' "bad, very bad", and putting her little hand across her chest said "Knife cut man's head off", alluding to the impression of the King's *head* only on the sixpence' (Thomas Philipps 252–3).
93. Saunders & Derricourt *Beyond the Cape Frontier* 110–12, 114–15.
94. Morse-Jones *Roll of British Settlers* 104; *The Lower Albany Chronicle* 69, part 3 (1841–1850). See chap 11 for more.
95. Appleyard *War of the Axe* 64.
96. Appleyard 64.
97. Adams *Buck Adams' Narrative* 159.
98. Adams 144.
99. Appleyard 51.
100. Appleyard 36, 50, 55, 57.
101. Appleyard 89; Harriet Ward *Five Years in Kaffirland* vol 2: 54.
102. Sketched from a photo in Mostert *Frontiers*, after 1120.
103. Pottinger to Grey, March 1847 (Le Cordeur & Saunders *War of the Axe* 31).
104. Quoted in Le Cordeur & Saunders 31.
105. Soga *SE Bantu* 225.
106. Theal *History of SA Since 1795* vol 7: 15.
107. Bisset *Sport and War* 89.
108. Bisset *Sport and War* 89.
109. Hook 12; SE *Bantu* 226, 229. Soga gives the Xhosa spelling as Mgwangqa.
110. Peires *House of Phalo* 148.
111. Appleyard *War of the Axe* 69.
112. Bisset 95.
113. Soga *SE Bantu* 227.
114. Harriet Ward vol 2: 97.
115. Appleyard 97–8, 100–1.
116. Napier *Excursions in Southern Africa* vol 2: 289
117. Napier *Excursions in Southern Africa* vol 2: 292–3.
118. Napier vol 2: 321.
119. Adams *Buck Adams' Narrative* 246.
120. Godlonton & Irving *Narrative of the Kaffir War* 65.
121. Godlonton & Irving *Narrative of the Kaffir War* 66.
122. Theal *History of SA Since 1795* vol 7: 60.
123. Stapleton *Maqoma* 173.
124. Fleming *Kaffraria* 24.
125. GH 8/45. Maclean to Woosnam, 2 April 1847.
126. Theal *History of SA Since 1795* vol 7: 100.
127. *History of SA Since 1795* vol 7: 100.
128. BK 15, Gaika Commission, Chiefs in British Kaffaria, January 1853.
129. Cathcart to Pakington, 12 October 1852 (Cathcart *Correspondence* 128).
130. Adams *Buck Adams' Narrative* 246 fn 3.
131. Deacon *The Island* 49–52.
132. Cathcart to Col Mackinnon, 24 July 1852 (Cathcart *Correspondence* 108).
133. Meintjies *Sandile* 233.
134. This is correct: Nonibe's grandfather was Sango, the Pondo prince, and her grandmother, of course, was Bessie (Cathcart to Darling, 4 September 1853 (Cathcart *Correspondence* 372)).
135. Cathcart to Pakington, 12 October 1852 (Cathcart *Correspondence* 129).
136. Cathcart to MLC, 20 May 1853 (Cathcart *Correspondence* 213–14).
137. Cathcart to MLC, Grahamstown, 20 May 1853 (Cathcart *Correspondence* 212–13).
138. Cathcart to Darling, 4 September 1853 (Cathcart *Correspondence* 374).

Chapter 10
1. As told by Nongqawuse to William Fynn (Cory *Conversations* 41).
2. Theal *History of SA Since 1795* vol 7: 198.
3. Broster and Bourn 22.
4. Theal *History of SA Since 1795* vol 7: 151–2.
5. Reverend Thomas, letter dated 3 June 1855 (Cory MS 6214).
6. Varley & Matthew *Cape Journals of Archdeacon Merriman* 224.
7. Peires *The Dead Will Arise* 34.
8. '… [H]e knew Dutch well…. But [his] desire of learning English was so great that we ended up usually conversing in that tongue' Varley & Matthew *Cape Journals of Archdeacon Merriman* 52.
9. *Cape Journals of Archdeacon Merriman* 53, 105–6, 123.
10. *Cape Journals of Archdeacon Merriman* 127.
11. Drawn from a contemporary sketch in Peires *The Dead Will Arise* 160.
12. Governor Harry Smith, quoted in *The Dead Will Arise* 12.
13. John Rich's diary, quoted in *The Dead Will Arise* 18.
14. Varley & Matthew *Cape Journals of Archdeacon Merriman* 64, 71, 77, 124 etc.
15. Varley & Matthew *Cape Journals of Archdeacon Merriman* 111.
16. *Cape Journals of Archdeacon Merriman* 205.
17. Map based on 'Gxarha River' by WO West in Kei Mouth Shell Museum and 3228CB/CD 1:50 000.

18. Peires *The Dead Will Arise* 36 & 44 fn 112.
19. Goldswain vol 2: 191 fn 355.
20. Charles Brownlee 127.
21. Charles Brownlee 127.
22. Charles Brownlee 127.
23. Charles Brownlee 133.
24. Peires *The Dead Will Arise* 121–2.
25. *The Dead Will Arise* x.
26. Alberti *Tribal Life and Customs of the Xhosa* 13.
27. BK 89, Report by George Shepstone, 18 October 1856.
28. *The Dead Will Arise* 79–80.
29. Hook 223.
30. Soga *SE Bantu* 239.
31. For Nomsa as unbeliever see Chalmers *Tiyo Soga* 117–18.
32. BK 89 'Secret Information 1856–1857', Report dated 20 June 1856; Charles Brownlee 133.
33. Gawler, magistrate to the Ndlambe, quoted in Peires *The Dead Will Arise* 145.
34. *The Dead Will Arise* 99.
35. Drawn from a photo in Mostert *Frontiers*, after 1120.
36. *The Dead Will Arise* 121.
37. *The Dead Will Arise* 118; Meintjies 249–50. Sandile tried to hide his support for the movement from the Ngqika commissioner, Brownlee, whose opposition had earned him the name 'Napakade', that is 'Never' (as in 'these prophecies will *never, never* come true' (Charles Brownlee 127).
38. Letter from Soga to John Henderson Soga, 2 September 1857 (Chalmers *Tiyo Soga* 142).
39. Mhala was chief of the Ndlambe around Fort Waterloo on the Geneka River, about 40 kilometres from King William's Town (Cory *Conversations* 44 fn 79). Dismissed by Archdeacon Merriman as a 'dirty, scrubby-looking savage in an old blanket, red with clay', he was in fact a shrewd politician.
40. *The Dead Will Arise* 121; Chalmers *Tiyo Soga* 109; Charles Brownlee 133.
41. Brownlee to Maclean, 18 October 1856 (Cory MS 8295).
42. Goldswain vol 2: 191–4.
43. Alexander vol 2: 222–3.
44. BK 89, Shepstone to Maclean, 8 August 1856.
45. BK 89, Shepstone to Maclean, 8 August 1856.
46. Peires *The Dead Will Arise* 16, 194.
47. BK 89, Shepstone to Maclean, 8 August 1856, and report from Fort Murray, 19 September 1856; Peires *The Dead Will Arise* 119, 176.
48. BK 15, Brownlee to Maclean, 21 March 1857.
49. *The Dead Will Arise* 171.
50. BK 89, Shepstone to Maclean, 8 August 1856.
51. Peires *The Dead Will Arise* 180.
52. BK 80: Kayser to Maclean, 20 June 1860.
53. *The Dead Will Arise* 87.
54. *The Dead Will Arise* 150.
55. BK 80, Agent with Siwani, 24 February, 3 March 1857.
56. Interview with Isiah Gwelala (Cory *Conversations* 97).
57. One such camp was on the Tshabo River in Siwani's uncle Mhala's country (*The Dead Will Arise* 209) and it is possible that Nonibi and Siwani sought refuge there.
58. Evidence of Sijako (Cory *Conversations* 121).
59. Evidence of Maseti (Cory *Conversations* 109).
60. Evidence of WFR Fynn (Cory MS 14600 vol 10: 131).
61. Mrs Brownlee, in Charles Brownlee 137.
62. Mrs Brownlee, in Charles Brownlee 138.
63. Interview with Mr Ralph, Cory *Conversations* 178.
64. From a photograph taken during his imprisonment on Robben Island c1860, in Charles Brownlee xxxix.
65. Peires *The Dead Will Arise* 245.
66. Theal *History of SA Since 1795* vol 7: 212-1-3; Cory *Conversations* 43 fn 68.
67. *The Dead Will Arise* 210, 212.
68. *Princess Emma* 46.
69. *The Dead Will Arise* 225.
70. Statement by Mhala's councillor, Kwitchi, to Major Gawler, January 1858 (Cape Parliamentary Papers, G5 of 1858).
71. Peires *The Dead Will Arise* 319.
72. *The Dead Will Arise* 335–6; Theal *History of SA Since 1795* vol 7: 213.
73. Map information from Bergh & Visagie 57.
74. Soga *SE Bantu* 373.
75. Interview with WRD Fynn (Cory *Conversations* 42).
76. Notes of WRD Fynn in Burton, Cory MS 14600 vol 10: 132.
77. Cape of Good Hope Parliamentary Papers, G5 of 1858.
78. Sketched from a photo in the South African Library, Ref INIL 8327.
79. Chalmers *Tiyo Soga* 146.
80. Testimony of Nombanda, 28 February 1858 (Cape of Good Hope Parliamentary Papers, G5 of 1858).
81. Chalmers *Tiyo Soga* 146.
82. Peires *The Dead Will Arise* 336.
83. Notes of WRD Fynn in Burton, Cory MS 14600 vol 10: 132.
84. On 'Glenshaw' farm, Alexandria, Eastern Cape Province.
85. Stanford 5.
86. Cape of Good Hope Parliamentary Papers, G5 of 1858, 'Statement of probable number of kraals, population and firearms…'; Theal *History of South Africa Since 1795* vol 7: 213 (1964 reprint).
87. Cape of Good Hope Parliamentary Papers, G5 of 1858.
88. *History of South Africa Since 1795* vol 7: 214.
89. BK 89, 5 October 1857.
90. Peires *The Dead Will Arise* 179–80.
91. *The Dead Will Arise* 214; BK 80, Kayser to Maclean 20 June 1860.
92. Soga *SE Bantu* 373–4.
93. BK 80 Statement by Siwani, 5 December 1859; Burton 41.
94. BK 80: Proceedings of a Board Assembled at Tamacha, evidence of Pali 24, and evidence of Kobi 29.
95. Bk 80: Proceedings of a Board, evidence of Notasi, 18, 19.
96. Soga *The ama-Xosa* 62 ; Molema 142.
97. Hunter 187–8.
98. Schoeman 22.
99. Stretch 61, 62.
100. Custom forbade a man from having sex with his wife until her child was weaned (Hunter 158–9).
101. BK 80, Proceedings of a Board, evidence of Nomkinti 33.
102. BK 80: Statement by Siwani taken at Fort Murray, 5 December 1859, and Proceedings of a Board, evidence of Njintsi 36.
103. BK 80: Proceedings of a Board, 17, 18.
104. BK 80: Proceedings of a Board, evidence of Nomanti 54; Statement by Siwani dated 5 December 1859.
105. BK 80: Proceedings of a Board, evidence of Nomanti 54; evidence of Nomvato 58–9; statement by Siwani dated 5 December 1859.
106. BK 80: Proceedings of a Board, evidence of Miti 27.
107. BK 80: Statement by Siwani, 5 December 1859.
108. BK 80: Proceedings of a Board, evidence of Nomvato 48, evidence of Siwani 46–7. Edye could not have been very young, since he had served as a lieutenant in the Fort Peddie Fingo Levy in 1852 – seven years before (*The Grahamstown Journal* 10 July 1852).
109. BK 80: letter dated 10 November 1859.
110. BK 80: Proceedings of a Board, Evidence of Nonibe 30.
111. BK 80: Proceedings of a Board, Evidence of Nonibe 22, Evidence of Miti, brother of Siwani 27, Statement by Umiyane dated 5 December 1859.
112. See eg BK 80 Proceedings of a Board 40.
113. BK 80: Proceedings of a Board, Evidence of Banyi (Bangayi) 38.
114. BK 80: Proceedings of a Board, evidence of Nomkinti 34.
115. BK 80: Report dated 23 December 1859.
116. Eg BK80: Proceedings of a Board 44.
117. BK 80: Report dated 23 December 1859.
118. BK 80: Report dated 23 December 1859.
119. *The Grahamstown Journal* 13 June 1870; Cory MS 14878/4 baptism No 3064. Edye died in Grahamstown

two years later, in 1874 (*Grahamstown Journal* 15 May 1874).

120. Dugmore 74.

121. Personal communication, 9 July 2003.

122. BK 89: Kaiser to Brownlee, 12 January 1863.

123. Trollope 160–1.

124. Trollope 160–1.

125. For promises see D'Urban to Cox, 12 May 1835 (Theal *Documents Relating to the Kaffir War of 1835* 157–8).

126. Hammond-Tooke *Tribes of King William's Town District* 75.

127. BK 80: Report dated 23 December 1859; Deacon 51–2.

128. Crealock *Frontier War Journal* 74 fn 138.

129. Crealock 35 fn 44, 57.

130. Trollope 160 fn 17 and Cory MS 14886, MS 14886/10.

131. Van Warmelo *History of Matiwane* 64.

132. Drawn from a photo in AM Duggan-Cronin *The Bantu Tribes of South Africa*.

133. The information in Soga *SE Bantu* opp 81 is largely incorrect. See instead Hammond-Tooke *Tribes of King William's Town District* 23.

Chapter 11

1. Evidence of WRD Fynn, 1883 Native Laws and Customs Commission 283.

2. Evidence of WRD Fynn, 1883 Native Laws and Customs Commission 283.

3. Frank Brownlee *Transkeian Native Territories* 28.

4. Evidence of WRD Fynn, 1883 Native Laws and Customs Commission 271.

5. Soga *The ama-Xosa* 72.

6. W T Brownlee *Reminiscences of a Transkeian* 72.

7. Soga *The ama-Xosa* 104–7.

8. Drawn from a photo in Mostert *Frontiers*, following 1120.

9. Hammond-Tooke *Tribes of Umtata District* 17. While he was in exile a large portion of his territory: 5 000 square miles of 'rich and varied scenery – crag, kloof and precipice, undulating plain and broad valley, forests of flowering trees, foaming rivers and streams and lustrous in the fervid bloom of semi-tropical shrubs a land of perpetual verdure, of pure and health-giving breezes...' had been seized by the British, renamed Fingoland and resettled with Mfengu and survivors of the Cattle-Killing. The rest remained uninhabited until Sarhili's return in 1865. The British appointed an Agent to the territory but his function was purely diplomatic and the king remained independent (Cory MS 14600 vol 10: 135, 137–8).

10. Soga *SE Bantu* 482.

11. Emma, letter to Miss Smart, her former headmistress, 26 March 1864 (Hodgeson *Princess Emma* 111).

12. Report in *The Great Eastern* and letter from Warner to Glover (*Princess Emma* 119–20).

13. Letter from Warner to Glover (*Princess Emma* 120).

14. Taylor *Christian Adventures in South Africa* 301.

15. Theal *History of South Africa Since 1795* vol 8: 57 (1964 edition).

16. Frank Brownlee *Transkeian Native Territories* 28.

17. Burton Notebooks, Cory MS 14600 vol 8: 1.

18. Burton Notebooks, Cory MS 14600 vol 2: 61.

19. She returned after the 1877 War of Ngcayecibi (Soga *SE Bantu* 249).

20. Frank Brownlee 30; *SE Bantu* 484–5.

21. Hodgeson *Princess Emma* 145; *SE Bantu* 485.

22. *Princess Emma* 144.

23. Pritchard *Friends and Foes in Transkei* 157–8.

24. Stanford vol 2: 10. See also *Selected Articles from the Cape Monthly Magazine* 170–1: Ngangelizwe was 'decidedly unable to take care of himself' after a 'great beer-drinking orgie'.

25. Callaway *Pioneers in Pondoland* 70.

26. Evidence of Xelo, 1883 Native Laws and Customs Commission 432.

27. See genealogy below.

28. Hodgeson *Princess Emma*, 107; W T Brownlee 71. The most famous member of the Thembu royal family,

incidentally, is the well-known revolutionary, jailbird and first democratic president of South Africa, Nelson Mandela. His clan name, Madiba, denotes his descent from the king of that name who ruled several generations before Ngangelizwe.

29. Evidence of Xelo, 1883 Native Laws and Customs Commission 432. See also Cory PR 1294.

30. 1883 Native Laws and Customs Commission 439.

31. Evidence of Xelo, 1883 Native Laws and Customs Commission 432.

32. Evidence of Bazley, *James Stuart Archives* vol 1 56.

33. He also collected fossils and was 'a great reader and scholar, a man of considerable mental and physical activity and a renowned Zulu linguist' (Bulpin *Natal and the Zulu Country* 376–82).

34. Quoted by Kirby *African Studies* vol 13: 18–19.

35. Kay 307.

36. Fynn 112.

37. Shaw *Journal* 133; Shrewsbury *Letters* 61.

38. Shepstone (*Methodist Missionary Notices* vol 4: 184).

39. Shepstone (*Methodist Missionary Notices* vol 4: 184).

40. Copy of letter from Reverend Jenkins, dated 29 April 1852, in Prof Percival Kirby's papers, Strange Library, Johannesburg.

41. Letter from Satchell, 14 October 1834, Buntingville, *Methodist Missionary Notices*.

42. Natal Archives, Bird papers vol 6: 55, 93.

43. Evidence of RPH King, 1942 (Killie Campbell Africana Library, MS 1026a).

44. Evidence of Ndongeni ka Xoki, 1905 (*James Stuart Archives* vol 4: 240).

45. Fynn 245.

46. His Great Wife was Fihlwase. Another was called Mdumayi. At least one child from these marriages, Henry King, was still alive in the 1920s. He lived at Ixopo and had 8 children. Evidence of Dinya ka Zokozwayo, 1905 (*James Stuart Archives* vol 1: 112); evidence of Ndongeni ka Xoki (*James Stuart Archives* vol 4: 240); Natal Archives, MSCE 2792/54.

47. Scallan 129.

48. Scallan 129.

49. *Bailie's Party of 1820 Settlers* 36, 149.

50. Morse-Jones *Roll of the British Settlers* 45.

51. Cory MS 1831.

52. See MD Davies *Twin Trails: the Story of the Fynn and Southey Families*, Salisbury, 1974.

53. Nash 83. It's now an instant-lawn farm and nursery, but still retains its original name, Standerwick

54. Butler 151.

55. Sketched from a survey by J Knoebel in 1820, 21 & 22 in Philipps' endpapers.

56. Beck (1987) 338, Appendix C, 294, 269 fn 41–2, 279 fn

57. Beck 333.

58. Beinart (1982) 24–5.

59. *The Council of Advice at the Cape of Good Hope* 320–1, 328; Beck 268, 289, 320.

60. Letter quoted by Reverend Kay 382.

61. Powell (Cory MS 7391) 94.

62. *Grahamstown Journal* 20 February 1847: 3.

63. Bazley, writing to Nochuku and John King's daughter in 1907, mentions a 'hut' belonging to her father near the 'St Johns' (Mzimvubu) River. William Bazley to Eliza King, 20 March 1907 ({Cory MS 1832).

64. Cory MS 15223.

65. Reverend Thomas, letter from Morley dated 20 April 1846 (Cory MS 6212).

66. *Grahamstown Journal* 2 October 1858, 9 October 1858.

67. Cory MS 15223 and MS 15015.

68. Pigot 40–2.

69. Stubbs 104.

70. *Lower Albany Chronicles* vol 1: 45, vol 2: 25 (revised ed), Nash 88; Cory map M/757/G1 MP 145.

71. Beck (1987) 338, Appendix C, 294, 269 fnn 41–2, 279 fn 63.

72. Beck 269 fnn 41–2. Beads went in and out of fashion

quickly, and Conway was probably hoping that his stock, of a colour or size no longer fashionable among the Xhosa of the border region, would still be in demand among the more remote Thembu.

73. Cory *Rise of SA* vol 2: 343.

74. Beck (1987) 323–4.

75. Fynn 321; Soga *SE Bantu* 442, Evidence of Mahaya (*James Stuart Archive* vol II: 114). Date based on Hammond-Tooke *Tribes of Mount Frere District* 38–9.

76. Beck 269, 338–9.

77. Beck 338; Morse-Jones *Roll of the British Settlers* 45; Nash 26; Cory MS 7391: 51. As Kew's trader's licence gives his occupation as 'tailor', he is probably the same P Kew who later did some tailoring for the Zulu King Dingane in Natal in 1835 (Beck 338; Fynn 255).

78. *Grahamstown Journal* 16 October 1837; *Roll of the British Settlers in South Africa* 104.

79. Heese & Lombard *SA Genealogies*, see under Conway.

80. Cory MS 15011.

81. BK 89, statements to the Chief Commissioner by Conway, Sharpley and others, 9 February 1857, and Crouch to Maclean 7 February 1857. See also Hook 25.

82. Hodgeson *Princess Emma* 36.

83. Beinart (1982) 29, 30; Margaret Donaldson *The Council of Advice at The Cape of Good Hope* 320–4.

84. Brigg 63.

85. *Grahamstown Journal* 2 November 1858.

86. Statute Law of the Cape… 1862, vol 1: 175–80.

87. Statute Law of the Cape… 1862 vol 1: 770–1.

88. Beinart (1982) 23, 24.

89. *Coelacanth* vol 17(2): 29.

90. Guthrie *Frontier Magistrate* 51.

91. Coulter 135.

92. Coulter 135–6.

93. See Appendix 2.

94. Holt *Where Rainbirds Call* 34.

95. Briggs 49.

96. Philipps to Major-General King, 20 Aug 1827 (Philipps 323).

97. Pringle 109, his italics.

98. Steedman (1935) vol 1: 300.

99. Pringle 108.

100. Pringle 109. His italics; I would have included '*with his own children*'.

101. For more see Sanni Metelerkamp's *George Rex of Knysna* (Howard Timmins) and Patricia Storrar's *George Rex: Death of a Legend* (Macmillan, 1974).

102. Beddy viii, quoting Victorin's *Travels in the Cape. The years 1853–1855*.

103. Storrar *George Rex* 99, 148, 151; Metrowich *Assegai Over the Hills* 184. Frederick was scathing in his opinions of and callous in his dealings with the Xhosa, but unlike many of his contemporary officers, had a high regard for the Khoi troops. He particularly admired their courage under fire: 'There is I assure you nothing equal to Tots [Khoi]', he wrote, 'they will run in the direction a shot is fired in spite of precipices thorny bushes or in fact any thing so much so that it is no uncommon sight in following them to find a sleeve of a jacket or part of their inexpressibles hanging on the boughs of the Wachtenbietjie' (literally the 'Wait-a-bit' – *Acacia* thornbush) (*Assegai Over the Hills* 184).

104. Beddy viii.

105. Beddy viii.

106. Briggs 49.

107. Records of the Natal Executive Council 1856–59: 100–2.

108. Eliza King to William Bazley, 18 March 1907 (Cory MS 1833).

109. Spaarman vol 1: 101.

110. Shell 186, 237.

111. Shell 288–9.

112. Angela is also known as Angila, Ansiela, Ansla and Hansela. Names were not standardised in those days (for more on this remarkable woman see Boeseken *Slaves*

and Free Blacks at the Cape 1658–1700 9, 22, 29, 79–81). She eventually became a slave-owner herself when she inherited the Kronendal Estate in Hout Bay from her late spouse. Her old Cape Dutch homestead still stands, in Main Rd.

113. Ross 14–15.

114. 'In the early decades of the eighteenth century, nearly 80 percent of all slaves imported came from the Indian subcontinent' (Shell 43).

115. I use the term here to mean 'East Indian' although it has been said that 'Malay was a term coined by whites in Cape Town as a synonym for Muslims…' (Worden & Rais *Breaking the Chains* 308).

116. Officially the Khoi could not be enslaved, but overt coercion was often applied to keep them at work (Shell 221).

117. Worden & Rais 308.

118. Merriman 3.

119. Gilbey *The Lady* 6, 31.

120. The Reverend Holt, visiting Gun Drift in 1954 wrote: 'I saw a tall, well-built man of about 50 years of age. The presence of European blood in him was evident, though it had been darkened by infusions of African blood for some generations. I judged him to be perhaps a great grandson of the original Lochenberg. He knew little of his family history. He was dressed in European clothes and spoke English quite well. He recognised the names of Klaas [Nicolaas] and Sarah Lochenberg as belonging to his family tradition, and was interested in what I was able to tell him about them' (*Where Rainbirds Call* 33).

121. Letters of Reverend Robert Callaway, 1912 (*Pioneers in Pondoland* 150–2).

122. Nelson Mandela, quoted by Donald Woods in *Biko* (Penguin Books, 1987): 24.

123. Mostly from Soga *SE Bantu* opp 466.

124. Genealogy from Hammond-Tooke *Tribes of Umtata District* 44 –8.

125. *Tribes of Umtata District* 17.

126. *Tribes of Umtata* District 43.

127. For drawing of Gqobile, see chap 7.

128. Evidence of Xelo, 1883 Native Laws and Customs Commission, 432.

129. *Roll of the British Settlers* 45.

130. At least for a time they were also resident at Tshinini: their infant son Joseph King was baptised at Tshinini on the same day, 1 September 1864, as his namesake, John and Nochuku's youngest son. A second son, Andrew Clark, was also baptised there, on 1 April 1865. Two more of their children were baptised at Morley on 18 July 1870, Benjamin de Fountain King (born 26 February 1868) and Sarah Elizabeth (born 11 March 1870), and another son, Edward James King, born 15 August 1872 at 'Embizani', was baptised at Xora (in abeLungu territory) on 17 October 1873 (Cory MSS 15223, 15015; Clarkbury Baptisms). He became a government dipping official at Colenso in Natal and died aged 47 on 24 October 1919. According to his estate (MSCE 4677/1919) his mother's maiden name was 'Hammon', or 'Hannon'. Mary Ann King may have been a daughter of Dan Hannon and his wife, traders whose boat was wrecked on the Wild Coast in 1853. Hannon then sought work at Palmerton Mission Station, just north of the Mzimvubu River ('Tour along the Coast', *The Natal Witness* 28 January 1853).

131. Possibly the same Thomas King who married Margaret or Mary, and whose son John King was born in King William's Town on 15 January 1871. A daughter, Eliza Florence, was born 2 December 1872, also in King William's Town (Cory MS 15920/2 Baptisms King William's Town Circuit 1865–1873).

132. Possibly the same John King whose son Henry (Harry) was born at Xora in abeLungu territory on 21 December 1871. Harry and his mother, Augusta, may have been the ones referred to in Bazley's note 40

133. In 1865 at the age of 17 William married Margaret

The Sunburnt Queen

Thompson. The bride may have been the daughter of another trader. When Reverend Holt interviewed members of the abeLungu and amaTshomane in the 1950s one of his informants was an elderly man, Tomsoni kaGojwela, 'named after an early trader called Thomson or Thompson' (*Where Rainbirds Call* 20).

134. Married Andrew John Conway: see Conway Genealogy for more.
135. Died July 1842 (Cape Archives 6/9/88 6553)
136. Hannah married a Mr Coester, living near Alice in 1851. (Cape Archives 6/9/88 6553). Eliza married Frederick Hawkes on 10 March 1828 (*Lower Albany Chronicles* vol 2 (revised): 25.
137. Heese & Lombard *South African Genealogies*, under Conway.
138. Evidence of Xelo, a Christian Headman, to 1883 Native Laws and Customs Commission, 432.
139. *South African Genealogies*, under Conway.
140. Cory MS 15015

Chapter 12

1. Child *Portrait of a Pioneer* 106.
2. Map and notes from Prof Kirby to Mr Basson, Secretary of the Grosvenor Salvage Co, 1955 (Kirby Papers, Strange Library, Johannesburg). The actual site lies close to 'X'.
3. Gill Vernon *Coelacanth* vol 38: 33–4.
4. Turner 105.
5. Kirby *True Story of the Grosvenor* 157.
6. Moodie *History of the Battles* vol 1: 168; Rochlin *Africana Notes & News* vol 7: 102.
7. Kirby *True Story of the Grosvenor* 185.
8. *The Natal Witness* 28 January 1853.
9. Evidence of Mdepa, 1830 (Kay 303).
10. Reverend Jenkins to Garden, 29 April 1852 (Kirby Papers, Strange Library, Jhb).
11. Bazley, note 22, *Africana Notes and News* vol 13: 18.
12. Soga *SE Bantu* 379.
13. Evidence of Zali, EW Pearce to Kirby, 8 June 1953 (Kirby Papers in the Strange Library, Jhb).
14. Evidence of Mantuhamba, Victor Mnto, Tomsoni kaGojwela (Holt *Where Rainbirds Call*) 19–23.
15. Kirby *True Story of the Grosvenor* 155.
16. Kirby *True Story of the Grosvenor* 241.
17. Fynn published diary 112, also her son Mdepa, Dr Cowie, etc (see Kirby *African Studies* 1–23).
18. Shaw *The Story of my Mission* 499.
19. Kay 307.
20. Andrea Cordani: www.ships.clara.net/ships/1shpntro.html.
21. Marshal *Ocean Traders* 108.
22. Fynn 112.
23. Van Reenen 101–2.
24. Carter 161.
25. See Van Reenen's journal entries for 4, 6 & 7 November, 1790: the original Dutch on 73 of *Jacob van Reenen and the Grosvenor Expedition* and in Kirby's translation, 101–2, and 116 fn 94 of the same volume.
26. Based on end map of the Malay Peninsula in Swettenham *British Malaya*.
27. Johnston *Dictionary of Geography* 925.
28. From Valentyn (1726).
29. Johnston 860–1.
30. Valentyn, quoted in Swettenham 27; Brookes 544.
31. Rapson *Cambridge History of India* vol 5: 85.
32. Scott *The Tea Story* 56; Rapson vol 5: 85.
33. Scott 56, 58.
34. Crowhurst *The Defence of British Trade* 219, 228.
35. Swettenham 30.
36. McCulloch vol 1: 76–7.
37. My thanks to Nidhi Raina for this information.
38. Stout *Loss of the Hercules* 23 fn 2.
39. Davies *Historical Atlas of the Indian Peninsula* 82.
40. Ross 74.
41. Letter from Vice-Admiral Curtis, May 1800 (*Records of the Ccape Colony* vol 4: 186).

42. William Bazley, note no 29 & 31 (*Africana Notes and News* vol 13: 18.); see also Xelo, 1883 Native Laws and Customs Commission 432; Cory MS 1294.
43. Ceylon and Batavia were Dutch colonies and the Philippines Spanish (Unstead 28–9).
44. Cross *The British Empire* 37.
45. Cross 44.
46. Chatterton *The Old East Indiamen* 21.
47. Fortescue *History of the British Army* vol 2: 171.
48. Willson *Ledger and Sword* 40.
49. Cross 41.
50. Unstead *Emerging Empire* 43.
51. After Philip Baldeus' 'Description of the coasts of Malabar and Coromandel', 1672, in Vincent *The Commerce and Navigation of the Ancients in the Indian Ocean*.
52. Abbe Raynal vol 1: 378.
53. Only two were younger – Eleanor Dennis (three years), and baby Hosea, who was about 16 months old and accompanied by his parents (Kirby *True Story* 44 and *Source Book* 81).
54. Kay *The Golden Calm* 49.
55. Fraser *Plain Tales from the Raj* 195.
56. Leibrandt *Rambles through the Archives* 44.
57. Fraser *Plain Tales from the Raj* 22.
58. Bazley, note 31 (*Africana Notes and News* vol 13: 18).
59. Garden, Monday, 28 July 1851, extract from his journal sent by Killie Campbell to Kirby in 1956 (Kirby papers, Strange Library, Jhb).
60. Crowhurst 221.
61. Crowhurst *The Defence of British Trade* 226–7, 242; Bulpin *Islands in a Forgotten Sea* 92.
62. Keay 264.
63. Andrea Cordani: www.ships.clara.net/ships/1shpntro.html.
64. Austen 26.
65. A woman passenger on the *Irwin*, for example, taken off Martinique by English pirates in about 1720, was gang-raped by 21 men, who broke her back and threw her into the sea. The captain of the pirates was Anstis or Anstey (Johnson 255–6).
66. Johnson *General History of the Robberies and Murders of the Most Notorious Pirates* 406.
67. Leibrandt *Rambles through the Archives* 44.
68. Holt *Africana Notes and News* vol 12: 134.
69. Holt *They Came Our Way* 137; and Kirby *True Story of the Grosvenor* 184–5; *Source Book* 197–201.
70. Adams *Buck Adams' Narrative* 245–6.
71. Maclean *Compendium* 14; WRD Fynn to Hook, 11 March 1907, reproduced in Hook 221–2..
72. Soga *SE Bantu* 482.
73. Adams' book was written in the 1870s, during the reign of Ngangelizwe, whose father's name was Mtirara. The latter had been king in the 1840s.
74. Harriet Ward *Five Years in Kaffirland* vol 1: 262.
75. Harriet Ward *Five Years in Kaffirland* vol 2: 54.
76. Napier vol 2: 305.
77. Capt Garden *Diary* 144, Killie Campbell Museum MS 65608.
78. *Records of Clan Campbell in the HEIC... 1600–1858* 50–3.
79. See List of passengers and crew, Kirby *Source Book* 197–201.
80. Cross *The British Empire* 41–2.
81. Margaret Campbell *Merchant Campbell* 15; Gardner *The East India Company* 50.
82. Duncan Campbell *Records of Clan Ccampbell in the HEIC... 1600–1858* 64, 162.
83. Dickson *Red John of the Battles* 83.
84. Hickey *Memoirs* vol 2: 200.
85. Unstead 43.
86. Campbell *Records of Clan Ccampbell in the HEIC 1600–1858...* lii.
87. Field 57.
88. Field 57.
89. *Burke's Landed Gentry* (1906 ed) 264.

90. For Xhosa see Soga.
91. Lenman *The Jacobite Risings in Britain 1689–1746* 141.
92. Lenman 141.
93. Lenman 147
94. Rennie *The Scottish People* 313–14.
95. Rennie *The Scottish People* 315.
96. Based on map of the East in Keay *The Honourable Company* viii–ix.
97. Rennie 112.
98. The lad, Donald Dhu, eventually escaped, but had the misfortune to be imprisoned by another rival just a few years later. By the time he died in about 1546 Donald had spent 66 years in captivity. (Rennie 55–7).
99. Campbell *Records of Clan Campbell in the HEIC* xxxvi; Buckland 68.
100. *Burke's Landed Gentry* (1906 ed) 267.
101. *Burke's Landed Gentry* (1906 ed) 267.
102. 'Chambers of Clough House', *Burke's Landed Gentry* (1937 ed) 381. Of all the genealogies I checked, only Stephen refers to his son having been on the *Grosvenor* (Stephen vol 10: 22).
103. Memoirs of William Hickey vol 3: 129–30. The exact location is unknown (see 'East India Company Lost Ships' (under 'P') http://www.ships.clara.net/lost/lost_p.htm
104. *Burkes' Landed Gentry* (1937 ed) 324.
105. Evidence of Xelo, 1883 Native Laws and Customs Commission1883 commission, 432.
106. *The Ochre People* 49.
107. It was Hammond-Tooke's *Tribes of King William's Town District*.

Appendix I

1. Holt *Where Rainbirds Call*, 19.
2. *Where Rainbirds Call* 19.
3. Stanford, Cory PR 1294.
4. Turner 213.
5. Stanford, Cory PR 1294.
6. Dennis Nameko, near Xora, 1989 (tapes in author's possession).
7. Turner 213
8. See chapter 1.
9. Dennis Nameko, near Xora, 1989.
10. AbeLungu, Xora mouth, Aug 1989 (tape in author's possession).

Appendix II

1. Bazley (*Natal Witness* 4 March 1907).
2. Bazley note 35 (*African Studies* vol 13(1): 19).
3. Holt *Africana Notes and News* vol 11: 3.
4. Bazley note 35 (*African Studies* vol 13(1): 19).
5. There was also one known only as Peter (*The Record* pt V: 41, *Records of the Cape Colony* vol 2: 399; DG van Reenen 164–5; Elphick & Giliomee (1979) 350; Bazley note 35 (*African Studies* vol 13(1): 19)).
6. DG van Reenen 164–5; Elphick & Giliomee (1979) 350.
7. Bazley note 38 (*African Studies* vol 13(1): 19).
8. *Transactions of the LMS* vol 1: 396–416.
9. *Transactions of the LMS* vol 1: 425; Cape Death Notices, vol number 6/9/535, ref 3400.
10. Prof Kirby believed that Mary Wilmot and three-year-old Eleanor Dennis were Anglo-Indian, though he did not state his sources. I have misplaced the reference, but believe it was in *The True Story of the 'Grosvenor'*.
11. *Shrewsbury Letters* 68, 76, 78–9, 94, 197 fn 100.
12. WT Brownlee 71.
13. *Transactions of the LMS* vol 1: 385).
14. Reverend Ayliffe, 17 July 1831 (*Methodist Missionary Notices* vol 5: 9–10).
15. Bazley (*Natal Witness* 4 March 1907) and Bazley note 35 (African Studies vol 13: 19). The place was still known as May's in the 1950s: 'where the road from Madonela to Harding crosses the stream' (*African Studies* vol 13: 19).
16. William Bazley's notebooks (*African Studies* vol 13: 19). Her death notice confirms the accuracy of the rest of Bazley's information, though, listing her mother as Lydia

Damoyi, and her father (described as a 'half-caste') as Poswa Gacula of Butterworth.
17. Cape Archives BK 91, letter from Barrington to Maclean, 7 October 1856.
18. Stanford *Reminiscences* vol 2: 50.
19. Cape Archives, Cape Death Notices 1834–1916, vol number 6/9/755, ref 1612.
20. Cape Archives, Cape Death Notices 1834–1916, vol number 6/9/755, ref 1612.
21. Cape Archives, Cape Death Notices 1834–1916, vol number 6/9/755, ref 1612.
22. Evidence of Mr Bond (*James Stuart Archives* vol 1: 75).
23. See fn 35 below.
24. Dominic Dunn (Ballard 224).
25. Cape Death Notices, vol number 6/9/535, ref 3400.
26. Poswa Gacula was a 'half-caste': see Cape Death Notices 1834–1916, vol number 6/9/755, ref 1612.
27. 1883 Native Laws and Customs Commission 464–467.
28. His brother signed his death notice with an 'X'. Cape Death Notices, 1834–1916 vol number 6/9/535, reference 3400. Francis was born in Pondoland, at Esihdontlwani, near Lusikisiki. There are still Canhams, the descendants of Minna, living in the district.
29. Mackeurtan p 172
30. Henry Ogle arrived at Port Natal in 1824 with Francis Farewell. He set himself up at Berea and had several large establishments and a number of Zulu wives. His Zulu name was 'Wohlo' (Mackeurtan 171; *James Stuart Archives* vol 4: 246, 434; *Andrew Smith and Natal* 32; Despatch from Captain Jervis at Port Natal to the Cape Governor (Bird 518–19).
31. Mackeurtan 275; Evidence of DC Toohey 'Native Commission of 1852' 550–1.
32. Evidence of Mbovu ka Mtshumayeli (*James Stuart Archives* vol 3: 25).
33. Morse-Jones (1969) 53.
34. Ballard 41, 223.
35. Ballard 223. At some stage he worked for the same firm that employed DC Toohey. Several of their families intermarried, as an elderly settler remarked in 1900: 'I know there are Pierces, Tooheys, ...etc. living near Dunn's place at Inyeane and close to the Matikulu river.... Some of these have married J. Dunn's daughters, a number being very good-looking.' (Evidence of Mr Antel, 1900 *James Stuart Archives* vol 1: 3).
36. Evidence of Dinya ka Zokozwayo 1905 (*James Stuart Archives* vol 1: 99; Ballard 25).
37. This must be the 'Dick Pierce (grandfather)' who was present, together with John Dunn, at Cetshwayo's battle with Mbulazi in December 1856. Also there was 'Dick Pierce (father)' and his son Joe Pierce who had the Zulu name 'Matu' (*James Stuart Archives* vol 1: 75).
38. John Dunn *Cetywayo and the Three Generals* 2.
39. Evidence of Mr Antel, 1900 (*James Stuart Archives* vol 1: 1).
40. Evidence of Mr Antel, 1900 (*James Stuart Archives* vol 1: 3).
41. Ballard 66.
42. Brooks and Webb 146.
43. Mitford visiting Dunn in 1880, quoted in Bulpin *Natal and the Zulu Country* 285.
44. Ballard 224.
45. Ballard 92.
46. Quoted in Ballard 225.
47. Ballard 223.
48. From a photo in Ballard, following 144.
49. Quoted in Ballard 240.
50. Ballard 242. In 1935 the John Dunn (Distribution of Land) Act was promulgated which awarded land to Dunn's descendants in the district of Mtunzini. In 1937 members of the Dunn family residing in Dunn's Reserve numbered 200 while 35 resided at Emoyeni. (Commission of Enquiry Regarding Coloured Population, 1937: 78–9. For more on the Dunn descendants up to the early 1980s see Charles Ballard's *John Dunn: The White Chief of Zululand*.) Relations with their Zulu neighbours

have never been entirely satisfactory, but the late 1980s, and the 1990s in particular, saw violent land clashes between the two communities.
51. MSCE 22/168 'Estate of Catherine Dunn (née Pierce) of eMangeti, Umlalazi.'.

Appendix III
1. Enklaar 92.
2. De Villiers & Pama 116–17. Another of Maria Louisz's daughters, Catherina Hoffman, married Frederik Hubner, brother of Hermanus Hubner, the trader killed at Phalo's Great Place in 1736 (De Villiers & Pama vol I: 334).
3. Holt *They Came Our Way* 57.
4. When Johannes married Christina Scheepers in 1752 she was already a widow twice over (De Villiers & Pama 116). On Johannes's death she became a widow for the third time. She must have been as tough as nails, a constitution that her son Coenraad inherited.
5. Mostert 238
6. Metrowich *Frontier Flames* 6.
7. Schoeman 22.
8. *Frontier Flames* 7. As an indication of how mixed the Afrikaners are, four of the rebel Boers were married to or lived with coloured women and another three had coloured grandmothers (Elphick & Giliomee 352 fn 53).
9. Schoeman 14.
10. He used a handful of tobacco to trick and slaughter the imiDange during the First Frontier War (see chap 5).
11. Theal *Records of Cape Colony* vol 2: 368–88.
12. Enklaar 87. The rebellion fizzled out; the remainder of the Boers laid down their weapons without firing a shot. For more see Elphick & Giliomee from 338.
13. Schoeman 49,
14. Lichtenstein vol 1: 261.
15. See Appendix 2.
16. Enklaar 10; Holt *They Came Our Way* 61–2; D G van Reenen 165.
17. Much of this information comes from DG van Reenen, who met De Buys in 1803 (164–5); Elphick & Giliomee (1979) 350.
18. Schoeman 54. In De Buys' genealogy her name is marked with a 'K', meaning 'van de Kaap', someone of slave stock born at the Cape (De Villiers & Pama). Interracial marriages were not at all uncommon in the Colony at that time; of 689 couples registered in 1798, 5–6 % had at least one grandparent of colour, of the 17 registered white company servants four had coloured wives, and of the 17 baptised coloured men five had white wives (Elphick & Giliomee 324–5).
19. Mostert 239, 276.
20. Mostert 318; Holt *They Came Our Way* 62.
21. Schoeman 62.
22. Schoeman 68.
23. Campbell's *Travels* (1815) quoted by Schoeman 83.
24. Dirk Gysbert van Reenen 167. Matola was where Morley Mission was later built, in Bessie's son Mdepa's territory (Kirby, *African Studies* vol 13: 5).
25. Paravicini 240.
26. Schoeman 68–9.
27. DG van Reenen 163; Schoeman 78.
28. My thanks to Biula van der Kaa for the translation from Dutch.
29. De Villiers & Pama 116. In the early days of the Cape Colony, all baptisms and marriages were solemnised in Cape Town. For those living in the outlying districts, the enormous distances prohibited frequent visits to Cape Town and it is not unusual to find whole families of children all with the same date of baptism, the result of a single journey to the capital.
30. De Villiers & Pama. The 'Makinas' were probably the amaGcina. (in the 1850s they were living near the Thembu, between the White Kei and Indwe rivers. See Stanford vol I: 4).
31. Schoeman, 67–8.
32. Enklaar 97.
33. De Villiers & Pama 117.
34. Lichtenstein vol 1: 259. See also chapter 8.
35. Schoeman 78–9; Campbell's *Travels*, in Schoeman 83.
36. Mostert 417–19.
37. Peires *House of Phalo* 117–18; Cory vol 1: 295; Schoeman 88.
38. Elphick & Giliomee (1979) 261–2.
39. Ross 90–1.
40. Mostert 239.
41. Schoeman 95–6.
42. Schoeman 97.
43. Stockenstrom 190.
44. Stockenstrom, quoted by Mostert 610.
45. Schoeman 97.
46. Mostert 238.
47. Schoeman 101.
48. Bergh & Bergh 27–9. The only thing wrong with Michael's story, much as he may have hoped to boost his own importance by claiming descent from the mighty Mzilikazi, is that, since he was born so much earlier, in 1812, the woman concerned could not have been his mother.
49. Schoeman 99; Ross 91.
50. Schoeman 99.
51. Commission of Enquiry Regarding Cape Coloured Population, Appendix 21, 286.
52. De Villiers & Pama 116–17; Elphick and Giliomee (1979) 325.
53. Commission of Enquiry Regarding Cape Coloured Population, 1937, Appendix 21, 287. By 1937 the 'Suiwers' numbered 218 while the 'Nie-suiwer' members totalled 340.
54. Commission of Enquiry Regarding Cape Coloured Population, 1937, Appendix 21, 289.

Appendix IV
1. Metrowich 268–9. Also Kirby *True Story of the Grosvenor* 223.
2. Metrowich 271.
3. See Kirby *Source Book* 175.

Appendix V
1. Maclennan *A Proper Degree of Terror* 186.
2. Soga *SE Bantu* 212.
3. Maclennan *A Proper Degree of Terror* 187–90.
4. Alberti *Tribal Life and Customs of the Xhosa* 13.
5. Maclennan *A Proper Degree of Terror* 189.
6. Maclennan *A Proper Degree of Terror* 207, 208.
7. Milton 75

Appendix VI
1. Soga *SE Bantu* 158, 178.
2. *SE Bantu* 178.
3. *SE Bantu* 235.
4. When Hintsa did arm himself, one of those who supplied him with guns was Louis Trichardt, later a trekker leader but at that time living under the king's protection on the upper Kei River (*House of Phalo* 118, 238 fn 83).
5. *SE Bantu* 17.
6. Stretch 75.
7. Stretch 71.
8. George Southey, 429–30.
9. Stretch 96, Naidoo 79.
10. Mostert *Frontiers* 726.
11. George Southey 429, Naidoo 77.
12. Stretch 187 fn 25.
13. Stretch 96.
14. Stretch 96. Southey had lost a lot in the war and nursed a deep and bitter hatred of the Xhosa: see extracts from his diary : George Southey 424 & 43.
15. For the findings of WA Ford, the assistant surgeon who examined Hintsa's body, see Naidoo 78.
16. *Minutes of the Proceedings of the Court of Inquiry…* quoted in *House of Phalo* 112 fn.
17. Stretch 94.
18. Holt *Where Rainbirds Call* 60.

Glossary, Notes, Pronunciation and Spelling

1. Soga (*SE Bantu* 161–20) describes a demonstration by Makana at Gompo Rock some time before the Battle of Grahamstown, which suggests the origins of the term. Makana claimed that he would raise the dead, and on the appointed day, summoned everyone to witness the miracle. He ordered each person to hop on one leg, exclaiming 'Tayi, Tayi'. The miracle didn't happen but the word seems to have mutated into the hopping dance-chant known as toyi-toyi.
2. Shaw *Story of My Mission* 396–7.
3. Hirst *'A quarrel between half-brothers'* 10.
4. 'Cha' means 'certainly not'.
5. See Soga *The ama-Xosa* 207, 211, 214.
6. See Hammond-Tooke *Tribes of Mount Frere District* 11.
7. See Moodie *The Record* pt III: 96; Brownlee *Reminiscences* 166.
8. DG van Reenen 175.
9. Steedman vol 2, appendix III: 269.
10. Henry Somerset, Report, 20 March 1833 (*Records of Natal* vol 2: 234).
11. Moodie *The Record* pt V: 45.
12. Moodie *The Record* pt V: 53.
13. Thomas Philipps 345.
14. Frances Farewell, letter to Campbell, 25 September 1829 (*Records of Natal* vol 2: 141).
15. Van Reenen's journal 161.
16. Capt D Campbell (*Records of Natal* vol 2: 174).
17. Van Reenen's journal 157.
18. Chirou's *Report on the Grosvenor* (Carter 190).
19. Carter 189–90.
20. Letter from Bell to Lt-Col Somerset, 13 June 1828 (*Records of Natal* vol 1: 171).
21. Letter from John Cane, 12 October 1829 (*Records of Natal* vol 2: 143).
22. Letter from Francis Farewell, 25 September 1829 (*Records of Natal* vol 2: 141).
23. Henry Francis Fynn (*Records of Natal* vol 2: 160).
24. Kay 173.
25. Lichtenstein vol 1: 407.

Index

Eddee & Crystal - Just you & I
From this moment on.
Take my breath away Beelen